Japan's Development Aid to China

Paradoxically, Japan provides massive amounts of development aid to China, despite Japan's clear perception of China as a prime competitor in the Asia-Pacific region.

This book provides an overview of the way Japan's aid to China has developed since 1979, explains the shifts that have taken place in Japan's China policy in the 1990s against the background of international changes and domestic changes in both countries, and offers new insights into the way Japanese aid policy-making functions, thereby providing an alternative view of Japanese policy-making that might be applied to other areas. Through a series of case studies, it shows Japan's increasing willingness to use development aid to China for strategic goals and explains a significant shift of priority project areas of Japan's China aid in the 1990s, from industrial infrastructure to socio-environmental infrastructure.

The book argues that, contrary to the widely held view that Japan's aid to China is given for reasons of commercial self-interest, the objectives are much more complex and dynamic. It shows especially how policy-making power within the Japanese government has shifted in recent years away from officials in the Ministry of Foreign Affairs to politicians in the Liberal Democratic Party.

Tsukasa Takamine is Postdoctoral Research Fellow in the School of Asian Studies, the University of Auckland and Research Associate of the Asia Research Centre, Murdoch University. His areas of research interest include Japanese foreign policy and policy-making, Japanese and Okinawan politics, political economy of the Asia Pacific and Sino-Japanese relations. He has published most recently in the *Pacific Review* and *Japanese Studies*. From April 2006 he will be Assistant Professor in the Department of Integrated Arts and Science, Okinawa National College of Technology, Japan.

Routledge Studies in the Growth Economies of Asia

Japan's Development Aid to China

The long-running foreign policy of engagement

Tsukasa Takamine

Routledge
Taylor & Francis Group

LONDON AND NEW YORK

First published 2006
by Routledge
2 Park Square, Milton Park, Abingdon, Oxon, OX14 4RN

Simultaneously published in the USA and Canada
by Routledge
711 Third Avenue, New York, NY 10017

Routledge is an imprint of the Taylor & Francis Group

First issued in paperback 2011

Typeset in Times New Roman by
Newgen Imaging Systems (P) Ltd, Chennai, India

British Library Cataloguing in Publication Data
A catalogue record for this book is available from the British Library

Library of Congress Cataloging in Publication Data
Takamine, Tsukasa.
    Japan's development aid to China : the long-running foreign policy
of engagement / Tsukasa Takamine.
      p. cm. – (Routledge studies in the growth economies of Asia ; 60)
    Includes bibliographical references and index.
    1. Economic assistance, Japanese – China. 2. Technical
assistance, Japanese – China. 3. Japan – Foreign relations – China.
4. China – Foreign relations – Japan. I. Title. II. Series.

HC427.92.T337 2006
338.91′52051–dc22   2005009578

Publisher's Note
The publisher has gone to great lengths to ensure the quality of this
reprint but points out that some imperfections in the original may
be apparent

ISBN13: 978-0-415-35203-1 (hbk)
ISBN13: 978-0-415-51146-9 (pbk)

For Chōki, Emiko, Yasunobu and Sumiko

Contents

Illustrations

Figures

Tables

Acknowledgements

Most of this research was carried out as part of a doctoral thesis undertaken at Murdoch University in Australia. Thus, debts incurred in the writing of this book go back for several years. Special thanks must go first and foremost to Sandra Wilson who supervised the doctoral thesis. I am deeply indebted to Sandra not only for her excellent intellectual guidance, but also for her motivational support during the entire research period. This book would not have been completed without her invaluable assistance.

I also owe gratitude to Yasuo Takao, Timothy Tsu Yun Hui, Hayden Lesbirel, Radha Krishnan, David Brown, Jane Hutchison, Ian Cook, David Wells and Jeff Harwood, scholars from various Australian and Asian universities who read all or part of the manuscript and provided helpful comments. Thanks also to Egami Takayoshi from Waseda University and Nakagawa Junji from the University of Tokyo for their encouragement and advice.

I very much appreciate the financial and other assistance provided by the School of Asian Studies at the University of Auckland. In particular, thanks to Richard Phillips for his generous help in converting Chinese personal names in the book into the Pinyin system and to Jennifer Devlin for her kind assistance in the final proofing process. I am also indebted to both the Asia Research Centre and the School of Social Science and Humanities of Murdoch University for financing much needed research trips to Japan.

My thanks are also extended to Motoyoshi Tadahiko from the National Diet Library; Hirano Atsushi and Shimomura Yasutami from the Japan Bank for International Cooperation; Tōyama Shigeru from the Ministry of Foreign Affairs; Kimata Yōichirō from the Japan International Cooperation Agency; Nakamaru Itaru from the Liberal Democratic Party; and Sugishita Tsuneo from the *Yomiuri* newspaper; who all kindly provided me with very useful primary research materials.

I am very grateful to all those who agreed to be interviewed for this project. They are listed in Appendix 2. Their special knowledge and insights constituted a critical resource for my research.

Finally, thanks to my wife, Miyuki, for her understanding and long period of patience. She was a source of great motivational support throughout the project. Both my daughter, Maho, and son, Kōta, who were born just before the start and at the ending stage of the project respectively, inspired me enormously too, simply by being there. I dedicate this book to my parents, Emiko and Chōki and my parents in law, Sumiko and Yasunobu, who consistently encouraged me from Okinawa.

Note on names

Japanese words have been romanised using the Hepburn system. Macrons have been used to denote long vowel sounds in Japanese words (e.g. Gaimushō, Chūō kōron). Chinese personal names have been given in Pinyin, rather than Wade–Giles (e.g. Zhou Enlai, instead of Chou En-Lai). Both Japanese and Chinese personal names are given in the conventional way, with surnames first followed by given name (e.g. Ōhira Masayoshi; Deng Xiaoping), except for Japanese and Chinese authors writing in English who have chosen to use the reverse order. With Japanese place names that are widely used in English, macrons have been omitted (e.g. Tokyo, Osaka), where they appear in the text, in translations of titles and organisations and as place of publication.

Abbreviations

ASEAN	Association of South-East Asian Nations
ASEM	Asia and Europe Meeting
BMD	ballistic missile defence
CCP	Chinese Communist Party
CHINCOM	China Committee of the COCOM
COCOM	Coordinating Committee for Multilateral Export Controls
CTBT	Comprehensive Test Ban Treaty
EEZ	exclusive economic zone
EPA	Economic Planning Agency (Japan)
ExIm Bank	Export and Import Bank
FDI	Foreign direct investment
FY	Fiscal Year
G7	Group of Seven (Canada, France, Germany, Italy, Japan, UK and US)
GDP	Gross Domestic Product
GNI	Gross National Income
IDA	International Development Association
IMF	International Monetary Fund
JBIC	Japan Bank for International Cooperation
JCP	Japan Communist Party
JETRO	Japan External Trade Organization
JICA	Japan International Cooperation Agency
JSP	Japan Socialist Party
Keidanren	Federation of Economic Organizations (Japan)
LDP	Liberal Democratic Party (Japan)
LTTA	Long-Term Trade Agreement
MITI	Ministry of International Trade and Industry (Japan)
MOF	Ministry of Finance (Japan)
MOFA	Ministry of Foreign Affairs (Japan)
MOFTEC	Ministry of Foreign Trade and Economic Cooperation (China)
MT Trade	Memorandum Trade
NATO	North Atlantic Treaty Organisation
NGO	Non Governmental Organization

NIEs	newly industrialised economies
NPT	Nuclear Non-Proliferation Treaty
ODA	official development assistance
OECD	Organisation for Economic Cooperation and Development
OECF	Overseas Economic Cooperation Fund (Japan)
OOF	other official flow
PF	private flow
PLA	People's Liberation Army (China)
PPP	purchasing power parity
PRC	People's Republic of China
SCAP	Supreme Commander for the Allied Powers
SDF	Self Defence Forces (Japan)
SDPJ	Social Democratic Party of Japan
SPC	State Planning Commission (China)
TMD	Theatre missile defence
UNCLOS	UN Convention of the Law of the Sea
UNDP	United Nations Development Programme
WFP	World Food Programme
WTO	World Trade Organization

1 Introduction

This book examines Japan's development aid policy to China since 1979. In December 1979, the Japanese Prime Minister, Ōhira Masayoshi, pledged ¥330 billion as development aid to China over the period 1979–83.[1] This was the beginning of official Japanese aid to China. Since then, successive Japanese governments have consistently provided China with official development assistance (ODA), in the form of government loans, grant aid and technical cooperation. The cumulative total of Japanese ODA to China from 1979 to 2002 reached ¥32,254 billion.[2] Among China's aid donors, Japan is easily the largest; since 1979 it has consistently provided more than half of China's total bilateral aid. Japan provided 56 per cent of China's bilateral ODA between 1979 and 1998 while Germany and France – the next most important ODA donors for China – provided 15 per cent and 5 per cent, respectively.[3] As a result, in financial and technological terms, the contribution of Japanese ODA to Chinese economic development over the last quarter of a century has been substantial.

In simple terms, ODA (or development aid) is a transfer of resources and knowledge from industrialised to developing countries. Japan has been, overall, the world's largest provider of development aid throughout the 1990s, and China has received the largest proportion of Japan's development aid during this period. The question arises as to why Japan provides so much development aid to China, despite Japan's clear perception of China as a strategic competitor in the East Asian region. This study seeks to answer that fundamental question. More particularly, the study examines the actual policy objectives of Japanese ODA to China and the broader interests behind it, together with the process of determining these objectives and interests.

Japanese aid to developing countries has often been regarded simply as an extension of Japan's national commercial interests, masquerading as humanitarianism. Many general analyses of Japanese aid, however, overlook or deal only briefly with the case of China as a recipient of Japanese aid. This study will show that a detailed examination of the China case suggests a much more complex range of policy goals on Japan's part than has commonly been recognised. Moreover, the objectives of and interests behind Japan's ODA to China have not remained static; rather, since 1979, they have evolved in response to critical changes in the domestic and international environments. The objectives of

Japanese development aid to China and the interests behind it, furthermore, stem at least as much from politico-strategic as from economic considerations.

The study situates itself broadly within studies of Japanese foreign policy, with an emphasis on the literature of Japanese foreign aid. Because the analytical emphasis is on ODA policy and policy-making, the study addresses Japan's ODA to China not from a recipient's perspective, but chiefly from a donor's, that is, from Japan's point of view. Moreover, though the study necessarily engages with economic aspects, it mainly concentrates on the politics behind Japan's ODA policy to China, and on broad perceptions of the economic, political and other effects of Japanese aid.

It is necessary to define ODA in order to clarify the analytical standpoint of the book. The strictest definition of ODA, which is provided by the Development Assistance Committee of the Organisation for Economic Cooperation and Development (OECD) – the international governing body of foreign aid – is based on three criteria. First, ODA is provided by official agencies; second, it is administered with promotion of economic development and the welfare of developing countries as its main objective; and third, it is concessional in character, that is, recipient-friendly, to avoid severe burdens on developing countries, and conveys a grant element of at least 25 per cent.[4] Therefore, ODA differs from the two other types of international development funding: the 'other official flow'(OOF), consisting of government loans with a grant element of less than 25 per cent, such as international loans from export and import banks of developed countries, and 'private flow' (PF), including commercial loans provided by private banks.

The normative expectation behind ODA, which is also emphasised by the OECD's Development Assistance Committee, is that 'rich governments should provide economic resources to poor ones while leaving aside any commercial, political, and strategic considerations in order to maximise their developmental impact.'[5] Despite this expectation, however, donor countries are in practice strongly interested in how and for what purpose their money and other resources are used in recipient countries. In fact, ODA is not 'an end in itself' but is 'an integral component' of the foreign policy of donor countries.[6] Unlike trade and foreign direct investment (FDI), which are primarily transactions by private businesses, ODA, whose source of funds is mostly taxpayers' money from donor countries, can hardly be separated from the foreign policy of the donor countries. ODA policies of major industrialised countries are largely 'influenced by different combinations of foreign policy interests'.[7]

Some analysts emphasise the importance of cultural influences on Japanese and Western aid activity, particularly in terms of motivation. With reference to the different socio-cultural contexts in Japan and Western countries, for example, 'the sense of *noblesse oblige* which forms an important part of the rationale of the aid programs of the West is said [by some observers] to be absent from that of Japan'.[8] This distinction between Japanese foreign aid, which is supposedly self-serving, and that of the West, which is said to be based on *noblesse oblige*, is, however, easily challenged by many empirical cases of Western foreign aid activity. France has used a significant amount of its ODA for the purpose of

French-language education in its former colonies in Africa to maintain its cultural influence over these countries.[9] From the late 1970s to the late 1990s, the US directed between 33 and 43 per cent of its total foreign aid to only two countries – Israel and Egypt – each of which is a very important country for US Middle East strategy.[10] One Australian official admitted that Australia's aid to China is a very useful tool to promote Australian firms' commercial interests in China.[11] The concept of *noblesse oblige* cannot explain the political, strategic and commercial interests clearly visible behind these Western countries' foreign aid activities.

Humanitarianism – surely – is one of the philosophical motivations of donor nations in giving foreign aid, and every year a considerable amount of Western and Japanese ODA funds is used for the purpose of emergency and poverty relief, food production, education and medical help in many developing countries.[12] However, while humanitarianism may not be the least important objective of Western and Japanese ODA policies, it is almost certainly not the prime motivation. On the basis of their comparative analysis of American, Japanese, French and Swedish aid flows, Schrader, Hook and Taylor conclude that 'our findings discounted the role of humanitarian need in the aid policies of these industrialised democracies'.[13] In reality, it is very difficult for donor governments to implement aid policies on a humanitarian basis when those governments are operating in the competitive global sphere. In actual practice, ODA can serve a variety of foreign policy objectives. In short, it is a 'flexible but widely misunderstood policy instrument'. Further, as David Arase observes, 'because it is so flexible, it is impossible to determine without reference to a donor's broader interests which purpose, or priority of purposes, will likely motivate that donor's interests'.[14]

Japan's ODA to China

There are three reasons why this book addresses Japan's ODA to 'China', rather than to other recipients of Japanese aid. The first, and most important, is that little, if any, detailed research has been undertaken into the actual goals of and broad interests behind Japan's ODA policy to that country, even though it has received the largest portion of Japanese ODA since 1979.[15] Japan's China ODA policy is only very briefly addressed in the existing literature on Japanese foreign aid and foreign economic policy, which will be reviewed below, either as an example of or an exception to the broad conclusions of those studies. While some official Japanese reports assess the impact of ODA to China at project level,[16] scholarly analysis of the context in which China ODA is provided, and the processes by which Japan's broad national interests are determined and policy goals are set, has not yet been undertaken. The second reason is that analysis of Japan's ODA policy to China clearly reveals the highly complex and dynamic nature of Japan's foreign aid policies. Japan's ODA to China constitutes a transfer of resources and knowledge, not between countries having common political and economic systems or values, but between countries that regard each other as important strategic competitors. This fact suggests the highly complex and strategic characteristics of Japan's aid policy towards China. Analysis of the aims of Japan's China ODA and interests behind it is made more challenging because of the highly complex and flexible nature of ODA as a foreign policy instrument. The third reason is that the case of Japanese ODA to China most fully reveals the intense bargaining between Ministry of Foreign Affairs (MOFA) bureaucrats and Liberal Democratic Party (LDP) parliamentarians at the policy level, a theme which has not yet been addressed in the broader literature on Japanese foreign aid.

Despite the lack of detailed scholarly analysis of Japan's development aid to China, various observations have been made, especially about the reasons for the initial decision to begin the aid programme. According to one Japanese China analyst, Japan started to direct ODA to China in 1979 'because of Beijing's request to Tokyo for financial assistance' to carry out its economic development policy.[17] An American specialist on China claims, on the other hand, that the Japanese decision was less altruistic: in this view, Japan first provided ODA to China because it had no option but to give financial help 'in order to salvage Japanese plant projects' in China,[18] most of which were under threat of suspension or cancellation at that time. One LDP official I interviewed links the China ODA programme directly with Japan's huge trade surplus in relation to its Western trading partners in the late 1970s. According to this argument, the Japanese government needed to recycle the surplus in the form of ODA, in the face of strong international criticism of Japan's trade surplus.[19] Given the extremely concessional characteristic of yen loans, which do not make sense commercially, one experienced banker in Hong Kong views Japanese development assistance to China as 'disguised war reparations'.[20] Robert M. Orr, Jr, in turn, points out the implicit strategic purpose behind Japan's China ODA provision, that is, during the 1980s, Japan wished to support China's effort to counter the increased Soviet military threat in the East Asian region, by means of ODA.[21] On the other hand, given Japan's suspension of ODA to China, India and Pakistan in protest against the nuclear tests conducted by those nations in the second half of the 1990s, William J. Long emphasises the use of Japanese ODA policy to support nuclear non-proliferation.[22] Some of these views remain as speculations rather than sound arguments supported by valid evidence, while others address only a few of the many aspects of Japanese aid to China. Obviously, any single line of interpretation is insufficient to explain the aims of Japan's China ODA and the motivation behind it in a comprehensive manner.

In order to carefully examine the objectives of Japan's China ODA and the interests behind it, it is very important to acknowledge three critical background factors unique to Japan. The first is China's geographical proximity, which is the fundamental source of Japan's security concerns in terms not only of military threat, but also of potential inflow of refugees, environmental destruction, and, recently, organised crime. The second is the history of wartime atrocities perpetrated by Japan in China, which has greatly affected Japan's moral and political stance in its relations with China. The third is the complementary nature of the economies of the two countries – in short, Japan is rich in capital and technology and China is rich in raw materials and labour – which determines Japan's economic interests in China. The significance of this last factor in particular will be illustrated in Chapter 5.

Quantitative overview

Before proceeding to a review of existing analytical approaches to Japanese foreign aid, I will provide a brief overview of Japan's development aid to China in order to assess its quantitative significance. Table 1.1 shows that during the period from 1992 to 2000, Japan was the biggest development aid donor to China, giving more than the total amount contributed by the top four Western aid donors. In 1998 alone, China received the equivalent of US$1,158 million, or 13.5 per cent of total Japanese ODA, making it the largest recipient of Japanese ODA, followed by Indonesia (US$828 million or 9.6 per cent) and Thailand (US$558 million or 6.5 per cent).[23]

Table 1.2 shows Japan's ODA provision to China by types – grant aid, technical cooperation and yen loans – between 1979 and 2001.[24] Japan's grant aid has mostly contributed to the development of basic social infrastructure and to the improvement of education and health care.[25] For example, since 1980, Japan has given ¥36 billion for the construction of the Japan–China Friendly Hospital, the Youth Exchange Centre and the Environmental Conservation Centre, all of which were built in Beijing city. Technical cooperation funds, on the other hand, have assisted the development of human resources in China. Throughout the period from 1979 to 1999, Japanese governments dispatched 4,158 technicians to China. In the same period, 9,712 Chinese technicians and officials were invited to Japan to take part in government-sponsored workshops and seminars to learn about Japanese technology and management.[26] Thus, technical cooperation funds have promoted the development of human resource in China, while grant aid has

Table 1.1 Amount of top five donors' ODA to China, 1992–2000 (net disbursement, US$ million)

Year	1		2		3		4		5	
1992	Japan	1,051	Italy	202	Germany	193	Spain	192	France	153
1993	Japan	1,351	Germany	248	Spain	140	Italy	136	France	103
1994	Japan	1,480	Germany	300	Spain	153	France	98	Australia	46
1995	Japan	1,380	Germany	684	France	91	Austria	66	Spain	56
1996	Japan	862	Germany	461	France	97	UK	57	Canada	38
1997	Japan	577	Germany	382	France	50	UK	46	Australia	36
1998	Japan	1,158	Germany	321	UK	55	Canada	52	France	30
1999	Japan	1,226	Germany	305	UK	59	France	46	USA	38
2000	Japan	769	Germany	213	UK	83	France	46	Spain	32

Source: Adapted from Economic Cooperation Bureau, Ministry of Foreign Affairs, *Japan's Official Development Assistance: White Paper 2002*, Tokyo, 2003; 'Taichū keizai kyōryoku (Japan's Economic Cooperation with China)', Tokyo, 2000.

Table 1.2 Japan's ODA to China by types, 1979–2001 (net disbursement base, US$ million)

Year	Grant aid	Technical cooperation	Yen loans	ODA total
1979	0	2.6	0	2.6
1980	0	3.4	0.9	4.3
1981	2.5	9.6	15.6	27.7
1982	25.1	13.5	33.02	368.8
1983	30.6	20.5	299.1	350.2
1984	14.3	27.2	347.9	389.4
1985	11.6	31.2	345.2	387.9
1986	25.7	61.2	410.1	497.0
1987	54.3	76.0	422.8	553.1
1988	52.0	102.7	519.0	673.7
1989	58.0	106.1	668.1	832.2
1990	37.8	163.5	521.7	723.0
1991	56.6	137.5	391.2	585.3
1992	72.1	187.5	791.2	1,050.8
1993	54.4	245.5	1,051.2	1,350.7
1994	99.4	246.9	1,133.1	1,479.4
1995	83.1	304.8	992.3	1,380.2
1996	25.0	303.7	533.0	861.7
1997	15.4	251.8	309.7	576.9
1998	38.2	301.6	818.3	1,158.2
1999	65.7	348.8	811.5	1,226.0
2000	53.1	319.0	397.2	769.2
2001	23.0	276.5	386.6	686.1
Total	897.9	3,540.4	11,495.7	15,934.0

Source: Compiled from Economic Cooperation Bureau, Ministry of Foreign Affairs, *Japan's Official Development Assistance: White Paper* (two issues), Tokyo, 2002–2003; *Wagakuni no seifu kaihatsu enjo* (Japan's ODA) (various issues), Tokyo, 1984–1999.

contributed more directly to improvements in the living conditions of the Chinese people.

Amongst the three types of Japanese ODA funds to China, the yen loans have most significantly assisted China's economic growth by supporting the country's industrial infrastructure development. For example, during the period from 1979 to 1998, yen loans contributed to the construction of 38 per cent (or 3,842 km) of China's total electric rail network, 25 per cent of its total chemical fertiliser production, 13 per cent of its total port facilities and 3 per cent of its total power-generating capability. During this period, yen loans also contributed to the building of 35 per cent of China's sewage control facilities (which can deal with 4 million tons of sewage per day).[27] It must be acknowledged, however, that during that period, the Chinese government limited foreign financing to less than a half of the total cost of each plant project.[28] Thus, at this time, Japanese ODA contributed at the most, half of the cost of the separate projects relating to railways, ports, fertiliser plants and so on. In financial, technological and knowledge terms, the contribution of Japanese ODA to Chinese industrial and social infrastructure development since 1979 has been extraordinary.

Analytical approaches to Japanese ODA policy

In addressing Japan's ODA policy to China, this study is informed by existing analytical approaches which have been developed for the analysis of Japanese foreign aid and foreign economic policy. I categorise these analytical approaches into five different groups: the *commercial instrument* approach, the *mercantile realism (or strategic pragmatism)* approach, the *reactive state* approach, the *proactive state* approach, and the *institutional analysis* approach.

It must be acknowledged that these five analytical approaches do not have exactly the same aims, but rather address three different questions concerning Japanese foreign aid policy and policy-making. First, the *commercial instrument* approach and the *mercantile realism* approach address the question of what policy objectives Japan pursues through its foreign aid and foreign economic policy. Second, the *reactive state* and the *proactive state* approaches ask whether it is foreign or domestic interests which primarily motivate Japan's foreign aid activities. Third, the *institutional analysis* approach investigates the question of what process (or institutional structure) actually makes Japan's foreign aid policy. I will now review these analytical approaches in turn, in order to clarify their value and limitations for the study. Then, I will select several key propositions which are useful to this research from these existing approaches.

Commercial instrument *approach*

The *commercial instrument* approach emphasises the commercial aspects of Japanese ODA activity. For the proponents of this approach, Japanese ODA is an instrument for advancing Japanese economic interests in developing countries.[29] According to David W. Neville, Japanese foreign aid programmes to many recipient countries during the 1970s were based on the desire to maximise Japan's commercial benefits in the international system. This is because:

> By supplying selected developing countries with aid, Japan expected reciprocal action from these countries.... The recipients of Japanese aid were expected to reciprocate by purchasing Japanese exports or by opening up their economies to Japanese corporate investment and by providing relatively unfettered access to raw materials.[30]

This view is derived largely from an emphasis on two historical facts relating to Japanese ODA practices. First, compared to ODA provided by Western countries, Japanese ODA, in terms of the percentage that is officially tied,[31] has largely been linked with the commercial interests of private Japanese companies; and second, Japanese governments have used ODA to Southeast Asian nations in order to increase Japan's access to mineral resources and develop markets for Japanese exports in the countries of the region.[32] In this paradigm, Japanese ODA as a whole is purely or very substantially a commercially motivated policy, and Japan's China ODA can also be explained as a policy aimed at increasing access to Chinese raw materials and markets.

However, this *commercial instrument* approach, focusing on aid-tying as the measure of economic and commercial interests in ODA, is insufficient to explain the complex aims of Japanese ODA activity and the multiple interests behind it. For example, this approach cannot explain Japanese governments' efforts to reduce the percentage of tied ODA since the 1970s. As a result of such efforts, the number of ODA projects carried out by private Japanese companies decreased consistently and dramatically in the 1970s and 1980s, a trend which contradicts the explanation of Japanese ODA policy that centres on commercial interest. In fact, by the mid-1980s some scholars had already pointed out that the commercial aspect seen in some of Japan's ODA programmes is 'the exception rather than the rule'.[33]

Besides commercial interests, it is quite clear that there are also certain political and strategic considerations behind Japan's ODA activities in Southeast Asian countries. In the 1950s and 1960s, for instance, Japan 'played a key role in supporting Southeast Asian economies [first through war reparations and then through ODA], thereby neutralising the appeal of China in that region'.[34] One example is provided by Japanese non-project ODA loans to Indonesia in this period in order to support the anti-Communist regime in that country.[35] The appropriate inference may be that commercial and resource interests are not the only purpose of Japanese ODA, but rather are included among the multiple motivations behind it.

In short, the proponents of the *commercial instrument* approach emphasise the primacy of economic advantage for Japan in providing foreign aid, but fail to recognise that the economic interests which are promoted by Japan's ODA often also have politico-strategic implications. In relation to China, for example, increased Japanese FDI also works to stabilise Sino-Japanese relations. ODA policy is undeniably 'a hybrid policy area, the axis of which runs between economic policy and foreign policy'.[36]

Whether it is commercial interests or strategic interests that most strongly motivate Japan's ODA activity has long been a subject of controversy. As discussed in the next section, the proponents of the *mercantile realism* approach recognise the political and strategic interests that are closely connected with economic-centred foreign policy actions of the Japanese state.

Mercantile realism/strategic pragmatism *approach*

The *mercantile realism* approach is essentially a modification of the *structural realist* theory, which contends that states' foreign policies are motivated primarily by the fundamental necessity of military security and that states frequently subordinate other objectives to that purpose.[37] Actual postwar Japanese foreign policy behaviour, however, is incompatible with the behaviour predicted by structural realism. In particular, Japan's support of Chinese modernisation by means of ODA, trade and other economic investment is difficult for structural realists to explain. In the paradigm of structural realism, 'concerns over relative gains and dependence on goods vital to national defence will convince most leaders to limit the scope of their state's economic engagement with those states deemed to represent the most imminent military threats'.[38] However, even though 'China is Japan's most important potential military challenger', Japan has not limited the scope of its economic engagement with the People's Republic of China (PRC), and rather has assisted China's industrialisation by means of ODA, direct investments and trade. Indeed, Japan has become the PRC's largest trading partner and, as we have seen, has long been the PRC's largest supplier of development aid.[39]

Thus, from a structural realism perspective, postwar Japanese foreign and foreign economic policies are *unorthodox*. It is true that in terms of defensive combat, the Japanese military force, with its technologically advanced conventional weapons, enjoys an advantage over all potential aggressors in the East Asian region. However, Japan's continued reluctance to increase the size and the power-projection capabilities of its military force indicates that 'Japan is not preparing to balance against Chinese military power comprehensively'.[40] Surprisingly, Japan is far more sensitive to competition with its Western allies such as the United States, Germany, France and the UK in the areas of trade, investment and technological innovation than it is to competition with China in the field of defence.[41]

In an attempt to explain Japanese policy and yet to remain within the *realist* framework, Eric Heginbotham and Richard J. Samuels developed the concept of *mercantile realism*, which reintegrates the economic and military security imperatives of state behaviour in a more comprehensive realist theory. The concept of mercantile realism describes the complexity of a state policy in which 'various economic and security interests have been balanced in the short and long term to maintain or advance the position of the state in the international system'.[42] On the basis of their *mercantile realism* approach, Heginbotham and Samuels argue that Japan's foreign and foreign economic policy is organised around the objective of advancing its technological and economic position, rather than its military position, in the global hierarchy.

In their account, Japan does not totally disregard its military security interests, but technological and economic security interests are the more important determinants of foreign policy behaviour. In other words, Japan's postwar foreign and foreign economic policy constantly show

> a more complex calculus, under which the maximization of military security frequently is subordinated in the pursuit of technoeconomic security interests. Military security is not ignored, but neither is it the predominant focus of a grand strategy designed to enhance comprehensive state power in the long run.[43]

In the paradigm of mercantile realism, economic security is very important because 'once economic security is gone, it is difficult to recover'.[44] The case of the US before the Second World War demonstrated that a state with a powerful technological and industrial base is able to transform its techno-economic capability into military power in a short period.[45] On the other hand, as the recent history of the former Soviet Union and more obviously the present situation of North Korea exemplify, a militarily overstretched state without an advanced industrial and technological base is unable to sustain its security and other interests for a long period.

Before and during the Second World War, Japan 'pursued policies designed to strengthen its economic base for the purposes of enhancing its military power'. However, given the disastrous consequences of these prewar and wartime policies, postwar Japanese governments have defined the concepts of security and power not in military terms but in relation to industry, technology and the economy.[46] Japanese mercantile realism, in the view of Heginbotham and Samuels, is intended 'to strengthen the technological, industrial and financial underpinning of power and measures crafted to insulate Japanese society from forces that might ultimately jeopardize the state's ability to pursue a mercantile policy in the long run'.[47]

Instead of mercantile realism, some scholars use the term *strategic pragmatism* to describe Japan's techno-economic-centred model of foreign and foreign economic policy action. Henrik Schmiegelow and Michèle Schmiegelow maintain that, in the 1980s, this Japanese model of action was so well established that it influenced the modernisation strategies of many developing countries in East Asia and Latin America as well as socialist countries, including China and the then Soviet Union, arguing that these countries took Japan's policy-making model as an inspiration in their effort to develop and modernise their own economies.[48] Both the mercantile realism and the *strategic pragmatism* approach emphasise the skill of the Japanese state in using its huge economic and technological capability, including its capability to provide ODA to many developing countries, as an important foreign policy instrument in order to advance Japan's political, economic and security interests in the world.

Reactive state *approach*

Given the crucial role of US governments in shaping postwar Japanese foreign and foreign economic policy, some analysts emphasise that Japanese foreign aid policy behaviour is mostly the product of US pressure.[49] This approach, most clearly articulated by Kent E. Calder, explains the formation of postwar Japanese foreign economic policy through the concept of the *reactive state*, and is particularly helpful in interpreting Japanese governments' foreign economic policy in the Cold War international system. Proponents of the *reactive state* approach claim that 'the impetus to policy change is typically supported by outside pressure, and ... reaction prevails over strategy in the relatively narrow range of cases where the two come into conflict'. The two essential characteristics of the reactive state are: first, that it 'fails to undertake major independent foreign economic policy initiatives when it has the power and national incentives to do so'; and second, that it 'responds to outside pressure for change, albeit erratically, unsystematically and often incompletely'. According to Calder, Japan is a reactive state whose postwar foreign economic policies show these two typical characteristics. In such a paradigm, Japanese ODA policies 'appear reactive to foreign pressure as well as broadly supportive of US strategic purposes in the global political economy'.[50]

Robert M. Orr, Jr supports the reactive state thesis in relation to Japanese ODA policy-making, arguing that when the US government puts pressure on the Japanese government to increase aid to particular countries or regions, 'there is a much greater likelihood that Tokyo will agree since it is assumed that Washington places relatively high priority on the matter'.[51] In this view, US pressure thus plays an important role in Japan's ODA policy. However, unlike Calder, Orr accepts the argument that rather than simply reacting to foreign pressure, the Japanese MOFA interprets pressure to suit its own policy goals and introduces it selectively in domestic debates over policy.[52] For example, the MOFA uses US pressure as a bargaining instrument in its battle with the Ministry of Finance (MOF) over budgets for its ODA programmes. Similarly, Miyashita Akitoshi contends that while US government pressure has played a decisive role in the formation of ODA policy, the Japanese government's reaction to such pressure 'reflects an *act of will* rather than a *lack of coherent policy* stemming from bureaucratic politics'.[53]

Some empirical evidence, however, raises questions about applying the *reactive state* approach to the analysis of Japan's foreign aid policy in relation to China in particular. First, the Japanese government's decision to start ODA to China in 1979 was clearly not the result of US pressure. Worried about the potential increase in Japan's economic presence in China, the US government in fact quickly expressed its concern about Japan's aid initiative to China when the Ōhira government announced it.[54] Second, the *reactive state* thesis cannot explain Japan's 1995 decision to freeze its grant aid to China in protest against China's repeated nuclear tests in that year.[55] In contrast to the 1989 Tiananmen Square incident when Japan joined Western governments' united aid sanction against China, in this case Japan applied an aid sanction against China unilaterally, rather than following the United States or any other major Western country.

Katada Saori uses this 1995 case of an ODA sanction to illustrate the 'increasing domestic influence on Japan's foreign aid in the post-Cold War era', arguing that 'the post-Cold War international environment, with the reduced overall amount of foreign aid and weakening of the united front among Western donors, provides more favourable conditions for Japan to make unilateral decisions'.[56] Actually, with respect to China policy, the degree of Tokyo's reactiveness to Washington had already decreased well before the end of the Cold War. One senior Foreign Ministry bureaucrat comments:

> Despite its large role in shaping Japan's China policy during the period from 1945 to 1972, US pressure has had very little influence on Japanese governments' China policymaking since 1972 when Japan normalised its diplomatic relations with China, except in the area of defence policy.[57]

In short, the proponents of the *reactive state* approach tend to overestimate the role of foreign pressure and underestimate the importance of domestic interests in determining Japan's foreign and foreign aid policy.

Proactive state *approach*

Dennis T. Yasutomo criticises the reactive state argument, pointing out that it 'fails to explain the direct relationship between Japanese ODA and its indigenous political interests independent of the United States'.[58] As an advocate of the *proactive state* approach, he downplays US and other foreign pressure as a major determinant of Japan's foreign and foreign aid policy. Rather, Yasutomo emphasises the autonomy and proactivity of Japan's foreign aid policy, maintaining that the Japanese state has a capacity to defend the national interest and to pursue coherent foreign aid policy, on the basis of its own agenda and strategy.[59] The contrast in views on Japanese foreign aid policy between the proponents of the *reactive* and *proactive state* approaches is thus based on disagreement over whether it is foreign or domestic interests that primarily motivate Japan's foreign aid activity. As we have seen, some empirical cases do indeed suggest that Japanese foreign aid policy to China is primarily motivated by Japan's domestic interests rather than by US and other foreign influences.

The advocates of the *proactive state* approach emphasise the concept of *comprehensive security* (*sōgō anzen hoshō*) as the basis of a direct relationship between Japanese domestic politico-security interests and foreign aid. In 1980, the Comprehensive National Security Group of the Policy Research Commission, an advisory group under the Ōhira administration, first enunciated a new concept of *comprehensive security*.[60] The report on comprehensive security submitted by the Group recommended that a comprehensive approach of combing military, economic and social policies should be carried out to assure peace and prosperity of Japanese citizens. The report urged to promote such goals as

> arms control, better North-South relations, and free trade at global level; good relations with political allies and key economic partners at the intermediate level; and military security as well as economic productivity and export competitiveness at the national self-help level.[61]

The Group's report highlighted the significance of ODA as a means to promote such goals, with the exception of military security. The Japanese government of the time accepted the notion of ODA as 'the cost of constructing an international order that secures Japan's comprehensive peace and security'.[62] In this context, ODA is seen as a foreign policy instrument to be used in response to a changing security environment, not reactively but proactively.

The proponents of the *proactive state* approach thus see the Japanese government as a purposive entity and understand its ODA decision-making as far more centralised than do those who follow other approaches.

Institutional analysis *approach*

Although the four analytical approaches discussed above provide some insight into the aims of Japanese ODA activity and the motives and interests that underpin it, the question of who, or what institutional procedure, actually determines these aims, motives and interests remained unclear. The *institutional analysis* approach addresses this question.

The four analytical approaches discussed above are based more or less on the assumption that the foreign aid policy of a state stems from a centralised policymaker which has concrete objectives and pursues clear-cut interests. In this *rational actor* paradigm, the state is a centralised entity that can present a consistent master plan for foreign aid policy and always, or at least usually, makes decisions rationally. On the other hand, some scholars approach government policy-making on the basis of a different paradigm – the *bureaucratic (or government) politics* model. This model, first articulated in full by Graham Allison, perceives no unitary actor, but instead many players who act not according to a consistent set of policy objectives, but rather in accordance with a range of conceptions of national, bureaucratic, electoral and personal interests; and who make government policy not according to 'a single, rational choice' but through 'pulling and hauling'.[63]

Alan Rix and Robert M. Orr, Jr both employ this bureaucratic politics model in their analyses of Japanese ODA. They emphasise the decentralisation of Japan's ODA decision-making, and the intensive bargaining among central government ministries in the making of policy.[64] In his 1980 study, Rix argues that ministerial interests are 'the main determinants of the articulation of Japan's aid and economic cooperation policies'. In his analysis, the MOFA, the MOF, the Ministry of International Trade and Industry (MITI) and the Economic Planning Agency (EPA) – which he calls collectively the Big Four – determine foreign aid policy through 'distinct channels and long established procedures.' Japan's ODA policy thus is 'built up on bureaucratic decisions and outcomes, ranging from determination of total aid volume goals to the type of funds committed to recipients and the terms on which they were provided.'[65]

As he acknowledges, Orr's 1990 study of Japanese foreign aid policy basically reconfirms Rix's 1980 findings. For example, Orr sees Japanese ODA policy as an outcome of intense bargaining among the three relevant ministries and one agency – the MOFA, the MOF, the MITI and the EPA – each of which approaches the process of ODA policy-making largely from 'its own parochial interests.'[66] However, what distinguishes Orr's study from Rix's is that Orr, in addition to his examination of 'the four ministerial decision-making system',[67] also addresses the importance of external influence in shaping Japanese aid policy. He particularly emphasises how pressure from the United States affects the Japanese ODA programme, demonstrating, in company with proponents of the *reactive state* approach, that the external factor in general, and US influence specifically, often becomes an integral component of Japan's bureaucratic policy-making process. In fact, Orr considers the relationship between bureaucratic politics and trans-governmental (Washington–Tokyo) relations to be a key part of the determination of Japanese foreign aid policy.[68]

The bureaucratic politics model emphasises that Japan's foreign aid policy is primarily formulated by a smaller bureaucracy within the central government. One weakness of this model is that in doing so, it fails to notice the proliferation of ODA policy-making authority within the larger governmental apparatus, including the ruling political party and the Diet, and also outside the government, in the business community and elsewhere. David Arase, on the other hand, addresses this gap in the literature on Japanese foreign aid policy, while retaining the focus on the institutional structures of the Japanese ODA system and the relative influence of the various policymaking actors. What makes Arase's institutional analysis approach different from the bureaucratic politics model of Rix and Orr is that Arase emphasises the relationship between the bureaucracy and the private sector rather than the relationship among the four ministries as the key mechanism in determining Japanese ODA policy. Thus his analysis of Japanese ODA policy-making goes beyond the focus on a smaller bureaucracy within the central government. Arase argues, for instance, that private business interests have played a central role in Japanese ODA policy-making: 'the network of public–private collaboration, combined with official funding and other policy measures, works to reduce information costs, install suitable infrastructure and regulatory environments in targeted economies, and socialize trade and investment risk'.[69] In Arase's account, ODA policy ultimately is 'the product of institutionalised structures and relations that link state and societal interests.'[70] On the basis of his institutional analysis, Arase concludes that successive Japanese governments have used ODA as a tool in their consistent efforts to increase Japan's position in global economic and political hierarchies.

Undeniably, Japan has used ODA to upgrade its position in the international division of labour by projecting 'its own industrial policy needs onto recipient economies', and by restructuring its trade and investment relations with many developing countries. In doing so, Japan has 'diversified its dependence on overseas resources and markets, improved its international competitiveness and growth prospects'.[71] Arase's study certainly illustrates the commercial and industrial benefits resulting from Japan's ODA policy implementation. However, unlike the commercial instrument thesis discussed above, in this version of the institutional analysis paradigm, commercial interests are only as important as diplomatic and security interests. Arase points out that ODA programmes have a unique ability to pursue various policy objectives simultaneously, remarking that Japanese ODA, while advancing national economic interests, also achieves a considerable political and security impact.[72]

What then are the important diplomatic and security interests pursued by Japanese ODA activity according to Arase? While referring to the ideal of 'the long-term use of economic aid to promote economic development in countries who then will come to share the political values of the donor and favour peace',[73] Arase maintains that because bilateral aid allows Japan 'to build strong relations with the governments of the developing world', it provides 'a form of political capital that will be increasingly important as Japan pursues an independent foreign policy agenda in the post-Cold War period'.[74] In his account, Japanese ODA has certainly served the nation's perceived economic, diplomatic and security needs.

This study is informed by the insights of several of the above scholars working within the institutional analysis paradigm, but seeks to go beyond the existing studies. I agree with Rix and Orr that Japanese ODA policy is primarily an outcome of intense bargaining among domestic policy-making institutions. However, I disagree with their emphasis on the central government bodies – the MOFA, the MOF, the MITI and the EPA – as the key players in this bargaining process. As we will see in later chapters, since the mid-1990s, Japanese ODA policy has not been determined by the politics practised among these four bodies but rather has been determined chiefly by intense policy-making competition between MOFA bureaucrats and LDP politicians. Arase, on the other hand, does acknowledge the LDP as one of the important players in Japanese ODA policy-making, though not as a central player equal in importance to the bureaucracy and the private sector. However, the shift in the balance of policy-making power between MOFA bureaucrats and LDP politicians which is identified in this book is not addressed in his 1995 study, doubtless because this phenomenon became visible only in the second half of the 1990s. In terms of the policy-making aspect, then, this book identifies a relatively new, yet crucial change in the process of deciding ODA policy in Japan, especially China ODA policy-making.

Implications of the five analytical approaches for this study

It is clear from the above discussion in the previous section of the different analytical approaches to Japanese foreign economic and foreign aid policy that the *commercial instrument* approach, which emphasises the commercial interests of Japanese foreign aid activity but fails to identify the political and strategic interests closely connected with, or hidden behind these commercial interests, is inadequate as a framework for analysing Japan's ODA policy to China. The *reactive state* approach, which underestimates the significance of domestic Japanese interests in shaping China ODA policy, is also of limited usefulness. As noted above, several empirical cases undermine the emphasis on US influence in the formulation and implementation of Japanese ODA policy to China. These examples rather suggest the primacy of Japan's domestic interests in determining policy objectives. Ultimately, the *mercantile realism* and the *proactive state* approaches more fully address the complexity of Japanese foreign aid policy and the divergent and varied domestic interests that motivate policy. The *mercantile realism* approach goes some way towards elucidating the complicated linkage between Japan's foreign aid and foreign economic policy and its effort to advance its political and strategic interests in the international community, while the *proactive state* approach rightly emphasises the significance of various indigenous interests in shaping Japan's ODA policy. Thus, these two approaches are useful in investigating both the objectives of Japanese ODA policy and the interests that motivate the policy.

On the other hand, although the *mercantile realism* and the *proactive state* approaches provide valid insights into the aims of Japan's ODA policy and the interests behind it, they tell us nothing about the process by which policy is made. Both approaches are based on the assumption that a centralised policymaker – that is, a state or a government – which appreciates objective national interests makes official policy according to a rational choice. However, this notion that a state makes a policy, and that policy is necessarily in the national interest, is incomplete and unsatisfying as an explanation of the process of foreign aid policy-making in democratic countries.

The *institutional analysis* approach outlined above addresses the importance of intensive bargaining (or politics) among various Japanese policy-making actors, each of which engages in ODA policy-making on the basis of different perceptions of national, organisational and personal interests. In fact, the politics of foreign aid is a battle among competing ideas that all claim to represent the national interest. The *institutional analysis* approach, which views the Japanese government as a battleground shared by different bureaucrats, politicians and business elites. thus supplements the shortcomings of the *mercantile realism* and the *proactive state* approaches. Hence it is a mixture of the mercantile realism, the *proactive state* and the *institutional analysis* approaches that can provide the most comprehensive and sophisticated picture of Japanese ODA policy and policy-making. Although these three analytical paradigms address different questions about Japanese foreign aid, they also serve as explicit points of reference when examining the aims of and interests behind Japan's ODA policy to a particular recipient country.

One contribution that this study makes to the literature of Japanese foreign aid policy is to bridge the gap between, on the one hand, analytical approaches based on the *rational actor* model (the mercantile realism and the *proactive state* approaches), and, on the other hand, the approach based on the *government politics* model (the *institutional analysis* approach). Moreover, the book also clarifies the linkage between the changing nature of the policy goals and interests of Japanese ODA and the politics that actually determines this change.

In sum, I will draw several key propositions from amongst the approaches described above. First, commercial interests are not the only factor, but are one of several types of interests that Japan pursues through its foreign aid activity. In other words, the fundamental aims of Japan's ODA activity are not only to advance commercial interests but also to develop a wide range of other perceived national interests, including political, diplomatic and strategic interests. The policy objectives of Japanese ODA are therefore more multiple and complex than has commonly been recognised. Second, ODA projects that promote commercial interests can also promote political and strategic interests at the same time. Thus. Japan's ODA activity can pursue various policy objectives simultaneously. Third. Japan's ODA policies are motivated and determined more by domestic (or internal) interests than by external influence. Fourth, Japan's ODA policies are not formulated by a centralised or single rational actor, but rather by policy-making bargaining (or politics) among different domestic actors with competing perceptions of national, organisational and personal interests. It is primarily the shift in the balance of aid policy-making power among these different actors that brings about changes in Japanese ODA policy and the goals of that policy.

Arguments

This book argues first, that there is no single aim or single interest encouraging Japanese governments actively to provide development assistance to China. Rather, aims and interests are multiple and highly complicated, and are often entwined with each other. Second, it is misleading to assume that the multiple and complex China ODA policy objectives have remained unchanged since 1979. On the contrary, they have evolved according to those changes in the domestic and international environments that impinge on Sino-Japanese relations. These include the changing phases of Chinese economic development, the new regional security environment following the end of the Cold War, and the changing domestic institutional structures responsible for formulating and implementing Japan's China ODA policy. Thus, Japan's policy of providing aid to China can be best understood in terms of the complex and evolving alliances of interests underlying it.

The book shows that during the 1980s, when the Chinese economy was comparatively underdeveloped and poverty was a significant threat to social stability, the major aims of Japan's China ODA policy were first, to assist in stabilising China's economic and social affairs by actively supporting the government's Reform and Liberalisation Policy through financial and technological assistance for industrial infrastructure development; and second, to support the integration of the Chinese economy into the market-based regional and global economic systems by promoting a market economy in China and by promoting China's trade with, and FDI from Japan and other countries around the world. During the first decade of the China ODA programme, therefore, Japanese governments mostly used ODA as a financial and technological tool in their attempt to promote a domestically stable and internationally engaged China, the emergence of which was construed to be in Japan's own strategic, political and economic interest.

Nevertheless, the policy objectives of Japan's China ODA had changed by the mid-1990s, by which time Chinese economic development had progressed significantly; the strategic relations between Japan and the PRC had radically altered following the Tiananmen Square Incident and the end of the Cold War international system; and Japan had attached clear political conditions to its foreign aid provision through the *ODA Charter* of 1992. Moreover, besides these external and internal changes, another crucial development within the process of Japan's China ODA policy-making also contributed to fundamental changes in China ODA policy – the shift in the balance of China ODA policy-making power from Foreign Ministry bureaucrats to LDP parliamentarians. This shift, evident from the mid-1990s onwards, has significantly changed the perception of what Japan's political, economic and strategic interests are in relation to the PRC, and thus has produced changes in the implementation of Japan's China ODA policy.

Since the mid-1990s, one major objective of Japan's China ODA has been to counter Chinese militarisation by using ODA sanctions, for example, to protest against provocative military action by the Chinese government in the East Asian region. At the same time, the Japanese government, on the basis of certain financial and strategic considerations, has also started to shift the priority areas of its China ODA from industrial infrastructure development to social infrastructure development, including environmental protection, poverty relief and the development of inland provinces to narrow the income inequalities between the people of the coastal and the inland regions. However, although there have been gradual increases since the mid-1990s in domestic pressure in Japan, particularly from the academic community and the media, to link ODA practices directly with the improvement of democratic conditions in China, the democratisation of China is not, so far, a formal policy objective of Japan's ODA.

The various policy objectives pursued by Japan's China ODA described above illustrate the striking flexibility of Japanese ODA as a foreign policy instrument. Nevertheless, certain key underlying concepts have remained consistent since 1979, notably the concept of *engagement*. In this book, the term engagement means a relationship of sustained interaction over a long period, intended by a state in order to promote positive relations with another state. In turn, such interaction is expected to promote or increase the national interests of the state which initiated it. A policy of engagement is potentially composed of a number of different dimensions, for example, political, economic, military and cultural. *Engagement* further implies a dynamic interaction and, of course, is a two-way relationship. Japan's engagement policy with China, addressed in this book, essentially consists of Japan's attempt to interact with China politically and economically, with military and cultural considerations less prominent. As Reinhard Drifte points out, sustained economic and political interaction with China are expected to 'steer China towards a peaceful and sustainable path ... while simultaneously hedging against any Chinese strategic breakout or policy failure'.[75] This book will also demonstrate, however, that engaging China is also expected to serve Japan's own economic and political interests. Of course, in this case as in others, *engagement* is a two-way street, and Chinese perceptions of Japan's policy of engagement must be expected to differ from Japan's.[76] Such considerations, however, are beyond the scope of this research.

Those most closely involved with ODA from the Japanese end, that is, Japanese ODA policy-makers and China specialists – both bureaucratic and academic – believe that an internationally isolated and domestically chaotic China would pose a threat to Japan. Like other countries at other times, Japan has found the spectre of a powerful and seemingly chaotic neighbour to be distinctly alarming. In fact, the view that an unruly China constitutes a potential danger to Japan has a long history among Japanese policy-makers. In the 1920s and 1930s, for example, this view was widespread.[77] China's internal and external situation is naturally still a cause for concern for Japanese policy-makers. But assessments of the options open to Japan have changed radically since the prewar period. Now policy-makers and analysts generally believe that Japan should assist its huge neighbour to tackle its own domestic problems, by providing ODA rather than by sending troops. The policy objectives of Japan's ODA as described above can be understood up to a point as diplomatic actions designed to prevent China from becoming isolated and disordered, while also promoting Japanese economic interests in the increasingly market-based and more open Chinese economy.

The evolution of the policy objectives of Japan's China ODA is also reflected in the change in the dominant view among Japanese policy-makers as to what constitutes the major factor obstructing the advancement of Japan's economic and political interests in China. During the 1980s, it was generally believed that the major factors were economic backwardness, the highly centralised, planned socialist economy, and the lack of economic interdependence between China and the countries in the *free world* bloc, including Japan. Now, by contrast, the main problems are perceived to be the widening wealth gap between the coastal and inland population, the rising unemployment levels, environmental destruction, and rapid militarisation. The target of Japan's long-running policy of engagement has shifted from an underdeveloped China which was *de facto* a strategic ally during the 1980s to a modernising China which has become a potential economic rival and a security threat from the mid-1990s onwards.

It is argued here that despite its inherently economic nature, Japan's ODA provision to China has in application been more politico-strategic than commercial. In the end, provision of China ODA is a proactive foreign policy on the part of Japan, which has the option of using its large economic and technological capability for the purpose of engaging China, and which on the other hand has significant domestic and external constraints on its freedom of action in security matters, especially the *peace* clause in the Constitution. ODA has been a very useful non-military strategic instrument for Japan in promoting its broad diplomatic, economic and security interests in relation to recipient countries, including China.

Arguably, Japanese ODA to China has had particular effects. Though it is not the aim of this study to chart those effects in detail, it is important to note that the perceived impact of Japanese aid in itself becomes a factor in formulating the future goals of the aid program. Thus, perceptions of the effect of Japanese aid are critical in any assessment of policy-making. Furthermore, certain basic conclusions about the effect of Japanese aid to China are inescapable. The start of Japan's China ODA in 1979 is undeniably one of the most important turning-points in postwar Sino-Japanese relations. It contributed significantly to China's remarkable economic development during the 1980s and 1990s, and the ability of the Chinese economy to engage with the regional and global economic systems. The Japanese ODA initiative added new dimensions to the traditionally trade-centred Sino-Japanese economic interactions – development cooperation and related investments. As a result, economic interdependence between the two nations has significantly deepened and diversified. Today, neither China nor Japan can afford to seriously confront the other because such a confrontation would fatally undermine their own country's economic interests. To have reached such a stage is probably the ultimate goal of Japan's policy of economically and politically engaging China. Sino-Japanese relations, which had been antagonistic for most of the twentieth century, have been relatively peaceful for some time. While many factors have doubtless contributed to such stability, the role of Japanese development aid since 1979 cannot be overlooked.

Japanese policy-makers have begun openly to discuss the possible termination of Japan's development aid to China. While criticising this move by Japan, the Chinese government persists in demanding continuation of Japanese aid on the basis that bilateral relations would be endangered without the aid connection. This view, which is also shared by some parts of the Japanese government, clearly illustrates the perceived political and strategic importance of Japan's ODA to China as a stabiliser of bilateral relations. Future outlook of Japan's development aid to China depends how and to which direction the economic, political and security environments that impinge Sino-Japanese relations change. It is most likely to be determined to a critical degree by changes in China's economic condition, its military behaviour in the East Asian region, the further shift in the balance of China aid policymaking power within the Japanese government and the Japanese public's perceptions of a modernising China.

Source materials

This book makes use of a range of primary research materials, especially documents from diplomatic archives, other official documents and statistics, and interviews with leading policy-makers and analysts. The use of archival materials concerning Sino-Japanese relations during the period from 1945 to the end of the 1960s. including those that were formerly unavailable for scrutiny and have now been opened to the public for the first time, has enabled me to explore, in depth, the historical background of Japan's political, economic, and other relations with China.[78] Official documents and statistics produced by institutions responsible for the formulation and implementation of Japanese ODA policy have also been proved very valuable.

Original materials were also collected through interviews with Japanese government and party officials, politicians, journalists and researchers in universities and think-tanks, all of whom are directly or indirectly involved in the process of China ODA policy formulation and implementation. In Japan, it should be noted, it is common for academics to be involved in government policy-making, through participation in high-level committees set up by the central government ministries and political parties. In this sense, no clear separation exists between the academic and the policy-making worlds, and academics have provided much valuable information for this study as direct informants as well as in their capacity as expert analysts. Some of my interviewees, across all categories, have actually been engaged in negotiations and discussions with their Chinese counterparts for more than two decades, and thus can be regarded as excellent sources of information in their own right, as well as providing indications of the motivations guiding those most closely involved with Japan's China ODA. The interview materials have been extensively used in this research, not only in constructing and in testing the arguments of the book, but also in order to understand how policy-makers and analysts assess the impact of Japan's development aid policy to China over the last two decades.

Government documents, for their part, pose particular issues for research into the goals and motivations of ODA. The ambiguity of Japanese government statements on the issue in fact makes it very difficult to discern the real aims of and actual interests behind the provision of aid to China. Unlike the US government, for example, the Japanese government is unwilling to use terms such as 'strategic goals' and 'national interest' in official statements explaining its foreign aid policy.[79] The MOFA apparently recognises that the use of such terms generates a negative impression among the Japanese public, because prewar and wartime Japanese governments frequently used such terms to justify Japan's military invasion and occupation of other Asian countries. In addition, the MOFA is very sensitive about how Japan's ODA is perceived overseas, and thus it is especially reluctant to disclose publicly the actual strategic and economic interests that Japan pursues through its foreign aid activities. The result is that the Ministry frequently uses a very generalised rhetoric in its efforts to explain and justify Japan's ODA policy, suppressing, in its official pronouncements, the real reasons for directing taxpayers' money to foreign countries in favour of reasons considered by the Ministry to be likely to gain taxpayers' support for ODA activity. While most governments of donor nations employ similar tactics for similar reasons,[80] consciousness on the part of bureaucrats of the ongoing legacies of recent history, combined with a long-standing tradition of bureaucratic aloofness, perhaps exacerbates the trend in Japan, deterring clearer articulation of policy goals. Moreover, as ODA comprises most of its annual budget, MOFA is especially keen to maintain public support for its foreign aid activity.[81] In this sense, the regular use of a rather imprecise policy rhetoric in the Ministry's statements is also connected with its willingness to protect its organisational interest.

Interviews with Japanese ODA policy-makers have proved helpful in disentangling official rhetoric from real motivations and interests, because such key individuals provide a less formal, in some cases more realistic, analysis than the official documents. In fact, some of the policy-makers whom I interviewed clearly distinguished between the *real* interests underlying Japanese ODA to China and what one of them called the *fiction* of certain official pronouncements.

In order to research Japanese ODA policy to China systematically. this book is divided into eight chapters. Chapter 2 elucidates the historical factors that encouraged the initial provision of official Japanese economic assistance to China. It is very important to understand this historical context because the provision of foreign aid to China is not a completely new policy which emerged after 1979, but rather is a development from pre-1979 Sino-Japanese relations. Chapter 2 thus reviews Japan's relations with China between 1945 and 1978, with particular focus on the China policies of the successive Japanese governments of this period. Chapter 3 investigates the goals of Japan's China ODA policy from 1979 onwards and the broader interests behind the policy, and explains how and why these goals and interests have evolved. In Chapter 4, the focus is on the institutional structures of the Japanese state that are concerned with China ODA policymaking and implementation. More specifically, this part looks at the policy goals of and interests behind Japan's ODA to China, and examines how various domestic institutions and actors actually participate in, and have influence over, the process of formulating these goals and furthering these interests, with particular reference to the changing balance of policy-making power between MOFA bureaucrats and LDP parliamentarians. Chapter 5 statistically analyses Japan's yen loans to China – one of the three types of Japanese ODA to China. In particular, it focuses on the use of the loans to contribute to the development of industrial infrastructure in China, in order to reveal the actual economic and political interests behind the disbursement of the huge amount of yen loans. Chapter 6 focuses on the three sets of aid sanctions that Japan has imposed on China in protest against specific instances of provocative military behaviour by Beijing between 1995 and 2000, in order to elucidate the strategic interests behind Japan's ODA policy to China. Chapter 7 assesses the perceived effects of Japan's China ODA policy and their implications for the current and future Sino-Japanese relations, analysing Japanese ODA policy-makers' and China analysts' own assessment of the contribution of ODA to the economic, social and political changes that have taken place in China since 1979. The aim is not to suggest a cause and effect relationship, but rather to highlight the perceived correlations. Chapter 8 presents some important theoretical and other implications of the findings of my research for the literature of Japanese foreign policy and of Sino-Japanese relations.

2 Japan's pursuit of economic and political engagement with China, 1945–78

This chapter examines Sino-Japanese relations during the years 1945–78, prior to the start of Japan's development aid to China. More specifically, the chapter examines the international and domestic conditions that affected Sino-Japanese relations during this period, along with the major China policies formulated by Japanese governments. This historical context is crucial because Japanese ODA policy towards China, the central theme of this book, emerged as a consequence of Japan's pre-ODA relations with China. As will be argued throughout the book, ODA has been the key policy instrument used by successive Japanese governments since 1979 in order to encourage the economic and political engagement of the PRC with Japan and with the global community. A careful examination of Sino-Japanese relations between 1945 and 1978 will clarify the background factors that motivated Japanese governments to pursue an engagement policy with China.

The following section examines Japan's relations with China during the Allied Occupation of Japan (1945–52), especially relations between the Yoshida Shigeru government and the US and their effect upon Sino-Japanese relations. The section on 'The search for an autonomous China policy, 1952–62' looks at the interactions between the Hatoyama Ichirō and Kishi Nobusuke governments and the PRC government during the period 1952–61, when political bargaining between Japan and China became more active and frequent in the wake of the establishment of unofficial trade relations and then the termination of those relations. The section on 'The political use of trade, 1962–71' investigates relations between the Ikeda Hayato and Satō Eisaku governments and the PRC government during the period from 1962 to 1971. The focus of this section is on the development of new unofficial bilateral trade relations and their impact on Japan's political relationship with China. The section on 'The end of external and domestic constraints on Japan's policy of China engagement, 1972–78' examines Sino-Japanese relations between 1972 and 1978, especially the negotiation processes leading to the normalisation of diplomatic relations in 1972 and the conclusion of a Peace and Friendship Treaty between the two countries in 1978, and the introduction of the Reform and Liberalisation Policy by the PRC government, also in 1978.

Japan's China policy in the Occupation era, 1945–52

Japan's defeat in the Second World War inevitably became the starting point of new relations with China. Not only had Japan attacked China militarily in the war, but several developments in Japanese and Chinese affairs during the period from 1945 to 1952, which will be described below, contributed to new difficulties in Japan's diplomatic dealings with China, difficulties which have in fact continued up until the present. With the Cold War dominating East Asian affairs by the end of the 1940s, Japan and China came to regard each other as enemies in a new way: because of their different political ideologies and economic systems. Japan thereby lost an opportunity to reconcile with China over past events – that is, Japan's invasion of China during the 1930s and 1940s, and the atrocities committed there by Japanese troops.

After Japan's defeat in August 1945, the US-dominated Allied forces occupied Japan. From then on, the Supreme Commander for the Allied Powers (SCAP), personified by General Douglas MacArthur, sought to destroy many of the pre-war state structures of Japan. With Japan's loss of full sovereignty in 1945, foreign policy also came under the control of the Allied Forces, or in reality, the US. Despite this circumstance, however, occupied Japan retained a strong central government, which, together with the SCAP, took very important steps to revitalise the devastated economy. The Japanese government started to allocate the nation's limited resources largely for the purpose of economic recovery, which became the government's highest priority, while totally relying on the US for its military security.[1]

On the other hand, in the immediate post-war period, China's Nationalist Party government led by Jiang Jieshi (Chiang Kai-shek) was by no means secure, and was subjected to armed challenge by the Chinese Communist Party (CCP) led by Mao Zedong (Mao Tse-tung). Eventually, this civil war between the two ideological rivals in China ended with the victory of Mao's Communist Party. The PRC was established in 1949. Mao signed an alliance with Stalin's Soviet Union in 1950 and the PRC became a second powerful country in the Communist bloc, which was in conflict with the *free world* bloc led by the US.

By the late 1940s, the SCAP, acknowledging the probable Communist victory in China and increasing Soviet influence in East Asia, started to reverse the thrust of its Occupation policy in Japan. The priority was drastically shifted from instituting radical reform to the reconstruction of a *new Japan* which in Washington's view had to become a Western ally in Asia.[2] On the basis of this *reverse course*, the US not only abandoned the requirement for Japan to pay reparations,[3] but also directly injected a large amount of money into Japan to help revitalise the nation's economy. Politically, the US government, fearful of the influence of Communism in Japan, began to support the conservative political force led by Yoshida Shigeru, which Washington had initially regarded as outdated 'old political power' from the pre-war era.[4] The conservative parties' dominance in Japanese domestic politics then began, as Yoshida became prime minister in January 1949 and the US started to give active support to the conservatives.

Reliance on the US for military security was not universally embraced in Japan.[5] In the end, however, the security alliance with the US was seen as overwhelmingly important for war-devastated Japan in order to assure military protection, security and internal order and to enable the allocation of limited resources for economic recovery rather than defence. The military alliance was formally ratified by the US–Japan Security Treaty of 1951. The cost of Japan's dependence on the US for its military security was political subordination to the US and comparative loss of autonomy in making foreign and security policy.

Accordingly, Japan's diplomatic and economic relations with China were subjected to US Cold War policy in East Asia. Despite the Japanese business community's desire to re-establish and develop economic relations with China, in practice its dealings with China were heavily under the influence of successive US administrations. Japan's attempts to pursue its economic interests in China were thus possible only within the framework of the US–Japan alliance; the US policy of China containment had a significant impact on Sino-Japanese relations in this period.

Even before the end of the Second World War, one of the most important questions in the East Asia policy of the US was which country – Japan or China – would be its main post-war strategic partner in the region.[6] Washington initially wished to make China its primary ally in East Asia, while American business elites dreamed of conquering the China market, which would then supposedly provide huge commercial benefits to them. President Franklin D. Roosevelt, for example, regarded China as likely to be the most important US ally in East Asia after the war.[7] The US government's idealism towards China was still intact at the end of the war. In fact, containing China was not considered necessary in Washington until 1950, when China began overtly to advocate intervention in foreign countries. The US view of China became more and more antagonistic as the CCP took greater control over Mainland territory and quickly implemented a series of provocative foreign policies, including the military alliance with the Soviet Union in February 1950, China's dispatch of military forces to help North Korea in October 1950 in the Korean War, and its military attack on Taiwan in the same year. American interests in Asia were further threatened by China's attempt to export Communist revolution to other non-Communist East Asian countries.[8]

Chinese intervention in the Korean War, which resulted in direct battle between the US and the Chinese armies, led to a dramatic turn in US China policy. When the United Nations branded Communist China as an aggressor, American opinion hardened, and the government adopted an anti-PRC stance.[9] The policy of containing Chinese Communism came to dominate US foreign policy for the next two decades. Japan's position in US East Asia policy was also dramatically changed. US Army Secretary Kenneth C. Royall was one who emphasised the strategic importance of Japan as a 'bulwark against Communism'.[10] As a consequence of this stance, the US dramatically overturned its early Occupation policy in Japan, as described above, seeking instead to incorporate Japan into the *free world* camp as its junior partner. Japan became the major US ally in Asia, and one of the most important countries in the non-Communist bloc.

The US policy of containing Communist China imposed severe restrictions on Japanese trade with China. While the US military fought against Asian Communists – North Korea and China – on the Korean peninsula, Congress passed the so-called Battle Act, or Mutual Defence Assistance Control Act in 1951. The Act denied American aid to any country failing to conform to American standards of control over exports to Communist countries. Accordingly, in December 1950, Japan, as a country occupied by the SCAP and needing American economic support, imposed an embargo on exports to China. As a result of the embargo, the volume of trade between Japan and China dropped sharply. Japanese trade with Communist China declined from US$39.6 million in imports and US$19.6 million in exports in 1950 to US$14.9 million and US$599,000 respectively in 1952.[11]

Further external constraints were imposed on Japan's economic relations with Communist China by the establishment of the Co-ordinating Committee for Multilateral Export Controls (COCOM), an international guiding body jointly created in 1949 by the US, the countries of the North Atlantic Treaty Organization (NATO) (except Iceland), Australia and Japan to regulate the export of strategic materials to the Soviet Union and other Communist countries.[12] As the Cold War deepened, the Western camp increasingly had the task of preventing Communist countries from developing high-technology weapons by stopping the transfer of Western high technology to these countries. As a result, Japanese exports to China became the subject of COCOM supervision.

The non-Communist camp's embargo against Communist countries was tightened after 1952, when the US established the China Committee (CHINCOM) as a branch body of the COCOM. The CHINCOM imposed further embargoes on Japanese trade with China,[13] introducing a list of 200 embargo items in addition to those already on the COCOM list. Actually, 'restrictions on exports to China were more extensive than those on exports to the Soviet Union and Eastern Europe'.[14] This was probably because the US regarded Mao's China as more dangerous to the West than Stalin's Soviet Union, because of the aggressive military behaviour clearly demonstrated by China in the Korean War.

Despite the desire of business elites to enter the Mainland China market, Japan's vulnerable position and the trade restrictions imposed by the COCOM and the CHINCOM put Japan's China trade policy strongly under the influence of Washington. In order to please the US, Japan abided fully by the COCOM list as the basis of its restriction on trade with China,[15] and added a further 400 embargo items to the standard list.[16] In fact, the limitation of Japan's China trade was stricter than that of any of the NATO nations except the US and Canada. As a result, most of the items that China wanted to import from Japan, including machinery and other industrial products, were on the embargo list.

More broadly, the externally imposed embargo meant the Japanese business community was unable to establish full economic relations with Communist China, and, consequently, was unable to secure Japan's commercial interests in the China market, which, it was believed, could potentially have 'absorbed a significant proportion of Japanese industrial output'.[17] The Japanese embargo against trading certain products with Communist China also prevented Japanese business from importing Chinese raw materials such as iron ore, coal and salt, as well as agricultural products such as soybean, oils and fats, for all of which Japan had largely depended on China before the war.[18]

The US became a major source of the raw materials that Japan had previously imported from China. In 1951, 33.6 per cent of Japan's total iron ore imports, 70.9 per cent of coal imports, 97.3 per cent of soybean imports and 10.6 per cent of salt imports came from the US, while Japan's imports of the same raw materials from China sharply dropped. In fact, Japan had not imported any of these raw materials from the US during the period 1934–36, the last *normal* period of trade before the war, while during that period China had supplied 34.0 per cent of Japan's imports of iron ore, 68.4 per cent of coal imports, 71.3 per cent of soybean imports and 38.6 per cent of salt imports.[19] The partial post-war embargo on trade with China, therefore, brought about a radical shift in the source of Japan's industrial raw material imports. This change, however, was not desirable from the point of view of the Japanese business community because American raw materials were imported at much higher prices than those from China.[20] Further, US raw materials and the US market alone were not enough to satisfy Japanese economic needs.

Southeast Asian factors

After losing much of its economic tie with Mainland China – Japan's traditional source of raw material imports and major pre-war destination of its industrial goods exports – both the Japanese business community's desire to restart trade with China and the government's concern about Japan's economic recovery were significantly intensified.[21] Given this situation, the US presented the 'US–Japan economic cooperation initiative', which aimed to develop economic relations between Japan and Southeast Asian countries by promoting Japan's machinery exports to and its raw material imports from that region. The initiative was based on Washington's concern that Japan, after regaining full sovereignty, might re-establish its economic ties with Communist China, unless it could secure sufficient markets and raw materials elsewhere for its economic recovery.[22] Consequently, Southeast Asian countries, together with the US, became Japan's major new trade partners. The US initiative aimed not only to separate Japan economically from Communist China, but also to develop the Southeast Asian economies and to incorporate Japan into US Cold War policy in the region. Washington thought that Japan's supply of industrial goods and military equipment to the region would be helpful in protecting Southeast Asian countries from Communism.[23] This logic later motivated Japan's own provision of ODA to Southeast Asian countries in the late 1950s and 1960s.

The US initiative to promote strong economic relations between Japan and Southeast Asian countries, however, could not immediately satisfy the Japanese business community's export needs. At that time, the Southeast Asian market was underdeveloped and could thus absorb only a small proportion of Japanese industrial output. Given this situation, the desire of Japanese business elites to enter the China market was strengthened, rather than weakened.[24]

The Yoshida governments and US pressure

A *prototype* of Japan's engagement policy towards China, later pursued by means of ODA, already existed in the era of the Yoshida Shigeru governments (1946–47, 1948–54). Prime Minister Yoshida believed that Japan should develop its economic relationship with the PRC despite the reality of the Cold War in Asia.[25] The basis of this idea was his realistic perception of Communist China, revealed by his famous pronouncement: 'Red or White: China remains our next-door neighbour. Geography and economic laws will, I believe, prevail in the long run over any ideological differences and artificial trade barriers.'[26] For him, Sino-Japanese economic relations and development were necessary not only for the sake of Japan's commercial interests in the China market, but also for achieving his diplomatic objective. He wanted to separate China *economically* from the Soviet bloc by deepening China's economic dependence on trade with Japan, and eventually to bring China into the Western camp.[27] For Yoshida, a strong economic interdependence between Japan and China, if achieved, could thus contribute significantly to Japan's economic and security interests.

Although the Yoshida government's policy was to establish and develop commercial ties with the newly established Communist China, in practice this was very difficult because of political constraints imposed by the US policy of containing China. To achieve his goal of economically engaging with the PRC, Yoshida personally supported Great Britain's *Two China* policy,[28] which officially recognised both the Communist government in Mainland China and the Nationalist government in Taiwan. However, John Foster Dulles, adviser to the US Department of State and the chief American negotiator of the 1951–52 San Francisco Peace Treaty and US–Japan Security Treaty, put strong pressure on the Yoshida government to take the same diplomatic stance towards the two Chinas as the US, that is, to recognise the Nationalist government in Taiwan as the sole legitimate government of China and to ignore the Communist regime which controlled the Mainland Chinese territory.

In April 1952, Yoshida, although very reluctantly, made a concession to Dulles in recognising the Nationalist Party government in Taiwan as the formal Chinese government.[29] For diplomatic reasons, Yoshida also accepted the US demand to conclude the Japan–Republic of China (Taiwan) Peace Treaty ending the state of war between Japan and Taiwan and establishing official relations with Jiang Jieshi's Nationalist government. Yoshida recognised that it would be politically very risky for Japan if his government rejected the US demand for formal recognition of the Taiwan government. The most serious risk was the probability that if Japan rejected the US demand, the US Senate would not ratify the San Francisco Peace Treaty which was to ensure the return of Japan's full sovereignty and independent status. Yoshida was also well aware that the recognition of Taiwan would serve Japan's national interests because it would ensure both Taiwan's support for Japan's entry into the United Nations and other international organisations,[30] and continuation of US military protection of Japan.

On 22 December 1951 Yoshida sent a memorandum to Dulles that assured the US government that Japan had no intention of recognising Communist China diplomatically. This memorandum was designed to 'influence the American public to favour the ratification of the [San Francisco] peace treaty'.[31] In the memorandum, Yoshida stated that Japan was prepared to conclude 'with the National [Nationalist] government of China, if that government so desires, a Treaty which will re-establish normal relations between the two Governments' while assuring the US that Japan had 'no intention to conclude a bilateral Treaty with the Communist regime of China'. Yoshida's letter outlined the reasons for choosing the National Government of the Republic of China as its counterpart in diplomatic normalisation: it was apparently because the Republic of China 'has the seat, voice and vote of China in the United Nations', and it 'maintains diplomatic relations with most of the members of the United Nations'. In contrast, the reasons not to recognise the Communist regime in Mainland China as the legitimate governmental authority were: first, the Communist regime 'stands actually condemned by the United Nations as an aggressor'; second, it 'is backing the Japan Communist Party in its program of seeking violently to overthrow the constitutional system and the present Government of Japan'; and finally, 'the Sino-Soviet Treaty of Friendship, Alliance and Mutual Assistance concluded in Moscow in 1950 is virtually a military alliance aimed against Japan'.[32]

The startling truth behind this history is that the memorandum sent from Yoshida to Dulles was not actually written by Prime Minister Yoshida or his advisers. In fact, there is evidence indicating that the memorandum was carefully drafted by Dulles himself and handed to Yoshida for signature.[33] Yoshida, after making some minor amendments, then sent it back to Dulles, who evidently thought that a memorandum stating Japan's anti-Beijing policy would help to overcome any reluctance on the part of the US Senate to ratify the San Francisco Peace Treaty. Since the Chinese military's entry into the Korean War, sentiment against Communist China had dominated the US Senate. Thus, Japan's ambivalent stance towards Beijing had indeed made the Senate very reluctant to ratify the peace treaty.[34] This story shows the strength of the US influence over Japan's foreign policy-making and particularly its China policy-making. Successive Japanese governments in the period of the Occupation were, without exception, similarly vulnerable to US pressure.

Tokyo fully acknowledged the strategic importance of keeping Taiwan in the *free world* bloc, and of separating Taiwan from Communist China.[35] This was not necessarily interpreted to mean, however, that Japan must stay away from Mainland China. Japanese policy-makers thought that as long as Taiwan remained in the non-Communist bloc, Japan could pursue its economic interests in Mainland China by re-establishing its official ties with China. As described above, however, Tokyo's strong wish to re-establish official trade ties with China could not be fulfilled due to the US objection. US influence on Japan's China policy continued after Japan regained its full sovereignty in 1952, though the degree of American influence gradually weakened thereafter.

The search for an autonomous China policy, 1952–62

Japan's search for an autonomous China policy gradually took shape after the restoration of sovereignty and independent status in 1952. Prime Minister Hatoyama Ichirō (1954–56), the successor of Yoshida, strongly advocated a foreign policy for Japan that would be independent of the US. This section first addresses the Hatoyama government's search for an autonomous diplomacy with China and then looks at the political interactions between the Kishi Nobusuke government and the Chinese government that were aimed first at establishing and then at ending early bilateral trade relations.

The Hatoyama government and the two China policy

Aspiring to achieve a foreign policy that was not a derivative of US foreign policy, Hatoyama pursued normalisation of diplomatic relations with both of the two major Cold War enemies – the Soviet Union and China. Hatoyama's search for an autonomous Japanese diplomacy was only a partial success, however, as despite his government's realisation of diplomatic normalisation with the Soviet Union in October 1956, it failed to achieve normalisation with China. In fact, the issue with the greater public profile in Japan was not rapprochement with the Soviet Union, but rapprochement with China. But in this period, the normalisation of diplomatic relations with China was ultimately prevented by Washington's strong objections. Conversely, the normalisation of relations with the Soviet Union was possible because the US already had diplomatic relations with the Soviet Union, and thus its opposition to Japan–Soviet rapprochement was minimal. In the end, Hatoyama's diplomatic agenda of pursuing an autonomous foreign policy was possible only if it did not challenge American interests.

Like his predecessor Yoshida, Prime Minister Hatoyama also advocated Great Britain's *two China* policy to enable Japan to develop economic relations with the PRC while maintaining its existing diplomatic and economic relations with Taiwan. As far as Hatoyama was concerned, it would not be necessary to cut official ties with the Nationalist government in Taiwan in exchange for Japan's formal recognition of Communist China; he saw no contradiction in having official relations with both the PRC and Taiwan governments.[36] Again, however, his policy was inconsistent with US China policy, which did not recognise the Communist government in Mainland China. Despite his independent agenda, Hatoyama's search for an autonomous China policy was premature. Japanese initiatives to establish economic relations with Communist China were in fact taken by non-governmental actors in Japan that, compared to the government, were relatively free from US and other external constraints.

Trade agreement: the beginning of Sino-Japanese economic relations

The first trade agreement between Japan and Communist China was reached *unofficially* in June 1952. This agreement was concluded between the Chinese government's International Trade Promotion Committee and pro-Beijing Japanese Diet members – Takara Tomi, Hoashi Kei and Miyagoshi Kisuke[37] – who visited China despite opposition from the Japanese government. The second and third unofficial trade agreements were concluded in October 1953 and May 1955, respectively. Both sides agreed to trade goods (including both exports and imports) worth about £60 million in each period of the second and third trade agreements.[38]

In Japan, pro-PRC non-governmental actors included those who had ideological sympathy with the PRC, those who were nostalgic for the period of pre-war and wartime Japanese dominance in Manchuria or the Japanese puppet state in Northeast China, and those who had had business experience with pre-war China. A number of them requested permission to establish official trade relations with Communist China. Members of Japanese business elites were particularly active in encouraging re-establishment of Sino-Japanese trade relations. For members of Japanese business who had had experience of the pre-war China trade, the recollection that China had once absorbed more than 20 per cent of total Japanese exports was still fresh. In 1929, for instance, China had absorbed 24 per cent of Japan's exports and was Japan's second largest export market, after the US, which accounted for 43 per cent of Japanese exports.[39]

The unofficial trade between Japan and China which started in 1952, however, did not operate under the same conditions for the Japanese business community as the pre-war trade had done. As noted earlier, most of the materials for plant construction and industrial machines that China wanted to import from Japan were on the embargo lists of the COCOM and CHINCOM. Nevertheless, it is notable that the volume of Sino-Japanese trade, except for the strategic materials on the embargo list, steadily increased after 1952.[40] During the 1950s, the number of Japanese people visiting China and Chinese people visiting Japan also increased. In 1955, Chinese delegations visited Japan to attend Chinese goods fairs, and participated in the Sixth World Congress against Atomic and Hydrogen Bombs, while about 600 Japanese visited the PRC. From then on, a thousand Japanese visited the PRC each year until bilateral trade relations were broken off in May 1958.[41]

In the mid-1950s, the PRC government took the initiative to normalise diplomatic relations with the Japanese government. The English-language diplomatic document sent in August 1955 from the Chinese Consul-General in Geneva, Chen Pei, to the Japanese Consul-General in Geneva, Tamura Keiichi, noted:

> For the sake of furthering the normalisation of relations between Chima [China] and Japan, and facilitating further relations of international situation, the Chinese government deems it necessary for the Government of China and Japan to hold talks on the question of trade between our two countries, the question of civilian residents of the both sides, the question of contact between the people of both countries and other major question affecting interests of the people of both countries. If the Japanese Government shares the same desire, the Government of the p[P]eople's Republic of China

welcomes a delegation to be despatched by the Japanese Government to Peking to hold such talks. It is requested that afore-mentioned proposal of my Government be transmitted to the Japanese Government.[42]

Conversely, other diplomatic documents suggest that Tokyo also wished to open up official relations with the Chinese government during the same period. In August 1956, one policy study group of the Japanese MOFA conducted research on a strategy to re-establish official contacts with Beijing, and on the likely US response. Interestingly, the study group's report suggested that Japanese policymaking should be more independent of the US:

It is not necessary to explain to the United States about the Japanese policy of making formal contact with Communist China. If Japan started, first, technical contacts such as postal exchange with Communist China, and then expanded contacts into other areas little by little, the possibility of the United States giving an all or nothing response to Japan would be small.[43]

The report thus indicates that in the mid-1950s, officials of the Japanese MOFA had begun to map out a China policy that would be independent of the US. In other words, Japan was engaged in a quest for official relations with the PRC despite the strong US influence over Japan's China policy-making at this time.

The Kishi government and the breaking off of trade

Changes in both Japanese and Chinese domestic politics in the late 1950s brought about a deterioration of relations between Tokyo and Beijing. In Japan, Kishi Nobusuke (1957–60), who had been an official in the Japanese puppet state of Manchukuo and had been listed (though not tried) as a Class A war criminal soon after the end of the Second World War, became Prime Minister following the resignation of Ishibashi Tanzan due to illness.[44] Although Kishi understood the importance of trade relations with Mainland China, he was unwilling to give up relations with the Nationalist government in Taiwan, and soon after he took the Prime Minister's office, he visited Taiwan in his official capacity. Given Kishi's formal visit to Taiwan, the Communist Chinese government started a series of diplomatic attacks on him.

The official visit to Taiwan was not the only reason that China started its campaigns of Kishi-bashing. There was also a domestic reason to do so. In general terms, China's Japan policy became radical and aggressive when its domestic politics were chaotic, while its policy tended to be moderate, or even somewhat friendly, at times of internal stability. In the late 1950s, conditions were far from stable. Mao's disastrous Great Leap Forward campaign (1958–60), whose 'utopian ideology envisioned a spiritually mobilised populace simultaneously bringing about the full-scale modernisation of China and its transition from socialism to communism within a few decades',[45] ended with tremendous human and economic costs. Approximately 20 million Chinese people died, mostly from famine caused by the campaign, and the nation's economy was largely destroyed.[46] With the start of the Great Leap Forward campaign, China's attitude to countries in the *free world* bloc became more radical and hostile. Beijing's diplomatic stance towards the Kishi government was no exception.[47]

In concluding the Fourth Japan–China Private Trade Agreement in 1958, the Kishi government initially approved China's demands for semi-diplomatic status for Chinese trade representatives in Japan and for permission to raise the PRC's national flag at their office in Japan. This decision caused a diplomatic backlash from Taipei and Washington because to agree to such practices meant the partial recognition of the PRC by Japan. John Foster Dulles, who by that time had become US Secretary of State, applied strong pressure on the Kishi government to reverse the decision to allow the raising of the Chinese flag on Japanese soil. On 12 March 1958, Jiang Jieshi's Taiwan government also warned that Taiwan would cut its diplomatic tie with Japan if Kishi did not reverse his government's decision.[48] As a result, on 9 April 1958, the Kishi government overturned its earlier decision, with regard both to the flag and to the status of Chinese trade representatives. Kishi feared that otherwise, the coming renewal of the US–Japan Security Treaty, which was due by 1960, might be endangered. He regarded renewal of the treaty as the most important foreign policy goal of his government.[49] Meanwhile, the Kishi government's reversal of its earlier decision caused renewed anger against Kishi in the Chinese government.

The *Nagasaki Flag Incident* (*Nagasaki kokki jiken*), which was the direct cause of the termination of Sino-Japanese trade relations, further inflamed the situation. In May 1958, an anti-Communist Japanese youth pulled down a PRC flag which had been flying at a Chinese goods fair in a department store in Nagasaki city. This incident led to a serious political confrontation between Beijing and Tokyo. China expressed its strong anger, stating that the Kishi government had deliberately ignored the flag incident, which had insulted the PRC. Kishi responded that Beijing was using the incident as a diplomatic weapon to attack his government.[50] Eventually, the Chinese government unilaterally terminated its trade relations with Japan, only six years after the trade had started.

Japanese officials believed that as a result of the termination of the trade connection, Beijing had lost its means of intervening in Japanese domestic affairs, as well as an opportunity to gain commercial benefits.[51] The fact that trade with Mainland China had formed a very small part of total Japanese trade during this period, on the other hand, enabled Japan to avoid serious economic damage resulting from the end of its China trade. For example, in 1956, the proportion of China trade in Japan's total trade was only 2.5 per cent, while trade with the US was 17 per cent in 1954 and 24 per cent in 1958. Japan's exports to Southeast Asian countries reached 30 per cent of total Japanese exports in 1958 and 48 per cent in 1953, while its imports from these countries accounted for 18 per cent of total imports in 1957 and 27 per cent in 1955.[52] Clearly, there was no pressing need for Japan to develop its economic relations with Communist China at the expense of political relations with its important allies – the US and the non-Communist Southeast Asian countries.[53] By the same token, however, and despite the minimal economic damage sustained at state level, the financial losses of individual Japanese firms actively engaged in the trade with the PRC proved to be large. In the year after the Nagasaki Flag incident, 'Japan's exports to China dropped by one-fourteenth, and imports dropped a little over one-third'.[54] Japanese firms had to wait for another four years to resume trade with China.

In August 1958, Zhou Enlai, then the head of the Chinese Foreign Ministry, attacked the Kishi government by presenting it with the *Three Political Principles* (*seiji san-gensoku*), which stipulated that Tokyo should first, immediately abandon words and behaviour which are hostile to China; second, cease to engage in any plan to create two Chinas; and, third, cease to obstruct the normalisation of diplomatic relations between the two nations.[55] Zhou's *three principles* aimed to have binding effects on future relations between China and Japan, and manifested Beijing's continued willingness to intervene in Japan's domestic politics in an attempt to change Japan's China policy in its own favour.

The motivations of the Japanese government in attempting to establish official relations with China differed between the Yoshida government era and that of the Hatoyama and the Kishi governments. Two major factors motivated the Hatoyama and Kishi governments to pursue official diplomatic and economic relations. First, these conservative governments wanted to contain the increasing power of domestic left-wing parties – the Japan Communist Party (JCP) and the Japan Socialist Party (JSP) – by establishing official relations with Communist China. They feared Beijing's intervention in domestic Japanese politics through its informal channels in the JCP and the JSP. and amongst that section of the Japanese public which had strong sympathy with Communist China.[56] The Japanese governments thought that establishing official relations with Beijing would weaken the informal connections between the CCP and these left-wing Japanese political parties and activists, because Beijing would be able to communicate through official channels rather than relying on the JCP and JSP. Thus, the establishment of official relations was considered likely to damage radical leftist movements within Japanese society.[57] Second, as mentioned earlier, the strong feeling of nostalgia among Japanese business elites who had been involved in business in China in the pre-war period also encouraged governments to establish economic relations with China, though they did so through *unofficial* trade in deference to Washington.

The political use of trade, 1962–71

Several international and domestic factors encouraged the resumption of Japan–China economic relations in 1962. First, China needed a new source of trade, since its trade with and foreign aid from the Soviet Union had ended in the wake of the Sino-Soviet split in the late 1950s. The devastation of China's domestic economy caused by the disastrous Great Leap Forward had also added urgency to the search for a donor of financial and technological aid to reconstruct the economy. The change of Japanese prime minister in July 1960 from Kishi to Ikeda Hayato, who took a softer and more positive stance to trade with China, also facilitated the resumption of Sino-Japanese trade relations. This section first examines the Sino-Soviet split and the Great Leap Forward, in terms of their impact on Sino-Japanese relations. It then analyses the diplomatic and political interaction between the Ikeda and the Chinese governments which resulted in the resumption of unofficial trade relations between Japan and China in a new setting. Finally, we will consider the relations between the Satō Eisaku government and the Chinese government, with particular focus on Beijing's use of unofficial trade relations with Japan as a political weapon against Tokyo.

The Sino-Soviet split, the Great Leap Forward and Sino-Japanese relations

China's confidence in practising hardline diplomacy with Japan during the 1950s was based on the existence of the Sino-Soviet alliance. As a major recipient of financial and technological support from the Soviet Union and East European Communist countries, there was little need for the PRC to seek Japanese economic assistance. However, after the beginning of the 1960s, when the Sino-Soviet confrontation intensified, China's Japan policy – especially its trade policy with Japan – suddenly shifted from a hardline to a softer approach. Thus the Sino-Soviet split, which had become obvious by the late 1950s, fundamentally changed not only China's relations with the Soviet Union, but also its relations with Japan.

Beijing initially chose the Soviet Union as a partner that could assure its national security and supply the economic assistance that was vital for the construction of the *new China*. The 1950 Sino-Soviet Treaty of Friendship, Alliance and Mutual Assistance guaranteed Soviet assistance in protecting the PRC from foreign aggressors.[58] In addition, an agreement on providing aid to China, also signed in February 1950 in the Kremlin, secured China's modernisation under the guidance of the most advanced socialist economy.[59] The Soviet Union's advanced military technology, characterised by the possession of inter-continental ballistic missiles and satellites, was very important for Chinese national defence, while the connection with the Soviet Union also assisted China's industrial modernisation.[60] The Soviet Union had provided about US$2.2 billion to China, including aid, by 1957, and China's trade with Communist countries had reached about 75 per cent of its total foreign trade by that time.[61]

Khrushchev's sudden criticism of his predecessor, Stalin, in the Twentieth Soviet Communist Party Meeting in 1956, without previous consultation with the CCP, and the Soviet Union's military intervention in Hungary in the same year, precipitated change in Sino-Soviet relations. In 1958, China decided to minimise its economic and military dependence on the Soviet Union and take an independent approach to economic development by initiating the Great Leap Forward. In return, in June 1959, the Soviet Union unilaterally cancelled the promised provision of its nuclear weapon production technology to China. Moreover, 1,390 Soviet technicians were withdrawn from China[62] and more than three hundred contracts with China were abrogated, including many contracts for plant construction. This ideological confrontation between China and the Soviet Union eventually escalated into military confrontation in the late 1960s, in the northeast and northwest of China.[63]

The strong Soviet military threat changed China's foreign and security policy dramatically. It was very hard for China to lose the economic and technological assistance provided by the Soviet Union because under the Cold War international system, the Soviet Union was the only country in the Communist bloc that had the capacity substantially to assist China's economic and military development. Soviet financial aid was thus very important for the Chinese government. For example, China received 270 million Russian roubles (about US$300 million) in developmental loans at extremely low interest rates (1 per cent annual interest) during the five-year period starting in 1950. Furthermore, the Soviet Union provided 431 million roubles in February and 233 million roubles in November 1952 as special loans to support the People's Liberation Army (PLA), which was fighting the Korean War.[64] With its urgent need to find an alternative source of foreign aid outside the Communist bloc, the Chinese government started to reverse its aggressive stance towards the Japanese government.

In addition to the Sino-Soviet split, the economic and social devastation caused by the disastrous Great Leap Forward campaign also contributed to China's urgent need to obtain Japan's development assistance. Quite soon after Beijing initiated the campaign, Japanese officials had already foreseen disastrous consequences. One document predicted:

> Communist China's industrialisation under the Great Leap Forward campaign totally ignores economic efficiency. Thus it will, in the long run, cause exhaustion of industrial resources and will eventually create tremendous costs for the Chinese nation. In fact, the largest problems embedded in Communist China's economy are its backward transportation and energy infrastructure. This means that even if China's industrial output increased, the outputs would not easily reach consumers. Thus, it is extremely questionable how much longer China can continue this highly irrational [Great Leap Forward] campaign that uses the politically mobilised mass as the only driving force for the nation's industrialisation.[65]

As will be examined in detail in Chapter 5, when Japan started to provide ODA to China two decades after this document was produced, the prime target of the ODA was in fact the development of China's *transportation and energy infrastructure*, which had been pointed out in the document as the greatest weakness of the Chinese economy.

Given these circumstances, the Chinese government had few realistic options but to take the diplomatic initiative to re-establish trade relations with Japan. Thus, the dramatic change in China's diplomatic stance towards Japan at the beginning of the 1960s was based not on political grounds, but on economic realism and the will to survive. The reasons that Beijing wanted Japan, rather than other industrialised countries, to replace the Soviet Union as financial and technological donor were first, that Chinese leaders highly appreciated Japanese economic strength, especially its industrial capability;[66] and second, that Japan was the only industrialised country having a long-standing historical tie with China.

Chinese Premier Zhou Enlai, at his August 1960 meeting with Suzuki Kazuo, a visiting representative of the China–Japan Trade Promotion League, disclosed China's new and less stringent trade policy towards Japan. The so-called *Three Principles of Trade* (*bōeki sangensoku*) allowed for

> (1) trade guaranteed by official agreement between the two governments; (2) trade supported by non-governmental agreements and contracts between private Japanese firms and appropriate Chinese corporations; (3) trade specially designed to suit the interests of small Japanese enterprises wholly dependent on Chinese supplies of raw materials and arranged by particular organizations, such as the Japan Council of Trade Unions (Sōhyō) and the All China Federation of Trade and Unions.[67]

In stark contrast to the harsh tone of the three political principles of 1958, discussed earlier, the presentation of the *Three Principles of Trade* meant that China had abandoned its attempt to establish official trade relations, which had been aimed at obtaining official Japanese recognition of the PRC. By indicating the three possible forms of trade between China and Japan listed earlier, the PRC government allowed private Japanese firms to develop unofficial trade relations with China. This initiative by Zhou was one of the factors that triggered the two years of diplomacy leading to the resumption of Japan–China trade relations in 1962.

The Ikeda government

Changes in Japanese domestic politics also promoted an atmosphere conducive to the resumption of Sino-Japanese trade relations. The change of Japanese prime minister from Kishi to Ikeda Hayato (1960–64) had a direct impact on the re-establishment of trade channels between the two countries. The Kishi government was forced to resign after the 1960 controversy over renewal of the US–Japan Mutual Security Treaty.[68] The economic bureaucrat Ikeda then took the prime minister's office. Ikeda's flexible approach towards the PRC, and the end of the Kishi government, which the PRC regarded as anti-Beijing and pro-Taipei, helped to facilitate the re-establishment of Sino-Japanese trade.

Soon after he became prime minister, Ikeda displayed his government's positive attitude towards the improvement of Sino-Japanese relations and in particular showed his willingness to resume and develop economic relations.[69] In turn, Beijing's response to Ikeda's soft diplomatic stance towards China was quick. In 1960, Liu Ningyi, the head of the All-China Federation of Trade Unions, visiting Japan to participate in the Sixth World Congress Against Atomic and Hydrogen Bombs, hinted at Beijing's willingness to reconcile with Tokyo, observing 'now that Kishi is overthrown, I can meet the people of Japan'.[70] Thus, the Chinese government capitalised on the change of Japanese cabinets as an opportunity to improve Sino-Japanese relations.

The Ikeda government's policy of supporting Japan's economic engagement with China facilitated the resumption of trade relations. In September 1962, an informal Japanese delegation to China agreed with the Chinese government to resume trade between Japan and China after several days of discussion. The delegation was led by Matsumura Kenzō, the LDP politician, rival of Kishi, and head of his own faction. Matsumura had strong personal connections with Chinese leaders, and was in fact one of the most pro-PRC politicians in the history of the LDP.[71] On the basis of the agreement brokered by his delegation, the so-called *LT Trade* – named after the initials of the two signatories, Liao Chengzhi of China and Takasaki Tatsunosuke of Japan – commenced in November 1962.[72] In addition, the two parties agreed to develop trade between private Japanese firms and the Chinese government based on Zhou Enlai's Three Principles of Trade. This policy produced the so-called *Friendship Trade*. At the beginning of the 1960s, therefore, Japan–China trade transactions were resumed under new arrangements: the Friendship Trade that was promoted by private Japanese firms and the Chinese government; and the LT Trade, the quasi-governmental trade,[73] based on an annual trade agreement.

Although it was non-governmental Japanese delegations that actually negotiated and contributed to the establishment of the two trade channels with China, the Ikeda government's full support of the Matsumura delegation was crucial to the success of the negotiation. In fact, Japanese delegation members included an LDP politician and a business leader who were advisers of Ikeda himself. Further, the Japanese MITI's heavy involvement in the trade process indicates that the LT trade had an official blessing.[74]

The increased number of friendly firms and their active trade transactions with China brought about a change in the balance of Japan's foreign trade. As the number of Japanese friendly firms handling trade transactions with China increased from 11 in 1960 to approximately 320 in 1966, the annual volume of Japan's trade with China between 1964 and 1967 surpassed the annual volume of trade with Taiwan for the first time since 1949. The share of Japan's trade with China out of Japan's total world trade dramatically increased from 1.6 per cent (US$48 million) in 1961 to 16.2 per cent (US$625 million) in 1969.[75] Japan also became China's leading trade partner in 1964, and Japan's share in China's foreign trade reached 14 per cent by 1966. Furthermore, by 1965 China had become Japan's fourth-largest trading partner behind the US, Australia and Canada.[76]

Despite his supportive stance towards the development of economic relations with China, Prime Minister Ikeda still maintained Japan's policy of separating political matters from economic relations (*seikei bunri*), which had been a pillar of Japan's China policy since the beginning of the 1950s. This policy was aimed at preventing China from harnessing trade relations with Japan to its political objective of gaining Tokyo's official recognition of the PRC and forcing Tokyo to cut its diplomatic relations with Taipei.[77] The Chinese principle of integrating political affairs and economic relations for political purposes was, in contrast to *seikei bunri* – called in Japanese *seikei fukabun*. The Ikeda government's rationale in holding to the *seikei bunri* policy was that it enabled Japan to sustain official relations with Taiwan, which was desirable not only to appease the US, but also because of Japan's very important trade connection with Taiwan, while deriving economic benefit from its unofficial trade with the PRC.[78]

While keeping the principle of *seikei fukabun* in mind, the Chinese government publicly displayed its *de facto* acceptance of Japan's *seikei bunri* policy.[79] The Chinese government, for instance, made considerable diplomatic concessions to Tokyo in order to bring about the resumption of bilateral trade relations. They included accepting that the PRC's national flag could not be raised in Japan and accepting the obligation to provide the Japanese government with fingerprints of all Chinese officials in its trade office.[80] Nevertheless, this did not mean that Beijing gave up its attempt to obtain official Japanese recognition of China. The PRC's political use of both the LT Trade and Friendship Trade will be discussed later.

The Satō government and China's political use of trade

After the resignation of Ikeda due to illness in November 1964, Satō Eisaku (1964–72) became the prime minister of Japan. Though the Chinese government later criticised the Satō government to a considerable extent, Satō's initial stance towards China was even more positive than that of Ikeda. Several months before he took the prime minister's office, Satō hinted to Nan Hanchen, the Chinese trade representative in Japan, that he would abandon the Japanese policy of separating politics from economic relations with China. He was also prepared to meet Zhou Enlai in Myanmar in 1964, although this meeting did not in fact eventuate.[81] Satō also requested his foreign policy advisers to undertake a fundamental review of Japan's PRC policy. Furthermore, at a press conference held on the day he became prime minister, Satō expressed his willingness to place the China issue at the top of the foreign policy agenda of his government. The positive stance taken by Satō pleased Chinese leaders at that time.

However, despite Satō's willingness to improve Sino-Japanese relations, international conditions and domestic political circumstances both in China and Japan prevented him from implementing his China initiative. On the contrary, relations between the Chinese and the Satō governments gradually deteriorated. By the mid-1960s, the Vietnam War had intensified. The Satō government's support for Washington undermined Chinese leaders' initial good impression of the Japanese administration. Moreover, it was unfortunate for Satō that China's Cultural Revolution (1966–76) occurred during his prime ministership. The Cultural Revolution, which is now regarded as 'the decade of chaos', originated in a domestic power struggle in which Mao Zedong fought to recapture leadership from his political rivals.[82] This terrible catastrophe made Chinese foreign policy, including its policy towards Japan, extremely radical and ideologically-based. Eventually, the Chinese government put the Satō government on the list of its four major enemies, along with the US, the Soviet Union and the JCP.[83]

In Japan, pro-Taiwan LDP politicians, who had been very disappointed by Satō's initial pro-PRC stance, formed a policy research group called the *Ajia mondai Kenkyū-kai (Asian Issues Research Group)* in December 1964. The increasing influence of this group within the LDP began to constrain the implementation of Satō's policy of improving Japan's relations with the PRC.[84] In February 1965, the Satō government failed to approve a plan to provide Japanese Export and Import Bank loans for a Japanese plant export to China. The deterioration of Sino-Japanese relations became even more visible with Satō's visit to Taiwan in September 1967. The Chinese government had arrested several Japanese businessmen as spies in July, and in September 1967 expelled several Japanese newspaper correspondents from the PRC.[85]

Unlike the case of the Kishi government as described above, the diplomatic confrontation between the Satō government and Beijing did not result in a break-off of bilateral trade because China needed to maintain the economic benefits brought by the trade. However, the Chinese government did start actively to harness trade relations with Japan as a political instrument to criticise and force change in Japan's stance towards the PRC. In 1968, the LT Trade, which had been based on a five-year agreement, was transformed into *MT Trade* (*Memorandum Trade*), with a new memorandum to be signed every year. China subsequently used the annual trade meeting with Japanese delegations as a political tool. The usual pattern of the meeting was that Japanese non-governmental trade representatives criticised the Satō government's China policy, in accordance with the practice of *self-denunciation*, and in compliance with Beijing's strong demand that they should do so. Then the two sides reached an agreement. Eventually, this MT Trade functioned as China's main diplomatic instrument against the Satō government.[86]

In addition to the politicisation of the LT/MT Trade described above, Friendship Trade was also used by the PRC as a political weapon. In fact, it was in the Friendship Trade that Beijing's use of the trade connection as a weapon against Japan could be most clearly observed. After the start of the Friendship Trade in 1962, the Chinese government changed the target of political pressure from the Japanese government to the non-governmental Japanese actors which actually handled trade transactions with China – the so-called *friendship firms*. These mostly consisted of small to medium-sized Japanese trading firms, which, after careful selection and screening by the Chinese government, became the primary trade route between the two countries. They were obliged by China to fully respect Zhou Enlai's Three Principles of Trade mentioned above and, in general, to show their loyalty to the PRC by obeying Beijing's political demands. For example, in August 1967 in the face of the PRC's strong condemnation of Satō's plan to visit Taiwan, almost all Japanese friendly firms mobilised their employees for a protest rally in Tokyo.[87] In short, the Chinese government manipulated these firms 'as a weapon to be used to force Japan to re-establish official or *de facto* diplomatic relations with it'.[88]

It seems that, already by the mid-1950s, officials of the Japanese MOFA were well aware of the risk involved in having China trade dealt with by private

Japanese actors.[89] Foreign Ministry officials also pointed to the intention behind China's trade with private Japanese actors. One diplomatic document noted that:

> Private trade contact is a part of Communist China's Japan policy.... Communist China is in a position freely to use these private [Japanese] organizations for its own objectives. It is very likely that Communist China is attempting to separate private Japanese organizations from the Japanese government and to increase its influence among the Japanese public by penetrating domestic politics.... The goal of Communist China would be to create pro-Communist China actors in Japan and to promote a change in the Japanese political system in the direction of neutrality or socialism.[90]

Clearly, the Japanese government was worried about the loyalties of private companies and organizations handling the China trade.

Apart from Japan's firm attachment to the US Cold War policy in East Asia, it was Beijing's active use of unofficial trade relations as a political instrument to intervene in Japanese domestic affairs that made it difficult for Japanese governments, especially the Satō government, to transform unofficial trade relations with China into *official* ones. Despite the wishes of Japanese governments and the business community, the establishment of truly official economic and diplomatic relations between Japan and China was a very difficult task. Japanese governments' long-held policy of engaging China, which had been first pursued by Prime Minister Yoshida Shigeru, was therefore still impossible to implement.

It is also notable that by the time of the Ikeda and Satō governments, Japan's security concern in relation to China had become a new motivation for the policy of engaging China. In the 1962 Diet session, Foreign Minister Miki Takeo, for example, expressed the Ikeda government's policy of encouraging China to become a member of the United Nations. He argued that it was desirable to include the PRC in the framework of international politics in order to stabilise the region, and to encourage the retention of China's nuclear test ban and its endorsement of international armaments reduction.[91] But the PRC developed a nuclear weapon during the 1960s, successfully conducting its first nuclear test in October 1964. In March 1969, Prime Minister Satō acknowledged the strong security concerns of Association of South East Asian Nations (ASEAN) member countries about the PRC's acquisition of a nuclear weapon, expressing his wish that the PRC should take its place as a full member of international society.[92] These official statements encouraging China's inclusion in international political institutions, particularly its participation in the United Nations, were based on Japanese leaders' perceptions of the threat posed to Japan by a newly emerged, politically isolated nuclear power. Such official views in the 1960s clearly foreshadow the stance that would again be taken by Japanese leaders in the uncertain conditions of the 1990s, as Chapter 3 will show.

Despite the difficulties of earlier years, the dramatic changes in the international and domestic environments surrounding Sino-Japanese relations after the beginning of the 1970s eventually removed the constraints on Japan's long-held policy of China engagement, as we will see in the next section.

The end of external and domestic constraints on Japan's policy of China engagement, 1972–78

The Sino-American détente and China's entry into the United Nations in 1971 on the one hand, and the change of prime minister in Japan from Satō to Tanaka Kakuei in July 1972 on the other, first weakened and then removed the constraints on Japan's freedom of action on China matters, eventually leading to the normalisation of Sino-Japanese diplomatic relations in September 1972. The conclusion of the Sino-Japanese Peace and Friendship Treaty and China's introduction of the Reform and Liberalisation Policy in 1978 paved the way for a new phase of Sino-Japanese relations, marked above all by the introduction of ODA.

The road to normalisation of diplomatic relations

External factors

The joint communiqué signed by Japanese Prime Minister Tanaka Kakuei (1972–74) and Chinese Premier Zhou Enlai on 29 September 1972 in Beijing ended more than two decades of diplomatic estrangement between the neighbouring countries. Two international developments had a large impact on developments in Japanese domestic politics, and consequently, created the political atmosphere that enabled prompt normalisation of diplomatic relations. They were US President Richard Nixon's announcement in July 1971 that he planned to visit the PRC, which is known as the *Nixon shock* in Japan, and the entry of the PRC into the United Nations in October 1971.

President Nixon's dramatic reversal of US China policy greatly surprised the government of Japan, together with that section of the public which took an interest in China issues. Although Nixon claimed that the initial reaction abroad, especially in Europe, was generally favourable, his announcement caused great commotion in Japan.[93] It was resented not because of the reversal of the American position on China, but because Nixon informed Prime Minister Satō about his plan to visit the PRC only two hours before his public declaration on 15 July 1971. The Satō government and many Japanese people outside government felt betrayed, especially those who had not doubted the solidity of the Japan–US alliance. This reversal in US China policy, which had been carefully arranged by Nixon and his adviser Henry Kissinger, was designed to maximise American interests in the international environment at that time. More particularly, it was intended both to facilitate America's withdrawal from the Vietnam War and to counter Soviet expansionism.[94]

Though neither Nixon nor Kissinger set out to harm Satō's political leadership,[95] the dramatic reversal of the US position on China did damage both the international and the domestic credibility of the Satō government, and caused it considerable embarrassment. It is noteworthy, however, that Satō's *personal* reaction to Nixon's announcement was not particularly bitter. His diary entry on the day of Nixon's announcement (in Japan it was on 16 July 1971) reveals that he understood that Nixon's China initiative was aimed at ending America's involvement in the Vietnam War. Satō was chiefly surprised by the fact that the Chinese government did not attach any political conditions to Nixon's visit. While expressing his sympathy towards the Taiwan government, Satō appreciated the indication of the PRC government's flexible diplomatic stance towards the US.[96]

As explained in the previous section, Prime Minister Satō had wished to establish official relations with the PRC well before Nixon's initiative. At the National Diet session on 22 January 1971, Satō had publicly offered to increase trade and press contacts with the PRC government and to initiate talks at the government level.[97] Up until the time he left the prime minister's office in July 1972, Satō had used several channels – the Consul-General in Hong Kong, Okada Akira;[98] the Governor of Tokyo, Minobe Ryōkichi; the official representative of MT Trade, Watanabe Yoheiji;[99] and a secret envoy, Eguchi Mahiko[100] – to make official contact with Chinese leaders. However, Satō's initiative had not succeeded due to Beijing's persistent distrust of and hostility towards him. Zhou Enlai, for example, said that China 'shall not accept Satō as a negotiating partner', adding, however, that 'any successor of Satō will be welcomed in Beijing'.[101] The Chinese government's hostility was based on its perception of Satō's foreign policy orientation, which was characterised as pro-Washington and pro-Taiwan, and was also due to the fact that he is the natural brother of former Prime Minister Kishi (1957–60), who had been a minister of the wartime Tōjō Hideki government, and had been listed as a Class A war criminal.[102]

In addition to the *Nixon shock*, China's acquisition of United Nations membership in October 1971 also significantly damaged the Satō government's domestic credibility and contributed to Satō's resignation. The Satō government had continued to support the US policy of keeping Taiwan in and the PRC out of the United Nations, despite opposition by some LDP members and the Japanese Foreign Ministry's pessimistic assessment of this policy.[103] Although Nixon's China initiative opened the way for direct discussions with Chinese leaders, the US government renounced neither its defence commitment to nor its diplomatic relations with the Taiwan government.[104] Thus the US government maintained its effort to keep Taiwan in and the PRC out of the UN General Assembly, even though a majority of the Assembly members, mostly Third World countries, supported the proposal to allow the PRC's membership. Eventually, in October 1971, the PRC became an official member of the UN Assembly and Taiwan lost its membership. The credibility of Satō, who had strongly supported the US over the issue, was significantly undermined. He announced his plan to resign in June 1972, eight months after the PRC's entry into the United Nations.

The reason that Satō supported US government policy on the PRC and Taiwan, despite opposition from quarters in Japan, was his desire to facilitate the reversion of the Okinawa Islands to Japanese sovereignty,[105] which he now considered to be the most important foreign policy goal of his cabinet, even though he had at first expressed his willingness to give priority to relations with the PRC, as noted earlier. Despite the end of the Allied Occupation of Japan in 1952, the Okinawa

Islands remained under the direct control of the US and were used as a frontline military base against the PRC and North Korea, until May 1972 when they returned to Japan. Recognising the importance of support from pro-Taiwan LDP politicians and pro-Taiwan members in the US Senate in order to realise the return of the Okinawa Islands, Satō had no option but to support US efforts to keep Taiwan in the United Nations and the PRC out.[106] The pattern by which the Japanese government conceded to the US in order to achieve in exchange a policy goal that required American support was again repeated here, in a manner that was quite similar to the situation two decades earlier when the Yoshida government had abandoned its attempt to establish official economic relations with the PRC in the face of the implicit US threat that it might not ratify the San Francisco Peace Treaty.

Another important result of the Nixon shock for Japanese relations with China was that it motivated officials of the MOFA to normalise diplomatic relations with the PRC quicker than the US. The loosening of the external constraints on Japan's foreign policy to China, together with a strong feeling that they had been betrayed by Nixon, made these officials determined to see that 'Japan got ahead of the US in the actual normalisation'.[107]

Domestic factors

In addition to the altered international environment surrounding Sino-Japanese relations, a rapid succession of changes in Japanese domestic politics played its part, in the process leading to Japan's normalisation of diplomatic relations with the PRC. The most important domestic factor was the elevation of Tanaka Kakuei to prime minister, a move welcomed by the Chinese government.

After Satō's resignation, Tanaka was elected president of the ruling LDP on 5 July 1972,[108] and formed his cabinet two days later. The emergence of the Tanaka government (1972–74) delighted Chinese leaders, who had been carefully watching post-Satō Japanese politics. They repeatedly questioned pro-PRC LDP politicians, such as Furui Yoshimi and Tagawa Seiichi, about the personalities of the candidates for prime minister, as well as their political attitudes to China.[109] Tanaka was their preferred negotiating partner for rapprochement, partly because as MITI Minister he had established the China Division within the Ministry, and had stated his willingness to allow the Import–Export Bank to lend money to China.[110]

Tanaka's move to start normalisation talks with China was immediate. On 7 July 1972, the day that he became prime minister, he announced that his government 'will initiate normalisation talks with the PRC as soon as possible'. Two days later, Zhou Enlai expressed great appreciation of the Tanaka initiative.[111] The next day, Zhou dispatched the deputy secretary of the Sino–Japanese Friendship Association, Sun Pinghua, to Tokyo. On 20 July 1972 Sun met Foreign Minister Ōhira Masayoshi. This was the first official contact between Japanese and Chinese officials since 1949.[112] On 24 July, Tanaka established the Council for Normalisation of Japan–China Diplomatic Relations within the LDP as the place for political debate between pro-PRC and pro-Taiwan party members.

With the help of Foreign Minister Ōhira and his advisers, however, Tanaka quickly decided to proceed with normalisation. In a conversation with Tagawa Seiichi, Tanaka said:

> It will be impossible to reach a decision if we want to create a consensus among LDP members, who have different positions on China. I therefore will exercise strong leadership to make a decision to normalise diplomatic relations within a short period of time.[113]

Fearful of bureaucratic delay, Tanaka rejected the involvement of Foreign Ministry officials in the discussions until later stages of the process of diplomatic normalisation.[114]

The Tanaka government was initially concerned that the commencement of normalisation talks would focus upon Japan's war reparations to China and the Japan–US defence treaty, and thus, the goal of Sino-Japanese rapprochement would be jeopardised. In the event, however, the PRC offered to renounce both war reparations claims against Japan, and any objection to the established defence alliance.[115] The decision to accept the alliance was partly the result of a February 1972 meeting between Nixon and Zhou, in which Nixon convinced Zhou that abrogation of the treaty might lead to a Japanese military build-up.[116]

More than two decades of an *abnormal* state of affairs between Japan and China finally ended in Beijing on 29 September 1972 when Tanaka and Zhou jointly signed the rapprochement communiqué. It is striking that Tanaka managed to achieve normalisation of diplomatic relations with the PRC only three months after becoming prime minister. On the other hand, regardless of who had succeeded Satō as prime minister, it is likely that Japan's rapprochement with China would eventually have been realised. At that time, significant voices in the public arena, as well as the majority of parliamentarians and business elites, supported rapprochement,[117] and a newly elected prime minister might have been unable to choose any other option. However, in terms of the speed of decision-making, Tanaka's contribution was remarkable.

After the normalisation of diplomatic relations

It might be reasonable to assume that normalisation of Sino-Japanese relations would have removed the political constraints on Japanese economic activities in China and enabled Japan to begin providing ODA. However, the 1972 rapprochement did not result in the immediate implementation of economic assistance to China. Political and economic considerations still prevented the Japanese government from initiating any large-scale economic commitment, and it was only after further changes in circumstances, particularly China's 1978 introduction of the Reform and Liberalisation Policy, which considerably opened up the Chinese economy to the outside world, that the Japanese government was able to begin to provide substantial development assistance to China.

Normalisation of Sino-Japanese diplomatic relations contributed to an increase in the volume of bilateral trade, but the increase was much smaller than might have been expected.[118] The volume of trade between Japan and China increased from US$1.1 billion in 1972 to $2 billion in 1973 and $3.79 billion in 1975. Yet, Japanese trade with South Korea and Taiwan during the same period also grew in similar proportion. Trade with South Korea increased from US$1.4 billion in 1972 to $3 billion in 1973 and $3.6 billion in 1975, while trade with Taiwan increased from US$1.5 billion in 1972 to $2.5 billion in 1973 and $2.6 billion in 1975. Neither was there any dramatic increase in the share of Sino-Japanese trade in Japan's total trade with Northeast Asia – namely, China, Hong Kong, North and South Korea, Taiwan and the Soviet Union – during the 1970s.[119] Clearly, the normalisation of diplomatic relations did not immediately bring about economic conditions favourable for Japanese businesses seeking to boost their trade transactions with and investments in China.

One factor restricting post-1972 Japanese economic interaction with China was China's lack of foreign currency reserves to pay for purchases of Japanese goods. But the biggest reason was Japan's cautiousness in expanding its trade with and investment in a China then undergoing considerable turbulence. The kick-off of Japan's extensive economic commitment to China did not happen until 1979, when the political and social disturbance caused by the Cultural Revolution began to die down and the PRC's Reform and Liberalisation Policy took effect.

Socio-political conditions in China during this period were far from ideal if the Japanese business community and government were to boost their economic activities there. The risk associated with business investment in China was simply too high to ignore. Political dominance by the Gang of Four in the mid-1970s resulted in social chaos in China,[120] making it impossible for Japanese businesses and the government to contemplate any large-scale economic commitment. In addition, the possibility of Japan's active economic commitment to China was being undermined by the so-called *anti-hegemony clause* of the Sino-Japanese Peace and Friendship Treaty. In 1974, the Japanese and Chinese governments agreed to initiate peace treaty negotiations, as the two countries had never formally ended the state of war between them after 1945. However, Tokyo's initial expectation that the issue would be quickly resolved soon evaporated when the Chinese government suddenly demanded the inclusion of an anti-hegemony clause, with the aim of forming a united front against the Soviet Union, in February 1975. The clause stated:

> Normalisation of relations between China and Japan is not directed against third countries. Neither of the two countries should seek hegemony in the Asia-Pacific region and each country is opposed to efforts by any country or group of countries to establish such hegemony.[121]

The Soviet Union and the international community interpreted the clause as providing for a virtual military alliance between Japan and China against the Soviet Union. While the Soviet government put strong diplomatic pressure on the

Japanese government not to accept China's demand, the PRC government showed no sign of compromise over the issue. By the beginning of 1975, negotiation of the Sino-Japanese Peace and Friendship Treaty had ceased.

Japanese business leaders advocated an early settlement of the Sino-Japanese negotiations, making their pro-PRC stance clear to both governments. For example, in October 1975, Dokō Toshio, the chairman of the Keidanren (Federation of Economic Organizations), told Chinese leaders that the Japanese government 'should not fear the Soviet Union in making major decisions on Sino-Japanese trade'.[122] Inayama Yoshihiro of Shin Nittetsu (New Japan Steel) Corporation, together with some pro-PRC LDP politicians, formed the Sino-Japanese Consultative Committee to encourage early settlement of the treaty negotiation. Despite pressure by such business leaders, the Japanese government was determined to avoid being caught alone in the cross-fire created by the Sino-Soviet confrontation. Disagreement between the Japanese and the PRC governments over the anti-hegemony clause continued up until 1978, when China accepted Tokyo's offer to include in the treaty a so-called *third country clause*, which confirmed that the anti-hegemony clause was not directed against any specific third party. The Sino-Japanese Peace and Friendship treaty was then concluded.[123]

The PRC's Reform and Liberalisation Policy and new economic relations

The emergence of a more development-oriented post-Mao leadership in China in the late 1970s was one of the most important factors that led to Japan's plant investments in the PRC and provision of ODA. The radical change in China's development policy in 1978, expressed in the Reform and Liberalisation Policy, facilitated a more proactive economic commitment to China by the Japanese government. China's new policy was designed to create a powerful socialist nation by modernising its industries, agriculture, transportation and national defence. These goals had been first articulated by Zhou Enlai in September 1954 at the First National People's Congress as the *Four Modernisation Policy*; the content of this earlier modernisation policy was redeveloped by Deng Xiaoping as the *Reform and Liberalisation Policy*.[124]

The Reform and Liberalisation Policy represented a significant policy change because CCP leaders, for the first time, admitted that development driven by Western technology should take priority over national pride in self-development. Some termed it the 'Great Leap to the Outside World'[125] in a comparison with the Great Leap Forward campaign of 1958–60. The effect of the policy was substantially to open up the Chinese economy to capitalist countries, including Japan, for the first time since the introduction of the socialist economy in 1949.

Chinese leaders implemented the policy because they wanted to reduce the economic and technological gap between the PRC and the industrialised countries of Europe, the US and Japan. They had become fully aware that China's position in the international economic and technological hierarchy was far behind that of the industrialised economies. China had isolated itself economically from the outside world in the 1950s and 1960s – the period in which the world economy recovered from the damage caused by the Second World War and grew rapidly – and this self-isolation had greatly contributed to the delay in the nation's economic and industrial modernisation. Thus, the Reform and Liberalisation policy was based on the conviction that it was necessary to develop the economy and technology if China was to become a great power.[126]

In comparison to Sino-Japanese trade from 1972 to 1978, the volume of bilateral trade from 1979 to 1981 grew sharply. This was largely because of the Long-Term Trade Agreement (LTTA) signed by the Japanese and Chinese governments in 1978. The agreement was based on the principle of balanced exchange, stipulating first, a total trade of US$20 billion during the eight-year period from 1978 to 1985; second, that in this period Japan was to export plant and industrial technology worth US$7–8 billion and construction machinery and materials worth US$2–3 billion on the basis of deferred payments; third, in return, China was to export crude oil and coal to the value of US$10 billion to Japan.[127] Although Chinese oil exports to Japan remained well below the agreed amount of US$47.1 million due to stagnant Chinese oil output, the trade agreement successfully contributed to an increase in both bilateral trade and contracts for construction of new plants.

China's efforts to attract Japanese economic investment were exemplified in statements made by Deng Xiaoping during his visit to Japan in 1978 to ratify the Sino-Japanese Peace and Friendship Treaty. Deng announced that China

> would invite many Japanese experts in science, technology and finance. The Sino-Japanese Long-Term Trade Agreement (LTTA) is not enough. I would not mind even if the US$20 billion [the amount of total bilateral exports agreed during the period from 1978 to 1985] were doubled or tripled.[128]

While travelling by *Shinkansen* (the bullet train; the world's fastest train at that time), Deng also expressed his determination to achieve rapid economic development in China, saying 'what is the most necessary for us [China] is to run as fast as possible'.[129] Obviously, Deng's statements were intended to counter the Japanese business community's concerns about China's willingness and ability to implement reform and liberalisation of its economy. More than most countries, Japan was well pleased to provide the capital and technological assistance necessary for China's development.

Conclusion

During the period from 1945 to 1971, successive Japanese governments, led by Yoshida, Hatoyama, Kishi, Ikeda and Satō, consistently pursued a policy of engagement with China. However, the subordination of Japan's foreign policy to that of the US, diplomatic pressure from the Taiwan government not to recognise the PRC, and China's political use of its informal connections with non-governmental

Japanese actors made it impossible for these Japanese governments to forge official economic and diplomatic relations with China. In the end, it was too risky for these Japanese governments to establish official relations with the PRC, which would have been very likely to damage the overwhelmingly important Japan–US defence alliance, which in turn guaranteed Japan's national security.

The reasons that these Japanese governments wished to establish official relations with China vary. The Yoshida government sought official economic relations in an attempt to regain Japan's share of the Mainland China market, which had absorbed more than one-fifth of Japan's total exports in the pre-Second World War period and which Japan had lost as a result of the war. Yoshida also pursued official trade relations with China in order to separate China economically from the Communist bloc led by the Soviet Union, by deepening China's economic dependence on trade with Japan. The Hatoyama and Kishi governments sought to establish official economic relations with China in a search for an autonomous foreign policy; because of the Japanese business community's persistent dream of regaining and extending a China market; and in an attempt to undermine China's increasing penetration of Japanese politics through its informal connections with the JCP and the JSP. In addition to economic interests, the emergence of China as a nuclear power in the mid-1960s also motivated the Ikeda and Satō governments to seek official diplomatic relations, as it was considered dangerous not to create new channels of communication with a neighbouring country that had developed nuclear weapons. Thus, despite the Cold War international system that separated Japan and China into different and rival ideological camps, economic interests and geographical proximity, the fundamental sources of Japan's security concerns, consistently encouraged Japanese governments to pursue official relations with China during the period 1945–71.

Dramatic changes in the international environment, as well as critical changes in Japanese and Chinese domestic politics in the 1970s, provided more favourable conditions for Japanese policy-makers to further their long-held policy of China engagement. The 1971 US–China détente removed the biggest external constraint on Japan's freedom of action on China matters, that is, the US Cold War policy of containing the PRC. The 1972 normalisation of diplomatic relations between Japan and China provided an opportunity to boost Japan's economic commitment to China, although this did not happen to any great degree until after 1978, when the bilateral peace treaty was concluded, China's domestic affairs had stabilised somewhat, and the Chinese government had introduced its new Reform and Liberalisation Policy. Benefiting from the removal of external and domestic constraints on Japan's China policy, the Ōhira government made a decision to provide ODA in 1979. Thus, Japan's policy of engaging China could finally be implemented by means of ODA.

The next chapter analyses the process that led to Japan's first provision of ODA to China, and elucidates the policy objectives of Japan's transfer of financial resources and knowledge to China as well as the broader interests behind it.

3 Policy objectives and underlying interests since 1979

This chapter investigates the complex policy objectives of Japanese ODA to China since 1979 and the broader interests behind it, with reference to major external and internal factors that encouraged the evolution of these objectives and interests. It argues that first, since 1979 Japan's policy of providing ODA to China has been intended to promote various perceived Japanese economic, political and strategic interests; and second, that policy objectives have evolved according to certain changes in the international and domestic environments. While some of the economic objectives that Japan has pursued through ODA provision to China have remained static, political and strategic goals have dramatically changed during the period in question. In particular, several external and internal developments that occurred between 1989 and the mid-1990s contributed to the change in Japanese policy-makers' perceptions of China, and eventually led to changes in the goals of Japanese ODA and the interests behind the provision of aid. Third, it is argued here that despite this evolution of Japan's policy goals, the underlying concept of *engagement* has remained consistent since 1979, although the perception of China as a partner has changed from a poor *de facto* strategic ally – China in the 1980s – to a rapidly modernising potential military challenger – China after the mid-1990s.

The first section of the chapter investigates the event that triggered the start of Japan's ODA programme to China, and then provides a brief overview of the quantitative significance of Japanese ODA. The second section examines the actual policy objectives of Japanese ODA to China and the broader political, strategic and economic interests behind it during the decade between 1979 and 1988. The third section analyses the international and domestic developments that produced changes in the policy objectives of Japanese ODA to China during the transitional period between 1989 and the mid-1990s. The fourth section elucidates the new policy objectives of Japan's China ODA, from the mid-1990s onwards, with reference to the actual implementation of the aid programme.

The beginning of Japanese aid to China

As noted briefly in Chapter 1, interpretations of Japan's motives for initiating the China ODA programme differ. Some observers regard Japanese aid to China as a form of disguised war reparations. Although they never expressed such a view officially, at least in 1979, some senior Japanese officials, especially those with a strong sense of war guilt towards the Chinese people, felt obliged to assist Chinese economic development.[1] Moreover, Chinese leaders clearly did regard Japanese ODA to China as a form of war reparations.[2] However, as several Japanese officials currently responsible for the formulation and implementation of China ODA policy remark, Japan's development aid to China should be considered separately from war reparations.[3] Thus, Japanese officials' lingering feelings of war guilt in 1979 should be regarded as part of the *ethical background* rather than as the real motive of the Japanese government in initiating the China ODA programme.

A second interpretation emphasises the linkage between the commencement of the China ODA programme in 1979 and Japan's huge trade surplus in relation to its Western trading partners in the late 1970s. That is, in light of the strong criticism by Western countries, the Japanese government needed to recycle its trade surplus in the form of foreign aid to developing countries,[4] and the PRC was a new and excellent destination for Japanese aid flow.[5] However, although the trade surplus did facilitate an increase in the overall amount of Japanese foreign aid, there is no conclusive evidence of a direct link between the issue of the surplus and the initiation of ODA to China. It is more reasonable to regard Japan's huge trade surplus in the 1970s as part of the financial background that enabled the Japanese government to provide a large amount of ODA to China, rather than as the actual target of the aid programme.

In fact, it was the suspension of Japanese plant project contracts by China that triggered Japan's ODA provision to China. Suspension of the contracts provided a direct opportunity for the Japanese government to initiate ODA. We will now examine the issue of the suspension of plant contracts, with particular reference to the Baoshan steel plant project.

In the late 1970s, the Chinese government asked the biggest Japanese steel manufacturer, Shin Nihon Seitetsu, to provide technological support for the construction of a gigantic steel plant in Baoshan, a city near Shanghai. After careful technical assessment by Japanese engineers, the company agreed to construct a plant with an annual capacity of 6 million tons in 1978 as the first project of the Sino-Japanese LTTA.[6] Hua Guofeng, the then Chinese head of state, wanted to make the Baoshan project a symbol of China's Reform and Liberalisation Policy, which advocated the introduction of foreign high technology to advance Chinese modernisation.[7] In fact, in 1978 China signed seventy-four plant project contracts with Japan under the LTTA. Among these, the Baoshan steel plant project was the biggest, and it was expected to play a major role in transferring Japanese steel production technology to China.

Payment for Japan's plant exports was to be made by exports of Chinese crude oil and coal to Japan. However, China failed to increase its oil output because of technological problems and as a result, its foreign earnings fell far short of expectations.[8] Although China had agreed under the LTTA to export 471 billion tons of crude oil to Japan during the period from 1978 to 1982, actual exports during this five-year period remained at 392 billion tons. The annual growth rate of Chinese oil output decreased sharply from 20 per cent in the early 1970s to 11 per cent in 1978 and −4.5 per cent in 1981.[9] In addition, China also had serious problems of inflation and budget deficits.[10] The failure to earn foreign exchange through oil sales, combined with the serious problems of inflation and budget deficits, put pressure on Chinese leaders to suspend the Baoshan project and other plant projects with Japan and other countries. Consequently, the Chinese government told the Japanese government in February 1979 of its decision to cancel various plant contracts with Japanese companies, including the Baoshan project.

The financial difficulty was not the only reason for this decision. As illustrated by a Central Committee meeting of the CCP held in April 1979, a certain political atmosphere within the Chinese government also contributed to the cancellation of the contracts. At this meeting, Chen Yun, China's top economic planning official, questioned the economic effectiveness of the Reform and Liberalisation Policy by pointing out the large financial risks in depending significantly on foreign loans to import massive amounts of technology and equipment. Chen urged that China maintain budget capability for repayments and for operating the constructed plants.[11] Deng Xiaoping, the deputy general secretary of the Party, supported Chen's criticism. Furthermore, in the same meeting, Premier Zhao Ziyang criticised China's huge plant investments as 'the source of the massive budget deficit that has become apparent over the last five years', insisting that 'China should reduce the introduction of plant projects while increasing the introduction of foreign technology.'[12] As criticism of these plant projects began to dominate deliberations within the CCP, the leaders implementing the projects began to change their positions. For instance, Li Xiannian, who was responsible for China's plant projects with foreign countries, criticised himself, admitting his responsibility for the budget deficit as a result of very large investments in such projects.

Japan's response to China's decision to cancel the Baoshan and other plant project contracts was to initiate ODA to China. In fact, soon after cancelling the Baoshan project, Deng Xiaoping hinted that the Chinese government would reverse the decision if Japan could provide financial assistance to China.[13] In December 1979, ten months after the cancellation, Prime Minister Ōhira announced in Beijing the disbursement of a 300 billion yen loan to China for five years (1979–83), with an annual interest rate of 3 per cent and repayment over thirty years with a ten-year grace period.[14] This first yen loan package rescued the first phase of the Baoshan steel plant project from cancellation, together with many other Japanese plant contracts.

The issue of the plant project suspension described above directly triggered Japan's ODA provision to China. However, this first yen loan provision does not mean that Japan simply responded to China's request without any consideration of its own national interests. Particular diplomatic, economic and strategic interests motivated Japanese leaders to initiate development assistance to China at that time. Indeed, the Ōhira government's decision to provide financial assistance to

China was a highly political decision; the initiation of the ODA programme in 1979 was a proactive policy on the part of Japan based on commercial, political and strategic calculations, aimed at advancing not only immediate self-interest but also longer-term interests in relation to the PRC.

Policy objectives and underlying interests, 1979–88

According to the Japanese MOFA,

> Our economic cooperation with China has been based on the recognition that our support of China's economic reforms and open-market policy will contribute to the stability and development of the Chinese economy, further strengthen the friendly relations between the two countries, and will eventually lead to peace, stability, and prosperity of the region.[15]

Over the last two decades. the Ministry has repeatedly stated the general point that 'the stability of the most isolated and populous country in the region is important to the security interests of Japan' as well as to the stability of the region as a whole. In a less formal situation, a senior official of the Foreign Ministry identified one of the specific fears underlying this stance: domestic instability 'might provoke a massive outflow of Chinese refugees into Japan that would be beyond Japanese capacity to control'.[16] However, the attempt to connect the stability of China directly with both a possible refugee crisis and the peace of the whole region must be regarded more as official justification by the MOFA, rather than a reflection of the actual aim of China ODA activity.

As will be argued in the following pages, the major aim of Japan's development assistance to China between 1979 and 1988 was to support China's Reform and Liberalisation Policy.[17] Nevertheless, Japan supported this policy not because it wanted to assist in the development of the Chinese economy and maintain the peace of the region for altruistic reasons, but rather to advance its own political, strategic and economic interests in relation to China. The self-interest that Japan pursued through provision of money and knowledge to the PRC was hidden behind the rhetoric of promoting China's economic development and the stability and peace of the region. In reality, a healthier dose of a narrower kind of self-interest played a large part in ODA policy-making.

Politico-strategic interests

During the first decade of Japan's ODA programme to China (1979–88), when the Cold War still dominated international relations, the political and strategic interests that Japanese governments pursued through ODA provision to China were first, to separate the PRC economically from the Communist camp led by the Soviet Union; second, to support the domestic political power of reformist Chinese leaders; and third, to prevent China from becoming a chaotic and isolated country.

Bringing China into the 'free world' *bloc*

Through the provision of ODA to China, Japanese leaders aimed eventually to bring the country into the *free world* bloc, by significantly increasing the PRC's foreign aid and trade dependence on Japan. The introduction of the Reform and Liberalisation Policy by the post-Mao Chinese government in 1978 provided an excellent opportunity for the Japanese government to implement its long-held policy of economic engagement with China.[18] As explained in Chapter 2, although Prime Minister Yoshida had desired to implement this policy at the beginning of the 1950s in order to separate the PRC economically from the Soviet Union, it was impossible to do so because of strong opposition by the US government and China's self-reliant development policy. However, the situation changed with the 1971 Sino-American détente and the introduction of the Reform and Liberalisation Policy. As will be discussed in Chapter 5, Japanese ODA has indeed contributed to an increase in China's trade and technological dependence on Japan and on Western countries and, hence, eventually did help separate China economically from the Communist bloc.

Between 1979 and 1988, Japanese ODA to China also had security implications for both countries, given the Soviet Union's rapid military build-up in the East Asian region. That is, through economic cooperation, Japan supported China's military effort to counter the Soviet military forces along its long borderlines.[19] During this period of the Cold War, the US government treated the PRC as an informal American ally against the Soviet Union and actively provided various forms of military support to China, including the transfer of some defence technology.[20] Thus, it is no surprise that as a formal American ally, Japan also treated China as its *de facto* ally against the Soviet Union. As one Japanese defence analyst remarks, a *de facto* anti-Soviet alliance between Japan and China had already existed throughout the 1970s and the 1980s.[21] During this period, the Japanese and the Chinese government even regarded each other's military build-up favourably. For example, Beijing did not object to the future renewal of the Japan–US security alliance in 1972, when the two countries normalised their diplomatic relations, and Deng Xiaoping and other Chinese leaders even encouraged a Japanese military build-up in the 1980s.[22] In this context, Japan attempted to use China ODA in order to promote its security interest in the region in the Cold War strategic environment.

Supporting the political power of reformist Chinese leaders

The second major policy objective that Japanese governments pursued through China ODA activity between 1979 and 1988 was support of the domestic political power of reformist Chinese leaders. To achieve this objective, Japanese governments actively supported the implementation of the Reform and Liberalisation Policy, by means of ODA.[23] Reformist Chinese leaders such as Deng Xiaoping, Hu Yaobang and Zhao Ziyang were a major driving force of the Reform and Liberalisation Policy and, therefore, the success of the policy was crucial for their leadership within the Chinese government. Failure of the policy would not only threaten the authority of such reformist leaders, but would also suggest the possibility that more conservative leaders might usurp the reformists. In this context, it is no coincidence that the Japanese government began providing ODA to China a year after the introduction of China's new policy.

The support of reformist Chinese leaders was clearly in Japan's political interest as they were more likely than conservative leaders to guide the PRC in an open, liberal and cooperative direction through further reform of the Chinese economic system. The successful implementation of the Reform and Liberalisation Policy was also in Japan's economic interest, as it would further open the Chinese economy and consequently create lucrative trade and investment opportunities for private Japanese companies in China.

Sustaining the stability of China

Japanese leaders between 1979 and 1988 also aimed to help maintain stability in China's political and economic affairs through the provision of ODA. Like China's other neighbours, Japan was concerned about political and economic collapse in China, which could conceivably cause territorial fragmentation, civil war and a resultant outflow of millions of Chinese refugees towards Japan and other neighbouring countries.[24] There is no doubt that such an outflow of refugees from a chaotic and collapsed China would put a severe strain on the limited resources of other countries.[25] In view of China's population of 1.2 billion, any breakdown of the Chinese economy and society would inevitably have a negative impact not only on Japan, but also on the region and indeed the whole world.[26] From this perspective, instability in the PRC's political and economic affairs posed a threat to Japan, and thus, was naturally a cause for concern for Japanese policy-makers. One can conclude that Japan provided ODA partly to help prevent China from disintegrating.

It is also clear, however, that the emphasis by Japanese officials on the potential inflow of Chinese refugees into Japan between 1979 and 1988 was rhetorical, or at least represented an exaggerated argument, intended to gain the public's support for China aid activity.[27] Apart from this broad perception of the threat from a collapsed China, there were several more precise reasons why Japanese policy-makers feared instability in China's political and economic affairs. First, Japanese policy-makers had commercial reasons for wanting to sustain stability in China. As one senior official of the MOFA commented, 'a disintegrated and unruly China would inevitably increase trade and investment risks for private Japanese companies and thus damage Japanese commercial interests involved with China.'[28] Without political stability and economic growth, it was highly unlikely that the PRC would have been able to provide Japanese companies with either trade or investment opportunities.

Second, Japanese policy-makers also believed that a politically and economically chaotic China was likely to adopt aggressive foreign and military policies. The history of the PRC certainly suggests that chaos in domestic politics can precipitate radical and aggressive foreign policy. As described in Chapter 2, during both the Great Leap Forward (1958–60) and the Cultural Revolution (1966–76), Chinese foreign and security policy had largely been dominated by radical ideology, rather than the accepted rules and norms of orthodox international relations. As a result, the PRC's foreign and defence policy towards Japan and other countries became very aggressive, and China experienced profound international isolation during both periods.[29] Japanese observers are keenly aware that Chinese leaders, especially when involved in a domestic power struggle, have tended to adopt a foreign policy that benefits their domestic power, even if it undermines state interests and endangers foreign relations.

Third Japanese officials believed that if China became fragmented and chaotic, anti-Japanese nationalism among the Chinese public would increase because the restraining hand of the CCP would be removed or weakened.[30] They particularly feared a large increase in the number of war reparations claims made against the Japanese government by Chinese war victims.[31] Such a situation constituted a worst case scenario for the Japanese government.[32] In this context, the CCP's ability to use its political authority to control the escalation of anti-Japanese nationalism within China, often exercised in the past, was, and in fact is still, very useful for the Japanese government.

The irony of Japan's China ODA is that it has functioned to support the continuation of one-party political control by the CCP through its assistance to Chinese economic development. Nevertheless, this does not mean that the Japanese government is uncritical of the Communist Party's political dictatorship in China; rather, the Japanese government does not want drastic and rapid change in the Chinese political system that might produce chaos in political and economic affairs. Although democratisation has not been the goal of Japan's China ODA policy, Japanese governments have in fact favoured the democratic transformation of the Chinese political system – but only if it progresses step by step without political upheaval and economic damage.[33] Japan's active support of the Reform and Liberalisation Policy through ODA can also be understood in this context.

In the end, it is in Japan's commercial, political and security interests to promote a politically stable and economically open China. Maintaining the stability of Chinese domestic affairs was thus an important aim of the Japanese government in implementing its development assistance policy to China between 1979 and 1988.[34]

Official Japanese statements after the Tiananmen Square Incident

The series of statements made by Japanese political leaders and officials after the 1989 Tiananmen Square Incident revealed the real interests that Japan had pursued through its ODA policy to China between 1979 and 1988. With the strong sense of crisis caused by this event, Japanese leaders and officials spoke out much more clearly than usual about the actual policy goals and interests behind ODA provision to China. This section reviews these statements in order to provide evidence for the arguments presented above on the politico-strategic objectives of China ODA. The concrete implications of the Tiananmen Square Incident for Japanese ODA policy towards China in the 1990s will be discussed separately in the next section.

The immediate trigger for the demonstrations that preceded the Tiananmen Square Incident of June 1989 was the death of Hu Yaobang, a reformist and former secretary-general of the CCP, in April 1989. Students, members of the industrial working class and intellectuals, who were suffering from the effects of inflation and market-based economic reforms and who were also frustrated by the slow pace of political reform and the level of official corruption, took to the streets to become the driving force of a mass protest against Chinese leaders. The establishment of the Beijing Students' Autonomous Federation in April and the Beijing Workers' Autonomous Federation in May, the first social organisations to be created outside the influence of the CCP since 1949, presented a fundamental challenge to the CCP's political dictatorship. Communist Party leaders such as Deng Xiaoping, the actual head of the CCP whose official position was as a member of the Party's Central Political Bureau, and Premier Li Peng, who maintained a hardline stance on the demonstrations, were victorious in an inner-party power struggle against the liberal group gathered around Secretary-General Zhao Ziyang, who sympathised with the demonstrators. Consequently, martial law was introduced on 20 May 1989 and the Chinese army crushed the demonstrations in Tiananmen Square on 4 June. The estimated number of students and other demonstrators killed in the military crackdown ranges from a few hundred to over a thousand.[35] The Chinese government's abuse of human rights shocked people around the world and led to a united aid sanction against China by the Group of Seven (G7) nations – the US, Germany, France, the UK, Canada, Italy and Japan.

Japanese leaders reacted to the events in Tiananmen Square with a carefully measured expression of concern. The first official reaction from the Japanese government came from Foreign Ministry spokesman Watanabe Taizō on 4 June – the day of the military crackdown. He said that 'it was unfortunate that force had been used to quell the political unrest' and hoped that 'the situation would not lead to more bloodshed'.[36] On the same day, Foreign Minister Mitsuzuka Hiroshi stated: 'it is very regrettable that such bloodshed occurred even though China is experiencing steady economic development based on its Liberalisation Policy.'[37] On 7 June, Prime Minister Uno Sōsuke emphasised the difference between Japan and the US in their relations with China by saying Japan could not blindly follow the US as it had to keep in mind its history of war aggression against China and thus would not like to make a black-and-white judgement.[38] On 18 June, Uno expressed his hope that China would not be pushed into a position of international isolation. Following the execution of three Chinese activists implicated in the Incident by the Chinese government, Uno also said on 22 June: 'From the point of view of a country which has supported China's Reform and Liberalisation Policy, it is deeply regrettable that such a thing happened.'[39] On 26 June, after a discussion with President George Bush and Secretary of State James Baker in Washington, Foreign Minister Mitsuzuka Hiroshi said that Japan and the US

> can not tolerate the Chinese government's human rights abuse, but also should not push China into a position of isolation from the international community. Thus we should convince China that it would be in its own interest to implement effectively its modernisation and liberalisation programs.[40]

Mitsuzuka repeated this position at an ASEAN foreign ministers' conference held in Brunei on 6 July, stating 'If we isolate China, we will drive it closer to the Soviet Union. It may not be wise policy.'[41] It is obvious from the statements above that the Japanese government was especially concerned about China's possible international isolation and the resurgence of the Sino-Soviet alliance that could have been caused by the Incident.

If sanctions were to be considered, the Japanese government was particularly reluctant to freeze the yen loans, which constituted the largest proportion of ODA funds provided to China. Soon after the Tiananmen Square Incident, both the MOFA and the MOF expressed their unwillingness to suspend yen loans to China, saying that it was too early to decide what to do. Furthermore, on 13 June, the Foreign Ministry stated that Japan's promise to support Chinese modernisation should be separated from humanitarian issues and that Japan would honour its commitment.[42] A week later. however, the Japanese government announced that it would freeze the third yen loan package to China, which was worth a total of ¥810 billion for 1990–95. As former Japanese ambassador to China Nakae Yōsuke remarks, Japanese governments have traditionally been reluctant to use economic sanctions as a diplomatic instrument.[43] In the face of increasing domestic and international criticism, however, the Japanese government eventually agreed to freeze its yen loans and join the Western countries' aid sanction against China. Japan's acquiescence was crucial to the effectiveness of the sanction because Japanese ODA constituted a significant proportion of China's foreign aid receipts. In 1986, for example, Japanese ODA comprised 75 per cent of China's total bilateral foreign aid receipts and 45 per cent of China's total aid receipts,[44] including aid from the World Bank, the United Nations Development Programme (UNDP), and other multilateral development institutions.

The Japanese government took an unusual international initiative to prevent China's isolation in the international community when it formally lifted its seventeen-month ODA sanction against China in November 1990. Japan's aims for its China ODA policy can be clearly observed in the process of implementing this initiative. During the G7 summit held in July 1989 in Paris, Japan had succeeded in persuading the other members of the G7 to insert the following sentence into the final communiqué: 'We expect China to create the conditions that will promote the resumption of cooperative relations and that will avoid China's further international isolation, by resuming its effort towards political and economic reforms.'[45] On 7 August 1989, the Japanese government decided to provide China with ¥200 million of emergency aid as disaster relief for a flood in a western province of China. By 18 August, the MOFA had resumed Japan's various cultural and youth exchange programmes with China, apparently in order to avoid isolating China and to encourage implementation of China's Reform and Liberalisation Policy.[46]

Japan was not alone in taking such a stance. By the end of 1989, some Western countries were also renewing relations with China. For example, West Germany indicated its willingness to provide ODA for a Shanghai subway project and US President George Bush sent National Security Adviser Brent Scowcroft to Beijing on a diplomatic mission on 10 December 1989. A week later, Bush approved the sale of three communication satellites to China and authorised US Export and Import Bank loans to American domestic firms doing business in China. In this context, the Japanese government, on 5 December 1989, resumed grant aid for projects in China worth ¥4.9 billion, which had been agreed before the Tiananmen Square Incident. At a meeting between the Japanese and US foreign ministers held on 5 July 1990, Foreign Minister Nakayama Tarō revealed Japan's plan to resume its frozen yen loans to China and Washington showed its understanding of the plan. Finally, during the G7 summit meeting held in Houston in the same month, Prime Minister Kaifu Toshiki explained the Japanese plan to lift all ODA sanctions against China and encouraged other G7 leaders to follow the Japanese initiative, emphasising the importance of supporting Chinese reformist leaders and China's Reform and Liberalisation Policy.[47]

The series of statements and actions by Japanese leaders and officials in the aftermath of the Tiananmen Square Incident described above highlights the aims of Japanese ODA to China and the interests behind the aid program at that time. In their statements, Japanese leaders and officials repeatedly emphasised the risk that pushing China into a position of isolation posed for the international community. They also strongly urged the importance of the survival of China's Reform and Liberalisation Policy. Japan used these two arguments to justify its reluctance to apply ODA sanctions against China and its willingness to lift the sanction as soon as possible. Japan's effort during the two G7 summit meetings in 1989 and 1990 to convince the other G7 member countries not to push China into a position of international isolation and to continue to support China's programme of reform and liberalisation further indicates the importance that Japan placed on these factors in its own relations with China.

To sum up, during the 1980s, Japanese policy-makers believed that if the Reform and Liberalisation Policy failed, China would be destabilised and isolated.[48] This would be a nightmare for Japan because it would damage the domestic power of reformist Chinese leaders and ultimately Japan's trade and investment interests in relation to China.[49] Moreover, if internationally isolated, the PRC was highly likely to become disruptive and combative, as North Korea had been over the last few decades. Thus, it is clear that the aims of Japanese policy-makers in providing ODA to China were not solely altruistic. Japan's active commitment, through aid, to the successful implementation of the Reform and Liberalisation Policy, which had 'already placed China on the road to [economic] reform and [social] openness',[50] can be understood in this context.

Economic interests

Apart from the politico-strategic interests discussed in the previous section, Japanese governments also pursued certain considerations of economic self-interest through the provision of ODA to China between 1979 and 1988. However, it was not a straightforward case of pursuing narrow commercial advantage.

The dominant view of Japanese foreign aid activity is that it aims to provide commercial opportunities for private Japanese companies.[51] On the basis of this perception, when the Ōhira government announced that it planned to initiate government-level economic cooperation with the PRC in 1979, the US and French governments quickly expressed their concern about the likely increase in Japan's economic presence in China. Contrary to US and French expectations, however, the Ōhira government made Japan's first yen loans to China *untied*.[52] As the provision of untied yen loans provided Japanese companies and their Western competitors with an equal opportunity to sell their plant and machinery to China, the commercial interests of private Japanese business would be minimised rather than advanced. Thus, if the major aim of Japanese ODA to China was to benefit private Japanese companies commercially, then this decision by the Ōhira government is difficult to comprehend.[53] Indeed, the major economic aims Japan pursued through the provision of foreign aid to China between 1979 and 1988 were not to advance the narrow and immediate commercial benefits of private Japanese companies through ODA project contracts, but rather to access China's energy resources and markets and, hence, to advance broader and longer-term national economic interests.

Securing a stable supply of Chinese oil and coal for Japan

The economic self-interest that Japan chiefly pursued through its China ODA policy during the first decade after the start of the policy was to secure a stable supply of Chinese oil and coal for Japan. The specific international environment of the 1970s particularly encouraged Japan to diversify its import sources of oil and coal. The 1973 *oil shock*, caused by the large reduction of oil exports from the petroleum-producing Arab countries to industrialised countries, brought about tremendous panic among the Japanese public. Furthermore, the second *oil shock* in the late 1970s – that is, the sharp oil price increase and uncertainty of supply caused by political upheaval in Iran – undermined Japanese industrial operations.[54] As stable access to oil and oil products was crucial for both the Japanese industrial and consumer sectors, the oil shocks presented a challenge for Japanese energy security. Given the oil shocks, Japan not only began to pay more attention to alternative energy resources, including nuclear energy, but also started to diversify its import sources of oil to reduce its large dependence on the Arab countries. Besides Indonesia, China was the closest and cheapest source of oil and coal imports for Japan. To ensure the supply of oil and coal, Japan actively provided a large portion of its yen loans for the development of that part of China's industrial infrastructure that facilitated the export of these resources to Japan, including railroads and ports.[55] As most of the first yen loan package to China was used to construct such transport infrastructure, Japan's need to secure energy imports had largely been met by the late 1970s.[56]

Expanding Japan's trade and investment interests in China

Apart from securing a stable supply of energy resources, Japan also pursued trade and investment interests in China through provision of ODA funds between 1979 and 1988. As will be demonstrated in Chapter 5, during this period, yen loan projects were concentrated on the development of transportation, energy and telecommunication infrastructure in China. These developments in turn helped promote Japanese business investments by reducing investment costs for those private Japanese companies that were seeking new markets. In 1992, Edward J. Lincoln argued that 'A major increase in direct investment, supported by large amounts of foreign aid helping to create the necessary infrastructure for that investment, is the principal vehicle for the increasing Japanese investment in Asia', and thus, 'Japanese bilateral foreign aid remains closely coordinated with, and connected to, other Japanese commercial interests.'[57]

The level of Japanese direct investment in China certainly did increase from US$22 billion in 1984 to US$51 billion in 1988.[58] In turn, the increase in investments facilitated Sino-Japanese trade, which rapidly increased from US$10 billion in 1983 to US$13 billion in 1984.[59] Furthermore, in 1985, Japanese exports to China doubled in the first half of the year compared to the same period in the previous year, reaching US$60 billion. China thereby became the second largest destination of Japanese exports after the US. By 1988, trade with Japan consisted of more than 20 per cent of China's total trade.[60] Though it is impossible to pinpoint the exact causes of the increase in trade, it seems clear that the provision of the first and second yen loan packages between 1979 and 1988, together with the Japanese investment which followed, was partly responsible, as was the generally good state of bilateral relations at the time. Thus, during the period 1979–88, the first decade of Japan's China ODA implementation, ODA arguably helped to deepen economic interdependence and to diversify economic relations between Japan and China, while also advancing Japanese trade and investment intersests.

In sum, during the first decade of the China ODA programme, Japanese governments mostly used ODA to support the PRC's Reform and Liberalisation Policy. This was construed to be in Japan's own politico-strategic and economic interests because first, it provided Japan with a chance to encourage the economic separation of China from the Communist bloc; and second, it advanced the political power of reformist Chinese leaders. By contributing to China's modernisation programme, and in particular, to the development of economic infrastructure, ODA also served Japan's commercial interests because it helped to secure a stable supply of Chinese energy resources to Japan and advanced Japanese investment and trade interests in China. Ultimately, Japan's support for the PRC's Reform and Liberalisation Policy by means of ODA during this period was thus based on

Japanese policy-makers' conviction that failure of the policy would damage Japan's political and economic interests in China.

Changing policy objectives and interests, 1989–94

Despite the smooth implementation of China ODA between 1979 and 1988, a number of international and domestic developments in 1989 and the early 1990s encouraged Japanese policy-makers to reassess the perceived national interests that Japan had pursued through China ODA policy. Such reassessment eventually led to changes in the policy objectives of China ODA after the mid-1990s. This section examines the impact of the 1989 Tiananmen Square Incident, the profound change in Sino-Japanese security relations during the early 1990s, and the 1992 attachment of political conditions to Japanese foreign aid to China. The period from 1989 to 1994, in short, can be regarded as a transitional period in which a re-evaluation of the Japanese interests pursued through China ODA activity was gradually undertaken.

Impact of the Tiananmen Square Incident

The Tiananmen Square Incident had significant implications for China ODA policy in the 1990s. First, the Chinese government's abuse of human rights in Tiananmen Square undermined Japanese policy-makers' idealism about modernising China, which was expected to have become more open and moderate. It forcefully reminded Japanese policy-makers of the diplomatic and security risk embedded in Japan's programme of aid to China, which had, after all, supported the modernisation programme of a strong authoritarian regime. As will be argued further in Chapter 4, this change in Japanese policy-makers' and the public's perception of China has become a very important factor leading to changes in the implementation of Japan's China ODA policy since the mid-1990s.

Second, Japan's ODA sanction, which was applied for the first time to China at the time of the Incident, revealed a new diplomatic option for Japanese policy-makers. The surprising vulnerability of the Chinese government to the aid sanctions applied by Japan and Western countries caused Japanese policy-makers to reflect on the usefulness of ODA sanctions as a diplomatic instrument against recipient countries, including China. In the face of sanctions, the Chinese government changed its commercial laws to make them favourable to Western and Japanese investors and freed jailed Chinese leaders of democratic movements less than one year after the Tiananmen Square Incident.[61] Despite Japan's lack of enthusiasm in applying ODA sanctions against recipient countries before the Incident, the number of Japanese ODA sanctions dramatically increased throughout the 1990s.[62] Subsequently, Japanese governments imposed three ODA sanctions upon China to counter provocative military behaviour by Beijing after the mid-1990s, as will be discussed in detail in Chapter 6.

Before the Tiananmen Square Incident, the major goal that the Japanese government had pursued through economic assistance to China had been to prevent

China from fragmenting and becoming isolated. After the Incident, on the other hand, preventing China from becoming a military power in the region also became an important objective of ODA policy.[63]

The changed strategic environment and the 'China threat thesis'

The profound change in the East Asian strategic environment following the end of the Cold War fundamentally affected Japan's ODA policy towards China. With the decrease in the Soviet military threat following the collapse of the Soviet Union at the beginning of the 1990s, came the end of the *de facto* anti-Soviet security alliance between Japan and China which had existed during the 1980s. This led to a resurgence of the traditional Sino-Japanese strategic rivalry from the beginning of the 1990s onwards. Furthermore, China's rapid modernisation and the sharp increase in its military expenditure since the beginning of the 1990s caused consternation among Japanese policy-makers about China's intentions in the region.[64] These dramatic changes in Sino-Japanese strategic relations contributed to a reconsideration of the policy objectives of Japan's China ODA and the strategic interests behind it.

From the beginning of the 1990s, the Chinese and Japanese governments started to regard each other's military development as a source of concern, largely because of the diminution of the common security threat formerly represented by the Soviet Union. In the 1990s, Beijing repeatedly condemned Japan's attempts to strengthen the Japan–US defence alliance, including revision of the Japanese Defence Guidelines and Japan's participation in the US ballistic missile defence (BMD) system development project, while the Japanese government became increasingly sensitive about China's military build-up and disruptive military behaviour in the region. The history of Japanese war-time aggression in China is one source of Chinese fear of Japanese militarisation,[65] while the CCP's repeated human rights violations and aggressive Taiwan policy are sources of Japan's scepticism about the PRC's military build-up.

One clear manifestation of concern about Chinese military modernisation, grounded in the country's fast economic growth, is the so-called *China threat thesis*, which has been articulated in the Western and the Japanese academic community and media since the early 1990s.[66] The China threat thesis first emerged in 1993 when the World Bank reported that, in terms of purchasing power parity (PPP) and if Hong Kong and Taiwan were included, China would surpass the US in total Gross Domestic Product (GDP) and become the world's largest economy by the year 2002.[67] At the same time, the International Monetary Fund (IMF) presented a similar report saying that in PPP terms, in 1992 China had already become the third largest economy in the world after the US and Japan.[68] These reports unnerved many analysts around the world who believed that the PRC would quickly turn its enhanced economic capability into military power, and subsequently, fulfill the China threat thesis.

China's increased expenditure on its military budget and weapons acquisitions specifically, together with the lack of transparency in its military policy,[69] are the major sources of concern for proponents of the China threat thesis. Rapid economic development during the 1980s and 1990s gave the Chinese government considerable financial capacity to develop its military power by modernising both conventional and nuclear weapons. Since the beginning of the 1990s, the PRC has indeed rapidly and consistently increased its military expenditure: the average annual growth rate of Chinese defence budgets between 1989 and 2002 has been well over 15 per cent.[70] In particular, there has been a large effort to modernise air and naval capabilities, which, if necessary, can be used to threaten neighbouring countries, especially those engaged in territorial disputes with China.[71] In fact, China is one of the few nations that has been rapidly increasing its military expenditure and consistently enhancing its nuclear and conventional military capabilities in the post-Cold War era, while other military powers, including the US and Russia, have been cutting their defence expenditure and decreasing the number of their nuclear missiles.

Furthermore, Japanese critics, such as Komori Yoshihisa and Hiramatsu Shigeo, argue that the Japanese government has been indirectly assisting China's military development by providing ODA.[72] They contend that Japanese development assistance to the PRC has supported Chinese military power by indirectly subsidising the country's defence budget and by helping to construct many airports, ports, railways, highways and telecommunication facilities in China. These critics emphasise the point that this infrastructure can be used for military as well as civilian purposes.

The China threat thesis and the argument that Japan's ODA has assisted Chinese militarisation have undeniably contributed to increasing suspicion of the Chinese government's military ambitions in the region among Japanese politicians and the public since the early 1990s, and thus have influenced Japanese governments' China ODA policy-making.[73] In the 1990s, as a result, Japan's implementation of the China aid programme became increasingly cautious, as we will see in Chapter 4.

Attachment of political conditions to Japan's development aid: the ODA Charter

Not only have changes in perceptions of China among Japanese policy-makers and academics affected China ODA policy, but the related attachment of clear political conditions to Japanese ODA provision in 1992 has also significantly changed the ODA approach to China. With the launch of an *ODA Charter* in 1992, Japan made the political and strategic aims of its ODA evident. The Four ODA Principles of the Charter began to be used as a critical diplomatic instrument to check China's military development and disruptive military behaviour in the East Asian region.

The *ODA Charter* was a statement of the underlying philosophy of Japanese ODA, expressed as a set of political conditions which would govern decisions about the provision of aid. It was produced in 1992 by the MOFA, but only after significant pressure from the LDP, which in turn was reacting to pressure from outside the Diet to make Japanese ODA more transparent and more explicitly responsive to the new international conditions of the early 1990s.

The *ODA Charter* states that after full consideration of each recipient country's requests, its socio-economic conditions and its bilateral relations with Japan, ODA will be provided in accordance with the following four principles. First, environmental conservation and development should be pursued in tandem. Second, any use of ODA for military purposes or for aggravation of international conflicts should be avoided. Third, full attention should be paid to trends in recipient countries' military expenditures, their development and production of weapons of mass destruction and missiles, and their export and import of military armaments. Fourth, full attention should be paid to efforts to promote democratisation and the introduction of a market-oriented economy, and the situation regarding the preservation of basic human rights and freedoms in the recipient country.[74] Unlike a *law*, the Charter is a flexible instrument whose application varies in actual practice. Nonetheless, the introduction of the Four Principles of Japanese foreign aid in 1992 did demonstrate Tokyo's determination to attach clear political conditions to its foreign aid activity.

The most significant characteristic of the ODA Principles is that they openly expressed concern over recipient countries' military build-up. Although other industrialised countries used their aid policies to express their concern about abuses of human rights in recipient countries, Japan was the first donor to connect military development with its foreign aid programme.[75]

The 1992 introduction of the *ODA Charter* raises the question of why the Japanese government so clearly attached political conditions to its ODA provision, despite its traditional reluctance to link political issues with its aid policy. In short, two major external factors had triggered a fundamental reassessment of Japan's ODA policy: the Gulf War (1990–91) and the end of the Cold War international system at the beginning of the 1990s.[76] It is no coincidence that the *ODA Charter* was announced soon after these external developments occurred or began to occur. In the face of international and domestic criticism of Japan's inability to deal with these events speedily and efficiently, Japanese policy-makers realised that an immediate overhaul of Japan's traditional diplomacy was needed. The strategic use of ODA was to be situated at the core of the new diplomacy.

The Gulf War between Iraq and a US-led multinational force demonstrated the limitations of Japan's *cheque-book diplomacy* and gave the Japanese government a strong incentive to overhaul its approach of giving money without making its underlying philosophy clear. Despite its US$13 billion financial contribution to the anti-Iraqi allied force, Japan was condemned by the international community over its role in the war.[77] The US Congress, for instance, criticised the Japanese contribution to the Gulf War as 'too little and too late'.[78] Furthermore, Kuwait, the country Iraq had invaded, omitted Japan from the list of countries it thanked in a letter published in the *New York Times* soon after the war. Japan's financial contribution to the multinational force had in fact been huge. Indeed, it was the largest financial contribution of all those made to operation *Desert Storm*.[79] Direct participation in battle outside Japanese territory by the Self Defence Forces (SDF) is firmly prohibited by the Constitution, regardless of the wishes of the Japanese government. Despite these circumstances, however, Japan's financial contribution won little international respect. In addition, Japan's pre-Gulf War aid for fertiliser factory construction in Iraq was criticised for indirectly assisting that country's militarisation, as fertiliser factories can be transformed to produce chemical weapons.[80] These diplomatic shocks generated a domestic debate about both the credibility of Japanese diplomacy and the risk of ODA activity unintentionally assisting a recipient country's militarisation.

The end of the Cold War also had implications for Japanese ODA. Basically, liberal democracy and the market economy have become more generally accepted in the international community, and now constitute more or less universal values. Even the former Soviet Union has begun to introduce democratic processes and a market-oriented economy. This profound change in the international environment redefined Japanese ODA policy in two respects. First, Japan made its ODA provision conditional on the protection of human rights, and second, the promotion of a market-based economy in Communist countries became a more solid objective of ODA policy. These two objectives were later incorporated into the Four ODA Principles and became political conditions of Japanese foreign aid.

During the Cold War era, Japan and Western aid donors were reluctant, except in cases of civil war, to cut or suspend their aid to non-Communist developing countries, even if the governments of those countries abused the human rights of their populations. For donor nations, the strategic importance of keeping such developing countries in the *free-world* camp had priority over their democratisation. Japan's ODA relations with Indonesia under the Suharto regime and the Philippines under the Marcos government are typical examples of this aid practice. The end of the Cold War, however, weakened the incentive to provide strategic aid to those countries previously supposed to be in the frontline against Communism. Human rights protection, which had been virtually discounted in favour of the strategic objective of winning the ideological battle against Communism, became an important condition of both Japanese and Western foreign aid. At various times since the end of the Cold War, Japan has reduced or withheld aid to Nicaragua, Zaire, Haiti and Kenya because of human rights violations, although its approach to human rights in China, as we have seen, has been very cautious.

Although a domestic debate seeking to clarify the philosophical basis of foreign aid activities had been sporadically evident inside and outside the Diet since the end of the 1970s, it had contributed little to any redefinition of Japan's ODA policy. The external developments described above, however, facilitated and raised the level of this domestic debate. In 1989, the Upper House of the Diet passed a resolution to ban the military use of Japanese foreign aid and to promote human rights and freedom in recipient countries.[81] In the same year, the ODA Research Group (ODA chōsa kenkyū-kai), formed by a citizens' group, requested the government to promote ideas such as pacifism, human rights, democracy and environmental conservation as basic aims of Japanese ODA.[82] The Keidanren also urged the government to establish a Japanese ODA Charter to clarify its aid philosophy, identifying the Canadian Charter as a possible model.[83] Furthermore, by 1990 there was growing intellectual argument among foreign policy specialists in favour of situating ODA as the core instrument of Japan's post-Cold War diplomacy and encouraging its political and strategic use.[84] The increasing prominence of such arguments in many parts of Japanese society contributed greatly to the creation of a national consensus calling for an overhaul of ODA policy. This developing consensus put pressure on the government to initiate and accelerate a new aid policy.

As will be discussed in Chapter 4, the governing LDP and the MOFA were the most important institutions holding actual power to make foreign aid policy. Thus, the decision-making processes in these two institutions were crucial to the establishment of the *ODA Charter*. In February 1991, the LDP started a debate over Japan's post-Gulf War ODA policy, and decided to formulate new ODA guidelines as an important philosophical basis for Japanese aid. In the aftermath of the Gulf War, the Party was very enthusiastic about linking ODA with recipient countries' military development. Kōno Yōhei, the head of the LDP Foreign Policy Council, for example, expressed his desire to counter military build-up in countries receiving Japanese ODA.[85] In the April 1991 Diet session, Prime Minister Kaifu Toshiki stated that his government would pay attention to the military expenditure of recipient countries, research on and development of weapons of mass destruction, arms trade, democratisation (that is, the promotion of human rights) and introduction of a market economy. In this way, the underlying ideas of the Four ODA Principles were made public for the first time.

At the July 1991 London summit of the G7 countries, the Kaifu government took the initiative to offer the Principles as a possible basis for a common foreign aid philosophy of the G7 countries. This initiative resulted in the so-called 'communiqué concerning transfer of conventional weapons and non-proliferation of nuclear, biological and chemical weapons' at the summit.[86] In December 1991, the LDP decided to establish Japan's ODA Charter by accepting a policy recommendation presented by the government's Third Administrative Reform Committee.[87] The LDP then put pressure on the MOFA to produce a suitable document.

Fearing the loss of its autonomy in foreign aid policy-making and implementation, the MOFA at first took a cautious stance towards making Japanese ODA conditional on the military and political affairs of recipient countries. The Ministry particularly feared the negative impact on its China and East European diplomacy that was expected to be caused by the conditionality of ODA.[88] In response to the increasing demands from LDP politicians to reform ODA policy, however, the MOFA eventually came to be committed to substantive reforms.[89] In March 1991, it coordinated an inter-ministerial meeting to discuss ODA matters. Despite concerns expressed by the MOF and the MITI, the assembled ministries agreed to attach political conditionality to ODA. In February 1992, the MOFA invited experts to Japan from the Stockholm International Peace Research Institute to a workshop on the relationship between foreign aid and militarisation. The Ministry then formulated a draft of the *ODA Charter*, which was promptly presented to LDP members at the Party's General Assembly in June 1992, where it received LDP approval. In the same month, the Miyazawa Kiichi cabinet officially introduced the Charter, with the Four ODA Principles as its pillar.[90]

The introduction of the Four ODA Principles in 1992 as a result of pressure from LDP politicians, rather than as an original initiative by Foreign Ministry bureaucrats, significantly constrained the degree of autonomy Foreign Ministry officials had in implementing ODA policy towards China as well as other countries. Consequently, the Japanese government's ODA approach to China gradually changed, as we will see in more detail in Chapter 6. In particular, it became very difficult for Foreign Ministry bureaucrats to continue their traditionally non-confrontational stance towards provocative military behaviour by China.

To sum up, the external and internal developments that impinged on Sino-Japanese relations between 1989 and 1994 encouraged a reassessment of the interests pursued by Japan through China ODA policy. The 1989 Tiananmen Square Incident greatly changed the perception held by Japanese policy-makers and the public of modernising China. The resurgence of the traditional Sino-Japanese strategic rivalry, following the collapse of the Soviet Union and the rapid expansion of China's economic and military capability, forced Japan to provide ODA to China more judiciously than it had in the past. The 1992 introduction of the Four ODA Principles represented a major change in Japan's approach to foreign aid, including China aid. The Charter was to promote the Japanese government's use of ODA as a strategic instrument, eventually leading Japan to impose aid sanctions against China in the latter part of the 1990s. During the period from 1989 to 1994, then, the fundamental goal behind Japan's China ODA policy gradually shifted from engaging a *weak* China (but a *de facto* military ally) to engaging a *modernising* China (that posed a potential military threat). This reassessment eventually led to the changes in the policy goals of Japanese ODA to China which became obvious after the mid-1990s.

New objectives and new interests, 1995 onwards

Since the mid-1990s, there have been three major developments with regard to Japan's ODA policy to China. First, for several reasons the Japanese government has shifted the priority project areas of China ODA from economic to socio-environmental infrastructure development. Second, Japanese governments have started to use ODA as a strategic weapon to counter Chinese militarisation. Third, the incorporation of the Chinese economy into the market-based regional and global economic system, in particular into the World Trade Organisation (WTO) framework, became a key policy goal of Japan's ODA. This section gives a brief overview of these three goals, which will be examined in more detail through case studies in Chapters 5 and 6.

Shifting the priority project areas of China ODA

Since the mid-1990s, Japanese governments have changed the major target project areas of China ODA. Instead of industrial infrastructure development, the new focus is on environmental infrastructure development. More particularly. the major project areas of Japanese yen loans have shifted from the traditional areas of railways, ports, power plants, water supply and sewerage construction to environmental protection, the improvement of food production and the development of inland provinces. For example, in 1996, eight environmental and three agricultural projects were included in the total list of twenty-two yen loan projects, worth a total of about ¥176 billion. Among the total twenty-two projects, seventeen were in inland provinces. In 1997, 6 environmental and 1 agricultural project out of the total of 14 projects, worth in all about ¥203 billion, were carried out. Among the 14, 11 were implemented in inland areas.[91] This trend towards yen loan provision for various environmental, agricultural and inland projects in China has continued: 20 out of the total of 28 projects, worth in all ¥390 billion, which were carried out in 1999 and 2000 were related to the environment or agriculture.[92]

The MOFA has stated that this shift in ODA policy is intended to help prevent the worsening of the socio-economic problems that have been created in the process of China's transition from a highly centralised planned economy to a more market-oriented one. Indeed, rapid economic growth in the 1980s and the first half of the 1990s, which Japanese ODA had helped to stimulate. did reduce the potential for instability in domestic affairs caused by China's economic backwardness and overall poverty. However, China's radical transformation into a market economy and the uneven distribution of wealth among its population in turn produced various socio-economic problems, including the widened income gap between inland and coastal provinces, massive unemployment created by the policy of closing uncompetitive state enterprises, the accumulation of non-performing loans in the private and state financial sectors, rapid environmental degradation and the absence of a social safety net for the unemployed.[93]

In the early 1990s, Japanese policy-makers acknowledged that these new domestic problems would put great strain on the sustainability of China's economic development and, hence, were likely to undermine the stability of China's economic and social affairs in the near future.[94] Increasing numbers of unemployed Chinese people in urban areas have indeed become a destabilising factor in China's social and political affairs. Moreover, the Japanese government further explains that the change in the priority areas of China ODA partly constitutes an attempt to promote a more institutionalised market economic system in China, through the promotion amongst other things of macro control mechanisms, financial systems for market integration, a financial control system through a central bank, and an institutionalised social safety net for the unemployed.[95] In this context, the Japanese government is using ODA more to provide knowledge and expertise to help create a more institutionalised market economy in China, than for the development of further economic infrastructure.

Government pronouncements on this subject are more likely, however. to reflect official reasoning, or at least secondary objectives, that hide the real policy goals pursued by the Japanese government through its China ODA. In other words, they constitute the kind of rhetoric that is deliberately emphasised by the

Japanese government in order to gain public support for the continuation of its China aid activity. The actual motives behind the Japanese government's decision to change the priority project areas of its China ODA from economic to social and environmental infrastructure development are the evident progress in China's economic development, the budgetary interest of the Japanese MOFA and a consideration of Japan's security interests.

First, China's rapid economic development in the 1980s and early 1990s decreased the importance of Japanese ODA as a source of foreign aid to supplement China's shortage of domestic savings. Given the shortage in the 1980s of both domestic savings and foreign currency, Japanese ODA policy-makers thought that the provision of ODA for construction of economic infrastructure was the most efficient use of development funds. By 1993, however, China's rapidly increasing trade surplus was responsible for vastly improved foreign currency reserves and domestic savings.[96] This meant that by that time the Chinese government already had a sufficient financial capacity to develop industrial infrastructure independently. Thus, according to the conventional wisdom of development economics, it was inevitable that the Japanese government would shift the priority areas of China ODA from industrial infrastructure development to other project areas.[97]

Second, the strong need of MOFA bureaucrats to protect their organisational interest also encouraged the shift in the priority project areas of Japanese development assistance to China. As ODA accounts for most of the Ministry's annual budget,[98] Foreign Ministry bureaucrats are keen to prevent any reduction of the ODA budget, including the budget for ODA to China.[99] Some opinion polls conducted between 1991 and 1996 revealed, however, that the Japanese public was reluctant to support any increase in the ODA budget. For example, according to one poll, the proportion of those who supported an increase in the overall ODA budget dropped from 41.4 per cent in 1991 to 32.9 per cent in 1996, while those who supported a cut in the ODA budget grew from 8 to 12.9 per cent.[100] The overall ODA budget was reduced for the first time in 1996 by 10 per cent and, since then, the decline in public support for ODA activity has put significant pressure on the Japanese government to cut the budget further. In fact, the government decided to reduce the ODA budget by another 10 per cent in 2002.[101] The economic recession that started in Japan at the beginning of the 1990s, and the resultant national budget deficit, has made Japanese taxpayers increasingly reluctant to allocate their money overseas.

In the face of such domestic pressure to reduce the total ODA budget, the MOFA was forced in the mid-1990s to shift the priority project areas of China ODA, in an effort to sustain public support for the ODA policy. Since China's economic development has progressed to a considerable degree, it has become increasingly difficult for Foreign Ministry officials to justify continued assistance for infrastructure development. The shift towards social and environmental infrastructure development in China, which is based more on humanitarian need than economic need, has proved a very useful way of gaining public and parliamentary support for the continuation of China ODA.

Third, the perceived new imperative for the Japanese government to restrain China's military development has also promoted the shift in the priority project areas of ODA to China. As explained in the previous pages, the resurgent Sino-Japanese strategic rivalry and China's rapid military development, which became evident in the early 1990s, motivated Japanese policy-makers to restrain the further militarisation of China. Moreover, the *China threat thesis* and the claim that Japanese ODA had indirectly contributed to the military development of China also made Japanese policy-makers more aware of the indirect linkage between Japanese ODA and Chinese militarisation. Japanese policy-makers were thus encouraged to change ODA funding areas in China to prevent Japanese ODA from indirectly assisting Chinese militarisation.[102] Unlike the development of highways, ports, airports and telecommunication facilities which can also be used for military purposes, the provision of ODA for environmental conservation and poverty relief projects can hardly be linked with the military operations of the Chinese army.[103]

Restraining Chinese militarisation

The attempt to discourage militarisation is thus partly responsible for the change in priority project areas. Japanese governments, however, have also taken more explicit action in this area. In particular, on several occasions, Japanese governments have suspended disbursements of ODA to China in protest against that country's disruptive military behaviour. Chapter 6 will examine in detail three cases of aid sanctions: a 1995 sanction in protest against Chinese nuclear tests, a 1996 sanction in protest against the military intimidation of Taiwan by the PRC, and a sanction imposed in 2000 in protest against China's naval activities inside Japan's exclusive economic zone (EEZ).

Incorporating China into the global economic system

Since the mid-1990s, the integration of the Chinese economy into the market-based global economic system, particularly into the WTO framework, has been a further policy goal of Japanese ODA to China. Prior to 1979, the major reason that many Japanese and Euro-American multinational companies did not invest in China was the absence of adequate industrial infrastructure. By contributing to the development of Chinese industrial infrastructure during the 1980s, Japanese ODA facilitated direct investments in China by Japanese and Euro-American companies. Consequently, China's foreign trade expanded and diversified and China's economic interdependence with these countries has significantly deepened, as will be explained in Chapter 5 in detail. For Japanese policy-makers, promotion of China's trade transactions with and FDI from a variety of countries was critical to their attempt to incorporate China into the market-based global economic system. China's recent entry into the WTO in 2001 already provided private companies from Japan and elsewhere with further investment and export opportunities. According to figures from the IMF, Japanese exports to China increased 61 per cent from US$29.7 billion in 1998 to US$48.5 billion in 2002, while the US exports to China increased 54 per cent during the same period from US$38.0 billion to US$70.1 billion.[104]

The first reason for Japan's efforts to incorporate China into the WTO frame-work was to encourage China to respect global economic norms and rules and base its behaviour on them, rather than on its own distinctive values and rules.[105] This would enable the two countries to negotiate and resolve any bilateral issue on the basis of accepted international rules. In other words, the Japanese govern-ment prefers to handle China within multilateral frameworks, rather than to do so by itself.[106] Second, Japanese governments have also sought to facilitate China's transition from a highly centralised socialist economy to a more market-oriented economy. In fact, in March 1999, Chinese leaders changed the Constitution to allow 'individual and private ownership', an important aspect of the market economy.[107] The transition of China to a more market-oriented economy is considered to be in Japan's political as well as economic interest, as it would guide China in a more open and liberal direction, in the long run. Once again, this example shows that the economic, political and strategic interests behind Japan's ODA to China are often entwined.

Conclusion

This chapter has argued, first, that the policy objectives of Japan's China ODA have evolved according to changes in the international and domestic environments. Second, although policy objectives have changed, the fundamental concept which underlies Japan's China ODA policy, *engagement* with China, has remained consistent.

During the period between 1978 and 1988, Japan's support of the Reform and Liberalisation Policy by means of ODA was based on the belief of Japanese policy-makers that failure of the policy would harm Japan's political and commercial interests in relation to the PRC. They believed that such a failure would likely destabilise China's socio-economic affairs and greatly undermine the political power of reformist Chinese leaders. They further considered that the successful implementation of the Reform and Liberalisation Policy would be in Japan's economic interests, as it would provide Japanese companies with a greater opportunity to access Chinese oil and coal and promote both exports of Japanese industrial products to China and direct Japanese investments in the developing China market. Support of the policy also gave Japan a chance to encourage the economic separation of China from the Communist bloc by enhancing China's economic dependence on Japan and Western countries and by promoting a market economy in China itself.

However, crucial external and internal developments surrounding Sino-Japanese relations between 1989 and 1994 modified the policy objectives of Japan's ODA to China. The Tiananmen Square Incident undermined Japanese ide-alism towards a China that now seemed to be refusing to change politically even while developing economically. The end of the Cold War and the rapid expansion of China's defence expenditure also caused Japan to adopt a more cautious ODA policy in relation to China. Furthermore, Japan's attachment of clear political conditions to its ODA provision through the *ODA Charter* of 1992 facilitated the use of ODA as a means to restrain Chinese militarisation in the 1990s.

Given these changes, Japanese governments began to pursue new policy goals through China ODA. Acknowledging the potential threat posed by the PRC's rapid militarisation, Japanese governments have started to use ODA as a strategic weapon to restrain China's military expansion and have imposed three sets of ODA sanctions not only as a carrot to promote favourable developments in China, but also, by use of sanctions, as a stick to counter unsettling behaviour by China. Japanese policy-makers also shifted the priority project areas of China ODA based on economic and strategic calculations. At the same time, the incorporation of the Chinese economy into the market-based global economic system, in order to encourage China to act more in accordance with international norms and rules and to encourage the further advancement of a market economy, became an important policy objective of Japan's China ODA.

Though the underlying concept of *engagement* has remained fundamentally consistent, as noted in the previous section, the primary purpose of Japan's commitment to engaging China has changed since 1979. From using ODA to engage a *weak* China which was an implicit ally in the 1980s, the priority has changed to engaging an economically developing China which has posed a potential security threat from the mid-1990s onwards.

Besides the external and internal developments reviewed in this chapter, another crucial development within the process of Japan's China ODA policy-making also contributed to fundamental changes in China ODA policy. The next Chapter 4 will address the shift in the balance of China aid policy-making power between MOFA bureaucrats and LDP politicians, in order to focus on the process of actually formulating Japan's ODA policy to China.

4 Aid policy-making

Institutions, processes and power relations

Although Chapter 3 provided insights into the complex and divergent goals of Japan's ODA policy and the interests behind it, the question of who, or what institutional process, actually determines Japan's development aid policy to China remains to be answered. This chapter investigates the process of formulating that policy, with particular reference to the changing balance of policy-making power between MOFA bureaucrats and LDP parliamentarians. In seeking to understand policy-making, it is important not only to consider what institutional changes have occurred, but also to identify the pressures responsible for such change.[1] In particular, this chapter analyses how the MOFA and the LDP – now the two most powerful foreign policy-making actors in Japan – actually participate in and influence the process of making Japan's ODA policy to China, and why the balance between them has changed.[2]

One might assume that the ODA policies of the Japanese state are formulated by a centralised policy-maker, which has concrete objectives and pursues precise interests. However, as suggested earlier, this conception that the Japanese government consistently acts on the basis of a master plan for foreign aid policy does not accurately reflect the actual process of ODA policy-making. As Hayden Lesbirel has argued in another context, the key concepts necessary to understand Japanese policy-making are the 'complex nature of bargaining' among various actors and in particular, 'the intensity of conflict, power relationships and the effectiveness of conflict resolution mechanisms, within the same policy arena'.[3] Japan's foreign aid policies, including China aid policy, are indeed the product of complex bargaining among many policy-making actors with different interests.

What kind of actors, then, actually determine Japan's development aid policies? As we have seen, in their respective studies, Alan Rix and Robert Orr identified the four central government bodies – the MOFA, the MOF the MITI and the EPA – as the key players that chiefly decide Japan's foreign aid policies.[4] While this explanation goes some way towards elucidating the policy-making process during the first decade or so of Japan's provision of foreign aid to China, it is less useful for the later period. Major changes in the process of formulating and implementing Japanese ODA have since undermined the credibility of this bureaucrat-centred model of policy-making, which for some time has constituted the prevailing explanation of Japanese policy-making more generally.[5] In fact, during the 1990s, there was a shift in the balance of foreign aid policy-making power from state bureaucrats to government party politicians. After discussing the earlier period, this chapter highlights this critical change in the process of Japan's aid policy-making in general, and China aid policy-making in particular.

It is necessary to explain why much of the focus of my analysis is on the LDP and the MOFA, rather than other important actors involved in China ODA policy-making such as the prime minister, opposition parties, the Keidanren, and researchers in universities and think-tanks. As head of the Japanese government, the prime minister plays a crucial role in making the final decisions of the government. For instance, Prime Minister Tanaka Kakuei (1972–74) demonstrated notable leadership in normalising Japan's diplomatic relations with China in 1972, and the 1978 conclusion of the Sino-Japanese Peace and Friendship Treaty would have been impossible without the strong initiatives of Fukuda Takeo (1976–77). However, it is the MOFA that controls the important diplomatic information which largely affects the prime minister's final decisions.[6] For its part, the Keidanren, as the representative of Japanese big businesses, is financially the most powerful pressure group in Japan. However, as its influence over the formal process of China ODA policy-making depends largely on its lobby activities in relation to key politicians and bureaucrats, its power in this area is minor relative to that of the MOFA and the LDP.

Opposition parties also play a crucial role in examining the government's ODA policies in Diet sessions, but have limited access to important policy information[7] and lack foreign policy-making knowledge. Thus, they normally operate outside the formal policy-making process. Academics and researchers, as policy advisers to the government, are often directly involved in the formal process of China ODA policy formulation. However, despite their considerable influence through provision of advice and recommendations, they are excluded from actual decision-making processes. In the end, the MOFA and the LDP are the only two institutions that have the capacity to develop China ODA policy. They monopolise the human and information resources that are crucial to the formulation of policy and have the power to formulate foreign and foreign aid policy more or less independently.

The first section of the chapter discusses Japanese foreign policy-making processes from 1979 to the mid-1990s, with particular focus on the roles and capabilities of the MOFA and the LDP. It is difficult to determine exactly when new trends in Japanese foreign aid and foreign policy-making became apparent, following the shift of balance from the MOFA to the LDP. However, it is clear that the new trend is associated with the circumstances of the mid-1990s, because the series of domestic events that triggered and facilitated the shift in foreign policy-making power occurred mostly in the first half of that decade. The second section examines these changes in the policy-making roles and capabilities of the MOFA and the LDP, as well as relevant changes in the interaction between the two bodies. The third section discusses recent tensions between the LDP and the MOFA over leadership in making new China ODA policies, and the chapter concludes with an assessment of the implications of this tension for the process of China ODA policy-making.

The China ODA policy-making process, 1979 to the mid-1990s

According to conventional wisdom, the governing party in a parliamentary system has authority to pass legislation and decide official policies. The degree of policy-making power is even greater if a governing party controls the majority of the seats in a national parliament. The LDP was the governing party controlling the majority of seats in both the Upper and the Lower House of the Japanese national Diet during the period from 1955 to 1993. Despite the conventional wisdom, however, the LDP did not play a large role in formulating policies. Rather, it gave central ministries a mandate to formulate policies, and as a result, bureaucrats in those ministries enjoyed a significant degree of policy-making autonomy. This does not mean, however, that the LDP's role in policy-making was as small as some observers have been quick to conclude. Even if the central ministries enjoyed a great deal of policy-making autonomy, it was still necessary to get the LDP's approval to make their policies *official*.[8] In other words, the LDP had a veto power over ministries even though that veto power was rarely used.

In the area of foreign and foreign aid policy-making, the MOFA enjoyed a large degree of autonomy in formulating and implementing policy before the mid-1990s. As Nishihara Masashi has established, the MOFA did not completely dominate Japanese foreign policy-making.[9] Undoubtedly, however, the ministry played a more central and significant role than any other single institution or actor. It is correct to say that the role of the LDP in formulating foreign policy became prominent in certain highly political cases, such as the decision to normalise diplomatic relations with China. Such cases, however, were very rare. The usual division of labour between the LDP and the MOFA before the mid-1990s was that the MOFA played a central role in formulating Japanese foreign and foreign aid policy, including China ODA policy; the LDP decided which policies to approve; and then the MOFA implemented the approved policies. This system, however, has been gradually changing since the 1980s, with particularly rapid change occurring after the mid-1990s. The policy-making roles and capabilities of the two institutions from 1979 to the mid-1990s will now be considered separately.

Liberal Democratic Party

Between 1979 and the mid-1990s, the LDP effectively handed the MOFA a mandate to formulate China ODA policy. Two questions need to be answered in order to understand the unique characteristics of the LDP's foreign aid policy-making. Why did LDP parliamentarians not actively involve themselves in the process of foreign aid policy-making? And why did they give MOFA officials such a great degree of autonomy in formulating China ODA policy? The answers to these questions lie in the following four characteristics of Japanese and LDP politics during this period: LDP parliamentarians' belief that diplomatic activity does not lead to votes in elections; an electoral system comprising multi-member constituency seats; strong factionalism within the LDP; and a lack of foreign policy-making capability within the LDP.

First, the belief that diplomacy does not win elections significantly contributed to LDP parliamentarians' passive stance towards the process of foreign policy-making and lack of motivation to participate in it. As one senior Finance Ministry official remarked, unlike domestic policy areas such as construction, transportation, agriculture and fisheries, education and telecommunications, which are directly linked with public spending, 'diplomacy does not lead to votes (*gaikō wa hyō ni naranai*)'.[10] The so-called *pork-barrel politics* by which politicians spend large amounts of public funds on local projects in order to win the votes of the people who are favourably affected has been evident in Japan for many decades, not least from the 1960s, when the country started to experience rapid economic growth and the amount of money available to government increased rapidly.[11] To gain votes in the electorates that they represented, LDP parliamentarians were especially eager, and able as members of government, to commit themselves to the politics of large-scale public spending. Areas of politics which directly benefited the voters were those which most influenced elections. Foreign aid policy remained distanced from *pork-barrel politics* as public funds allocated for this purpose are spent mostly overseas, rather than in local areas of Japan.

Second, the electoral system comprising multi-member constituency seats (*chūsenkyoku-sei*), which was used for the powerful Lower House of the Diet up until 1994,[12] resulted in elections where personality and personal networks were more central than policy. This system, in which each district elected between 3 and 5 representatives, meant that LDP candidates competed against each other in common electoral districts, inevitably reducing the importance of the party label as a tool in generating votes[13] and promoting personality- and network-oriented, rather than policy- and issue-oriented, election campaigns.[14] Consequently, the system of multi-member constituency seats encouraged greater pork-barrel spending by LDP parliamentarians, and enabled parliamentarians: as Yasuo Takao points out, the absence of a competitive party system produces politicians who are 'eager to demonstrate their ability to deliver particular benefits... to their local constituents'.[15] The system of multi-member constituency seats also enabled parliamentarians virtually to ignore diplomatic issues, including China ODA. Japanese public opinion, under this electoral system, was not normally influential enough to encourage LDP parliamentarians to take an active interest in foreign policy, even in diplomatic issues associated with strong public debates.[16]

Third, factionalism within the LDP also led to a lack of involvement in foreign and foreign aid policy-making by LDP parliamentarians, because it provided a ready route for pressure from bureaucrats. Since 1955, when the party was formed following the unification of the two main conservative parties – the Liberal Party and the Democratic Party – factionalism has been one of the distinctive characteristics of LDP politics.[17] The LDP has always consisted of several large and distinct factions, each of which operates under the leadership of a powerful politician. Furthermore, there are important informal links between LDP politicians and central ministry bureaucrats.[18] On occasions when there were objections by LDP parliamentarians to foreign policies formulated by the MOFA, senior ministry bureaucrats used the power of factional leaders to silence these parliamentarians.[19] It was very difficult for junior faction members, for example, to confront the leaders of their factions with objections to MOFA's policies. This meant that even when LDP parliamentarians attempted to commit themselves to foreign policy-making, the established personal networks between MOFA bureaucrats and LDP factional leaders held them back. In this context, only senior parliamentarians who were either factional leaders or had a certain degree of influence within factions were able to commit themselves to foreign policy-making.[20]

Fourth, and arguably the greatest factor explaining the LDP's passive involvement in foreign and foreign aid policy-making, was the lack of appropriate policy-making capacity within the party. Without adequate access to diplomatic information and the technical know-how to formulate foreign policy, the party had no option but to hand the MOFA a mandate to formulate foreign policy, including China ODA policy. The LDP acknowledged the MOFA's greater degree of foreign policy-making autonomy,[21] and the party's veto power over the MOFA was very rarely used in practice.

Ministry of Foreign Affairs

The MOFA thus enjoyed a considerable degree of foreign and foreign aid policy-making autonomy until the mid-1990s. From the MOFA side, the reasons for this autonomy are first, as noted earlier, that the Ministry had an unchallengeable foreign policy-making capability, which was far larger than that of any other official agency or political party; and second, that the complex bureaucratic decision-making mechanism underlying China ODA policy development helped further to insulate the MOFA from intervention by LDP parliamentarians.

As the government agency primarily responsible for diplomatic relations with all foreign states, as well as governmental and non-governmental international organisations, the MOFA monopolised all officials with enough technical expertise for foreign policy formulation, as well as diplomatic information and other resources.[22] Neither the LDP nor any other agency could seriously compete with the MOFA in this respect. Therefore, it was unthinkable for the LDP to take control of foreign and foreign aid policy-making away from the MOFA.

The complexity of the decision-making system underlying Japanese ODA policy-making helped the MOFA to shield its formulation of China ODA policy from intervention by LDP parliamentarians. As noted earlier, aside from the MOFA, three other branches of government – the MOF, the MITI and the EPA – had important roles in developing ODA policy, with this system being known as 'the four ministerial decision-making system (*yonshōchō-taisei*)'. The MOFA was largely responsible for policy-making in relation to grant aid and technical cooperation programmes, while all four ministries participated in the policy-making process regarding yen loans.[23]

Each ministry's position on questions of ODA was primarily related to its own policy mandate. The MOFA approached ODA activity from a general foreign policy perspective consistent with its perceived diplomatic and strategic interests. It controlled the Japan International Cooperation Agency (JICA), which essentially handles both grant aid and technical cooperation programmes to many recipient countries, including China. The MOF oversaw decision-making relating to the ODA budget and had strong veto power over excessive requests of ODA budgets. It had detailed information about the recipients' borrowing and repayment records, and took a cautious approach to approving yen loans to countries having a debt problem.[24] The MOF also controlled the Export and Import (ExIm) Bank of Japan, which provided the so-called *untied loans*, non-ODA government loans whose grant element was less than 25 per cent, to many countries. The MITI approached ODA from a commercial perspective and, as the bureaucratic representative of the Japanese business community, it had considerable influence within the four ministerial decision-making system. Finally, the EPA, though it supervised the Overseas Economic Cooperation Fund (OECF), which implemented yen loan transactions, was the weakest of the four bodies and had a somewhat more vague agenda concerning Japanese ODA.[25] Meetings of officials from the four branches of government were coordinated by the MOFA on a regular basis, and information relating to ODA was exchanged and decisions were made based on high-level discussions by deputy ministers.[26]

With a total of four ministries and agencies involved in the formulation of ODA policy, it was inevitable that the LDP would struggle to have any substantial influence. If LDP parliamentarians wanted to have any influence over ODA policy formulation they needed to negotiate with, and put pressure on, all of the four bodies, each with its different interests. As several MOFA officials commented, by maintaining its leadership over such a complex bureaucratic decision-making system, the MOFA was further advantaged in the policy-making process.[27]

The MOFA's power over ODA policy-making was in practice concentrated in particular pockets of the organisation, and divisional politics within the MOFA also had considerable impact on Japan's foreign aid diplomacy towards China. Until recently, according to a senior MOFA official, one division within the MOFA – the China Division – enjoyed almost exclusive power to decide the Ministry's China-related policies.[28] It is true to say that as it has primary responsibility for the entire gamut of Japanese foreign aid policies, the Economic Cooperation Bureau within the MOFA could also play an important role in formulating China ODA policies. However, the China Division had supremacy over the Bureau in making the MOFA's final decisions on China aid specifically. The policy-making dominance of the China Division, in turn, led to the MOFA's remarkably cautious and non-confrontational China ODA policy: the Division is still perceived as very much pro-China, and is often cynically referred to by the media and academics as the *China School*.[29] As one Japanese newspaper journalist remarked, officials in the China Division are especially fearful of Beijing's veto power over the appointment of Japanese ambassadors to China.[30] For example, the current Japanese ambassador to China, Anan Koreshige, has once in the past had his appointment as a diplomat to the Japanese embassy in Beijing rejected by the Chinese government because of his criticism of the Cultural

Revolution.[31] Not willing to damage their promotion opportunities within the MOFA, officials in the China Division tended to avoid formulating China ODA policies that would not be supported by the Chinese government.

In fact, a certain degree of informal policy-making corroboration did occur between senior bureaucrats and influential LDP parliamentarians. The system by which retired public servants entered politics provided one useful channel of communication. In the 1960s, especially, many senior ministerial officials entered politics after early retirement with the support of influential LDP politicians, mostly factional leaders.[32] For example, during that period, about a quarter of Lower House LDP parliamentarians had retired from government ministries in order to stand for parliament, and been elected using the LDP label. The proportion was even higher in the Upper House, and at that time, most significantly, as many as one half of cabinet ministers had previously had public service careers.[33] This practice led to the creation of informal channels between senior MOFA bureaucrats and LDP leaders, which enabled such bureaucrats easily to influence the LDP's decision-making process.[34]

One major result of the MOFA's considerable degree of autonomy in formulating China policies between 1979 and the mid-1990s was Japan's non-confrontational approach to China, as noted earlier, and a relative inflexibility in China aid policy despite a changing environment. Because of its own budgetary interests, the MOFA was unwilling to change traditional ODA practices, which continually increased the amount of ODA funds directed to China despite Japan's increasing national budget deficit. According to one senior LDP official, this practice led the Chinese government to believe that Japanese aid would always be secure and would never decrease.[35]

The policy-making autonomy of the MOFA was gradually undermined in the 1990s as a result of structural and functional changes in both the MOFA and the LDP in the first half of that decade. The following section addresses these changes.

The China ODA policy-making process, mid-1990s onwards

In the first half of the 1990s a series of important domestic events occurred, including the introduction of a new electoral system, the start of an era of coalition governments and the implementation of administrative reforms. These events led to changes in the separate foreign policy-making roles and capabilities of the LDP and the MOFA. In turn, these changes, combined with the LDP's strengthened foreign policy-making capability, triggered and facilitated a shift in the balance of China ODA policy-making power from the MOFA to the LDP. Eventually, LDP parliamentarians started actively to participate in the process of China ODA policy-making and to challenge the MOFA's monopoly over it. Conversely, the MOFA gradually lost its China ODA policy-making autonomy and is now struggling to protect its remaining power in that area. As a result, tensions between these two powerful foreign policy-making actors over the leadership of China ODA policy-making have increased.

Liberal Democratic Party

The LDP's intervention in the MOFA's China ODA policy-making became more frequent and stronger from the mid-1990s, as a result of LDP parliamentarians' growing motivation to influence policy in this area and the party's enhanced foreign aid policy-making capabilities in general. Several specific factors were responsible.

The new electoral system introduced in 1994 significantly changed the attitude of LDP politicians towards foreign policy-making overall, and China ODA policy-making in particular. In 1994, the eight-party coalition government led by Hosokawa Morihiro, the first non-LDP prime minister since 1955, implemented electoral reform, changing the electoral system for the powerful Lower House of the Diet from multi-member constituency seats to a combination of single-member constituency seats (*shōsenkyoku sei*) and seats elected by proportional representation (*hireidaihyō sei*).[36] Under the new system of single-member constituency seats, where each district elects only one representative, LDP candidates do not compete against each other in the same electoral districts, but instead compete against other parties' candidates. As a result, Japanese elections have become more policy oriented rather than personality and network oriented. This change, together with the increased electoral competition,[37] as one parliamentarian mentioned, has encouraged LDP parliamentarians to become involved in foreign and foreign aid policies associated with major public debates.[38] LDP parliamentarians have become more sensitive to public opinion, especially in their own electorates. Further, the successive formation of LDP-led coalition governments since 1994 has provided the LDP with a new incentive to enhance its independent policy-making capabilities in relation to both domestic and foreign issues. Unlike in the era of LDP majority governments, it has become necessary for the LDP to present impressive and unique policies,[39] which differ from those presented by coalition partners, to demonstrate its leadership within coalition governments.

Under the new electoral system, Japanese ODA to China, like other issues, is directly linked to the electoral fortunes of LDP parliamentarians if there is sufficient public interest in it.[40] As China ODA policy has become a public issue in Japan, especially since the Tiananmen Square Incident, it is now difficult for LDP parliamentarians to ignore it. Several prominent figures who are involved in or who comment on ODA issues confirm that there is a direct link between the changed electoral system and LDP parliamentarians' changed attitude to China ODA policy. As one newspaper journalist observed, the key factor in understanding this link is the increased direct dialogue between LDP parliamentarians and their electorate since the introduction of the new system. In practice, many LDP politicians experience difficulty in responding to questions by their constituents about the provision of taxpayers' funds to Japan's problematic neighbour.[41]

Japanese public resentment of the Chinese government has increased for several reasons, and in turn has led to increasing demands for a reduction of, or an end to, ODA funding to China. First, Japanese citizens are increasingly demanding that public money not be provided to a country that has engaged in specific instances of provocative domestic and international behaviour. Opinion

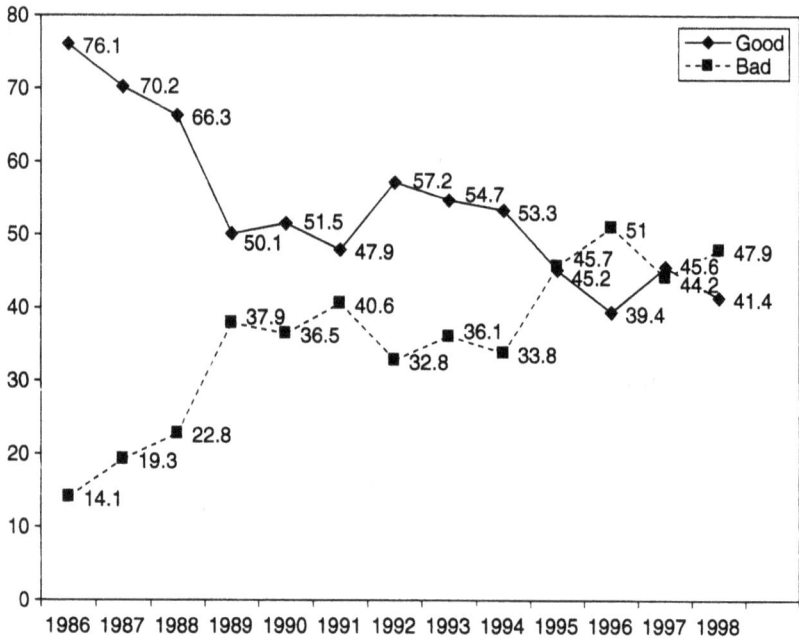

Figure 4.1 Japanese public perceptions of Sino-Japanese relations, 1986–98.

Source: Adapted from Sōrifu (Prime Minister's Office), *Gaikō ni kansuru yoron chōsa (Opinion Polls Regarding Diplomacy)*, Tokyo, 1998.

polls conducted by the Prime Minister's Office (see Figure 4.1) reveal an increasing ambivalence towards China on the part of many Japanese. According to these polls, between 1986 and 1998, the proportion of Japanese having a favourable view of Sino-Japanese relations decreased dramatically, from 76 per cent to 41 per cent, while the proportion having an unfavourable view increased from 14 per cent to 48 per cent. In particular, the Chinese government's human rights abuses in the Tiananmen Square Incident damaged Japanese idealism towards China. In the polls conducted by the Prime Minister's Office, the proportion of Japanese holding a favourable view of China dropped sharply, from 66 per cent in 1988 to 50 per cent in October 1989, 4 months after the Tiananmen Square Incident, while those with the opposite view increased from 23 per cent to 38 per cent.[42] Besides the shock of Tiananmen, recent international actions by the Chinese government – nuclear tests (1994–96), missiles being fired near Taiwan (1996), and frequent naval activities inside Japanese waters (2000) – have all contributed to growing Japanese pessimism towards a modernising China. Given these events, in 1996 Japanese holding a negative perception of China surpassed for the first time those holding positive views, according to an official poll.[43] Clearly, increasing numbers of Japanese have come to view China as problematic, and are becoming sceptical of China's strategic ambitions in the East Asian region.

A second reason for public calls to slash, and in some instance to cease, ODA to China has been China's rapidly increasing military expenditure.[44] The official growth rate of China's defence expenditure has been well over 10 per cent for each of the past fourteen years, with 18 per cent increase in 2002.[45] Having greater financial resources, Beijing is clearly making a concerted effort to modernise its conventional and nuclear weapons.

A third factor that has led to domestic criticism of ODA to China is the fact that the Chinese government has always been reluctant to inform its citizens of these aid flows. When in Japan, both Chinese President Jiang Zemin (in 1998) and Premier Zhu Rongji (in 2000) conceded the need openly and officially to acknowledge Japan's economic assistance,[46] yet once back in China they have not made any such acknowledgement.[47]

Fourth, many Japanese fail to understand why their government continues to provide economic assistance to a country whose economy has, in Gross National Income (GNI) terms,[48] become the sixth largest in the world, while Japan has been in deep recession for the last decade, with resultant large budget deficits.[49] The frustration of the Japanese public is also fuelled by the fact that China has long provided foreign aid to other developing countries while justifying its right to receive such funds itself.[50]

Watanabe Toshio, a prominent development economist and former ODA policy adviser to the LDP, experienced the LDP politicians' own strong resentment towards the Chinese government in a meeting of the party's China ODA review committee held in late 2000. He remarks that the degree of anti-China sentiment among LDP parliamentarians was far stronger than he had expected. The Japanese public's increased resentment towards China was clearly reflected in the attitude of LDP politicians, and motivated them to overhaul Japan's China aid policy.[51]

LDP politicians' willingness to be involved in ODA policy-making has thus clearly increased due to greater public attention to China ODA policy. Not only have attitudes within the LDP changed, however, but also the LDP's capacity to influence foreign policy-making has itself significantly increased since the mid-1990s. During its thirty-eight years in power (1955–93), the Party in fact had acquired a store of foreign policy-making knowledge, though for a long time it was not sufficient to challenge the expertise of the MOFA. One of the most important reasons for the increase in expertise is the enhancement of the foreign policy-making capacity of the LDP Policy Research Council (*seimu chōsakai*), which is the actual policy-making body of the Party, through its frequent interaction and collaboration with central government ministries over many years. In 2001, the Council had 50 full-time policy-making staff in 17 divisions and 1 special committee covering all policy areas.[52] Japanese ODA policy to China was dealt with in the Special Committee on Overseas Economic Cooperation (Taigai keizai kyōryoku tokubetsu iinkai) and the Division of Foreign Affairs (Gaikōbukai).[53]

Officials of the LDP Policy Research Council have undoubtedly strengthened their capability to formulate foreign policy.[54] Nakamaru Itaru, a veteran Council official who has interacted with MOFA bureaucrats for more than three decades, is one individual who has acquired a detailed knowledge of ODA policy-making and now has tremendous influence not only on ODA policy-making within the party but also on that of the MOFA.[55] With the aid of officials like Nakamaru, the LDP has enhanced its foreign policy-making capabilities to the point where it is able to challenge the MOFA's monopoly of China aid policy-making. Further, as the foreign policy-making capability of the central LDP Policy Research Council has strengthened, the policy-making power of the LDP factions in this area has correspondingly diminished.[56] Consequently, MOFA bureaucrats' tactic of using the power of factional leaders to sway LDP parliamentarians opposed to MOFA-formulated China policies has become less effective.

Other factors also contributed to the increase in LDP expertise in foreign policy matters. Those LDP parliamentarians who became ministers or vice-ministers of the MOFA inevitably learned about the policy-making operations of the Ministry, and developed personal connections with MOFA officials. For example, Takemi Keizō, a member of the Upper House of the Diet and an influential member of the *gaikō-zoku* (*diplomatic tribe*, or group of politicians who operate enthusiastically in the Division of Foreign Affairs of the LDP Policy Research Council), has strong ties with MOFA bureaucrats, and considerable influence over them, as a result of his experience as the MOFA vice-minister (July 1998–October 1999). Takemi makes good use of his connections as a source of important diplomatic information. As one high-level MOFA official commented, Takemi has gained deep insights into the complex Sino-Japanese relations and profound knowledge of both Chinese and Taiwanese affairs, and he is the most active and influential LDP politician in the area of China policy-making.[57]

As is well established in the literature on Japanese politics, the *zoku* (tribes) have been an active component in the Japanese policy-making process at least since the 1980s.[58] However, as Inoguchi and Iwai point out, unlike in the industrial and agricultural policy-making area where large numbers of LDP parliamentarians formed *zoku* in order to influence the policy-making process, in the foreign policy-making area, *zoku* were not formed before the late 1980s at the earliest.[59] Clearly, then, it was the new conditions of that period onwards that promoted the formation of the *diplomatic tribe* within the LDP and that have given its members particular prominence in the Japanese foreign policy-making process.

The LDP has also grown increasingly frustrated over the MOFA's inability to develop China ODA policies according to changing domestic and international conditions. The issue of the suspension of special yen loans[60] to China illustrates this weakness. In 2000, China repeatedly conducted naval activities inside Japan's EEZ around the disputed Senkaku Islands near Okinawa. Despite requests by the Japanese Maritime Safety Agency and the Maritime Self Defence Forces for tougher diplomatic action, the MOFA did not suspend the already scheduled disbursement of special yen loans to China. One of my informants, a senior official of the LDP, condemned the MOFA's behaviour at that time as 'very insensitive', commenting that such insensitive behaviour was 'in the nature of Japanese bureaucracy'.[61] Eventually the LDP compelled the MOFA to suspend the loan disbursement.

It needs to be acknowledged here that the LDP is not acting as a unitary, rational actor on issues relating to Sino-Japanese relations. Rather, there still are divisions among LDP politicians in their attitude towards China. However, the division between the pro-PRC and the pro-Taiwan groups within the LDP has gradually become less and less significant in shaping the party's China policy than it was during the 1970s and 1980s.[62] As LDP parliamentarians' political stances to the PRC government have become increasingly unified since the mid-1990s, the LDP's China policy-making is hardly influenced by the weakening pro-PRC and pro-Taiwan division.[63]

In addition to the demise of the division, the generation change which has taken place among LDP China policy-makers over the last decade has also led to a change in party's diplomatic dealing with China. Within the LDP, the initiative in relation to Japanese ODA policy to China has shifted from the older to the younger generation of parliamentarians. Apart from the case of Takemi Keizō noted earlier, Kōno Tarō, Shiozaki Yasuhisa, Etō Seishirō, Asō Tarō and Abe Shinzō are amongst the new generation of the *diplomatic tribe* who have been increasing their influence over China ODA policy-making within the LDP.[64] On the other hand, the influence of older LDP leaders like Nonaka Hiromu, Hayashi Yoshirō, Katō Kōichi and Koga Makoto, who have strong personal ties with Chinese leaders and who consider Sino-Japanese relations as *special* on the basis of Japan's wartime aggression in China, has been diminishing.[65] These new generation LDP leaders of the *diplomatic tribe*, by contrast, consider Sino-Japanese relations to be one of many sets of bilateral relations that Japan has around the globe. They tend to formulate Japan's China policy more on the basis of notions of 'global standards' and 'democracy', rather than the conception of 'special relations'.[66] Thus, they do not hesitate to adopt a tougher diplomatic approach to China, if it is considered necessary. In 1995, for example, conservative Japanese politicians, including these younger members of the LDP's *diplomatic tribe*, called upon the Japanese government to 'admonish China for its chauvinism' in its military actions in the South and East China Seas and 'advocated the use of ODA and other policy tools to influence errant Chinese behaviour'.[67]

Ministry of Foreign Affairs

A series of administrative reforms carried out in the 1980s and the 1990s weakened the overwhelming policy-making power of central ministries, and simplified, in particular, the mechanism underlying bureaucratic ODA decision-making. As a result, LDP intervention in the MOFA's China ODA policy-making has become easier. It is now very difficult for the MOFA to decide China ODA policy without the political intervention of the LDP.

One of the most important objectives of Japanese administrative reforms was in fact to place a check on the policy-making power of the central ministries. In 1981, the Nakasone Yasuhiro government established the First Administrative Reform Council to privatise three gigantic state-owned enterprises which were under the control of central ministries. They are currently known as Nippon

Telegraph and Telephone Corporation, Japan Tobacco Inc., and Japan Railways. The Second Council, established by the Takeshita Noboru government in 1987, carried out extensive economic deregulation to reduce the ministries' over-whelming regulatory power over private businesses.[68] The Third Council, estab-lished in 1990 under the Kaifu Toshiki government, called for a strengthening of the diplomatic capability of the Prime Minister's Office in order to check the MOFA's monopoly over foreign policy-making.[69] Interestingly, the chairs of these three councils were all occupied by the then heads of the Keidanren, that is, the most powerful business leaders of the time.[70] This suggests that LDP politicians and business leaders had joined forces to reduce the policy-making powers of Japanese bureaucrats.

The so-called Hashimoto administrative reforms started by the Hashimoto Ryūtarō coalition government in 1997 seem to have had a significant impact on the Japanese ODA bureaucracy. For one thing, the Hashimoto government closed down a large number of ministries and agencies, reducing the total number of central government ministries from 22 to 13. Amongst the casualties was the EPA, with the result that the traditionally complex bureaucratic ODA policy-making mechanism was simplified, as the four-ministerial ODA decision-making system was transformed into the much simpler 'three-ministerial system (*sanshōchō taisei*)'.[71] The government also made Japanese bureaucratic transactions more transparent by introducing a law in 1998 that allowed public access to some bureaucratic information.[72] The Hashimoto reform made LDP intervention into the process of ODA policy-making easier, and as a result increased the ability of the LDP to limit the MOFA's China ODA policy-making power.[73] For MOFA bureaucrats, on the other hand, the LDP's increased intervention is nothing but a disturbance of their work.[74]

The MOFA's traditionally inflexible and low-profile China ODA policy has also changed as the China Division's influence within the Ministry has been eroded. The recent MOFA review of China ODA policy, for example, was an ini-tiative not of the China Division, but of the MOFA's Economic Cooperation Bureau,[75] which has a central role within the MOFA's new China ODA policy development framework. Moreover, according to some who are heavily involved in the process of the MOFA's ODA policy-making, certain officials who take a particularly hardline stance against the Chinese government have emerged within the China Division itself.[76] This development is very likely to create a more plu-ralistic decision-making structure within the Division and to promote a tougher diplomatic stance by the Division towards the Chinese government in the near future.

The MOFA's evolving China ODA framework has already been observed in some spheres. In terms of the Japanese public, the Ministry, for example, is improving both the quality and the quantity of information it releases on ODA policies. It uses electronic mail as a means to communicate with the public, and provides more detailed information relating to China ODA on its website.[77] In terms of actual ODA practice, the JICA (*Kokusai kyōryoku jigyōdan*), the MOFA's ODA implementation agency, has started to use ODA as a strategic instrument in order to support pro-Japanese political elites within the CCP and to encourage improved relations between the two nations. In 2001, the Agency invited fifty Chinese youth leaders from an elite school for the CCP to Japan, and arranged exchange meetings with young Japanese political and business leaders.[78] Clearly, the MOFA is beginning openly and progressively to use ODA for strategic purposes.

The foreign aid policy-making interaction between the MOFA and the LDP has also changed, largely due to changes in the separate roles and capabilities of the two institutions. In place of the old division of labour between the MOFA and the LDP, there is now a degree of competition between these two bodies in taking policy-making initiatives. The LDP now formulates China ODA policy independently of the MOFA, thus putting pressure on MOFA's policy-making autonomy. The Party routinely requests MOFA officials to provide bureaucratic information relating to Japan's China ODA. It also asks Japanese and foreign academics to provide opinion and advice on Japan's China ODA. Based on this information, members of the LDP Policy Research Council – that is, LDP parliamentarians and officials – formulate the Party's China ODA policy and present it as LDP policy in an attempt to influence China ODA policy-making.[79] This results in the MOFA having to take LDP policy proposals into account when formulating its own China ODA policies, so that the MOFA policies can eventually obtain the LDP's formal approval.[80] As one senior LDP official remarked, the LDP's veto power has become a more practical tool than it used to be, in terms of influence over the MOFA's China ODA policy-making process.[81]

As a consequence of the developments reviewed above, Japan's traditionally low-profile and conciliatory diplomatic approach to China is now changing. Tokyo's decision in April 2001 to grant a visa to the former Taiwan president, Lee Denghui, after having previously declined to issue a visa due to Beijing's objection, clearly illustrates this changed diplomatic attitude. This decision was a result of some LDP leaders' strong pressure on MOFA bureaucrats, who had been very reluctant at first to issue the visa.[82]

From interviews, it is obvious that some Japanese academics who are former policy advisers to the LDP and the MOFA view the decline of bureaucratic power and the enhanced influence of LDP politicians very positively. They believe that LDP politicians' active involvement in the process of China policy-making improves the transparency and accountability of bureaucratic decision-making and, in a positive sense, also increases the influence of public opinion over Japan's China ODA.[83]

Tension between the LDP and the MOFA

Two foreign policy reports presented by the MOFA and the LDP respectively in December 2000 clearly illustrate the different approaches of the two institutions to China ODA, and increasing tensions over who should be responsible for overhauling China ODA policy. In these reports, the LDP and the MOFA both reviewed Japan's ODA policy to China, with both institutions presenting their reports at the same time. Although the two review committees shared some members, the reports are worded quite differently and outline different positions. The report presented by the MOFA committee, called '21seiki ni muketa taichū keizai kyōryoku no arikata ni kansuru kondankai (Policy Recommendation Report by the MOFA Committee on Japanese Economic Assistance to China for the 21st Century)', uses very sensitive and cautious expressions when discussing the political issues and problems Japan encounters in its implementation of China ODA. On the other hand, the LDP report, 'Chūgoku ni taisuru keizai enjo oyobi kyōryoku no sōkatsu to shishin (Review and Guidelines of Japanese Economic Aid and Assistance to China)', employs much more direct language.[84] Of course, both institutions claim to be representing the national interest.

The different positions over China ODA policy can be clearly observed from the two reports. First, the LDP wishes to enhance the political effect of aid to China by including ExIm loans (or the so-called *untied loans*) – non-ODA government loans provided by the former Export and Import Bank[85] – as a component of Japanese development funds to China.[86] In fact, the cumulative amount of ExIm loans to China up to 1999 – ¥3,430 billion – was larger than that of the separate ODA to China – ¥2,688 billion –, and apart from the repayment period (shorter in the case of ExIm loans), the conditions of these two types of government loan, including the interest rate, were very similar.[87] The main difference is that ExIm loans are controlled by the MOF rather than the MOFA. The MOFA, on the other hand, is very reluctant to combine these two funds[88] because the Ministry wants to protect its bureaucratic capacity to control ODA transactions exclusively. If the bureaucratic transactions of ODA and untied loans were combined, the influence of the MOF on MOFA's ODA activity would inevitably increase greatly.

Second, the LDP points to the problem of continuing to give ODA to China in light of China's recent naval activities inside Japan's EEZ. By contrast, the MOFA deliberately avoids directly linking China ODA to this issue. Whereas the LDP report explains the issue of the naval activities in some detail, the MOFA devotes only one sentence to the issue in its thirty-page report.[89] Given that China's naval activity is certainly an issue for the MOFA as well as the LDP, this fact raises the question of MOFA's bureaucratic transparency in general and the transparency of its China diplomacy in particular.

Third, the LDP clearly expresses its displeasure with China's practice of providing foreign aid to Asian and African countries despite China being the largest recipient of Japanese aid. The LDP is also concerned about the lack of transparency in the distribution of this Chinese foreign aid and in the politico-strategic ambitions behind Beijing's aid activities.[90] Conversely, the MOFA defends China's use of foreign aid by emphasising the developmental impact it has on the recipient countries. The Ministry even recommends that Japan embark on joint foreign aid programmes with China for the benefit of poor Asian and African countries.[91]

Fourth, the LDP makes mention of the fact that Chinese nationals are not being informed by their own government about Japanese ODA, whereas the MOFA points out that Chinese leaders have recently been making efforts to rectify this omission. The MOFA notes Premier Zhu Rongji's statement, in a press conference held during his official visit to Japan in October 2000, that the Chinese government would make an effort in future to provide information to the Chinese public about Japan's ODA contributions.[92] In contrast to the MOFA's optimistic view concerning the likely implementation of this promise, the LDP has a more modest expectation.[93]

The MOFA would clearly like to maintain the existing framework of China ODA policy despite enhanced public pressure for change. On the other hand, the LDP would like to overhaul the existing framework as a response to this public pressure and because it now has the capability to formulate its own China ODA policy. The different style of language of the two reports not only reflects policy differences, but also, as some academics have observed, indicates tension between the two over the review of China ODA policy,[94] a tension which is surely also reflected in the fact that the two institutions undertook reviews and issued reports simultaneously. The current politics of Japan's China aid policy-making can be understood to a great degree in terms of this tension between the LDP and the MOFA.

The implication of this tension for Sino-Japanese relations is clear. The Chinese government has become increasingly sensitive to the current Japanese politics of China ODA. It is particularly concerned about the shift of policy-making power from the MOFA, with its conciliatory diplomatic approach, to the LDP, which prefers more straightforward diplomacy. My request to a Chinese diplomat staying in Tokyo in April 2001 for an interview was rejected due to this diplomat's reluctance to talk about Japan's China ODA issues. He said that ODA matters were too sensitive to discuss. This episode indicates the Chinese government's cautiousness towards the politics of China ODA in Japan. Several Chinese leaders have begun to engage in the so-called *gratitude diplomacy* towards Japan: in addition to Chinese President Jiang Zemin and Premier Zhu Rongji, who were mentioned earlier, the Foreign Minister, Tang Jiaxuan, also openly expressed China's gratitude for Japanese foreign aid provision in 2001. The Chinese government now understands very well that Japanese public opinion towards China is one of the most important factors influencing the LDP's China ODA decision-making, and that the balance has swung a long way towards the LDP in the policy-making process.

Conclusion

This chapter argues that since the mid-1990s, Japanese China ODA policy has ceased to be determined primarily by policy-making bargaining among central government ministries, but rather has been determined chiefly by intense competition between the LDP and the MOFA. Following institutional and functional changes in both the LDP and the MOFA during the first half of the 1990s, the power to formulate China ODA policy has shifted dramatically from MOFA bureaucrats towards LDP parliamentarians. Various factors – the LDP's steady accumulation of foreign policy-making knowledge, its enhanced access to important diplomatic information previously monopolised by the MOFA and the political will of LDP parliamentarians to take a leading role in China ODA policy-making – have contributed to this important development. While LDP politicians' intervention in the area of China ODA policy-making has become more frequent and effective, MOFA bureaucrats struggle to protect their already undermined autonomy. The result is an increased tension between the two institutions over leadership in formulating new China ODA policy.

At the level of ideas, from the mid-1990s, Japan's China ODA policy-making has seen a battle between the competing views presented by LDP politicians and MOFA bureaucrats. The dramatic and ongoing shift in the balance of ODA policy-making power towards the LDP and away from the MOFA produced a change in the way that the Japanese government used ODA in its strategic dealing with China between 1995 and 2000, will be discussed in detail in Chapter 6. The shift also has the potential to cause a fundamental redefinition of Japan's China ODA policy in the near future. Japan is now experiencing a transitional period, with increasing domestic pressure for a fundamental review of China ODA policy, but a new and coherent policy framework has not yet emerged. It is very likely that Japanese public perceptions of China, more so than bureaucratic and other political interests, will have a large influence over Japan's future ODA policy to China. It may be some time, however, before the LDP and the MOFA can fully cooperate to overhaul China ODA policy.

Chapter 5 examines the actual transactions of Japan's ODA programmes to China, focusing on the role of yen loans (or government loans) in developing industrial infrastructure, in order to reveal the actual economic and political interests behind the disbursement of the huge amount of development aid that is provided to China.

5 Yen loans to China

Development, globalisation and interdependence

This chapter elucidates the broader economic and political interests that Japanese governments have pursued through ODA to China, by means of a specific study of yen loans. In the process, it engages with the argument about whether Japanese ODA should be seen primarily as an instrument to advance the commercial interests of Japanese firms. The chapter also suggests answers to the question of whether Japanese policy-makers have successfully achieved their objectives, by statistically analysing the effect that yen loans have had upon the development of the Chinese economy and the integration of the Chinese economy into the market-based global economic system. Ultimately, it provides empirical evidence to support the argument that ODA has indeed helped advance Japanese economic and political interests at the national level in relation to China over the last two decades.

My statistical analysis indicates that there is a positive, albeit indirect, link between Japanese ODA and the development and globalisation of the Chinese economy. The linkage works in this way: first, Japanese yen loans contributed to the development of China's industrial infrastructure; second, the strengthening of Chinese infrastructure attracted and facilitated the inflow of FDI from Japan and other countries into China; third, these FDI encouraged the expansion and diversification of China's foreign trade; and fourth, the expanded and diversified Chinese foreign trade promoted economic development and the incorporation of the Chinese economy into the market-based global economic system. Of course, it must be acknowledged that Japanese ODA is only one of many factors that have contributed to the development and globalisation of the Chinese economy. Nonetheless, as is evident from the fact that Japan has been the single largest source of development assistance to China of all donor nations and international aid organisations over the last two decades, the impact of Japanese ODA should not be underestimated. Furthermore, as the linkage explained above indicates, Japanese ODA has itself helped to promote China's trade with other East Asian countries, Western countries and other countries around the world.

My research also indicates that there is no clear evidence showing that ODA to China has improved Japan's share of China's foreign trade or Japan's share of the world's direct investments in China. Through its China ODA activity, it is apparent that Japan has advanced its broader national economic and political interests, rather than the narrow commercial interests of particular private Japanese companies. This case study of yen loans also provides concrete evidence of the shift in priority target areas of Japanese ODA in China since the mid-1990s from economic to socio-environmental infrastructure development.

The primary reason for my focus on the effect of yen loans, rather than the two other types of Japanese ODA – grant aid and technical cooperation – is that, until 1999, yen loans comprised the largest component (indeed, 91 per cent) of the cumulative amount of Japanese ODA to China. Thus, among the three types of ODA, yen loans have had the greatest impact on China's economic development. This chapter deals with all the yen loan projects undertaken in China between 1979 and 2000, rather than focusing on one particular ODA project. In other words, the analytical method is to look at the entire forest, rather than a single tree. The major source materials used in this chapter are official economic statistics and data concerning Japan's yen loan projects in China, collected by the OECD, the IMF and various Japanese and Chinese government institutions.

The first section of the chapter assesses the quantitative significance of the whole of Japanese ODA to China, first, by comparing the amount of ODA provided to China by Japan with the amount provided by other major donor nations and international aid organisations, and second, by investigating the proportion of Japanese ODA funds in China's total national budget and in its budget for capital construction. The second section examines yen loans to China by project and sector, in order to elucidate the impact that yen loans have had on the development of Chinese economic infrastructure. It then analyses the commercial and political interests behind Japan's China ODA activities by looking at the correlations among ODA, FDI and trade. The third section evaluates the shift in the priority areas of yen loans which had become evident by the mid-1990s, in order to highlight changes in the policy objectives of Japan's China ODA.

A comparative analysis of ODA to China and the three types of aid

China's foreign aid absorption policy over the last half century can roughly be categorised into three phases. During the first decade after the establishment of the People's Republic (from 1949 to the beginning of the 1960s), China regularly received foreign loans and technology from the Soviet Union and East European Communist countries to facilitate the construction of heavy industrial factories. From the beginning of the 1960s to 1978, a period in which China experienced international isolation largely due to the Sino-Soviet split, Chinese leaders rejected all foreign capital and technology. During this period, Chinese leaders insisted on *self-reliance* as the basic philosophy for economic development, and foreign capital was regarded as a manifestation of economic imperialism. After 1978, China dramatically changed its former development policy of self-reliance and adopted a more active foreign capital absorption policy. When they opened the door to the world in 1978, following the end of the domestic disturbances caused by the Cultural Revolution, Chinese leaders were shocked by the success of the outward-looking development strategy of the newly industrialised economies (NIEs) – Taiwan, Singapore, Korea and Hong Kong – which had attracted enormous amounts of foreign capital.[1] China's new policy of using foreign capital, including ODA, for economic development – under the Reform and Liberalisation Policy – has continued up until now.

Comparative analysis

Table 5.1 shows ODA flows to China by major OECD countries and major international aid organisations. The system under which donor countries provide development funds directly to developing countries is called *bilateral ODA*, and the system under which donor countries provide funds to international aid organisations, which then channel the aid to developing countries, is called *multilateral ODA*.

Table 5.1 ODA flows to China by major donors, 1979–98 (net disbursements, US$ million)

	1979–82	1983–86	1987–90	1991–94	1995–98	1979–98
Japan	403.4	1,624.5	2,782.0	4,466.2	3,977.0	13,253.1
Germany	76.1	303.0	415.7	847.7	1,848.4	3,490.9
France	5.0	26.9	448.8	492.2	268.3	1,241.2
Italy	3.4	67.5	382.4	461.6	17.0	931.9
Canada	4.5	45.2	172.9	240.6	189.4	652.6
Australia	4.6	49.0	91.0	194.2	139.3	478.1
Belgium	25.9	21.0	46.3	33.0	30.5	156.7
(A): bilateral ODA total	537.4	2,229.4	5,065.4	7,957.1	7,834.3	23,623.6
Japan's share in A (%)	75	73	55	56	51	56
IDA	0.9	686.8	1,955.6	2,936.0	2,829.8	8,409.1
WFP	32.8	257.1	221.0	98.4	66.9	676.2
UNDP	46.6	67.8	138.0	178.0	92.5	522.9
EC (EU)	7.2	8.4	148.3	91.7	104.7	360.3
IFAD	3.9	56.0	67.9	45.7	67.4	240.9
(B): multilateral ODA total	546.7	1,182.8	2,617.9	3,551.2	3,317.2	11,215.8
(C): Arab countries	—	129.7	16.7	43.3	12.7	202.4
(D): total (A + B + C)	1,084.1	3,541.9	7,700.0	11,551.6	11,164.2	35,041.8
Japan's share in D (%)	37	46	36	39	36	38

Source: Compiled from Organisation for Economic Cooperation and Development (OECD), *Geographical Distribution of Financial Flows to Developing Countries* (various issues), Paris, 1981–2000.

Note
IDA (International Development Association), WFP (World Food Programme), UNDP (United Nations Development Programme), EC (European Community (currently, European Union)), IFAD (International Fund for Agricultural Development).

It can be observed that Japan was, by far, China's largest bilateral aid donor during the two decades between 1979 and 1998. During this period, Japan provided a total of US$13.3 billion or 56 per cent of the total bilateral ODA (US$23.6 billion) that China received from twenty-one OECD countries. Japanese aid to China even exceeds the total amount of multilateral ODA funds to China (US$11.2 billion) provided by more than fifteen international aid organisations, including the five major organisations which are listed in Table 5.1, in that period. The second-and third-largest bilateral aid donors to China were Germany and France, which provided 15 per cent (US$3.5 billion) and 5 per cent (US$1.2 billion), respectively, of total bilateral ODA between 1979 and 1998.

It is striking that Japan has consistently provided more than half of China's bilateral ODA receipts, even though its share has gradually decreased from three-quarters in the period 1979–82 to half between 1995 and 1998 (Table 5.1). On the other hand, over the past two decades, Japan's share in the grand total – that is, the sum of the total bilateral, multilateral and Arab countries' ODA funds provided to China – has been relatively steady at 36 per cent to 46 per cent.[2] Between 1979 and 1998, Japan's share in the grand total of China ODA (US$35 billion) was 38 per cent. This is larger than the share of the International Development Association (IDA), which is the development assistance arm of the World Bank and is the biggest multilateral aid donor to China, a fact which again illustrates the comparative significance of Japanese ODA to China. Thus, in financial terms, Japan is easily the biggest and most important source of China's development assistance funds.

It is noteworthy that the US, the world's second-largest foreign aid donor until 2001 and the largest after 2002, is not included in Table 5.1 because it has not provided ODA to China. The reason is that during the 1980s and 1990s, the US Foreign Aid Law strictly banned any foreign aid activity to Communist countries. On the other hand, the US has directed a large amount of ExIm Bank funds to China in order to facilitate US exports to China.[3] For example, it provided US$1.9 billion to China in this way in 1997.[4] Such international funding is not counted as development assistance, however, due to its commercial nature. Instead, it is recognised as *other official flow (OOF)*.

ODA in the Chinese national budget

Another possible way to evaluate Japanese ODA's contribution to China's industrialisation quantitatively is to examine the ratio of Japanese ODA to China's national budget expenditure. Table 5.2 shows the percentages of foreign aid funds received from Japan in China's total central government expenditure and in its expenditure on capital construction (not including capital formation) between 1990 and 1998. It can be seen that the percentages of Japanese ODA in China's total budget expenditures vary from 0.5 per cent in 1997 to 2.2 per cent in 1994. The average between 1990 and 1998 was 1.3 per cent. On the other hand, the proportion of Japanese ODA in Chinese expenditure on capital construction, which is used for infrastructure development, ranges between 4.5 per cent in 1997

Table 5.2 Contribution of Japanese ODA to the Chinese national budget, 1990–98 (US$ million, %)

Year	(A): Japanese ODA to China	(B): China's central government budget (total)	% of A in B	(C): China's budget for capital construction	% of A in C
1990	723	64,467	1.1	11,444	6.3
1991	585	63,618	0.9	10,512	5.6
1992	1,051	67,860	1.6	10,080	10.4
1993	1,351	80,568	1.7	10,273	13.2
1994	1,480	67,210	2.2	7,424	19.9
1995	1,380	81,708	1.7	9,450	14.6
1996	862	95,470	0.9	10,914	7.9
1997	577	111,385	0.5	12,298	4.5
1998	1,158	130,429	0.9	16,762	6.9

Source: Compiled from National Bureau of Statistics of China, *China Statistical Yearbook 2001*, Beijing: China Statistics Press, 2001; Organisation for Economic Cooperation and Developmnt (OECD), *Geographical Distribution of Financial Flows to Developing Countries* (various issues), Paris, 1991–2000.

and 19.9 per cent in 1994, with an average of 10.4 per cent throughout the period. From these figures, it is safe to say that, while the financial contribution of Japanese ODA to China's total budget expenditure is not big, its contribution to expenditure on capital construction is impressive. In fact, the real impact of Japanese ODA on China's economic development is undoubtedly larger than that indicated by the figures above. In addition to its direct financial contribution, Japanese ODA has also made a significant, if unquantifiable contribution to China in terms of knowledge, through project technology transfer and human resource development.[5]

Three types of Japanese ODA to China

As briefly noted in Chapter 1, Japanese bilateral ODA to China can be categorised into three types: grant aid, technical cooperation and yen loans. From 1979 to 1999 Japan directed ¥2,453 billion of yen loans, ¥119 billion of grant aid, and ¥116 billion of technical cooperation to China.[6] Grant aid schemes are implemented across a wide range of areas, such as environmental protection, health and medical care, education, agriculture and forestry, with the improvement of living conditions in China being their primary focus. Technical cooperation schemes aim to transfer the necessary technical knowledge and expertise needed for development, mostly by inviting Chinese trainees to Japan and dispatching Japanese experts to China for the purpose of training and educating Chinese technicians and officials. ODA loans, or yen loans, allow the provision of substantial amounts of funding to China at low-interest rates and with lenient repayment conditions, to facilitate the development of China's economic and social infrastructure.

Table 5.3 Japan's grant aid projects in China in FY 1997 (¥ million)

Project	Amount
Virus Examination Equipment Supply	104
Improvement of Agricultural Water Management of Dong Ting Hu Lake	1,127
Provision of Medical Equipment for Inner Mongolia Region	1,364
Provision of Medical Equipment for Emergency Centres in Sichuan, Hubei and Dalian	1,848
Provision of Educational Equipment for Secondary Schools for Minority Ethnic Groups	720
Disaster Relief	64
Supply of Equipment for Production of TV Programs by Tianjin Television Station	50
Improvement of Food Production	1,170
56 Grassroots Aid Projects	439
Total	6,886

Source: Adapted from Economic Cooperation Bureau, Japanese Ministry of Foreign Affairs, *Japan's Official Development Assistance Annual Report 1999*, Tokyo. 2000.

Grant aid

Table 5.3 gives details of the grant aid projects that Japan committed to China in 1997. During this year, Japan provided grant aid worth about ¥6.9 billion, which comprised 3.1 per cent of the total Japanese ODA to China, for the implementation of a variety of projects, including the provision of medical equipment and food production improvement projects. Notably, fifty-six grants were provided for grassroots projects in 1997. Despite their relatively small scale, grassroots projects, in most cases meaning projects that are implemented by Japanese non-governmental organisations (NGOs), have become increasingly important as an effective aid approach. Such projects are appreciated by local Chinese people because they have close contact with the projects and because these projects can quickly improve living conditions.[7] In 1997, Japan also provided grant aid as relief after two disasters, and one grant for educational and cultural activity, specifically, the supply of equipment necessary for secondary school education and television programme production. Despite the relatively small amounts of money involved, the grant aid programmes in China implemented by the JICA probably have the most direct and immediate impact on the living conditions of Chinese people.

Technical cooperation

Japan's technical cooperation projects in China extend over various areas. including the transfer of computer technology, the development of legislation. and the training of local personnel in the areas of medical care and education. One of the main technical cooperation programmes is the Japan Overseas Cooperation Volunteer (*Kaigai seinen kyōryokutai*) programme, under which young Japanese volunteers live and work alongside local people in developing countries for two years in order to assist in the economic and social development of those countries.

Japan's most recent technical cooperation project in China involves reducing water pollution in Taihu Lake, near the Chang Jiang River in Jiangsu Province. Starting in 2001, this project is scheduled to run for five years. The water in Taihu Lake has been contaminated by domestic and industrial waste water, which has been increasing with rapid economic development, and this has had detrimental effects on the lake's ecosystem. In order to help solve this serious problem, the JICA dispatched Japanese experts to undertake a pollution assessment of the lake. and invited Chinese scientists and officials to come to Japan to be trained in the analysis of water quality.[8]

Yen loans

Japanese ODA loans – the so-called *yen loans* – are long-term, low-interest, concessional credits that the Japan Bank for International Cooperation (JBIC. formerly known as the Overseas Economic Cooperation Fund) provides to developing countries, including China, to assist their development. The basic approach of the JBIC in providing ODA loans is to assist self-help efforts towards economic growth. In the 1990s, the annual interest rates of yen loans to China. which ranged between 0.7 and 2.5 per cent, depending on the type of project. were much lower than those provided by the World Bank, which ranged between 1.5 and 7.8 per cent.[9] The repayment conditions of yen loans – thirty years, with a period of grace of ten years – are advantageous to China because many transportation projects, such as construction of railways and ports, require several years to complete. Typically, it then takes several more years before the project is operating smoothly and producing sufficient earnings to repay the loan.[10] As will be demonstrated later, Japan's yen loans to China have contributed greatly to China's economic infrastructure development.

Different development approaches are employed by the JICA, which supervises the grant aids programme, and the JBIC which oversees yen loans projects. Yen loans are intended to have a long-term economic impact, while grant aid is designed to have a short-term social effect. The direct objectives of Japan's grant aid programmes have been to improve the living conditions of the Chinese people through medical and educational assistance; emergency and poverty relief; and to improve agricultural productivity. Yen loans have also been used for the development of China's basic economic infrastructure, which has an indirect impact on the Chinese people's well-being. This indirect development approach through yen loans is very important in promoting China's economic development, which in turn will increase the wealth of individual Chinese in the long run. Moreover, the significance of the yen loans is indicated by the fact that, until 1999, 91 per cent of the cumulative amount of Japanese ODA to China was used for yen loan projects.[11] Hence the main focus of this chapter is on the yen loan projects.

Yen loan commitments to China, 1979–2000

All of the yen loan projects carried out in China between 1979 and 2000 are listed in Appendix 1, attached at the end of this book. During this period, a total

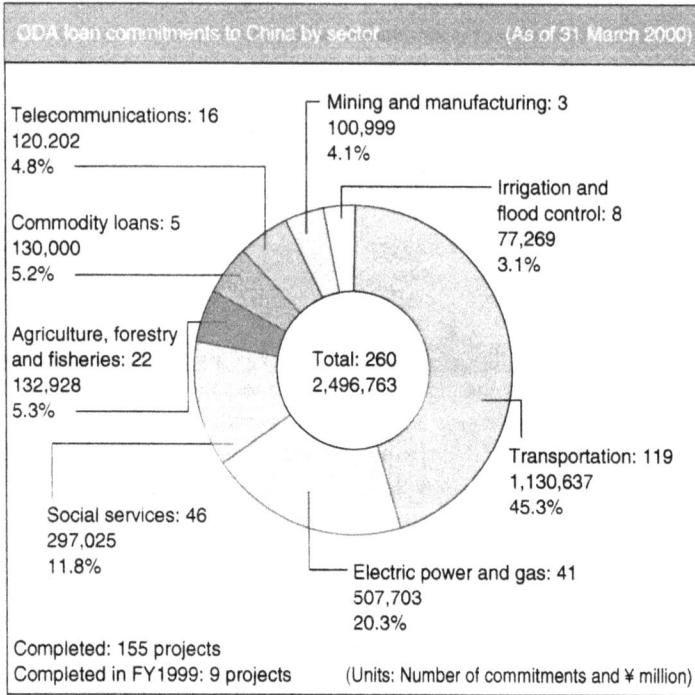

ODA loan commitments to China by sector   (As of 31 March 2000)

Telecommunications: 16
120,202
4.8%

Mining and manufacturing: 3
100,999
4.1%

Commodity loans: 5
130,000
5.2%

Irrigation and
flood control: 8
77,269
3.1%

Agriculture, forestry
and fisheries: 22
132,928
5.3%

Total: 260
2,496,763

Transportation: 119
1,130,637
45.3%

Social services: 46
297,025
11.8%

Electric power and gas: 41
507,703
20.3%

Completed: 155 projects
Completed in FY1999: 9 projects   (Units: Number of commitments and ¥ million)

Figure 5.1 ODA loan commitments to China by sector, 1979–2000.

Source: Japan Bank for International Cooperation, *ODA Loan Report 2000*, Tokyo, 2001.

of 152 projects, worth about ¥2,668 billion, was implemented. This section first examines these yen loan projects in China from several perspectives – by sector, by relationship to trade and FDI, by loan procedure and by tying status.

Figure 5.1 shows Japan's yen loan commitments to China by sector from 1979 to 2000. It is apparent that yen loans have been heavily used to facilitate the development of industrial infrastructure in China, particularly transportation and energy infrastructure. For example, during this period, the cumulative amount of loans spent on transportation projects reached ¥1,130 billion, accounting for 45.3 per cent of the total yen loans to China. Similarly, a total of forty-one energy infrastructure projects – relating particularly to the development of electric power and gas infrastructure and worth about ¥508 billion – had been financed by Japanese yen loans by March 2000. Thus, the transportation and energy infrastructure sectors accounted for 66 per cent of the total ODA loan budget and 62 per cent of the total number of ODA projects.

Between 1979 and 2000, Japanese and Chinese governments both gave priority to transportation and energy infrastructure projects, because such projects were essential to China's overall economic development. As noted in Chapter 2, in discussing Japanese officials' criticism of the Great Leap Forward campaign, the lack of domestic industrial infrastructure had been the single most important structural problem for China in developing its economy. In particular, the lack of transportation and energy infrastructure had to be addressed if further modernisation were to occur. Recognising this, Chinese and Japanese governments used yen loans in an effort to remove *bottlenecks* in the energy and transportation sectors and to promote sustainable economic development in China.[12]

ODA and the development and globalisation of the Chinese economy

The above section highlighted the significant role that Japanese ODA has played in developing China's industrial infrastructure. However, it is FDI and trade that most directly stimulated the Chinese economy.[13] Therefore, it is necessary to clarify the relationship among Japan's ODA, FDI and trade with China in order to examine the actual impact of Japanese ODA on the Chinese economy. The relationship among Japan's ODA, FDI and trade is as follows. Yen loans facilitated and increased Japanese companies' direct investments in China through improvement of the industrial infrastructure which is necessary for foreign investment. The expansion of Japanese FDI flow into China led, in turn, to an increase in the volume of bilateral trade and, hence, promoted Japanese economic interests in China. As a result, the economic interdependence between the two countries has significantly deepened.

Table 5.4 shows the development of Japanese and other major countries' FDI in China by actual value from 1990 to 1997. During this period, Japanese direct investments into China consistently increased, except for a drop in 1989 following the Tiananmen Square Incident. In particular, Japanese investments rose sharply after 1993, reaching US$4.3 billion in 1997. One of the major factors that contributed to the dramatic increase of Japanese FDI in China after the beginning of the 1990s was the development of Chinese economic infrastructure in the 1980s, supported by a large amount of foreign aid from many donor nations and international aid organisations as shown earlier. As the single largest aid donor,

Table 5.4 FDI into China by major countries and Hong Kong, 1990–97 (US$ million)

	1990	1991	1992	1993	1994	1995	1996	1997
HK	1,880	2,410	7,507	17,275	509	20,060	20,680	20,632
Japan	503	533	710	1,324	2,075	3,108	3,679	4,326
Taiwan	222	466	151	3,139	3,391	3,161	3,475	3,289
US	456	323	511	2,063	2,490	3,083	3,443	3,239
Singapore	50	58	122	490	1,180	1,851	2,244	2,606
S. Korea	13	40	119	374	723	1,043	1,358	2,142
UK	13	35	38	221	689	914	1,301	1,858
Germany	64	161	89	56	259	386	518	993

Source: Compiled from Nihon bōeki shinkō kyōkai (JETRO), *Chūgoku deita fairu 1999/2000* (China Data File 1999/2000), Tokyo, 2000.

Table 5.5 FDI into China by top six source countries and Hong Kong (as of December 1999)

	Number of contracts	Share (%)	Total actual value (US$ billion)	Share
Hong Kong	185,798	54.4	154.28	50.1
US	28,721	8.4	25.82	8.4
Japan	18,737	5.5	24.91	8.1
Taiwan	43,540	12.7	23.89	7.8
South Korea	12,827	3.8	9.01	2.9
Germany	2,126	0.6	4.79	1.6
France	1,586	0.5	3.59	1.2
Total	341,720	100.0	307.71	100.0

Source: Compiled from Zai-Chūgoku Nihonkoku taishikan keizaibu (Economics Division, Japanese Embassy in China), 'Saikin no Chūgoku keizai jōsei to Nitchū keizai kankei (Current Chinese Economic Affairs and Japan–China Economic Relations)', 2001.

the relative importance of Japanese ODA in creating the necessary infrastructure for FDI was also large. Yen loans greatly helped to minimise the costs of investments in China for private companies, including Japanese companies, by supporting the development of industrial infrastructure.[14]

Table 5.5 shows the total flow of FDI into China as of the end of 1999 from the top six source countries and Hong Kong by number and value of investments. In terms of the number of contracts, Japan is the fourth-largest source (5.5 per cent) behind Hong Kong, Taiwan and the US. It is also the third-largest (8.1 per cent) investor in China in terms of monetary value, after Hong Kong and the US. Interestingly, Hong Kong's share in China's total FDI inflow is, by far, larger than that of any other country. This is because many foreign multinational companies and Chinese companies channel their China investment through Hong Kong 'in order to reap valuable tax concessions'.[15] Thus, Hong Kong's own FDI in China is greatly overestimated.

The rising level of FDI in China from the early 1990s promoted and accelerated China's economic development for the remainder of that decade. FDI directly or indirectly accelerates economic growth in developing countries.[16] FDI contributed greatly to China's economic growth by introducing new technology and managerial expertise, creating employment for local people and bringing in a large amount of foreign capital. Furthermore, FDI promotes developing countries' exports to and imports from the industrialised countries that are investing in those developing countries. For example, direct investments by private Japanese companies in China encourage Chinese imports in the form of 'industrial plant and machinery, industrial components and other intermediate products' from Japan, while many Japanese manufacturing companies operating in China are 'increasingly producing consumer goods for the Japanese market'.[17]

As Japan is the third-largest source of Chinese FDI (Table 5.5), it can therefore be argued that Japanese investments have supported China's economic growth, at least to the same extent as its share in China's total FDI inflow. Moreover, if we take into account the large contribution of Japanese ODA in increasing overall China FDI inflow from many multinational companies around the world through economic infrastructure development in China, we should note that Japan's actual contribution to China's economic development and foreign trade expansion is larger than simple FDI statistics indicate. Furthermore, as mentioned earlier, ODA's role in transferring knowledge and technological expertise for economic development from Japan to China is arguably as important as its role in providing finance for economic infrastructure development.

Increased Japanese FDI in China has also increased bilateral trade between Japan and China. Table 5.6 shows the development of Sino-Japanese trade by absolute value from 1979, when Japan's China ODA programme started, to 1999. It is apparent from the table that, apart from some fluctuations, Japan's exports to, imports from, and total trade with China have all greatly increased during that period. The financial value of Japanese exports to China increased from US$3.7 billion in 1979 to US$23.3 billion in 1999. During the same period, Japanese

Table 5.6 Japan's trade with China: exports and imports, 1979–99 (US$ million, %)

Fiscal Year	Exports		Imports		Total trade		Trade balance
	Amount	Increase (%)	Amount	Increase (%)	Amount	Increase (%)	Amount
1979	3,699	21.3	2,955	45.5	6,653	31.0	744
1980	5,078	37.3	4.323	46.3	9,402	41.3	755
1981	5,095	0.3	5.292	22.4	10,387	10.5	−196
1982	3,511	−31.1	5,352	1.1	8.863	−14.7	−1,842
1983	4,912	39.9	5,087	−5.0	10,000	12.8	2 175
1984	7,217	46.9	5,958	17.1	13,174	31.7	1,259
1985	12,477	72.9	6,483	8.8	18,960	43.9	5,994
1986	9,856	−21.0	5,652	−12.8	15,509	−18.2	4,204
1987	8,250	−16.3	7,401	30.9	15,651	0.9	848
1988	9,476	14.9	9,859	33.2	19,335	23.5	−383
1989	8,516	−10.1	11,146	13.1	19,662	1.7	−2,630
1990	6,130	−28.0	12,054	8.1	18,183	−7.5	−5,924
1991	8,593	40.2	14,216	17.9	22,809	25.4	−5,623
1992	11,949	39.1	16,953	19.3	28,902	26.7	−5,004
1993	17,273	44.6	20,565	21.3	37,838	30.9	−3,292
1994	18,682	8.2	27,566	34.0	46,248	22.2	−8,884
1995	21,931	17.4	35,922	30.3	57,853	25.1	−13,991
1996	21,890	−0.2	40,550	12.9	62,440	7.9	−18,660
1997	21,785	−0.5	42,066	3.7	63,851	2.3	−20,281
1998	20,022	−8.1	36,896	−12.3	56,917	−10.9	−16.874
1999	23,329	0.9	42,850	2.1	66,179	16.3	−19.521

Source: Compiled from Zaimushō (Ministry of Finance), *Kanzei nenpō Heisei 12-nen ban* (Customs Annual Report 2000), Tokyo, 2000.

imports from China increased fifteen times, from US$3 billion to US$42.9 billion, and the volume of total bilateral trade rose ten times, from about US$6.7 billion to US$66.2 billion. Consequently, Japan has become China's largest trading partner, while China is Japan's second-biggest trading partner, behind the US.[18] Specifically, Japan is China's most important import source and its second-biggest export market after the US, while China is Japan's second-largest import source and the third-biggest export destination for industrial output, following the US and Taiwan.

A positive correlation between Japanese companies' increased FDI into China and the boosted bilateral trade in the 1990s can be observed from the statistics provided earlier. Japanese development assistance to China, through the promotion of FDI and trade, led to an increase in Japanese investment and trade interests in relation to China in the 1980s and, more significantly, in the 1990s. It is safe to say that the provision of China ODA over the last two decades has helped advance Japanese economic interests in China.

Did Japan's China ODA promote Japan's economic interests unilaterally? That is, did it only assist the increase of Japanese investment in and trade with China? The analysis presented here suggests that this is not the case. In fact, it suggests that Japanese ODA facilitated and increased FDI in China not only by Japanese companies, but also by Euro-American and other East Asian companies. In turn, this FDI in China promoted the expansion and diversification of China's overall foreign trade and, hence, contributed to the development and globalisation of the Chinese economy. Thus, Japanese ODA promoted the economic interests not only of Japan but also of other countries, and in doing so, encouraged China's economic interdependence with these countries.

Figure 5.2 shows China FDI inflows by major source countries, excluding Hong Kong, from 1990 to 1997. It is immediately apparent from this figure that China FDI by major source countries dramatically increased after 1992. In particular, Taiwan's investments in the PRC grew sharply from US$151 million in 1992 to US$3.1 billion in 1993. Similarly, US investment increased from US$511 million to US$2.1 billion and Japanese investment surged from US$710 million to US$1.3 billion during the same period. Clearly, the China investment boom began in the early 1990s and since then, the increasing FDI from multinational companies around the world has been a major driving force of China's rapid economic growth. China's improved industrial infrastructure in the 1980s, which had been greatly assisted by yen loans and by ODA from other donor countries and aid organisations, contributed to this increase in FDI inflow into the country after the beginning of the 1990s. More significantly, Figure 5.2 shows that while Japanese direct investment in China climbed dramatically from 1992 to 1997, investments by other countries increased equally dramatically during the same period. Thus, it can be argued that Japanese ODA encouraged not only Japanese, but also other East Asian, American and European multinational companies' direct investment in China.[19] Of course, it is also correct to say that ODA by other countries and by international aid organisations to China similarly promoted Japanese investment interests.

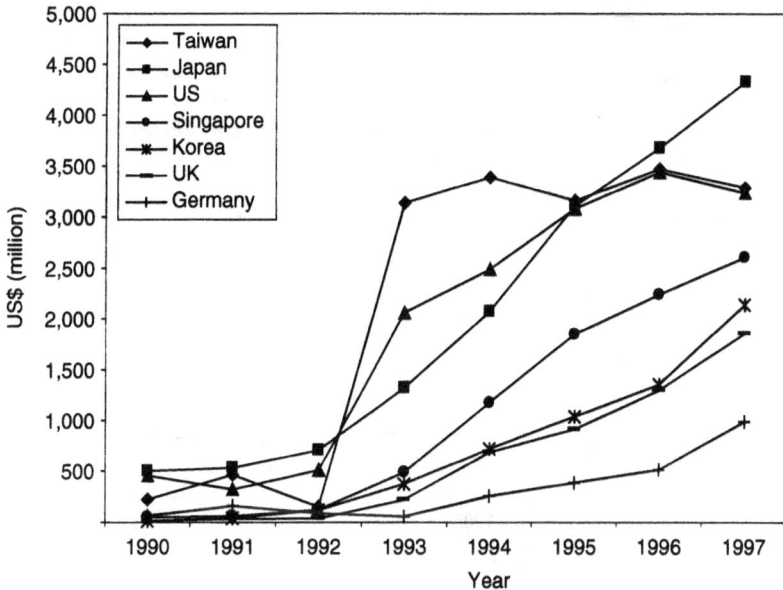

Figure 5.2 Trend of FDI into China by major source countries, 1990–97 (US$ million).

Source: Complied from Nihon bōeki shinkō kyōkai (JETRO), *Chūgoku deita fairu 1999/2000* (China Data File 1999/2000), Tokyo, 2000.

Note
Hong Kong's FDI in China is excluded from this graph because it is greatly overestimated, as explained earlier.

Figure 5.3 shows the relative trade share (total trade volume) of China's major trading partners between 1980 and 1999.[20] Apart from some fluctuations, Japan's share of China's total foreign trade declined from 24.4 per cent in 1980 to 18.3 per cent in 1999. On the other hand, the relative trade share of the three newly indus-trialised Asian economies – Taiwan, Singapore and South Korea – on the one hand, and the US and Canada on the other, increased over the same period: from 1.6 per cent to 15.8 per cent and from 15.3 per cent to 18.4 per cent, respectively. The fact that, despite the dramatically increased volume of total bilateral trade and Japan's status as China's largest single trading partner, Japan's share in China's total for-eign trade between 1980 and 1999 declined, rather than increased, was due to the expansion and diversification of Chinese foreign trade after the mid-1980s.[21] Therefore, there is no indication that the increase in Japanese ODA to China has led solely to an expansion of Sino-Japanese trade. The increasing FDI flow into China, which has come from a variety of sources, has promoted the expansion and diversification of China's foreign trade as a whole, and thus has contributed to the overall development and globalisation of the Chinese economy.[22]

There is, therefore, no clear sign that Japanese ODA to China has primarily resulted in Japan's unilateral economic gain, especially as yen loans are essentially

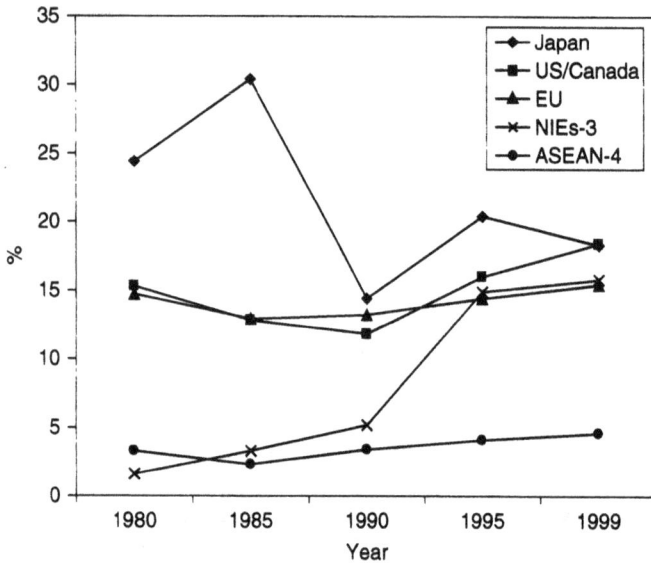

Figure 5.3 China's foreign trade (total volume) by partners, 1980–99 (%).

Source: International Monetary Fund, *Direction of Trade Statistics*, (various issues), Washington, DC, 1981–2001.

Note
NIEs-3 refers to Taiwan, Singapore and Korea; ASEAN-4 refers to Thailand, Indonesia, The Philippines and Malaysia.

untied, as explained later. By providing yen loans for projects in China, Japanese governments have supported the expansion and diversification of China's international trade, rather than pursuing the immediate commercial interests of private Japanese companies. In this context, it is unsurprising that Japan's ODA provision to China has not led to an increase in Japan's share in China's international trade over the last two decades. Ultimately, Japanese ODA to China increased China's economic interdependence with other countries as well as Japan and thus, promoted the incorporation of the Chinese economy into the global economic system. From this point of view, it is clear that in the case of China, Japan's policy of providing ODA is not primarily a commercially constructed one, as some scholars have argued or implied. Rather, it is based on broader politico-strategic objectives.

The dramatic increase in the amount of FDI into China and the expansion and diversification of China's foreign trade in the 1980s and 1990s have also facilitated China's transition from a socialist economy to a market-based economy. The fact that such a transition is taking place is quite clear. For example, the share of production by state-owned enterprises in China's total industrial output dramatically decreased from 80 per cent in 1978 to 38 per cent in 1996.[23] On the other hand, the share of non-state-owned enterprises, including foreign and private enterprises, in China's total industrial output has consistently increased, reaching 53 per cent in 2000 and 59 per cent in 2002.[24] These figures show China's rapid transition to a market-oriented economy over the last two decades. Mark Beeson and Leong Liew emphasise the great importance of this change, arguing that with respect to China, 'the fact that capitalism has "Chinese characteristics" is less significant than the fact that China has *capitalist* characteristics'. They continue: 'That a fifth of the world's population has been integrated increasingly into the wider world system organised along market-centred principles is clearly of enormous long-term historical significance'.[25] Japanese yen loans indirectly contributed to the promotion of capitalism in China through their contribution to the development and globalisation of the Chinese economy, as described earlier.

In the end, China's economic development, the incorporation of the Chinese economy into the global economic framework and China's transition to a market-based economy are in Japan's economic as well as political interests. First, China's economic development does not result in Japan's economic loss, but rather, Japan's gain, because of the complementarity of the two economies – that is, China is rich in raw materials and in cheap labour, which is important for Japanese economic security, and Japan is abundant in capital and technology, which China needs for its industrialisation. Thus, probably more than other states, Japan is likely to benefit economically from China's economic growth.[26] Second, China's transition from a socialist to a market economy is in Japan's economic and political interests as China increasingly shares a similar economic system and liberal economic values with Japan. China's economic development and its transition into a market economy also provide more opportunities for private Japanese companies to benefit from the increasingly expanded, open and capitalist China. Finally, the incorporation of China into the global economic framework is in Japan's politico-strategic interest because it inevitably imposes global economic norms and rules on China. Thus, it constrains China's traditional unilateralism and encourages more cooperative international behaviour. An internationally engaged China sharing common economic values and interests with other Asia-Pacific countries is less likely to jeopardise the stability of the region.

Have yen loans directly benefited private Japanese companies?

The earlier section addressed the relationship among ODA, FDI and trade. It demonstrated that there is an indirect, but positive, linkage among Japan's China ODA, the increase of Japanese investments in China and the expansion of bilateral trade. This section, on the other hand, investigates whether yen loan projects promoted the direct and immediate commercial interests of private Japanese companies. The question is approached through an examination of the implementation procedures and tying status of yen loan projects in China.

Implementation of yen loan projects

In general, yen loans to developing countries are provided in accordance with a series of steps starting from project preparation and proceeding to appraisal, signing of a loan agreement and project implementation.[27] In the case of China, yen loans are provided in line with the following procedures.[28] First, the Chinese government, on the basis of the objectives and strategies of its five-year economic planning, identifies a list of projects for which yen loans are needed. The Chinese agency responsible for yen loan and other foreign loan aid – the State Planning Commission (SPC) – plans the allocation of yen loans across sectors in terms of the total five-year commitment by the Japanese government and decides the amount that China wishes to borrow. During this project preparation stage, the JBIC engages in policy dialogues with the Chinese government to exchange opinions on the relative urgency and priority of different projects, and conducts a feasibility study of the economic, social, technical and environmental aspects of each yen loan project. The SPC then presents a list of yen loan projects for the Chinese State Council's approval.

Second, as the representatives of the Chinese government, the SPC and the Ministry of Foreign Trade and Economic Cooperation (MOFTEC) submit their formal loan requests to the Japanese government, together with other materials produced in the preparation stage, such as the results of the feasibility study and other loan application documents.

Third, the JBIC makes a preliminary examination of the projects proposed by the Chinese government (*yōsei anken*). A Japanese government delegation, consisting of representatives from the MOFA, the MOF and the MITI, then dispatches missions which consult with the SPC and the MOFTEC and determine the urgency and priority of the different projects. The JBIC then dispatches a project appraisal team, comprising technical experts and economists, to make a more detailed analysis of the project from economic, technical and environmental perspectives based on discussions with Chinese staff and surveys at the project site.

Fourth, the Japanese MOFA checks the proposed projects on the basis of diplomatic and strategic considerations. The MOF checks them on the basis of budgetary considerations and examines the repayment capacity of China by ascertaining the country's foreign debt.[29] Details of the proposed projects are then forwarded to a meeting of the cabinet, administratively the highest decision-making body of the Japanese government.[30] On the basis of the appraisal by the JBIC, the Japanese government determines the amount and the conditions of the loans. The Japanese and Chinese governments then conclude an *exchange of notes*, which are the diplomatic documents that specify the projects, the monetary value of each of the loans and the conditions attached to each loan. Finally, on behalf of the two governments, the JBIC and the MOFTEC sign a loan agreement.

After the conclusion of the loan agreement, the project in China enters the implementation stage. Goods and services necessary for the project are procured through international competitive bidding conducted by the Chinese authorities. Money is disbursed in response to requests from China as demand for funds arises. Each project is implemented by the relevant Chinese ministry. For example, the Ministry of Railways oversees railway construction projects. However, the JBIC supervises and monitors the implementation of the whole project to ensure smooth progress and provides advice, if necessary. Based on this monitoring, the JBIC may amend the loan agreement on a yearly basis as it prepares for disbursement of funds in the subsequent year. In order to improve the effectiveness and performance of the China aid programme, the JBIC evaluates each completed yen loan project.

From an examination of the procedures associated with yen loan projects in China, there is no evidence that the Japanese government provides yen loans to support the direct and immediate commercial interests of private Japanese companies. Although the Japanese government can exchange opinions with the Chinese government on the priority of different yen loan projects through policy dialogue, China's control over the international competitive bidding for the procurement of goods and services means that the Japanese government has no influence over deciding the actual project contracts. On the basis of his case study of a railway construction project funded by yen loans in China, Gang Zhang similarly concludes: 'This case study finds no sign indicating that the Japanese companies in this case have benefited from the fact that the project is financed by OECF [currently JBIC] yen loan.'[31]

Tying status

In reality, the share of contracts held by Japanese companies in yen loan projects in China has consistently and sharply declined over the last decade, while the percentage of Chinese contracts in the projects has increased dramatically. The declining share of Japanese companies' contracts contradicts the assertion that ODA to China actively promotes the interests of the Japanese private sector through project contracts. The share of Japanese contracts in total yen loan project contracts in China was 34 per cent in 1996, 36 per cent in 1997, 15 per cent in 1998 and only 4 per cent in 1999, while that of Chinese contracts was 30, 43, 60 and 80 per cent, respectively.[32]

The reasons for the sharp decline in the share of Japanese contracts in the yen loan projects are twofold. First, there is the comparative cost disadvantage of Japanese business – that is, for the Chinese government, project contracts with Japanese companies are much costlier than those with local Chinese companies.[33] Second, China's gradual accumulation of expertise and technology has in time enabled it to implement many of its yen loan projects without the need for Japanese assistance.[34] In fact, China's capacity to undertake plant construction projects was already well advanced by the late 1970s, compared to many of the other recipients of Japanese aid.[35]

In light of a decade-long recession and a declining share of yen loan project contracts, the Japanese business community has in fact become increasingly critical of Japanese ODA activities in China. On the strong initiative of the MOFA and the MOF, since 1978 Japanese governments have steadily untied their entire ODA yen loan provision, so that by 1997, 99 per cent of yen loans were untied.[36] In the late 1990s, politicians, the Keidanren and the MITI lobbied both ministries, seeking to promote more direct profits for private Japanese businesses through ODA in China.[37] Consequently, between 1999 and 2001, the Japanese government allocated ¥600 billion for new *special yen loans* to recipient countries under the condition that the contracts for the associated projects were fully tied to private Japanese businesses.[38] These *special yen loans*, however, should be considered completely separately from Japan's standard yen loans to China.

The widely held perception that Japanese ODA projects are closely tied to private Japanese business interests through project construction contracts is thus not well founded. In fact, recent trends in the contracts in yen loan projects in China and the pressure to arrange the special yen loans illustrates the point that, during the 1990s, the linkage between yen loan projects in China and participation by Japanese companies in these projects was weak.

ExIm loans to China

Why does the Japanese government not do more to promote the direct and immediate commercial interests of the private sector through China ODA programmes? One major reason is that it primarily uses another financial instrument to promote such interests – that is, ExIm loans provided by the Japan ExIm Bank.[39] As noted in Chapter 4, the name of this bank was changed to the JBIC in 1999 due to the ExIm Bank's merger with the OECF. The total value of the assets of the JBIC in 1999 was equal to that of the World Bank. Through provision of these loans, the Japanese government openly pursues the trade and investment interests of private Japanese companies in China and secures a supply of Chinese raw materials for Japan. As briefly mentioned earlier, ExIm loans with a grant element of less than 25 per cent are not counted as ODA;[40] instead, they are considered to be OOF. Although the current annual interest rate of ExIm loans to China is only slightly higher than that for ODA to China, the repayment period of ExIm loans (seven years) is much shorter than that of ODA (forty years). This is the reason that ExIm loans are not recognised as ODA. Thus, detailed consideration of Japan's ExIm loans to China does not fall within the scope of this research. However, I will briefly examine the ExIm loans here, in order to show that it is not yen loans but rather ExIm loans that are primarily aimed at promoting the direct commercial profits of private Japanese companies in China.

Japan's ExIm loan commitments to China started in 1979, when the Japanese government provided the first package of ExIm loans, worth ¥420 billion, in order to assist the development of oil, coal and natural gas fields in China and to promote exports of those energy resources to Japan. The second package of ExIm loans, amounting to ¥580 billion, and the third package of loans, worth ¥700 billion, were extended in 1984 and 1992, respectively, for the same purposes.[41] The Japanese government provided the fourth package, worth about ¥520 billion, in 1996, and from that time, the target project area of the loans was expanded from energy resource development to areas including the development of ports, airports, highways and power plants. Apart from the above loans, up to 1998, the Japan ExIm Bank also extended ¥1,100 billion as other types of loans to China in order to directly promote investment by private Japanese companies.[42]

The cumulative total of Japanese ExIm loans to China between 1979 and 1999 reached ¥3,420 billion, thus surpassing the total of ODA ¥2,688 billion disbursed during the same period.[43]

It is clear that the Japanese government used the ExIm loans, as well as ODA, to secure a stable supply of Chinese energy resources – oil, coal and natural gas – to Japan, allocating a further ¥1,100 billion in other loans in a form that would directly assist trade with and investment operations by private Japanese companies in China. The ExIm Bank (currently JBIC) openly acknowledges that the expansion of investment and trade by private Japanese companies overseas and the assurance of stable energy resource imports are the two major goals of its overseas loan operations.[44] ExIm loans and ODA are kept separate: they are not combined in any one project, but rather are used to fund separate projects and are subject to different implementation processes. While ExIm loans have been used to promote the immediate commercial interests of the Japanese private sector in relation to China, ODA has been allocated to advance broader and longer-term perceived national economic and political interests. This division of role between the two types of Japanese government funds to China allows ODA to be seen to be free from promoting the direct commercial interests of private Japanese businesses, and to respond more to political, diplomatic and strategic imperatives. As a result, the provision of ODA to China often has greater political implications for Sino-Japanese relations than does the provision of ExIm loans.

The shift in priority project areas

Since the mid-1990s, the priority project area of Japanese yen loans to China has changed from development of industrial infrastructure to development of socio-environmental infrastructure, reflecting the same shift in the ODA programme as a whole. In particular, yen loans now give priority to environmental protection, including support in such areas as flood control measures and reforestation; improvement in agricultural productivity to overcome food shortages and eliminate poverty; alleviation of regional disparities through inland development; and social infrastructure development, such as water supply and sewerage development, as a direct contribution to the improvement of living conditions.[45] This section provides evidence for the shift through a comparison between 1993 yen loan projects and 1999 projects, and through an examination of several environmental projects. It then investigates more broadly what kind of environmental and social projects have been actually implemented in China through Japanese yen loans.

The focus on new priority areas is clearly reflected in the sharply increased number of environmental projects and the greatly decreased number of industrial infrastructure projects in 1999 compared to 1993. Tables 5.7 and 5.8 show all yen loan projects approved for China in the fiscal years 1993 and 1999, respectively. It can be observed from Table 5.7 that ten out of the eighteen projects in 1993 were transportation and energy infrastructure development projects. The total loans provided for these projects that is, ¥99 billion comprise 71 per cent of the whole loans ¥139 billion, while environment-related projects worth about

Table 5.7 Yen loan projects in China, FY 1993 (¥ million)

No.	Yen loan project	Sector	Amount
1	Inner Mongolia Chemical Fertilizer Plant Construction	AG	4,509
2	Shenmu–Shuoxian Railway Construction	TP	11,614
3	Baoji–Zhongwei Railway Construction	TP	2,027
4	Hengshui–Shangqiu Railway Construction	TP	6,407
5	Yunnan Chemical Fertilizer Plant Construction	AG	5,745
6	Tianshengqiao First Hydropower Project	EG	16,647
7	Nanning–Kunming Railway Construction	TP	23,342
8	Luzhai Chemical Fertilizer Plant Construction	AG	3,700
9	Jiujiang Chemical Fertilizer Plant Construction	AG	9,757
10	Beijing Subway 2nd Phase Construction Project	TP	3,819
11	Hubei Ezhou Thermal Power Plant Project	EG	12,431
12	Beijing-Shenyang-Harbin Systems Project	TC	4,055
13	Qinhuangdao Port 4th Stage Coal Terminal Construction Project	TP	3,944
14	Wengfu Chemical Fertilizer Plant Construction Project	AG	8.820
15	Fujian Province Xhang Quan Railway Construction Project	TP	6,720
16	Qingdao Water Supply and Sewerage Development Project	SS	2,513
17	Xian Water Supply Project	SS	4,587
18	Beijing Capital Airport Terminal Area Expansion Project	TP	8,106
	Total		138,743

Source: Compiled from Economic Cooperation Bureau, Ministry of Foreign Affairs, *Japan's Official Development Assistance Annual Report 1998*, Tokyo, 1999.

Note
AG (Agriculture), EG (Energy), SS (Social Services), TC (Telecommunications), TP (Transporation).

¥7 billion account for only 5 per cent of the total loans.[46] On the other hand, in 1999, fourteen (74 per cent) out of a total of nineteen projects were environment-related (see Table 5.8). The total amount allocated for these fourteen yen loans was ¥125 billion, which accounted for 65 per cent of the total amount ¥193 billion, while for transportation and energy infrastructure projects was ¥68 billion, that comprised only 35 per cent of the total amount. More details of the increased number of environment-related projects are given in the following section.

Model city projects: overview

Rapid economic development in recent years has led to acute environmental pollution in China. From Japan's point of view, acid rain caused by the massive amount of sulphur dioxide emissions from Chinese factories is destroying forests in Japan, and, thus urgently needs to be addressed. In 1997, Japanese Prime Minister Hashimoto Ryūtarō proposed the Japan–China Environment Model City Initiative at a summit meeting held in Beijing. This initiative was designed to

Table 5.8 Yen loan projects in China, FY 1999 (with location map) (¥ million)

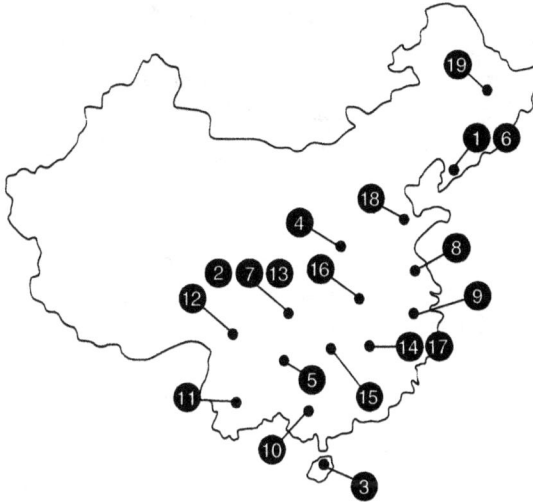

No.	Yen loan project	Sector	Amount
1	Benxi Enviromental Improvement Project	EV	1,160
2	Liangping–Changshou Highway Construction Project	TP	24,000
3	Hainan East Expressway Expansion Project	TP	5,274
4	Xinxiang–Zhengzhou Highway Construction Project	TP	23,491
5	Guiyang Environment Model City Project	EV	6,266
6	Dalian Environment Model City Project	EV	5,315
7	Chongqing Environment Model City Project	EV	4.412
8	Suzhou Water Environment Improvement Project	EV	6.261
9	Zhejiang Sewage Treatement Project	SS	11.556
10	Guangxi Water Supply Project	SS	3.641
11	Kunming Water Supply Project	SS	20.903
12	Chengdu Water Supply Project	SS	7.293
13	Chongqing Water Supply Project	SS	6.244
14	Jiangxi Water Supply Project	SS	4,147
15	Hunan Urban Flood Control Project	IF	24,000
16	Hubei Urban Flood Control Project	IF	13,000
17	Jiangxi Urban Flood Control Project	IF	11,000
18	Yellow River Delta Agricultural Development Project	AG	8,904
19	Harbin Electric Network Construction Project	EG	6,070
	Total		192,637

Source: Japan Bank for International Cooperation, *ODA Loan Report 2000*, Tokyo, 2001.

Note
AG (Agriculture), EG (Energy), EV (Environment), IF (Irrigation and Flood Control), SS (Social Services), TC (Telecommunications), TP (Transportation).

provide effective support to alleviate China's worsening environmental problems by implementing intensive environmental improvement measures in selected Chinese cities – Chongqing, Guiyang and Dalian – which were then expected to serve as models of success for other cities.[47]

In March 2000, the Japanese government provided ¥16.0 billion in yen loans for the *model cities* project. Japan made further contributions to the project by providing training and expertise. For example, the Japan–China Environmental Improvement Seminar was held in Japan in March 2001 in order to discuss Japan's experience of environmental management with Chinese environmental experts and to facilitate training of Chinese technicians by the JICA. The three city projects discussed later are all part of the Japan–China Environment Model City Initiative.

Guiyang projects

Guiyang, a designated model city (No. 5 in the map in Table 5.8), suffers from serious air pollution caused by the combustion of coal. The city relies heavily on coal for energy, and heavy chemical industries are predominant. Sulphur dioxide concentrations in Guiyang are very high, exceeding the 1967 average in Japan when air pollution was at its worst level there. Air pollution is further exacerbated by the city's location in a geographical basin.

This project involves the implementation of measures proposed by an expert committee in an effort to improve Guiyang's air quality. Specific measures consist of strategies to reduce air pollution at power plants, installing monitoring systems and constructing low-sulphur clean coal production facilities. The project is relevant to three priority areas targeted by Japanese policy-makers: environment, food and poverty, and the development of inland provinces in order to reduce regional disparities. In the first phase of the project, ¥6.3 billion in ODA loans was provided for exhaust gas cleaning facilities, monitoring equipment and clean coal production facilities, and to employ consulting services.

Dalian projects

The JICA conducted a development survey of Dalian (No. 6 in the map in Table 5.8) to help develop basic environmental plans and conduct other activities. Although the widespread use of central heating and gas are improving the environment, the city is still heavily reliant on coal for energy, and air pollution from coal-burning remains a serious problem. Sulphur dioxide concentrations are very high, especially in winter.

This project implements measures designed to reduce air pollution at steel and cement plants. These actions were again proposed by an expert committee in an effort to improve Dalian's air quality. In phase one, ¥5.3 billion was provided in loans in March 2000 for the construction of facilities to supply thermoelectric power and other projects, and for dust collectors, smelting furnaces, cement mills and other equipment, together with materials required to address pollution sources at industrial plants.

Chongqing projects

Chongqing (No. 7 in the map in Table 5.8) suffers from serious air pollution caused by the combustion of coal for energy, especially by heavy chemical industries. The city is surrounded by mountains, with the result that air circulation is low. Like Guiyang, Chongqing ranks among the worst cities in China for sulphur dioxide concentrations.

On the advice of a committee of experts on air quality, this project involves the construction of facilities to supply natural gas, the development of monitoring systems. and the installation of exhaust gas desulphurizers at power plants. In phase one, ¥4.4 billion in loans was provided in March 2000 for natural gas supply equipment, monitoring equipment and exhaust gas cleaning equipment.

Sewerage and water supply projects

The Zhejiang sewage treatment project (No. 9 in the map in Table 5.8), which cost about ¥11.6 billion, entailed construction of sewage treatment plants in three cities (Hangzhou, Shaoxing and Jiaxing) in the province of Zhejiang, where the quality of water has greatly deteriorated in recent years, amid increasing industrialisation and urbanisation.

To address the ever-worsening water shortage in Kunming and to prepare for future water demand in this city, the Kunming water supply project (No. 11 in the map in Table 5.8), which cost about ¥20.9 billion, entailed the construction of water supply facilities and of a dam planned upstream of Zhangiuhe in the northern part of Kunming. The Chengdu water supply project (No. 12 in the map in Table 5.8), which cost about ¥7.3 billion and involved the construction of the sixth water purification plant in Chengdu, was also intended to alleviate that city's water shortage.[48]

Flood control projects

The Hubei urban flood control project (No. 16 in the map in Table 5.8), which cost about ¥13 billion, comprised construction and repair of dikes, cofferdams and pump facilities in cities located around Jianghan in Hubei, in order to improve their flood control capacity and prevent floods from undermining the social and economic stability of the region. The Jiangxi urban flood control project (No. 17 in the map in Table 5.8), which cost about ¥11 billion, involved similar types of construction and repair around Poyang in Jiangxi, with the same aims.[49]

Table 5.8 also shows that thirteen out of the nineteen yen loan projects granted in 1999 were for development of inland provinces and accounted for 68 per cent of the total yen loan budget to China in that year. Some of these inland projects were designed to support flood control. The Yangtze River flooded during summer and autumn 1998, affecting 223 million people and causing an estimated ¥3 trillion in damage. Japan subsequently extended loans to strengthen riverbanks and construct urban drainage facilities in Hunan, Hubei and Jiangxi Provinces. the three provinces that suffered the greatest damage in the 1998 flood.[50]

As already discussed in Chapter 3, there are three major motives for the Japanese government to shift priority project areas of Japanese yen loans to China from industrial to socio-environmental infrastructure development. The first reason is the apparent progress in China's economic growth, which in turn increased the country's independent capacity to develop domestic industrial infrastructure. The second reason is the budgetary interest of the Japanese Foreign Ministry, which is keen to prevent any reduction of its ODA budget. The shift towards socio-environmental infrastructure development in China, which is based more on humanitarian need, has proved a very useful way of gaining both public and parliamentary support for the continuation of China aid. Finally, the Japanese government's consideration of its security interests also encourages the shift. Unlike the development of highways, ports, airports and telecommunication facilities which the Chinese army can use for military operations, the provision of yen loans for environmental conservation and poverty relief projects can hardly be linked with China's military development.

Conclusion

This case study of overall yen loans demonstrates that since 1979, yen loans, which consist of 91 per cent of Japan's total China ODA, have contributed to China's economic development through industrial infrastructure development, which was necessary to facilitate direct investment by Japanese and other multinational companies in China. In fact, since the early 1990s, yen loans have helped to increase FDI in China from multinational companies around the world, which have, in turn, contributed to a significant increase in China's foreign trade and a diversification in its trade channels. These increases in trade and FDI have been the major driving forces of China's industrialisation, its rapid transition to a market economy and its integration into the global economic system.

In the end, China's transition from a socialist economy to a market economy and the incorporation of the Chinese economy into the market-based global economic framework are in the economic and political interests of Japan. It needs to be understood that the bilateral economic relation between Japan and China is not a zero-sum game, but rather that China's economic development benefits Japan. The complementarity of the two economies means that Japan gains economic advantages from China's growing and increasingly open economy through trade and investments. The incorporation of China into the global economic framework is also seen to be in Japan's political interests because it inevitably imposes global economic norms and rules on China and, thus, promotes the emergence of a more responsible and cooperative China.

In contrast with Japan's use of ODA as a financial instrument to promote positive developments in China, the next chapter examines the use of ODA as a diplomatic weapon to counter disruptive behaviour by the Chinese government. In particular, it focuses on the three sets of aid sanctions that Japan imposed on China between 1995 and 2000, in order to elucidate the strategic interests behind Japan's ODA policy to China.

6 Aid as a strategic tool

Three cases of economic sanctions

This chapter considers Japan's use of ODA as a strategic instrument to counter provocative military behaviour by China. As shown in Chapter 5, since 1979, Japanese governments have continuously used ODA as an incentive to promote positive changes in China – the development of the Chinese economy, China's transition to a market economy and the integration of the Chinese economy into the global economic system – which are also perceived by Japanese policy-makers to be in Japan's own economic and political interests. While Japanese governments continue to use ODA to facilitate these changes, since the mid-1990s they have also used ODA as a diplomatic weapon in an attempt to restrain Chinese militarisation.

The chapter examines the aims of Japan's strategic use of aid as a diplomatic weapon against China, and clarifies the domestic political and bureaucratic interests that motivated aid sanctions and determined the decision-making process leading to these sanctions. Here an aid sanction is broadly defined as a reduction or cancellation of aid provision by a donor country in order to influence military, diplomatic or other behaviour of a recipient country in the pursuit of various foreign policy goals of the donor which applies the sanction. These matters are approached through three case studies of ODA sanctions applied by Japan between 1995 and 2000: in response to China's nuclear tests, its military intimidation of Taiwan and its naval activities inside Japan's EEZ. The chapter is chiefly designed to provide empirical evidence to support the overall arguments presented in Chapters 3 and 4.

The major factors that influence a decision to apply aid sanctions against China and the specific objectives in each case are bureaucratic and political interests, and public opinion. Within the Japanese government, however, the initiative in deciding on sanctions and the motivation in applying them vary depending on the case. The applications of ODA sanctions have been by no means uniform. For example, some ODA sanctions were symbolic and applied to appease the Japanese public, rather than to achieve a substantive diplomatic outcome. Others were more straightforward. Despite the limited influence that Japanese ODA sanctions have actually had on Chinese military behaviour in the region, Japan's strategic use of aid against China has undeniably created a new dynamism in the diplomatic relations between the two countries.

This chapter comprises five sections. The next section discusses Japanese governments' overall reasons for using aid sanctions in order to counter Chinese military development since the beginning of the 1990s. The section on Nuclear tests analyses the government's suspension of grant aid in protest against China's repeated testings of nuclear weapons in 1995. The section on Taiwan Strait crises examines the Japanese government's suspension of the implementation of the fourth yen loan package in protest against Beijing's military intimidation of Taiwan in 1996. The section on Naval activities investigates the Japanese government's withdrawal of special yen loans in an attempt to stop China's naval activities inside the Japanese EEZ around the disputed Senkaku Islands in the East China Sea in 2000. The chapter concludes with an analysis of the motivations and interests behind Japan's ODA sanctions against the PRC and an assessment of Japan's possible strategic use of China ODA in the future.

Aid diplomacy: background and practice

Before proceeding to the case studies, it is necessary to explain why Japanese governments first began to impose ODA sanctions in response to particular Chinese military actions. Three major factors encouraged the use of ODA as a strategic weapon against the Chinese government. They were, first, the resurgence of the strategic rivalry between Japan and China following the collapse of the Soviet Union; second, the shift of policy-making power from Foreign Ministry bureaucrats, with their traditionally non-confrontational diplomatic approach towards the PRC, to LDP politicians, who tend to prefer a more straightforward diplomacy; and third, the change in Japanese policy-makers' and China specialists' perceptions of a rapidly modernising China. As the first two factors were discussed in Chapters 3 and 4 respectively, this section mostly focuses on the third factor.

Changing perceptions of a militarily modernising China constitute a key factor that has encouraged Japanese governments to use ODA to deter China's military development, which progressed rapidly in the last decade of the twentieth century. As briefly mentioned in the previous chapters, the growth rate of China's defence expenditure was in double figures for fourteen consecutive years since 1989. The PRC's defence expenditure for the year 2001 was 17.6 per cent higher than that of the previous year, while that for 2002 was increased by 18 per cent compared to the previous year.[1] According to *The Military Balance*, China's defence expenditure in 2004 is expected to increase by 11.6 per cent compared to the previous year.[2] Thanks to its improved financial capability, the PLA has made great efforts to modernise its nuclear and conventional weapons since the beginning of the 1990s. The PLA has upgraded its long-range (intercontinental) and intermediate-range nuclear ballistic missile systems; enhanced its command, control, communication and information facilities; and strengthened the conventional weapons capability of its navy and air force by procuring technologically advanced warships and fighter aircrafts, mostly from Russia.[3] In addition, China has been active in developing the PLA's combat power to fight a high-tech war by integrating the PLA units with information networks and developing satellite-based communications.[4] Particularly since the beginning of the 1990s, as will be shown later, Japanese governments have begun to view the sharp increase in Chinese defence expenditure very negatively.

From Japan's perspective, China's military build-up in the 1990s is one negative consequence of that country's rapid modernisation over the last two decades. Economic growth and industrialisation have greatly strengthened China's financial and industrial capacity to modernise its military force. The irony, of course, is that Japan has used ODA as an instrument to apply sanctions against Chinese militarisation, which, arguably, might not have been possible in the first place without Japanese development assistance.

Rapid economic development of a nation does not necessarily lead to a speedy military build-up, as the case of post-war Japan demonstrates. Two major reasons, however, motivated the Chinese government actively and openly to implement its military development programmes, despite the strong concerns expressed by many countries in the region. The first reason was historical. During the hundred years from the Opium Wars (1839–42) to the end of the Second World War, China was the victim of repeated military invasions and partial colonisation by the Western powers and Japan. These harsh historical experiences convinced Chinese leaders that strong military power was vital in order to protect state sovereignty from foreign invasion and to reject foreign interference in China's domestic affairs.[5] Such an approach indicates that Chinese leaders have remained wedded to nineteenth-century concepts of international security.[6] Therefore, the willingness of Chinese leaders to increase China's military capability can be partly understood as a psychological defence mechanism, underpinned by the harsh reality of China's modern history.

The second reason relates to the security of energy supplies in the PRC. The rapid economic development of China in the 1980s and 1990s significantly increased the domestic demand for oil. Although China is an oil-producing country, the demand for oil by its industries exceeded domestic supply in 1993. Since then, China has become one of the world's major oil importers. For example, in 2003 China imported 90 million tonnes of oils mostly from the Middle East and the domestic demand for oil is expected to increase rapidly as the Chinese economy grows.[7] For China, the stable and secure supply of Middle Eastern oil for its domestic industries has thus become crucial in order to sustain its economic development. China must, therefore, protect its vital *sea-line*, which connects Chinese coastal areas and the Persian Gulf.[8] It also became desirable to develop submarine oil resources in the South and East China Seas to supplement domestic oil supply. Consequently, China has strengthened its naval and air power projection capability, which can be used to protect its energy interests, if necessary.[9] That is why China has given priority in weapons modernisation to its navy and air force, rather than to its army.

Mainstream China policy-makers and China specialists in Japan recognise that China's present military capability is still very limited compared to that of the US and Russia.[10] From their point of view, the power projection capability of Chinese conventional forces, as distinct from nuclear force, is still not a direct threat to Japanese security and will not become so for another few decades at least.[11] For these policy-makers and analysts, the *China threat thesis* is based on the vague fear of China's potential to become a dominant military and economic power in the region in the future, rather than on the reality of China's current military capability.[12] For such observers, the China threat thesis is, in fact, an over-reaction to China's rapid modernisation and rests on claims with little or no empirical substance.[13] Nonetheless, the China threat thesis and the argument that Japan's ODA has assisted Chinese militarisation, which were described in Chapter 3, have undeniably contributed to increasing suspicion of the Chinese government's military ambitions in the region, especially among the Japanese media and the public.[14] In one opinion poll conducted in September 2002 by the *Yomiuri shinbun*, a major Japanese daily newspaper, the proportion of Japanese who believe that the Chinese military build-up will pose a threat to Japan's national security in the future was as high as 70 per cent, while the proportion of those who disagree remained less than 24 per cent.[15] Moreover, although mainstream Japanese policy-makers and China specialists recognise the myths underlying the current China threat thesis, they acknowledge the longer-term potential of the military threat posed by the PRC. Thus it is necessary, in the view of these policy-makers, to take precautions in order to prevent China from seeking regional hegemony in the future. Such considerations influenced Japanese governments' implementation of China ODA policy in the 1990s.

Japanese policy-makers and China specialists have identified four possible scenarios in the future course of China's modernisation. These four scenarios are presented in Figure 6.1.[16] The first scenario (represented by A in the diagram) is that the PRC will become a country that has a high level of intention to threaten the stability of the East Asian region, but limited capability. The second scenario (represented by B) is that it will have both a high level of intention and a high capability to jeopardise the stability and peace of the region. The third scenario (represented by C) is that China will have a high capability to threaten other nation-states in the region, but a low level of intention. The fourth scenario (represented by D) is that China will have neither the capacity nor the intention to pursue regional hegemony. This last scenario is predicated upon China being unable to maintain its economic growth. China in the period from the mid-nineteenth century to the mid-twentieth century was an example of this case.

The best-case scenario for Japanese policy-makers and China specialists is scenario 'C', in which China will have the capacity to jeopardise the stability of the Asia-Pacific region, but little intention to do so. In other words, Japanese policy-makers would like to encourage China to take a more engaged and cooperative position within the international community, while supporting that country's sustainable economic development. Both aims are, in fact, in Japan's own interests, as described in Chapter 5. This outcome could be achieved if Chinese leaders considered regional stability and peace to be compatible with their nation's economic interests, and if China continues to be included in regional and global economic and security regimes. Thus, to constrain China's traditional unilateralism

High
(Y)

A   B

Low (X) ◄─────────────────► (X) High

D   C

(Y)
Low

(X): Capacity to threaten neighbouring states
(Y): Level of intention to threaten neighbouring states

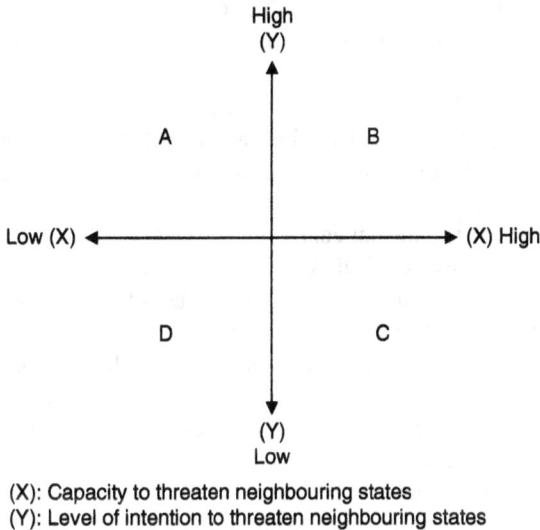

Figure 6.1 Japanese policy-makers' and specialists' perceptions of China.

in foreign policy, it is considered important that Japanese policy-makers endeavour to support stable economic development and encourage China's further incorporation into multilateral economic and political frameworks. This is the most desired course for Japanese policy-makers and China specialists in promoting a diplomatic framework for Japan's peaceful coexistence with China.

The worst-case scenario for Japanese policy-makers and China specialists is scenario 'B', that is, the emergence of a China that has both a high level of intention and a high capacity to threaten the stability of the Asia-Pacific region. A militarily developed China with a strong ambition to seek regional hegemony would cause nothing but trouble, especially for those countries in its immediate vicinity.[17] Avoiding this outcome necessitates that China's modernisation be guided in a more moderate, liberal and cooperative direction towards scenario 'C'. To this end, Japanese governments have used ODA not only as an incentive to promote positive developments in China, but also as a diplomatic card to restrain disruptive military behaviour. Since the beginning of the 1990s, Japanese policy-makers have thus openly pursued what they perceive to be Japan's security interests through China ODA and, since 1995, have imposed several ODA sanctions in attempts to dissuade the Chinese government from engaging in aggressive military behaviour.

The four ODA principles and actual practice of aid diplomacy

Japanese governments imposed aid sanctions on China not only because they perceived the modernisation of China's military forces as a potential threat to regional stability, but also because China's disruptive military behaviour was inconsistent with Japan's Four Principles of ODA. Or, at least, the fact that China's actions have contravened the Four Principles has allowed and provided justification for Japanese retaliation. The reasons for and the process leading to the introduction of the four ODA principles have been described in Chapter 3. Here I restate the four principles in order to elucidate the relationship between those principles and Japan's ODA sanctions against the PRC, which will be examined in detail later.

The principles are: first, environmental conservation and development should be pursued in tandem; second, any use of ODA for military purposes or for aggravation of international conflicts should be avoided; third, full attention should be paid to trends in recipient countries' military expenditures, their development and production of weapons of mass destruction and missiles and their export and import of armaments; and fourth, full attention should be paid to efforts to promote democratisation, the introduction of a market-oriented economy and the securing of basic human rights and freedoms in the recipient country. Japan states that it will provide ODA in accordance with these four principles.

Japanese governments have applied three types of pressure to address the problem of a recipient country breaching the ODA principles: diplomatic pressure, negative linkage and positive linkage. Diplomatic pressure consists of persuasion through various diplomatic channels and normally precedes an actual exercise of aid sanction.[18] It is mostly manifested by the use of terms such as *deep concern* and *regret* by Japan in relation to the negative actions taken by governments of recipient countries. Negative linkage (aid sanction) is a cut in or suspension of ODA to a recipient country which has acted contrary to one or more of the Four Principles. On the other hand, a positive linkage (incentive) initiates or increases ODA provision to a country that shows signs of improvement in such areas as human rights and restraint over military expenditure.

Since the introduction of the Four Principles in 1992, the Japanese government has used them in dramatic fashion as political and strategic weapons against China. Table 6.1 shows the actual applications of the four ODA principles by the Japanese government against the PRC between 1992 and 2000.[19] Since 1992, the Principles have been used on twelve occasions as a diplomatic weapon, mostly to counter Chinese military build-up and disruptive military actions. Thus, it is the third principle – that is, full attention should be paid to recipient countries' military expenditure, their development and production of weapons of mass destruction and missiles, their exports and imports of armaments – which has mostly been applied to China. While Japan's application of this principle indicates its determination to take clear action to restrain Chinese military expansion, at the same time, unlike some other nations, Japan has remained cautious about making ODA provision conditional on the furtherance of human rights and democratisation. The Japanese government mentioned democracy in only one case (see no. 1 in Table 6.1). This fact shows where the purpose of applying the ODA principles to China really lies.

Japan first made strategic use of ODA towards China in March 1992 when the Japanese government dispatched a high-level diplomatic mission, led by former

Table 6.1 Japan's strategic use of ODA to China, 1992–2000

No.	Month/Year	Measure(s) taken	Reason(s)	Approach
1	March 1992	Explained Japan's ODA principles regarding military development and democratisation	MD/DE	DIP
2	May 1993	Re-explained the ODA principles to Beijing	MD	DIP
3	March 1994	Expressed Japan's intention to monitor China's military development and weapons exports	MD/AT	DIP
4	June 1994	Expressed concern over the nuclear test which had been conducted	NP	DIP
5	October 1994	Expressed deep concern over the nuclear test which had been conducted	NP	DIP
6	May 1995	Expressed deep concern over nuclear test, and hinted at possible suspension of ODA	NP	DIP
7	August 1995	Froze grant aid	NP	NEG
8	March 1996	Suspended official talks on disbursement of the fourth yen loan package	MI/NP	NEG
9	December 1996	Resumed official talks on fourth yen loans package	MI/NP	POS
10	March 1997	Resumed disbursement of the frozen grant aid	NP	POS
11	August 2000	Froze the provision of special yen loans	TI/MI	NEG
12	October 2000	Resumed the provision of special yen loans	TI/MI	POS

Source: Compiled from Gaimushō keizai kyōryoku kyoku (Economic Cooperation Bureau, Ministry of Foreign Affairs), *Wagakuni no seifu kaihatsu enjo* (Japan's ODA) (various issues), Tokyo, 1994–2000; Zaidan hōjin kazankai (Kazankai Foundation) (ed.) *Chūgoku sōran 1998* (Biennial Comprehensive Analysis of China 1998), Tokyo, 1998; *Yomiuri shinbun*, 28 August 2000.

Note
AT (armaments trade), DE (democracy), DIP (diplomatic pressure), MD (military development), MI (military intimidation), NEG (negative linkage), NP (nuclear proliferation), POS (positive linkage), TI (territorial issue).

Foreign Minister Ōkita Saburō, to Beijing (case no. 1). The purpose was for delegates to hold discussions with their Chinese counterparts, and specifically to explain the third (military development) and the fourth (market economy and human rights) principles of the *ODA Charter*, stressing their importance as political conditions attached to Japan's ODA provision.[20] During the period from 1992 to 1994, Japanese governments also took 'various opportunities to explain the position outlined in... [the] ODA Charter on military spending and related issues', urging that China 'adopt a more transparent set of military policies'.[21] For instance, in May 1993, Japanese Foreign Minister Mutō Kabun explained that the Japanese government would implement China aid based on its four ODA principles, and hence the militarisation of recipient countries would become relevant to Japanese foreign aid provision (case no. 2).[22] In a further example, during his March 1994 visit to China, Prime Minister Hosokawa Morihiro expressed his government's intention to monitor carefully China's ongoing military development (case no. 3).[23] These diplomatic initiatives indicate that by the beginning of the 1990s, the Japanese government had become fully aware that China's rapid economic growth was being accompanied by an equally rapid increase in the military budget and an escalation of China's involvement in the armaments trade. Thus, Japanese leaders had a strong strategic motivation to try to retard further military expansion by China.

There were three issues that arose during the period from 1994 to 2000 which provided the Japanese government with further opportunities to use the Four ODA Principles as a diplomatic instrument against China. They were China's successive nuclear weapons tests from 1994 until July 1996; large military exercises by the Chinese army including the launch of missiles across the Taiwan Strait to intimidate the people of Taiwan in March 1996; and Chinese naval activities in disputed areas in the East China Sea, together with circumnavigation of the Japanese archipelago in 2000 by a PLA warship. These events and the Japanese response to them illustrate the new dynamics in relations between Japan and China and constitute excellent empirical tests of the effectiveness of the strategic use of ODA by Japan.

Nuclear tests

The changed attitude of the Japanese government towards China's military behaviour was clearly observed in its response to the nuclear tests conducted by China in the first half of the 1990s. During that period, China consistently conducted tests once or twice a year.[24] From June 1994 to May 1995, the Japanese government responded by applying diplomatic pressure on three occasions in an effort to stop the tests (nos 4–6 in Table 6.1).[25] In 1994, the Japanese government repeatedly warned China that the continuation of its weapons testing programme would have a negative effect upon bilateral relations, including the ODA programme. However, the Chinese government ignored these warnings and conducted further nuclear tests in June and October 1994.[26] The obvious inconsistency between Japan's ODA principles and China's nuclear tests greatly distressed many Japanese people and resulted in an increase in domestic pressure on the government to take tougher diplomatic action. In public opinion polls undertaken in 1995, 90 per cent of respondents indicated that they were 'very angry' about the repeated nuclear tests conducted by both China and France in that year.[27]

When China conducted another nuclear test on 15 May 1995, the Japanese government took stronger action than in previous cases, when simple diplomatic pressure had been applied. It decided to reduce, but not totally suspend, the grant aid portion of ODA to China. In addition to this action, Japanese Foreign Minister Kōno Yōhei also asked the US and the Russian governments to apply diplomatic pressure on the Chinese government to halt the nuclear tests.[28]

Three events surrounding the May 1995 Chinese nuclear test encouraged these actions by the Japanese government. First, the May 1995 test came straight after the Nuclear Non-Proliferation Treaty (NPT) was extended indefinitely on the condition that all the nuclear powers, including China, refrain from conducting nuclear tests. Second, it was also conducted shortly after Prime Minister Murayama Tomiichi had visited China and asked Chinese leaders to freeze nuclear weapons tests. Hence, Murayama was embarrassed by China's actions.[29] Third, that particular test was also conducted during the fiftieth anniversary of America's dropping of atomic bombs on the cities of Hiroshima and Nagasaki at the end of the Second World War, and thus this particular test greatly disturbed many Japanese people.[30]

However, the Japanese government's decision to reduce its grant aid had little influence on China, which conducted another nuclear test on 17 August 1995. Out of frustration, the Japanese government decided on 29 August to freeze its grant aid provision to China, except that portion used for humanitarian purposes,[31] until it became clear that China had ceased nuclear testing (case no. 7 in Table 6.1). This decision was based on the third ODA principle – that is, full attention should be paid to trends in recipient countries' military expenditures, their development and production of weapons of mass destruction and missiles and their export and import of armaments.[32] As a consequence, Japanese grant aid to China was cut back sharply from ¥7.79 billion in 1994 to ¥480 million, which was spent in 1995 on the campaign to eradicate poliomyelitis, two emergency relief efforts and twenty-five grassroots aid projects.[33] It is striking that Japan unilaterally sanctioned China without waiting for major Western ODA donors to take the same step. This action demonstrated the Japanese government's strong determination not to tolerate the further development of the PRC's nuclear weapons.

Coalition cabinet politicians and Foreign Ministry officials took different policy stances in responding to the nuclear tests by China. In acknowledgment of the Japanese public's anger about repeated Chinese nuclear tests,[34] politicians in the coalition government parties (the LDP, the Social Democratic Party of Japan (SDPJ) and the Sakigake Party) advocated strong diplomatic action against China, including the suspension of grant aid and of yen loans. These politicians believed that 'without the suspension of yen loans [which comprise a large portion of Japanese ODA to China], it is very difficult to convey Tokyo's determination to protest strongly against the nuclear tests by Beijing'.[35] On the other hand, officials of the MOFA initially opposed the call from politicians to apply sanctions against the PRC. The Ministry's bureaucrats objected to the aid sanction because 'it is not in Japan's interests to damage diplomatic relations with the PRC' and because 'there is very little possibility that Japanese ODA sanctions can actually stop China's nuclear tests'.[36] From the Ministry's point of view, it was not at all desirable to suspend the fourth yen loan package (1996–2000) because this would break the Japanese government's agreement with the Chinese government to provide ¥580 billion in yen loans for the three years from 1996 to 1998 as part of the overall package. The basic agreement concerning the provision of this loan package had already been reached in December 1994.[37]

The final decision to freeze grant aid in protest against nuclear tests by China constituted a political compromise between the coalition parties and the MOFA. Given the strong pressure applied by coalition party politicians, the Ministry had to accept the implementation of the grant aid sanction. However, it did success-fully convince the politicians not to include yen loans in the sanction.[38] It is also noteworthy that Murayama, the leader of the SDPJ, was the prime minister of the coalition government, which consisted of the SDPJ, the Sakigake Party and the LDP. The involvement of the SDPJ and the Sakigake Party, which took a strong anti-nuclear stance, was an important factor in the government's decision to apply the grant aid sanction.[39] Unlike the united aid sanction against China by G7 coun-tries following the 1989 Tiananmen Square Incident, in this case Japan was the only country that applied an aid sanction against China.[40]

China's reaction to the grant aid sanction was swift. On 29 August 1995, the same day that Tokyo announced the sanction, a Chinese Foreign Ministry spokesman expressed deep regret at the decision and stated that 'China opposes Japan's attempt to attach political conditions to the economic cooperation between the two countries because this attempt will harm the healthier develop-ment of bilateral relations.'[41] The *People's Daily*, China's government-controlled newspaper, linked the sanction with the history of Japanese invasion: 'China is the country that suffered most under Japanese aggression. That is why our receiv-ing of grant-in-aid has a special historical background.'[42] Moreover, the Chinese Ambassador to Japan expressed what he claimed to be the Chinese people's dis-appointment and anger at the sanction. He also criticised Japan on the grounds that while it had taken an anti-nuclear diplomatic stance, Japan itself had been protected by the US nuclear umbrella.[43]

Despite these initial rebuffs, however, the Chinese government gradually showed signs of diplomatic compromise. Although it did not cancel the forth-coming nuclear tests, the Chinese government, surprisingly, informed the Japanese government in advance about the nuclear tests it had scheduled for June and July 1996. It also promised the Japanese government that it would then cease testing its nuclear weapons.[44] In fact, the Chinese government declared a morato-rium on nuclear tests immediately after the July 1996 test and signed the Comprehensive Test Ban Treaty (CTBT) in September of that year.[45]

In light of these developments, the Japanese government resumed the disbursement of grant aid to China in March 1997 (case no. 10 in Table 6.1). The carrot (positive linkage) was thus provided after the stick (negative linkage). The suspension of grant aid appeared to have had an impact, but it is also notable that the Japanese government did not lift the grant aid suspension until nine months after the Chinese government declared a moratorium on nuclear tests. Hayashi Sadayuki, Vice-Minister of Foreign Affairs, explained that 'we are in no mood to resume grant aid to China so soon after the moratorium on nuclear tests'.[46]

Was China's moratorium on nuclear tests directly linked to Japan's grant aid sanction? In all likelihood, according to William Long, the sanction 'was linked only indirectly to China's decision to halt nuclear testing' in July 1996. In Long's view, China's decision came 'after substantial international pressure had been applied during the negotiations for the CTBT, concluded in September 1996, of which Japan's withdrawal of grant aid was but one factor'.[47] On the other hand, Katada Saori contends that 'The aid suspension decision itself shocked the Chinese government. ... despite the relatively small amount of money involved, the Chinese government was much more disturbed by this unilateral grant aid suspension' than it had been by Japan's participation in the international aid sanction following the 1989 Tiananmen Square Incident.[48] Similarly, the MOFA concluded that the grant aid suspension against China had proved to be more effective than it had initially thought.[49] It is very difficult to clarify the cause and effect in this case, because it can be assumed that many other factors contributed to the Chinese government's eventual decision to stop testing its nuclear weapons. It must be argued, however, that Japan's grant aid sanction against China produced a positive response, even though it did not bring about an immediate cessation of the tests. As the unprecedented advance official notification to Japan of subsequent scheduled nuclear tests indicates,[50] there was a link between Japan's sanction and China's concession.

Why did the Japanese government not suspend yen loans, rather than just grant aid, in protest against China's nuclear tests despite the fact that the suspension of such a large portion of Japan's ODA to China would undoubtedly have had a much greater impact than the grant aid sanction? Answers to this question are twofold. First, policy-makers within the MOFA were reluctant to apply any sanctions at all to China, and the suspension of grant aid was sufficient to satisfy those politicians, organs of the media and members of the public who were demanding tougher diplomatic action against China. Recognising the difficulty of actually influencing China's military behaviour, MOFA officials applied the grant aid sanction primarily in order to maintain domestic support for their China policy.[51] Thus, Japan's grant aid sanction in 1995 was applied more for domestic consumption than for any genuine strategic purpose.

Second, the Japanese government, particularly Foreign Ministry officials, were very reluctant to suspend yen loans because they feared that this would damage those Japanese interests that were pursued through yen loan provision to China, as described in Chapter 5. If the Japanese government suspended yen loans it would lose an important tool with which to promote Japanese interests in relation to China. Thus, while using yen loans as an incentive to promote positive developments in Chinese domestic affairs perceived to be in Japan's national interests, policy-makers in the Foreign Ministry on the other hand used grant aid, which was relatively a very small portion of Japanese ODA to China, as a diplomatic card to discourage further nuclear tests by the Chinese government.

The Taiwan Strait crisis

Less than a year after it suspended grant aid in response to China's nuclear weapons tests, the Japanese government imposed a new aid sanction on China, delaying the disbursement of the fourth yen loan package, which had originally been scheduled to be disbursed before mid-1996, until December of that year in protest against a series of military exercises that China had conducted in the Taiwan Strait in March 1996. Following the visit of Taiwanese President Lee Denghui to the US in mid-1995, political tension between the PRC and Taiwan had increased. The direct military aim of the Chinese exercises was to demonstrate the capacity of the PLA to blockade the Taiwan Strait. The political aim was to show clearly the PRC's determination to use military force as a means to annex Taiwan into the PRC, if Taiwan declared its formal independence from China. More particularly, the PLA's military exercises were intended to intimidate Taiwanese voters on the eve of Taiwan's presidential election and dissuade them from voting for pro-independence candidates, especially President Lee Denghui of the Nationalist Party and Chen Shuibian, the candidate of the pro-independence Democratic Progress Party (and the current President of Taiwan).[52]

When it became aware of the PRC's plan to conduct large-scale war games across the Taiwan Strait, the Japanese government in March 1996 initiated diplomatic efforts to persuade the Chinese government to cancel the exercises. For example, at the Asia and Europe Meeting (ASEM) held on 1 March 1996, Prime Minister Hashimoto Ryūtarō conveyed to Chinese Premier Li Peng his concerns about the PLA's planned missile tests and urged a peaceful resolution of the Taiwan issue.[53] The Japanese Foreign Ministry also repeatedly expressed its deep concern about the PRC's plans.[54] On 6 March 1996, Katō Ryōzō, the Director General of the Asian Bureau of the MOFA, requested that the Chinese government refrain from carrying out military exercises, saying 'it is not good for the peace and stability of the East Asian region deliberately to increase the tension between the PRC and Taiwan'.[55]

The Chinese government, however, ignored these requests to cancel the exercises. Form 8 to 15 of March 1996, the PLA proceeded to test-fire its DF15 missiles in the waters off two major international Taiwanese ports, Gaoxiong and Jilong, and conducted large-scale war games by mobilising '150,000 troops along China's southern border'.[56] In fact, one of the missiles fired by the PLA fell within 60 kilometres of the Japanese island of Yonaguni, which has about two thousand Japanese inhabitants.[57] The war games also directly affected Japanese air and sea traffic, as well as the fishing industry operating in and around the affected area, and thus created economic damages for Japan.

The PRC's military intimidation of Taiwan greatly distressed the Japanese government and caused a diplomatic backlash in Japan which took several forms. For example, the Chief Cabinet Secretary, Kajiyama Seiroku, strongly urged China to stop the military exercise and even pro-China Katō Kōichi, the Secretary-General of the LDP, warned the Chinese government that 'this crisis could have an impact on Japan's own security interest'.[58] Senior officials of the Japanese MOFA were unusually forthright, threatening the Chinese government that the Ministry 'would not ignore the Chinese military exercise'.[59] Some Japanese policy-makers advocated a tougher diplomatic stance against the Chinese government, and the call to freeze yen loans to China became stronger within the Japanese government.[60] Consequently, in March 1996, the Hashimoto government delayed official talks with Beijing on forty aid projects (case no. 8 in Table 6.1) worth about ¥580 billion, which had been allocated for the first three years (1996–98) of the fourth yen loan package (1996–2000). This sanction continued until December 1996, when the bilateral tension between the Japanese and Chinese governments eased (case no. 9).[61]

Despite the belief within the Japanese government that an aid sanction could influence China's military behaviour, the sanction did not in fact produce the desired result. The Chinese government responded to Japan's diplomatic pressure in due course with the statement that 'the Taiwan issue is an internal issue of China. [Therefore,] no other country can intervene in this issue'.[62] Although the Chinese government made no actual concession, however, it would probably be incorrect to argue that Japan's ODA sanction had no impact whatsoever. Chinese Foreign Minister Qian Qichen later told his Japanese counterpart, Ikeda Yukihiko, that the diplomatic pressure applied by the Japanese government during the crisis was the second strongest after that applied by the US,[63] suggesting that the yen loan sanction did, at least, shock Chinese leaders. In the end, it is extremely difficult for any country to influence the Taiwan policy of the Chinese government due to the apparently overwhelming importance that the PRC places on the Taiwan issue.[64]

To many observers, it is not clear whether the Japanese government applied this yen loan sanction to protest against the military intimidation of Taiwan by the PRC or to protest against China's programme of nuclear tests. As noted earlier, in 1996, the same year as the Taiwan Strait crisis, the PRC also conducted two nuclear tests and the Japanese government strongly protested against these tests. Kimata Yōichirō and Katada Saori both argue that the Japanese government intentionally delayed the implementation of the fourth yen loan package as a protest against the PRC's nuclear tests.[65] On the other hand, Tanaka Akihiko believes that the Japanese government delayed the disbursement of the yen loans primarily to protest against the military intimidation of Taiwan by the PRC.[66] My interview with one senior official of the Japanese MOFA supports Tanaka's argument. This official stated clearly that 'we [the Foreign Ministry] slowed down the formal procedure of the disbursement of the yen loans to China in protest against the military behaviour by Beijing at the time of the Taiwan Strait Crisis'.[67] The different timings of the lifting of the 1995 grant aid sanction and the 1996 yen loan sanction also support this argument. The 1995 grant aid suspension in protest against China's nuclear tests continued up until February 1997. If the 1996 yen loan sanction was also applied as a protest against the PRC's nuclear tests, it is therefore very difficult to explain why it was lifted in December 1996. All in all, it is more reasonable to conclude that these two sets of sanctions were imposed on China for different reasons.

The Japanese MOFA did not announce to the public the March 1996 decision to delay the disbursement of the fourth yen loan package, as it did the decision to suspend grant aid in August 1995. Such reticence on the part of the Ministry indicates that this sanction was actually implemented to demonstrate the determination of the Japanese government to prevent the Chinese government from using military force to resolve the Taiwan issue, rather than to satisfy politicians and the public at home who were demanding a yen loan sanction. As LDP Secretary-General Katō Kōichi implied in his remark noted earlier, there was a possibility that the PLA's large-scale military exercises near Taiwan could have triggered a war between the two Chinas, whether by accident or intent. If war had occurred, it would inevitably have damaged the peace and prosperity of the entire East and Southeast Asian region and, hence, would have put Japan's economic and security interests in the region at serious risk. It was not surprising that the Japanese government sought to prevent the tension between the PRC and Taiwan from escalating into war. One Taiwanese diplomatic document recently revealed that at the time of the crisis, President Lee Denghui secretly used Japanese Prime Minister Hashimoto as a go-between in order to request that the US government dispatch American aircraft carriers to the Strait.[68] In fact, US President Bill Clinton did send two aircraft carriers near Taiwan in order to monitor the PRC's war games and to put direct military pressure on the Chinese army.[69]

It is highly likely that Foreign Ministry bureaucrats and LDP parliamentarians were in agreement over the need to apply yen loan sanctions in response to the Taiwan Strait crisis, as is indicated by the responses noted earlier from within both organisations. Bureaucrats and politicians probably agreed about the necessity to send the PRC government the strongest possible warning, and were prepared to go as far as suspending the disbursement of the fourth yen loan package. It could even be the case that MOFA bureaucrats played the leading role in making the decision, rather than LDP politicians. Several Japanese diplomatic documents reveal that, as early as the late 1950s, MOFA bureaucrats had concluded that the military annexation of Taiwan by the PRC was unacceptable for Japan because it would fundamentally damage Japan's military and economic interests in the East and Southeast Asian region.[70] Given the continued overwhelming importance of regional stability for Japanese interests, officials of the MOFA advocated a strong protest against the PRC's military exercises in 1996. The US Department of Defence later revealed that when the US government asked about Japan's likely response if a military clash between the PRC and Taiwan were to occur, the Japanese government promised that it would give its full support to the US in any military action.[71] Therefore, it can be argued that the risk of war between the PRC and Taiwan perceived by Japanese policy-makers was the major factor that encouraged the Japanese government to apply the yen loan sanction against China, despite the diplomatic backlash expected and received from the Chinese government.

Naval activities

China's naval activities inside Japan's EEZ in Summer 2000 provoked the Japanese government into applying further aid sanctions. Japanese relations with China had deteriorated as a result of recent Chinese naval activities, including several contentious visits to disputed areas around the Senkaku Islands in the East

China Sea. In 2000, the first circumnavigation of the Japanese archipelago by a PLA warship further accelerated this deterioration.[72]

There is a link between China's naval activities and the issue of the Senkaku (or Diaoyu in Chinese) Islands. The Senkaku Islands, which consist of several small, uninhabited islands, is located 300 kilometres southwest of the island of Okinawa. Japan first claimed its sovereignty over the islands in 1895 after Japan's victory over China in the First Sino-Japanese War (1894–95). The islands had temporarily come under American control after the Second World War, but the sovereignty over the islands, was handed over to Japan in 1972 with the reversion of Okinawa. However, the PRC and Taiwan governments both made a territorial claim to the Senkaku Islands, soon after the United Nation Economic Commission issued in 1969 a report suggesting considerable reserve of submarine oil and gas resources around the islands.[73] This became an important issue in the 1978 negotiation between the Japanese and Chinese governments over the conclusion of the Peace and Friendship Treaty, but, at that time, a serious dispute was avoided when Deng Xiaoping told Japanese Foreign Minister Sonoda Sunao that 'China tacitly admitted Japan's practical control of the Senkaku Islands'.[74]

However, the territorial dispute over the Senkaku Islands escalated in the 1990s. The Japanese government was upset in February 1992, when China suddenly introduced a domestic law, which opened the islands to Chinese oil and natural gas exploration, and thus re-claimed the islands as Chinese territory, and hinted that military force might be used to protect its claim.[75] Following the ratification of the UN Convention of the Law of the Sea (UNCLOS) in 1996, both Japan and China established a 200-mile EEZ in the East China Sea.[76] As a result, the EEZ claimed by the Chinese and the Japanese governments in the East China Sea, which drew around the Senkaku Islands, overlapped. Despite Japan's attempts to persuade China in drawing a so-called *median line* on the overlapped zone and respect it as a temporary sea border, China has not yet agreed to the proposal.[77] This is because if China recognised the median line, both the Senkaku Islands and some oil and gas fields nearby remain within the Japanese side of EEZ. So far, the negotiations about the median line between the two countries has not reached to a conclusion.

Since the late 1990s, China has actively conducted mining exploration and naval activities not only inside its EEZ, but also inside the Japanese EEZ, that is, beyond the median line. The intention behind these naval activities is presumably to explore and develop the allegedly rich oil and natural gas resources in the area and to gather military data for the PLA's submarine operations.[78] Instances of Chinese naval activities inside Japan's EEZ increased rapidly from 4 in 1997 to 14 in 1998 and 30 in 1999,[79] an increase which provoked the Japanese government. In particular, the Maritime Safety Agency and the Maritime Self-Defence Forces, which patrol Japanese waters, were greatly concerned and in the late 1990s, started to report the details of the Chinese naval activities in their annual white papers in order to alert the wider public to the problem.[80]

In his first official visit to China in July 1999, Japanese Prime Minister Obuchi Keizō expressed to Chinese leaders his government's concern about the PRC's increasing naval activities inside the Japanese EEZ. However, Chinese Premier Zhu Rongji told Obuchi that 'there is nothing wrong with these Chinese activities'.[81] rejecting Obuchi's complaint. After this exchange, the number of Chinese naval activities conducted for military purposes and resource mining exploration inside the Japanese EEZ dramatically increased. According to the Japanese Maritime Self-Defence Forces, 64 Chinese naval vessels were active around Japan between April 1999 and May 2000.[82] Furthermore, the PRC had extended its naval activities to new areas around the Japanese archipelago. For example, in May 2000, one Chinese warship circumnavigated Japan, carrying out intensive military intelligence activities in both the Tsushima Strait, located between Japan and South Korea, and the Tsugaru Strait, located between mainland Japan and the northern island of Hokkaidō.[83]

Frustrated, in August 2000, Japan responded by suspending the disbursement of two special yen loans to the PRC worth about ¥17.2 billion,[84] which had been allocated for an airport and for railway construction projects (case no. 11 in Table 6.1).[85] As explained in Chapter 4, LDP leaders in this case clearly prevailed over Foreign Ministry officials, who had been proceeding with the scheduled disbursement of the loans despite calls for strong diplomatic action against the Chinese government by the Japanese Maritime Safety Agency and the Maritime Self-Defence Forces. According to one senior LDP official, LDP politicians were greatly frustrated in this case by the Foreign Ministry's inability to adjust its approach to China ODA in response to changes in the domestic and international environments.[86]

In August 2000, the Japanese government sent Foreign Minister Kōno Yōhei to Beijing to request the Chinese government to arrange a formal system of advance notification of the entry of Chinese naval and resource exploration ships into Japan's EEZ.[87] During his visit, Kōno met with Chinese President Jiang Zemin, Premier Zhu Rongji and Foreign Minister Tang Jiaxuan and expressed Japan's deep concern about the increased naval activities, linking the matter to the deteriorating support for the provision of ODA to China by the Japanese public.[88] Furthermore, in his speech at the Communist Party School, Kōno explained that the Japanese public had become increasingly worried about the rapid increases in China's defence budget and the lack of transparency of the PRC's military policy. He warned Chinese leaders that 'public support is essential if the Japanese government is to continue its development assistance to China'.[89]

The reactions of Chinese leaders to these diplomatic moves by Kōno were surprisingly restrained. During the meeting, President Jiang Zemin refrained from using the PRC's traditional tactic of linking a current bilateral diplomatic issue with the history of Japanese invasion of China.[90] Premier Zhu told Kōno that 'the naval activities did not aim to annoy Japan, but were implemented on the basis of international law. We did not think that these activities would generate Japanese concern and anger'.[91] In fact, the PRC government, in August 2000, acceded to the Japanese proposal to arrange an official system of advance notification for such naval and resource exploration activities in the 'zone of interests' where the EEZ borders claimed by China and Japan overlap.[92] As a result, the

Japanese government lifted the sanction on the special yen loans to China on 10 October 2000 (case no. 12 in Table 6.1).

The fact that the Foreign Affairs Division of the LDP forced the MOFA to freeze the disbursement of the special yen loans until Kōno would return from China had certainly shocked the Chinese government, which worried about the evident shift in balance of ODA policy-making power from MOFA bureaucrats to LDP politicians, and the unusually subdued response by Chinese leaders during Foreign Minister Kōno's visit indicates the Chinese government's concern about the apparent change in Japan's China aid policy-making. However, it is noteworthy that the introduction of the official advance notification system for naval activities did not lead to a decrease in the number of China's naval and marine research activities in Japan's EEZ. On the contrary, Chinese vessels started to conduct their activities inside Japanese waters more openly than before. Commanders of Chinese vessels understood advance notification as a system that automatically gave them Tokyo's formal approval of their activities inside Japanese waters. Furthermore, although China notified most of their activities in advance, it often arbitrarily changed times and locations.[93] It is ironic, then, that Japan's proposal produced the opposite result to that which had been intended.

Analysis of cases: interests, effectiveness and limitations

In Table 6.2. I present a comparison of some of the important aspects of Japan's three ODA sanctions against China between 1995 and 2000. The table indicates that the purpose of the sanction and the source of the decision-making initiative varied in each instance. In the case of the 1995 nuclear tests, the MOFA responded to strong domestic demand from cabinet politicians and the public, abandoning its usual reluctance to impose aid sanctions on China and playing a leading role in deciding on the suspension of grant aid. The Ministry needed to protect its autonomy in ODA policy-making and, hence, its own bureaucratic interests, which had already been undermined, from further challenge by LDP politicians. Thus, for MOFA bureaucrats, this sanction was intended to appease domestic dissatisfaction, rather than actually to stop China from testing nuclear weapons: an objective which the MOFA felt could not be achieved through sanctions.

In the case of the 1996 Taiwan Strait crisis, however, there was no obvious discord between MOFA officials and LDP parliamentarians over whether to impose a sanction involving yen loans. The reason for this unusual convergence of bureaucratic and political interests within the Japanese government was the shared awareness that Japan was facing a security crisis. Thus, there was agreement on the need to apply a strong ODA sanction in order to stop China's military intimidation of Taiwan.

In the case of the PRC's naval activities in 2000, LDP parliamentarians, who had been frustrated by MOFA officials' insensitivity in proceeding earlier in the same year with the special yen loan disbursement to China despite that country's disruptive naval activities, this time compelled the MOFA to freeze the disbursement

Table 6.2 Comparison of three cases of aid sanctions, 1995–2000

	Case (Year)		
	Nuclear tests (1995)	Taiwan Strait crisis (1996)	Naval activities (2000)
Type of sanction	Freeze of grant aid	Suspension of official yen loan talks with Beijing	Freeze of disbursement of special yen loans
Purpose	(1) Official: to stop the nuclear tests (2) Actual: MOFA's need to respond to domestic demands in order to protect its bureaucratic interests	To stop China's war games which could lead to a real war between the PRC and Taiwan	To stop naval activities by the PRC inside Japanese exclusive economic zone
Decision-making initiative	Decision led by MOFA officials: but under strong pressure from coalition cabinet politicians and the public	United decision by MOFA officials and LDP politicians, who shared a strong sense of security crisis	Policy led by LDP politicians: the LDP forced the MOFA to freeze ODA. A shift in policy-making power from the MOFA to the LDP enabled this
Degree of pressure	Weak	Very strong	Strong
Effect	Limited effect	No effect	Good effect
Main factors explaining success or limitations	(1) Only a small portion of Japanese ODA (grant aid) was suspended (2) PRC's strong pro-nuclear policy	No concession over the Taiwan policy due to PRC's resistance to other countries interference in the matter	PRC's shock at the LDP-led decision-making and weakened Japanese public support for China ODA

of the special yen loans. LDP parliamentarians, whose status is determined by election, did so because they were more sensitive to public opinion than MOFA bureaucrats. The LDP was able to prevail over the MOFA because by that time. as argued in Chapter 4, foreign policy-making power had already shifted to a considerable degree from MOFA officials to LDP parliamentarians.

Table 6.2 also suggests that the correlation between the strength of ODA sanctions and the actual effectiveness of those sanctions is weak. In other words, a strong ODA sanction does not necessarily have the intended effect. First, in the case of China's nuclear tests, Japan's aid sanction against the PRC was relatively weak, in that the grant aid frozen at that time constituted only a small portion of Japan's total ODA to China. Therefore, the sanction could only be expected to have had a minor influence over the PRC's behaviour. As described earlier, the sanction did indeed have only a limited impact on China's nuclear test programme. On the other hand, the Japanese government employed a very strong sanction during the 1996 Taiwan Strait crisis – by delaying the implementation of the crucial fourth yen loan package, worth about ¥580 billion. Although the Japanese government did not announce this action publicly as a sanction, it must be classed as a sanction because official talks on the implementation of the yen loan projects were not held.[94] Thus, it can be understood as an ODA sanction even though it was not articulated as such. In this case, however, the Japanese government gained no concession from the Chinese government despite the suspension of yen loans, which comprise a large portion of Japanese ODA to China. In fact, the sanction had no direct effect at all. In the case of China's naval activities, the Japanese government directly suspended disbursement of the special yen loans, which constituted a relatively small amount of money compared to the standard yen loans. While this sanction was not as strong as that applied in the case of the Taiwan Strait crisis, it produced a surprisingly positive outcome for the Japanese government.

My comparative analysis indicates that the Chinese government's reactions to Japan's ODA sanctions have been influenced primarily by domestic factors such as the PRC's own foreign and security policies, rather than by the strength of the sanctions themselves. Thus, it is clear that despite Japan's efforts, its ODA sanctions overall have had only a limited influence on the PRC's military behaviour. Other factors also explain the success or otherwise of Japan's tactic of using ODA sanctions against China.

The first factor that limited the effectiveness of the sanctions was that China rarely concedes on issues directly relating to 'state sovereignty' and 'internal affairs'.[95] This was evident during the Taiwan Strait crisis. The PRC government regards Taiwan as a renegade province, and thus the Taiwan issue is directly linked by the PRC to sovereignty and internal affairs. Consequently, the PRC government reaffirmed to the international community that it would use force to solve the Taiwan issue, if necessary. Thus the Japanese government's attempts to use its unilateral ODA sanctions against China had only an ephemeral impact on China's behaviour. The reality is that Japan, like other countries, has limited direct influence over the PRC government's domestic and international behaviour in such cases.

As the cases of both the nuclear tests and the naval activities illustrate, the Japanese Foreign Ministry's willingness to protect its own bureaucratic interest – that is, its autonomy in making Japan's foreign and foreign aid policies – from outside challenge is the second factor that restrains the effectiveness of Japan's aid sanctions against the PRC. As described in Chapter 4, up until the mid-1990s, the monopoly of China policy-making traditionally enjoyed by the MOFA had been the key factor contributing to Japan's usually prudent and conciliatory diplomatic attitude towards China. The Ministry's official explanation of why Japan reluctantly joined the multilateral moratorium on foreign aid to China after the 1989 Tiananmen Square Incident illustrates this attitude very well. According to the Ministry, ODA projects in China were suspended at that time because of 'China's introduction of martial law' and 'the resultant evacuation of Japanese ODA officials from China',[96] but not because of the *human rights abuse* cited by

Western democracies. This kind of attitude on the part of the MOFA gave the Chinese government the impression that the Japanese government was prone to relatively easy compromises.

The third factor that limits the effectiveness of Japan's ODA sanctions against China consists of a combination of Japan's geographical proximity to, history of wartime atrocities in and large economic interests in China. These factors have functioned as major impediments to Japan's freedom of political action in relation to the PRC. Before the mid-1990s, the MOFA justified its practice of not cutting ODA to China, the country which most clearly violated Japan's Four ODA Principles, by emphasising the flexibility of its criteria in determining ODA sanctions. For example, an official publication states that:

> Management of the Four Principles [governing Japan's foreign aid policy] is reviewed in a comprehensive way, taking into account various diplomatic considerations. ... it is necessary to evaluate a given case from broader perspectives by taking into account not only the situation in a recipient country in relation to the Four Principles, but also ... political and economic relations with Japan.[97]

It should be noted that while Japanese governments were reluctant to apply ODA sanctions to China before 1995, they had quite often sanctioned African and Latin American nations in the first half of the 1990s.[98] Clearly, China was a much more sensitive case, for the reasons cited earlier.

It is highly likely that the Japanese government will again freeze yen loans to China in the near future. During the period from 1979 to 2000, Japan's yen loan commitment to the PRC was based on a system of multi-year packages, in which yen loans were negotiated and contracted for five- to six-year periods to meet the needs of the PRC's five-year economic plans. Among the many Japanese yen loan recipients, China was the only one afforded this system. The major disadvantage of this system from Japan's point of view was that it made it difficult to suspend yen loans, when necessary. It was possible to impose yen loan sanctions on the PRC during the 1996 Taiwan Strait crisis without jeopardising an entire package because the crisis happened to coincide with the commencement of the new contract for the fourth yen loan package, which was provided for 1996–2000.[99] From 2001, however, yen loans were negotiated and disbursed to China on an annual basis, in line with the practice in the case of other recipient countries. The desire to be able to apply sanctions, or at least the recognition that there will be pressure to do so, has been a major factor in changing the system of yen loan contracts from five-yearly to annual. Thus, with the introduction of this annual system, Japan's yen loans to China have become more flexible and subject to use as an instrument of sanctions.

Conclusion

Since 1979, Japanese governments have primarily used ODA as a financial incentive to promote broad Japanese interests in relation to the PRC – the support of

China's economic development, China's transition to a market economy, and the incorporation of the Chinese economy into the global economic system. In a new development in the 1990s, however, Japanese governments also started to use ODA strategically to deter the PRC government from engaging in aggressive military behaviour in the East Asian region. Thus, ODA became not only a diplomatic instrument to advance Japan's perceived commercial and political interests, but also a strategic tool to promote its security interests in relation to China.

For Japanese policy-makers, it is becoming increasingly difficult to achieve a balance between the two different approaches to China ODA implementation: the use of ODA as both a *carrot* and as a *stick*. Foreign Ministry bureaucrats still believe that, in the long run, the provision of ODA (the *carrot*) is a more effective means to promote Japan's national commercial and political interests in relation to China than the imposition of ODA sanctions (the *stick*). However, given the deterioration in public perceptions of a modernising China which has often engaged in provocative domestic and international behaviour over the last decade, LDP politicians are highly likely to exert political pressure on the government to impose further aid sanctions against China, including an end of ODA provision in the future.

7 The effects of Japan's aid policy to China and implications for bilateral relations

This chapter assesses the perceived economic, social and political effects of Japan's development aid to China. It is, of course, impossible to prove any direct cause and effect relationship between Japanese ODA and the social and political changes that have undoubtedly occurred in China; even the purely economic impact of ODA is difficult to disentangle from the effects of other economic factors. What this chapter will do, however, is to investigate how China aid policy-makers themselves assess the economic, social and political effects that Japanese ODA has had upon China. Such an assessment will suggest at least the perceived correlations between Japanese ODA and China's economic development and political and social change, if not a direct causal effect. In turn, the perceptions that Japanese policy-makers and analysts have of the impact of ODA are crucial in their own right, as they affect subsequent decisions about the provision of aid in the future.

The central questions this chapter addresses are twofold. What do Japanese China aid policy-making elites, as well as specialist academics, consider to have been the effects of Japanese ODA in China? What is the relationship between the perceived effects of Japan's China ODA and the Japanese government's policy objectives, as expressed in its ODA to China?

My research shows that Japanese policy-makers and analysts believe that Japanese ODA to China since 1979 has had positive effects not only on China's economic development but also in terms of supporting social and political change implemented by the Chinese state. They contend that Japan's massive injections of foreign currency and technology into China have substantially assisted China's economic development, promoted an increasingly market-oriented economy and helped to integrate the Chinese economy into the global economic system. These dramatic changes in the Chinese economic system and in various institutions have produced corresponding social changes. Despite the difficulty of proving a cause and effect relation, Japanese China ODA policy-makers and China analysts certainly tend to believe that China's rapid economic development, together with the transformation from a highly centralised planned (or socialist) economy to a more market-based economy, have facilitated the emergence of a more pluralistic social order, in which different groups have obviously divergent social interests. The emergence of a pluralistic socio-economic order in China has, in turn, promoted corresponding political reforms. Despite continuing its strict one-party political dictatorship, the CCP has increasingly been compelled to employ a more liberal and transparent public policy to govern an increasingly organised, complex and informed Chinese society. Given this situation, many Japanese China specialists point to the possibility that '*de facto* democracy' has already emerged in China, and they believe that Japanese ODA has played its part in bringing it about.

Thus, in this chapter, I demonstrate that Japanese China ODA policy-makers and China analysts exhibit remarkably positive perceptions of the relationship between Japanese ODA and economic, social and political change in China. They believe that, though indirectly, the ODA policy they helped to formulate has had a positive impact on China socially and politically, as the success of economic reform and development has been the major, if not the sole, driving force for socio-political change in China. My research shows that over the last two decades, economic, social and political changes in China have, in fact, proceeded in line with the policy objectives pursued by Japanese governments during this period. It is therefore reasonable to suggest that Japan's ODA policy has successfully helped to guide China's modernisation in a more stable, transparent and liberal direction. On the other hand, Japanese governments have also recently used ODA as a means to deal with the various problems which have emerged as negative side-effects of China's modernisation. One of these problems is the rapidly increasing military expenditure arising from China's general approach to foreign relations, in a context of increased financial capacity following the substantial level of economic development over the last two decades. Other problems include increased unemployment, widened income and development gaps among the people and among provinces, and severe environmental degradation.

In order to examine the perceived effects of Japan's China ODA more comprehensively, this chapter is divided into four sections. The first section investigates the relationship perceived to exist between Japanese ODA and the structural and functional changes evident in the Chinese economy over the last two decades. The second explores the perceived socio-political effects on China of Japanese ODA, particularly its apparent role in stimulating the emergence of a more pluralistic social order and in facilitating the gradual and steady decline of the CCP's political control over society. Thus, the first two sections address the effects of Japan's use of ODA as an incentive to promote structural and functional changes in the Chinese economy, society and polity. The third section, by contrast, considers perceptions of the usefulness of ODA as a means to restrain China's rapid military expansion, and of the significance of the shift of ODA project areas from the development of industrial infrastructure to the development of socio-environmental infrastructure in China. The fourth section then considers the implications of ODA for Sino-Japanese relations. My assessment of Japanese policy-makers' and analysts' evaluation of the effects of Japan's China ODA is largely based on my recent interviews with Japanese officials, politicians, journalists and academics, most of whom have been involved in the process of formulating Japan's China ODA policy and who have interacted with their Chinese counterparts over a long period.

Economic effects of Japan's ODA policy

The key concept that has consistently underpinned the aims of Japan's China ODA policy is *engagement*. As explained in Chapter 3, Japan began to provide ODA to China in 1979 from a desire to support Deng Xiaoping's Reform and Liberalisation Policy, which aimed at the progressive use of available foreign capital and technology for modernisation. The policy objectives behind Japan's use of ODA to support the Reform and Liberalisation Policy were to separate China economically from the *Communist bloc* led by the Soviet Union by encouraging China's greater economic dependence on Japan; to assist reformist leaders within the CCP; and to prevent China from disintegrating and becoming isolated from the international community. In the Cold War international environment, the strategy of engaging China with the *free world* bloc and supporting reformist Chinese leaders within the Communist Party was thought by Japanese policy-makers to be consistent with Japan's own political and strategic interests.[1] Besides these perceived politico-strategic interests, Japanese governments also sought to promote economic interests through the provision of ODA to China, aiming to ensure a stable supply of raw materials from China, in particular oil and coal, and to promote the investment and trade interests of private Japanese companies in China through economic infrastructure development.

In pursuit of these multiple interests, Japanese governments supported China's economic reform policy, and hence, arguably, assisted the modernisation of China. One senior official of the MOFA says with confidence that 'Japanese ODA has succeeded in accelerating and stabilising Chinese modernisation.' While acknowledging that Chinese modernisation might have progressed without Japanese financial and technological assistance, he maintains that 'without the help of Japanese ODA, the modernisation of China would not have been as stable and quick as it actually has been'.[2] Other officials of the MOFA agree that ODA has had a significant impact on China's economic development[3] and thus has helped to ensure social stability by improving the living conditions of many Chinese people. Such assessments by Japanese China ODA policy-makers are also shared by many of Japan's academic China analysts. For example, the scholar Kokubun Ryōsei and journalist-scholar Sugishita Tsuneo both contend that the enormous amount of funds that Japan has provided in the form of ODA has contributed significantly to China's economic development and has provided stability during modernisation.[4]

The financial contribution of Japanese ODA to China's economic development was especially significant during the 1980s when China suffered a foreign currency shortage.[5] Although China now has the world's second largest foreign currency reserves after Japan,[6] in 1979, when Japan first provided ODA to China, that country desperately needed foreign currency to support the economic development required under the Reform and Liberalisation Policy.[7] As noted in Chapter 2, China had suffered from a shortage of foreign currency after the Soviet Union suddenly ceased its foreign aid provision to China in 1957 following the Sino-Soviet political confrontation. According to Soeya Yoshihide, the reason that

Chinese leaders asked the Japanese government to provide financial support for the Reform and Liberalisation Policy was probably that the Japanese business community (*zaikai*) had given the Chinese government the 'idea of using Japanese foreign loans as a useful tool for China's economic development'.[8]

The most important direct contribution of Japanese ODA to China has been in the form of funds for industrial infrastructure development.[9] Most of the yen loans provided to the PRC during the period from 1979 to 2000 were used for the development of transportation, energy and telecommunication infrastructure in China, as described in detail in Chapter 5. In turn, such infrastructure development not only promoted Japan's economic and energy supply interests in China, but also encouraged China's economic interdependence with other countries.[10] Japanese ODA to China certainly also supported the interests of those private Japanese businesses that were willing to invest in China, through industrial infrastructure development in China's coastal provinces.[11] For example, initial infrastructure development centred on the coal and oil sectors, in which Japanese private companies had direct interests.

Promotion of a market economy

Japanese policy-makers and China analysts believe that Japanese ODA to China has contributed to the promotion of a market economy in China,[12] although the relationship between ODA and the emergence of a market-based economy is less direct than the relationship between ODA and economic development. The major driving forces of China's transition from a socialist economy to a market economy have been FDI from and trade with foreign countries, including Japan. As FDI and trade transactions with market economies increased, Chinese governments acknowledged the advantages of market economy mechanisms for economic development. This acknowledgment has probably been the major motivation of Chinese governments in carrying out economic reform. It is necessary to recognise, however, that Japanese ODA significantly helped to promote the inflow of FDI from a variety of market economies into China, and thus assisted the resultant increase in trade. As Nakagawa Junji remarks, although the role of development funds provided by private foreign banks and FDI in promoting further development of the market economy system is becoming increasingly important, ODA's separate contribution to the development of a market-based economic system in China is undeniably large.[13]

The promotion of a market economy has been one of the most important ODA policy goals of Japan because, as we have seen, the transformation of the Chinese economy from an isolated socialist economy to one that is open and market-oriented is considered to be in Japan's economic interests. A market-oriented Chinese economy is more likely to provide foreign countries, including Japan, with opportunities to access its large and growing domestic market. Some Japanese business and bureaucratic elites, however, view China's rapid economic development under a market system as a threat to Japanese small and medium-sized companies because of the likelihood of intensified competition due to the low production costs associated with their Chinese counterparts in the low technology areas.[14] Nonetheless, mainstream Japanese policy-makers and particularly big businesses favour continuing ODA to help promote China's further transition to a market economy. For many Japanese companies the importance of the Chinese market as an export destination has significantly increased. In 2003, Japan's exports to China reached an all time high of US$57.2 billion, a 43.6 per cent increase from the previous year.[15]

The promotion of a market economy in China is also considered to be in the political interests of Japan, for reasons outlined later. As the emergence of a more pluralistic socio-economic order in China indicates, the effects of economic transition on social change have already become evident, especially in the prosperous coastal provinces. In the opinion of Yabuki Susumu, an academic specialist on Chinese political economy, that country is in effect no longer a Communist country, but already practises an 'authoritarian capitalism', which is similar to the pre-democratic regimes in South Korea and Taiwan.[16] Similarly, Soeya Yoshihide believes that Japanese ODA indirectly, but significantly, has helped transform China from a 'Communist state' to an 'authoritarian developmental state'.[17] The implication of this economic transformation for Sino-Japanese relations is thought to be positive by Japanese policy-makers, as the two countries increasingly share a common economic system and some common liberal economic values.

Incorporation of China into the market-based global economic system

Japanese ODA policy-makers and China analysts consider that Japanese diplomacy aimed at bringing China into the market-based global economic system, which today is institutionalised as the WTO, (formerly known as the General Agreement on Tariffs and Trade), has been very successful.[18] In this view, Japan's ODA contribution to China's FDI and trade promotion has greatly helped China's engagement with the regional and global economy.[19] As a result, China's economic interdependence with East Asian countries and Western countries has again deepened.[20] Of course, the Chinese government's willingness to join the WTO system in order to gain further economic benefits is the single most important factor encouraging the incorporation of China into the global economy. However, it can be argued that without economic reforms and development, to which Japanese ODA has contributed, the Chinese government might not so quickly have realised the benefits of involvement in the world economy and, thus, would not have pursued WTO membership in the first place.

While Japanese ODA has arguably played a particular part, incorporation of the Chinese economy into the regional and global economic systems also became the most important official objective of Japan's China policy as a whole during the 1990s. Official China ODA reports presented by the JICA in 1991 recommended for the first time that China should be enticed into global regimes and global institutions (*kokusai shakai ni hipparidasu*).[21] The Hashimoto and Obuchi governments made particularly large efforts to convince both Chinese leaders and other OECD countries to take a positive approach towards China's acquisition of

WTO membership during the second half of the 1990s. For example, the Hashimoto government reached an agreement with the PRC over trading goods in September 1997 and the Obuchi government reached a service trade agreement with the PRC in July 1999. Four months later, Australia and the US established similar trade agreements with the PRC.[22] On 11 December 2001, the WTO officially announced China's membership, and the *active engagement* that underpins Japan's China ODA policy moved to a new stage.

Japanese governments strongly supported China's acquisition of WTO membership because it is seen to be not only in Japan's economic interests, but also its strategic interests. While some Japanese officials question whether the Chinese government sufficiently respects and protects the intellectual property rights of foreign companies operating within China's domestic market,[23] the Japanese government remains remarkably positive about China's WTO membership. China's entry into the WTO is certainly expected to increase its integration into the market-based world economy and officially to impose the norms and rules of international economic activity on China. Thus, membership of the WTO is likely to make China a more constructive partner in the global system[24] and encourage it to share certain responsibilities and act more cooperatively.

To provide further encouragement to China to act in accordance with international norms and rules, Japanese governments have also endeavoured to facilitate the incorporation of China into other international and regional institutions, such as the ASEAN Regional Forum. These efforts constitute an implicit recognition that Japan cannot deal with China by itself and thus needs multilateral frameworks to direct China's modernisation in the *right* direction.[25] Moreover, the Japanese government is still reluctant to deal with the Chinese government on a bilateral basis because of the Chinese government's frequent use of the history of Japan's military invasions of China in the 1930s and 1940s as an effective negotiation card.

To summarise, in the opinion of Japanese policy-makers and analysts, Japanese ODA during the 1980s greatly contributed to the development of economic infrastructure in China through yen loan provision, thus contributing to an increase in FDI by Japanese and Euro-American companies in China and, hence, also contributing to the expansion and diversification of China's foreign trade. During the 1990s, on the other hand, Japanese ODA promoted the incorporation of the Chinese economy into the market-based global economic system. The results, in this view, were a greater economic interdependence between China and other countries in the world and a relatively peaceful regional environment. Despite these perceived achievements, however, Japanese governments continue to provide ODA to China because it is an essential element in managing their bilateral relations. The following section examines the correlation between the provision of ODA and social and political change in China.

Social and political effects of ODA policy

The democratisation of China is not an official aim of Japan's China ODA policy. Even China policy-makers in the MOFA do not want the sudden end of the

Communist Party's political control in China, since they believe that if the Communist Party regime ended at this early stage of China's social transformation, it would be more likely to create domestic turmoil than stable democracy, and to increase anti-Japanese nationalism among the Chinese public. However, China's economic development and its transformation into a market-based economy have indirectly promoted gradual democratic change. It is necessary to briefly address this social transformation in China in order to clarify the indirect linkage between Japanese development assistance and Chinese democratisation. This section first discusses the effect of economic development on social change within China, and then examines how social transformation has affected the domestic political environment in China.

Social change

China's economic development and the rapid expansion of a market-based economy over the last two decades have generated a profound social transformation in the PRC. This process, according to some Chinese sociologists, has comprised two different transformations – *institutional* and *structural* – which have occurred simultaneously. Institutional transformation in China refers to the change from a highly centralised planned economic system to a more market-oriented economic system, or what the Chinese government calls a socialist market economy. On the other hand, structural transformation means the change from a *traditional* China, characterised by agriculture, village and closed society, to a modern society, characterised by industry, urbanisation and openness.[26] In other words, structural transformation refers here to the transformation from a society that was totally or very substantially controlled by the state (or the CCP) to a society that includes various social and economic interests existing outside state control, such as private entrepreneurs and foreign companies. It is these newly emerged sectors that have actually created the economic dynamism of post-reform China.

The development of a market-based economy and the resultant social transformation have significantly expanded personal liberties in China. For example, Chinese people today have freedom to move around the country and to travel overseas. They can start their own businesses and express themselves on a wide range of issues,[27] unless they openly challenge the political authority of the Communist Party. Young Chinese are now even able to share Western popular culture by consuming McDonald hamburgers and Western fashions in cosmetics.[28] Such 'social deregulation' has helped to create a middle class and has 'offered both the means and incentive for new groups to form and organise'.[29] As the scholar Inada Jūichi puts it, more pluralistic social interest groups, which are capable of giving people a feeling of participation or investment in the governing system, have emerged in China as a consequence of economic development.[30]

There are also signs of an emergent freedom of expression within the Chinese academic community. Some Chinese scholars specialising on Japan now do not hesitate to break the taboo of criticising the Chinese government's official foreign policy towards Japan and have presented arguments that are inconsistent with the official Japan policy espoused by the CCP.[31] These Chinese scholars present their arguments on the basis of a more scientific and objective assessment of the PRC's economic and political interests with respect to Japan than they had been able to in the past, when the *official* assessment was more powerful. Clearly, social pluralism in contemporary China is to some extent being reflected in the emergence of pluralistic arguments among the Chinese academic community.[32]

However, the emerging social pluralism and freedom of expression in today's China are only allowed within a limited range. If emergent social groups, not dominated or controlled by the Communist Party, politically challenge the Communist Party's authority, they are quickly suppressed.[33] The case of the religious group Falun Gong starkly reveals the vulnerability of these self-organising social and economic entities. Fearing the strong loyalty that Falun Gong followers display towards the founder of the sect, and following a series of organised political demonstrations against the Communist Party's rule by its adherents, the Chinese government started a campaign in the late 1990s to destroy Falun Gong by making the sect illegal. Since then, thousands of Falun Gong leaders have been arrested and imprisoned.[34]

Political change

In light of the evidence of a new socio-economic pluralism in China, one Japanese China policy-maker predicts that a 'public-led democratisation (*shizen hasseiteki na minshuka*)' in China will eventually emerge.[35] Is the democratisation of China included in the policy objectives of Japan's China ODA? My research suggests that it is not. My interviews with officials of the Japanese Foreign Ministry dealing with actual China ODA transactions and Japanese China analysts indicate that the democratisation of China has never been an overt aim, or even a hidden aim, of Japanese China ODA. Foreign Ministry officials clearly state: 'The democratisation of China has not been the policy objective of Japanese China ODA.'[36] When the Japanese government introduced the Four ODA Principles in 1992, it unambiguously stated that it would monitor recipient countries' effort to promote democratisation and the protection of basic human rights. In practice, however, Japanese governments have been very reluctant to make provision of ODA conditional on a commitment to human rights by China, as noted in Chapter 6. Japanese specialists on China ODA in universities and the mass media also consider that the democratisation of China was not and is still not an objective of China ODA policy.[37]

Officials of the Japanese MOFA do not think that external (foreign) pressure on the Chinese government can be effective in promoting democratisation due to China's culture of 'pride and face (*mentsu*)'.[38] That is, the Chinese government cannot be seen to be acceding to external pressure. Moreover, despite the positive effects that economic development is expected to have on the political system, 'democratisation is simply too big an aim to be directly linked with ODA'.[39] The relationship between ODA and democratisation is, indeed, indirect. The idea of using ODA for the promotion of Chinese democratisation is not an official one; rather, it is a notion that has recently emerged within the Japanese academic community and in some sections of the media.[40]

Japanese policy-makers and academics thus acknowledge the practical difficulty of linking ODA with Chinese democratisation, and even the undesirability of doing so, as will be explained later. At the same time, however, they share an expectation that Japanese ODA's continuing assistance to China's economic development and expanding market system will eventually guide Chinese politics in a more liberal and democratic direction.[41] This liberal assumption is based on the conviction that 'economic development under a market economy system will encourage the emergence of a democratic political system in the long run'.[42] The so-called East Asian experience – that is, the cases of the democratisation of Thailand, South Korea and Taiwan – is taken as empirical evidence of the positive linkage between economic development and political democracy. According to the scholar Yabuki, Chinese democratisation will become more likely if China achieves the level of economic development that South Korea and Taiwan achieved before they became democratic.[43] The fact that Japanese policy-makers hold such beliefs indicates that the Japanese government has been more confident than Western governments about the general applicability of the East Asian model of democratisation.

There are problems, however, in implementing an ODA policy based on this liberal assumption. First, the assumption that economic development under a market economic system necessarily will lead to political liberalisation and democratisation is questionable, especially on theoretical grounds. Second, it is unclear whether the assumption is applicable to every nation-state in the world without exception.

While many theorists perceive a strong positive linkage between the development of a market-based economy and democracy, the direct relation between the two remains unclear. Jagdish Bhagwati argues that 'a market economy is a necessary, but not a sufficient, condition for democracy'.[44] Francis Fukuyama contends that 'economic development is neither a necessary nor a sufficient condition for stable democracy; it is, however, very helpful'.[45] According to both Bhagwati and Fukuyama, a market economy itself does not generate direct pressure for democracy, and economic development, despite its contribution to the emergence of the *new rich* (middle class), does not necessarily mean that democracy will prevail.[46]

Historical evidence indicates that while democracy requires a market economy, a market economy does not necessarily require democracy.[47] All contemporary industrialised democracies have market economic systems and there is 'no example of a democracy that is or was fully socialist'.[48] On the other hand, empirical evidence also shows that a market economy can 'exist in the absence of democracy'.[49] A market economy is 'perfectly compatible with many forms of authoritarianism (though obviously not with communist totalitarianism), and may even flourish better in non-democracies'.[50] The rapid economic development of pre-democratic Taiwan and South Korea, for example, demonstrates that a market economy is compatible with authoritarianism. As the case of Singapore also demonstrates, 'economic development and an authoritarian regime can coexist for a long time'.[51]

Although there is no direct relationship between democracy and a market economy, a market-based economy is more likely to promote democratisation than a socialist economy. A market economy is 'a more efficient engine of economic growth than socialism', and therefore it is 'more likely to generate the rapid socioeconomic change' that contributes to the emergence of a more democratic political system.[52] After accumulating economic and social wealth, South Korea in the late 1980s and Taiwan in the late 1990s, transformed from market-based authoritarianism regimes to democracies. Minxin Pei predicts that:

> The Chinese path toward democratisation will most likely follow the model of Taiwan and South Korea once China becomes a fully market-based authoritarian system.... The indirect route through market-based authoritarianism – an organic evolutionary process, time-consuming and unexciting on the surface – may eventually produce more enduring democratic systems with less political and economic trauma.[53]

Such optimistic views about Chinese democratisation are premised on a series of propositions presented by Seymore Lipset – that is, economic development creates a middle class; the middle class generates civil society because once its economic well-being has been secured, it seeks more *freedom* and starts to express a greater variety of social interests; civil society then promotes political change, and, finally, the process leads to democratisation.[54]

Most mainstream China analysts in Japan, however, question the applicability of such theoretical propositions to China. For example, Hishida Masaharu maintains that far from stimulating democratic development as suggested by Lipset's propositions, the emergent middle class or the so-called *new rich* in China's modernising urban coastal areas have neither promoted civil society nor challenged the political authority of the CCP. Hishida and other Japanese China analysts contend instead that members of the emergent middle class, such as private entrepreneurs, are more interested in creating personal networks with provincial and state officials in order to maximise their own business interests than in creating civil society. In other words, business elites (private entrepreneurs) and power elites (government officials) collaborate for mutual benefit – that is, money for officials and administrative assistance for business expansion for entrepreneurs – through their informal personal networks. This is the biggest factor generating the ever-increasing corruption in post-reform China. According to one report, the number of convictions in corruption cases involving government officials in China between 1998 and 2002 surpassed 200,000.[55] Hishida also questions the likelihood of Chinese democratisation in the near future by pointing out that an 'institutionalised civil society', formed by individuals or groups possessing a high degree of autonomy from the rulers, has never emerged in China's history.[56] Nakagane Katsuji emphasises that the belief among Chinese leaders and the middle class that the end of the Communist Party's political control would result in political, social and eventually economic chaos has considerably constrained the call for democratisation from the emergent middle class.[57] In the opinion of such China analysts, the single biggest obstacle to China's democratisation is the 'institutional involvement' of the PLA in the governing system in China and the Army's strong support for the CCP's continued political control over individual Chinese.[58] For example, a Chinese official interviewed by Inada Jūichi asserted with confidence that 'our military [the PLA] stabilises the nation and can prevent Chinese politics from becoming chaotic'.[59]

As far as the Japanese government is concerned, China's continued stability remains a more important policy goal of its ODA provision than *democratisation*.[60] This does not mean that the Japanese government is uncritical of the Communist Party's political dictatorship in China. Rather, the Japanese government does not want drastic and rapid change in the political system that might produce chaos in China's domestic affairs. In other words, the Japanese government favours the democratic transformation of the Chinese political system only if it progresses step by step, without political upheaval and economic damage. One senior Foreign Ministry official points to the rapid and radical changes in the Russian political system at the beginning of the 1990s, which resulted in economic and social instability, as an example of the unwanted scenario for Japanese policy-makers.[61]

For Japanese policy-makers and China analysts, the best-case scenario for Chinese democratisation involves the gradual democratisation of China led by a gradual transformation of the Communist Party itself, rather than the emergence of an unstable democracy created by the sudden end of the Communist Party's control.[62] The former is considered most likely to facilitate China's democratisation without leading to domestic upheaval. In the end, it is not in Japan's interest to promote radical change in Chinese politics, but it is in its interest to support the maintenance of a politically and economically well-ordered China.

The irony of Japan's China ODA is that so far, it has functioned to support the continuation of the Communist Party's political control through its contribution to the economic development of China. In fact, Japanese policy-makers prefer the continuation of the Communist regime if it can prevent the country from becoming fragmented and chaotic and if it can control anti-Japanese resentment among the Chinese people which might damage Japanese economic interests. Japanese policy-makers and China specialists are concerned about the possibility that in any process of Chinese democratisation, anti-Japanese nationalism could replace Communism as a marker of national identity.[63] In this context, Nakajima Mineo points out the dangers associated with the emergence of 'Great China Nationalism (*Dai Chūka nashonarizumu*)' and 'Neo-Sinocentrism (*Chūka shisō no gendai ban*)'.[64] Japanese officials also feel that if China were democratised today, anti-Japanese nationalism among the Chinese public would increase, rather than decrease, because the restraining hand of the CCP would be removed or weakened.[65] In the end, the CCP's political authority serves Japan's interests because the Party is apparently able to prevent the escalation of anti-Japanese nationalism within China, and has often acted in the past to do so.

It must be acknowledged that anti-Japanese nationalism is a double-edged sword for the CCP. On the one hand, anti-Japanese national sentiment has indeed been a very useful political instrument for the CCP to legitimise their authoritarian control over the Chinese population, and the Party is often guilty of whipping it up through anti-Japanese patriotic education. On the other hand, the CCP has often attempted to discourage any spontaneous anti-Japanese movements by the Chinese citizens for strong fear that such movements might easily turn against the Party itself.[66] The

CCP's effort to control spontaneous anti-Japanese movements during the Asian Cup soccer tournament held in China in 2004 clearly illustrated this irony or paradox.[67]

This orientation of the Japanese government (*Nihon dokuji no riron*) differs from that of Western governments, which officially advocate democratisation and the protection of human rights.[68] In this sense, the goals of Japan's China ODA policy have not been integrated with the US' China policy, which prioritises democratisation over stability. Thus, the Japanese and US governments consider China's political development from different viewpoints. Japanese governments certainly favour encouraging Chinese modernisation in a democratic direction in the long term, but only if it does not undermine the stability of China's domestic affairs. Japan's geographical proximity to and greater economic interdependence with China, which are not shared by Western countries, are the sources of Japan's strong concern about stability within China. This is the major reason that Japanese governments, unlike their Western counterparts, have not demanded the *speedy* democratisation of China.[69]

De facto *democracy*

Despite the apparent lack of commitment by the emergent Chinese middle class to the creation of a civil society and despite the continuing one-party political control by the CCP, Chinese politics today is becoming more democratic. The political power of the CCP has slowly but consistently weakened.[70] Watanabe Toshio observes that the expansion of the market economy in the PRC has been gradually but persistently undermining the motivation of local Communist Party leaders to engage themselves actively in local politics.[71] Many of these local Communist Party leaders are more concerned with furthering their own commercial interests than repeating the political slogans and propaganda that are imposed on them by the central government, which has proved unable to reverse the trend towards the meltdown of the Communist Party's authority at the local level. These circumstances have contributed to the decay of the CCP's tight political control over Chinese society. The CCP used to exercise strong one-party dictatorship, with a high degree of legitimacy based on Communist political ideology and the official version of the history of the Communist revolution. However, recent political campaigns by central Communist Party leaders, which emphasise terms such as *patriotism* and *Sino-centrism* as slogans to promote national unity, indicate an implicit acknowledgement by Communist Party leaders that *Marxism* will no longer suffice as the basis for the Party's legitimacy.[72]

We will now consider the evidence for the emergence of '*de facto* democracy' within some parts of Chinese society, as perceived by Japanese policy-makers and specialists on China. Then we will examine the impact of China's *de facto* democracy on Japan's current China ODA policy.

Some of the Japanese specialists on China's political economy whom I interviewed detected the emergence and development in contemporary China of a '*de facto* democracy', based not on democratic concepts and institutions, such as a multi-party system, universal suffrage, freedom of speech and the separation of the executive, legislature and judiciary, but rather on democratic functions. Watanabe and Soeya argue that in order to maintain social stability, the CCP must inevitably adopt a political system that can adjust to the 'increasingly divergent socio-economic interests (*tagen-ka suru rieki shudan*)' in China that have been created by economic development and increasing market-orientation.[73] Therefore, the Party is likely to institute more democratic practices, as democracy is apparently more effective than Communism for this purpose. Similarly, Yabuki points out the probability that CCP leaders will promote this functional (*de facto*) democracy due to the need to counter the corruption associated with the informal personal networks between political and business elites.[74] Actually, none of these analysts believe that the Communist Party's political dominance in China will end in the near future. Nevertheless, they think that, in practice, it is becoming increasingly necessary for Party leaders to employ more democratic approaches to governance, in order to adjust and satisfy a society that is becoming increasingly organised, complex, robust and informed, if they are to slow the decay of the Party's political control.

The free election system that has recently been employed for the election of village council members is one manifestation of this *de facto* democracy. Village elections in China are not totally free from central government control[75] and are still at an early stage of democratic development.[76] Nonetheless, these elections do, at least, provide Chinese villagers with an institutional framework in which to express their political demands and concerns. In the view of many policy-makers and analysts, if the Chinese political system reaches the stage where it can accommodate increasing numbers of social and economic entities beyond the control of the CCP, then China's social and political stability will be assured and *de facto* democracy will arrive. If it cannot accommodate such entities, the increasing social dynamism in China, which has been created by economic development and the market economy, will bring nothing but social and political instability.[77] The anger of some Chinese people over the widening income gap between the coastal and inland population, the widespread corruption of government officials and the increasing numbers of unemployed people[78] are examples of tensions that are causing socio-political instability in many parts of China and could conceivably cause nationwide socio-political instability in the near future.

Although the government is reluctant to make the promotion of democratisation and human rights an official policy goal of China ODA, Japanese Foreign Ministry officials are nevertheless coming under increasing pressure from the news media, the academic community and politicians to do so. As argued earlier, many observers believe that the emergence of '*de facto* democracy' has in fact promoted China's socio-political stability, rather than undermining it. In addition, Taiwan's rapid democratisation in the late 1990s made the Japanese public and politicians even more critical of the PRC's authoritarian regime.[79] For example, in May 1996, the Foreign Affairs Committee of the Upper House of the Diet, consisting of politicians from various parties, passed a resolution that was highly approving of democratic developments in Taiwanese politics, while urging the PRC government towards a peaceful resolution of the Taiwan issue.[80] These developments have made it more difficult for the MOFA to continue to separate ODA from the restriction of political freedom and human rights abuses by the Chinese government.

Despite its consciousness of the practical difficulty of linking ODA to China's democratisation, and the risks of doing so, it has become increasingly necessary for the MOFA to attach relevant conditions to its China ODA transactions, in order to convince Japanese politicians, the academic community and the public that Japan should continue to provide ODA to China at all.[81]

Indeed, the JICA, which is responsible for the implementation of ODA, has started to use ODA to support democratisation in some developing countries. For example, Japanese ODA has been used to facilitate civil lawmaking (*hōseibi*) in Vietnam. In fact, the Agency has accepted 756 trainees for programmes concerned with democratisation and has provided financial assistance for elections held in twenty-seven countries and regions in the 1990s.[82] According to one Agency official, however, China is still not a target of ODA support in this area as Japanese officials feel that such assistance would be rejected by Chinese leaders, because of their strong *pride (mentsu).*[83]

The assumption that China's ongoing social transformation will eventually lead to democratisation has become a useful piece of *policy logic (seisaku rojikku)* that enables the MOFA to justify its China ODA activity to Japanese taxpayers. The problem with this rhetoric, however, is that the Ministry will come under pressure to impose an ODA sanction on China whenever the Chinese government is perceived to have abused human rights. In other words, official emphasis on such rhetoric significantly limits the MOFA diplomatic options towards China. This is the major dilemma that the Foreign Ministry is currently facing with regard to its China ODA policy.[84]

Strategic effects of Japan's ODA policy: new developments

This section addresses evaluations by Japanese policy-makers and China analysts of Japan's use of ODA in an attempt to slow China's military development, and of the change in the priority areas of Japan's development assistance to China from the building of economic infrastructure to the development of socio-environmental infrastructure.

ODA sanctions are intended to express the Japanese government's concerns about China's behaviour, including that country's provocative military behaviour in the region.[85] Thus, Japan's actual withdrawal of ODA as a form of sanction against China has not been a proactive policy, but rather constitutes *reactive* diplomatic action, often resulting from the need of the MOFA to respond to domestic pressure from the public, the media and politicians. In fact, Japanese policy-makers have never intended to rely solely on aid sanctions to counter China's military build-up and the disruptive regional behaviour associated with it.

While using ODA as a diplomatic weapon against the PRC, Japanese governments have been quietly and steadily enhancing Japan's own military capability in order to deter the PRC's military development and prevent China from seeking regional hegemony in the future.[86] For example, since 1993, Japan has been developing a theatre missile defence (TMD) system with the US in response to potential ballistic missile threats posed by China and North Korea.[87] In March 2001, the Japanese government introduced a law that allows the Japanese Maritime Self-Defence Force (SDF) directly to inspect suspicious vessels operating around Japan.[88] One Japanese newspaper has revealed that the Japanese Defence Agency intends to construct a new air force base on Shimoji Island, which is very close to the disputed Senkaku Islands.[89] In March 2003, the Japanese government started its programme to launch spy satellites by using its newly developed H2A rockets. In this way, the Japanese government already began to use its space technology, which has been developed for peaceful use, for military purposes.[90] Furthermore, Japan's pro-gramme to increase SDF's power projection capability specially around the East China Sea has been underway. The major elements of the programme are to increase the number of military personnel stationed in the Okinawa Islands, replace F14 fighter airplanes at the Naha air-base with more powerful F15 fighters and build new submarines.[91] These developments indicate that ODA sanctions are not the only means, but are one of several strategic instruments available to Japan to counter the PRC's militarisation and disruptive military behaviour in the region.

Some Japanese China specialists argue that some of Beijing's military activity in the region in the 1990s was motivated primarily by the need of the CCP to consolidate its position by generating patriotic and nationalist fervour among the Chinese public. For example, Kokubun Ryōsei contends that China's naval activity inside Japan's EEZ in 2000 was 'a problem deliberately created by the Chinese government'. In implicit acknowledgement of their waning political authority, Communist Party leaders, according to this analyst, sought to evoke public support for the Party and recover its legitimacy by intentionally generating such regional political tensions. China, continues Kokubun, 'then wanted to resolve this problem in order to promote good relations with Japan'. However, this strategy 'produced the opposite outcome for the Chinese government, as it led to a political backlash from Japanese politicians and increased resentment of China among the Japanese public'.[92] Such Japanese observers and policy-makers thus consider that in its action in 2000, Beijing was employing a classic diplomatic tactic to stimulate nationalism at home. In this context, it was not necessary for Japan to respond severely to China's provocative behaviour. It is very interesting to note that according to this view, the Chinese government was creating international tensions for domestic political purposes, while the Japanese government was also applying sanctions against China for domestic political reasons.

As explained in Chapter 6, some of the ODA sanctions that Japanese governments imposed on China were symbolic sanctions that were intended to satisfy politicians and the public who had been calling for a tougher stance against the Chinese government, rather than to produce a specific diplomatic outcome. One senior Foreign Ministry bureaucrat remarks:

in the decade before the 1989 Tiananmen Square Incident [1979–89] there had been a broader consensus among the Japanese public and politicians in favour of providing full support for China's modernisation. Given the changed domestic and international environment since then [the post-Tiananmen resentment of the PRC government among the Japanese public, the rapid militarisation of China and the end of the Cold War], we will respond on a case-by-case basis to any disruptive behaviour by Beijing that could damage Japanese interests.[93]

Clearly, the changed perceptions of China by Japanese politicians and the public after Tiananmen have greatly influenced this MOFA bureaucrat's attitude towards China. Given such changed domestic conditions, MOFA bureaucrats have imposed ODA sanctions on China despite their acknowledgement that unilateral sanctions by Japan would produce only a marginal effect on Chinese behaviour.

As detailed in Chapter 5, the Japanese government has begun to concentrate in its China ODA provision on such areas as environmental protection, poverty relief and the development of inland provinces to narrow the income gap between the inhabitants of the coastal and inland regions.[94] Japanese policy-makers argue that although overall poverty and economic backwardness in China had been the major threats to Chinese stability during the 1980s, they have since been replaced by social and environmental problems caused by China's rapid and unbalanced development. Following this logic, it is in Japan's interest to use ODA as a financial instrument to alleviate China's social and environmental problems in order to facilitate stable economic development. However, this explanation of the shift in the priority areas of China ODA, which is regularly presented in official publications by the Japanese MOFA,[95] should be regarded primarily as rhetoric intended to justify government policy and gain public support. As explained in Chapter 3, the factors and interests that actually motivated the Japanese government to shift the priority project areas of China ODA were the progress in China's economic development, the budgetary interest of the Japanese MOFA and military considerations.

For officials of the Japanese MOFA, industrial infrastructure development in itself has become less and less important as a justification to gain public support for the policy of continuously directing taxpayers' money to China, especially since China has now undergone considerable economic growth. Facing the need to find a new explanation for Japan's China ODA policy, Foreign Ministry officials were highly likely to choose the mitigation of socio-economic and environmental problems as new priority areas of ODA. These areas, which are based more on humanitarian than on economic need, are very useful as a way of gaining public support for the continuation of China ODA by the Ministry.

Gaining or retaining public support has become a crucial issue. In 1996, Japan's overall ODA budget was reduced for the first time by 10 per cent. The Japanese government decided to reduce the ODA budget by another 10 per cent in 2002.[96] Moreover, increasing public opposition towards China ODA activity has put pressure on the government to cut the ODA budget even further. For example, according to one opinion poll conducted by the *Yomiuri shinbun* in September 2002, the proportion of Japanese who have a positive view of the government's China ODA activity over the last two decades was less than 22 per cent, while the proportion who view China ODA activity negatively was as high as 65 per cent. Moreover, in this poll, 56 per cent of the total respondents wished to either cut or cease the provision of Japanese ODA to China, while 36 per cent wished to maintain the current level or increase China ODA provision.[97] The Japanese public is now clearly taking a negative view of the government's ODA policy to China, and is demanding a reduction in the China ODA budget. Japanese policy-makers and China analysts generally believe that, in light of the budget constraints upon Japan's ODA provision to China and of the increasing public opposition towards China ODA provision, the Japanese government should target specific provinces and sectors for yen loan projects of a humanitarian nature.[98]

ODA, Sino-Japanese relations and the regional framework

The previous sections in this chapter presented an evaluation of the specific economic, socio-political and strategic effects that Japan's China ODA policy has had according to Japanese ODA policy-makers and China specialists. This section examines their assessment of the impact that ODA policy has had on Sino-Japanese relations as a whole.

As we have seen, Japanese ODA policy-makers and China analysts contend that Japanese ODA to China has helped to promote greater economic interdependence between the two countries, which, in turn, has helped to stabilise bilateral relations.[99] China has in fact become 'the most popular destination in the world for Japanese investors'.[100] One manifestation of this economic interdependence is the great growth in the number of Japanese multinational companies that assemble their products at their own factories in China, before exporting the products to Japan and other countries around the world. Not only small, labour-intensive companies, but also big Japanese high-tech businesses operate in China. By 1994, for example, Sony had invested in a new factory to manufacture camcorders in China; Canon had built a facility to produce fax machines and NEC had implemented a joint venture to make computer peripheral machines.[101]

Not surprisingly, Japan has become China's largest trading partner and China has become Japan's second biggest trading partner. Japanese policy-makers and China analysts believe that as a consequence of this interdependence, Sino-Japanese relations can now be described as '*ōgenka dekinai kankei* (relations between two countries that cannot afford a serious confrontation with each other)'.[102] On the one hand this is because, in view of its strong economic interests in relation to Japan, the Chinese government is likely to refrain from seriously confronting Japan because of the economic backlash which could be expected to result. On the other hand, if the Japanese government were to confront China seriously, bilateral relations would be endangered and this would lead to regional instability and, ultimately, '*keizaiteki sōgo kakushō hakai* (mutually assured economic destruction) might result'.[103] In this context, according to those most involved with policy formulation, ODA has thus functioned to stabilise bilateral relations and has helped to prevent political tensions from escalating into serious confrontations. From such a point of view, officials of the MOFA view Japan's China ODA as a '*futoi paipu* (fat pipe – an important connection)' that is essential in managing Sino-Japanese relations,[104] which had, after all, been antagonistic for most of the twentieth century.

In other words, the Chinese government would be more likely to take a hard line towards Japan if the economic interdependence between the two nations were weak. If Japan ceased its ODA provision to China, it is likely that there would be a rapid deterioration of bilateral relations, including serious diplomatic clashes over Taiwan, the Senkaku Islands and conflicting interpretations of historical issues.[105] This is one political reason why the MOFA prefers to maintain its ODA to China despite the problem of the national budget deficit[106] and despite the increasing domestic objections to the way in which China ODA works in practice.

ODA policy-makers and China analysts also believe Japanese ODA to China has had a salutary effect on China's status in the whole region. Japan's ODA has not only promoted greater economic interdependence between China and Japan, but has also encouraged economic interdependence between China and other East Asian countries as well.[107] Efforts by Japanese governments to support the PRC's Reform and Liberalisation Policy, which was the main objective of ODA provision for the first decade or so, amounted to a *de facto* engagement policy, because such efforts promoted the incorporation of China's economy into the East Asian regional economic system and enhanced economic interdependence between China and its neighbours, as described in Chapter 5. Watanabe Toshio terms this process '*Chūgoku keizai no higashiajia-ka* (East Asianization of the Chinese economy)'.[108] Chinese companies in the coastal provinces are no longer able to conduct economic transactions without interaction and cooperation with surrounding East Asian countries – Taiwan, South Korea and the South East Asian nations. As a consequence of its new economic dynamism, China has become increasingly integrated into the economic frameworks of the region.[109]

While Japanese policy-makers and academics support this use of ODA to engage China in regional and global politico-economic frameworks, they also acknowledge the possibility that their engagement policy towards China could fail.[110] They predict that Japan's attempt to incorporate China into regional and global frameworks may be unsuccessful because of the fundamental nature of China's international behaviour – Sino-centrism and its tendency to reject foreign pressure. The PRC is, in fact, one of the most difficult countries for Japan and other countries to engage with.

Why, then, do Japanese policy-makers continuously seek to engage China, despite the acknowledged risk of failure? It is because they consider that Japan has no realistic alternative policy options. A containment policy towards China – that is, an attempt to keep China's military and economic power within acceptable limits for Japan – is not an option for Japan because of the risk of damaging the domestic political power of Chinese reformist leaders[111] and due to Japan's relative lack of independent military capability.[112] If the Japanese government chose a containment policy towards China, it would also undoubtedly damage Japanese investment, trade and natural resource interests there. For the Japanese government, the Japan–US security alliance is, in fact, its ultimate insurance against failure of the engagement policy.[113]

The provision of Japanese yen loans is not considered excessively risky, because China is a highly reliable debtor. In the 1960s, for instance, China completed the repayment of its development loans from the Soviet Union earlier than scheduled, even though the two nations were engaged in serious political confrontation during this period. Without significant foreign currency at that time, China had to export agricultural products in order to obtain foreign currency to repay these loans, which placed a severe financial burden on the Chinese people.[114] However, China's prompt repayment greatly increased its perceived reliability as a borrower in the international community. As noted in Chapter 5, more than 90 per cent of the cumulative amount of Japanese ODA to China from 1979 to 1999 was in the form of yen loans that need to be repaid by China, although the figure was only 72.3 per cent during first decade, from 1979 to 1989. In other words, the proportion of yen loans increased in the second decade of Japan's ODA programme.[115] Such considerations reduce the risk of political backlash at home and contribute to Japanese governments' willingness to pursue China engagement despite the known risk of failure. In fact, the Chinese government has begun to repay its loans in accordance with the repayment schedule, and timely repayment has continued.[116]

Japanese policy-makers and China analysts assert that China has increasingly come to share the same economic and social values as Japan, including a commitment to the market economy system and the desire to foster social pluralism. These officials and academics, who have been engaged in negotiations and discussions with their Chinese counterparts for two decades now, emphasise how much more moderate and flexible the attitudes and language of their Chinese counterparts have become, compared to twenty years ago.[117] This new flexibility is considered to be partly the result of Japanese provision of ODA to China, and one of its most visible effects. It also has important implications for Japan's future relations with China. including security relations. The provision of yen loans with a repayment period of thirty years and a ten-year grace period has created a *forty-year relationship* between Japanese and Chinese officials and other individuals, and this, in itself, has made a major contribution to mutual understanding.[118] Although most of the Chinese public is still not informed about Japanese ODA contributions, my informants Inada and Watanabe, who have actually visited many ODA project sites in China, found that Chinese officials and other people who have had direct involvement in Japanese ODA projects, very much appreciated Japan's assistance.[119]

Despite the supposed promotion of common socio-economic values between Japanese and Chinese citizens, however, engagement with China – the most important underlying concept of Japanese development assistance to China – has not progressed as much as Japanese policy-makers expected or hoped. As the recent series of disruptive military actions in the East Asian region by China shows, China's foreign and military policy have become, if anything, even more assertive and disruptive than before.

Outlook: will Japan's development aid to China continue?

There are two major reasons for China, despite its remarkable economic growth, still needing development assistance from Japan. First, since 1999 China has not been eligible for loans from the IDA – the attached conditions of which include zero interest, and a repayment period of thirty-five years including a ten-year period of grace – because China no longer qualifies, on account of the remarkable progress of its economic development.[120] In addition, the World Food Program (WFP) recently announced its plan to terminate its aid program in China in 2005 due to the same reason.[121] The IDA had been the largest supplier of multilateral ODA to China since 1982 and the WFP has been the second-largest multilateral aid donor for China over the past two decades. Thus, the end of their provision of development aid to China inevitably increased, and will further increase, the importance of Japanese ODA.

Second, China's worsening budget deficit,[122] the large number of the unemployed in China, and the problem of a rapidly aging population have in fact increased the country's need for foreign aid, despite the overall economic growth which disqualifies it for development aid from the IDA and the WFP. For example, the Chinese government estimated that its budget deficit would increase from about US$33 billion in 2000 to US$40 billion in 2001 and issued about US$79 billion of national bonds in 2001.[123] Despite the budget deficit, the government is under huge pressure to increase expenditure on welfare, especially to create a social safety net for the unemployed. China's policy of shutting down uncompetitive and debt-creating state-owned enterprises has resulted in an enormous number of people becoming unemployed over the last decade. According to one Chinese study, by 1997 the number of the unemployed reached 5.6 million, while the number *temporarily* discharged was 11.5 million.[124] In practice, however, people who have been discharged on a supposedly temporary basis find it very difficult to return to the work in China and thus, these people must also be counted as unemployed. Furthermore. the Chinese government's recent announcement of the need to temporarily discharge 30 million of a workforce of 180–210 million means that China has 'a rate of functionally unemployed and on welfare of at least 15–16 percent'.[125] This problem has already led to riots in many parts of China.[126] For example, in March 2002, more than thirty thousand retrenched former employees of state-owned enterprises in Liaoning province protested against the labour and welfare policies of the provincial government.[127] Thus, the Chinese government is now making considerable efforts to create a social safety net to alleviate the anger and financial difficulty of the unemployed.[128] Given the above situation, the Chinese government needs foreign economic assistance to supplement its budget deficit and to establish an institutionalised welfare system.

As can be seen from Table 7.1, there is still a substantial economic disparity between Japan and China. Despite the widespread perception that a rapidly developing China is economically catching up with a stagnant Japan, the gap in economic size still remains considerable. Figures from the World Bank (Table 7.1) indicate that Japanese GNI in 2003 (US$4,390 billion) was about three times greater than China's (US$1,417 billion). A comparison of the wealth of the citizens suggests an even greater gap. China's per capita GNI in 2003 (US$1,100) was only one-thirtieth of that of Japan (US$34,510). Moreover, China's per capita GNI in 2003 (US$1,100) was even lower than that of major Southeast Asian countries – for example, Thailand (US$2,190), Malaysia (US$3,780) and Singapore

Table 7.1 Comparison of economic size between China and
         Japan, 2003

Items (Unit)	China	Japan
GNI, 2003 (billion US$)	1,417	4,390
GNI per capita, 2003 (US$)	1,100	34,510
Share of world GNI, 2003 (%)	4.1	12.7
GDP growth, 2001–02 (%)	8.0	0.3
GDP per capita growth, 2001–02 (%)	7.3	0.2
Population, 2003 (millions)	1,288	127

Source: Compiled from World Bank, *2004 World Development
Indicators, 2004 World Bank Atlas*, Washington, DC, 2004.

(21,230).[129] These statistics indicate that China still has a substantial need for developmental assistance and, on the basis of the remaining difference in wealth between the Japanese and Chinese people, the Japanese government still has sufficient *ethical* reason to direct development aid to China.

However, given the Japanese public's deteriorating perceptions of a modernising China which continues disruptive military behaviour in the region,[130] the Japanese government has begun to discuss openly the possible termination of its development aid to China.[131] While criticising this move by Japan, the Chinese government persists in demanding continuation of Japanese aid on the basis that bilateral relations would be endangered without the aid connection.[132] This view, which is also shared by some officials of the Japanese MOFA,[133] clearly illustrates the perceived political importance of Japan's ODA to China as a stabiliser of bilateral relations. On the one hand, the Chinese government acknowledges both the significance of Japanese ODA as an essential element in managing bilateral relations and the continuing need for Japanese ODA in order for China to alleviate its budget deficit and develop a reliable social security system, as discussed earlier. On the other hand, it continues with disruptive military and resource exploration policies in the East Asian region, which in turn is increasing domestic pressure on the Japanese government to terminate its aid provision to China. The PRC continues with their policies because of the overwhelming importance that China puts on its unification policy with Taiwan and its necessity to develop submarine resources in the region to ease the domestic problem of energy shortages. Whether Japan's development aid to China will continue depends on how and to which direction the economic, political and security situations surrounding Sino-Japanese relations change in the future.

Conclusion

My research shows that Japanese policy-makers and China analysts make the following judgements. First, since 1979 Japanese governments have achieved the ODA policy objective of contributing to the stabilisation of China by supporting the PRC's Reform and Liberalisation Policy through active provision of funds and technology. Second, while supporting China's overall economic development, Japanese governments have also successfully promoted a market economy in China and the incorporation of the Chinese economy into the global economic system through ODA. Most of the ODA funds provided have been used for industrial infrastructure development in China, and, in turn, this infrastructure has contributed significantly to ensuring a stable supply of Chinese oil and coal for Japan in the first instance, and has then contributed to an increase in China's trade with and FDI from Japan and other countries. Thus, in the view of those who administer and comment on Japan's ODA programmes, Japan's development assistance to China has helped to produce greater economic interdependence between China and Japan and between China and a number of other countries.

Japanese China ODA policy-makers and China analysts think that China's economic development and transition to a market economy, which Japanese ODA has helped to facilitate, have had positive effects on China's social affairs. The improved wealth of Chinese individuals and the emergence of a market-based domestic economic system have, in turn, promoted the growth of more pluralistic socio-economic interests in China. The emergent middle class, mostly business entrepreneurs in urban districts who have benefited from China's transition to a market-oriented economy, have demanded further freedom in economic and social activities. Moreover, the increasingly divergent socio-economic interests in contemporary China have offered both the means and the incentives for new groups to form and organise, including those groups that are neither dominated nor controlled by the CCP, thus creating an environment for further political reform.

Although the democratisation of China has not been a direct objective of Japan's ODA policy to China, it is desired by Japanese policy-makers in the long term. Unlike economic development, however, democratisation is considered to be simply too distant from ODA activities, and thus it is very difficult to link Japan's ODA directly with the democratisation of China. Despite their recognition of this fact, however, many of the Japanese policy-makers and academics whom I interviewed were optimistic that Japan's continued support for China's economic growth through ODA, together with the promotion of a more market-oriented economy and the further globalisation of the Chinese economy, will eventually lead to the liberalisation and democratisation of China's polity. They argue that it has already become necessary for CCP leaders to introduce more democratic approaches to governance to adjust and satisfy the various elements within an increasingly pluralistic, educated and demanding society in China.

The implications of ODA for Sino-Japanese relations are clear. Japanese ODA policy-makers and China analysts believe that Japanese ODA to China has greatly assisted the transformation of the PRC from a Communist totalitarian state to an *authoritarian developmental state*, while at the same time advancing Japan's economic and other interests. As a consequence, they further believe that Sino-Japanese relations, despite a sorry history during the first half of the twentieth century, have become so economically entangled that neither country can afford to confront the other in any hard-line fashion.

8   Final comments

The book is designed to provide an answer to the question of why successive Japanese governments have steadily directed development aid to China, despite the fact that the governments of these two countries regard each other as important politico-strategic competitors. In other words, the research sought to elucidate the policy objectives of Japan's development aid to China and the interests underlying the policy. Findings of my research indicate that successive Japanese governments have provided considerable financial resources and expertise to China in order to advance Japan's perceived economic, political and strategic interests in relation to China. Contrary to the dominant view that Japanese foreign aid activity is primarily motivated by a desire to increase Japanese commercial interests overseas, this research suggests that the picture is more complicated. Japanese aid policy-makers are willing to advance not only commercial but also perceived political and security interests in relation to recipient countries. In this respect, the unique capacity of aid to enable a donor to pursue various foreign policy objectives simultaneously in the recipient country is clearly visible in the case of Japan's China ODA. While Japanese governments have used ODA as a financial incentive to promote positive economic and political developments in China, since the mid-1990s they have also used it as a crucial diplomatic weapon to promote Japan's security interests in relation to China.

Moreover, the various policy objectives that the Japanese government has pursued through ODA provision are often entwined in complex ways, and they have not been static but have evolved in response to changes in the domestic and external environments that redefined Japan's perceived national interests. However, despite changing policy goals, the concept of *engagement* that underlies Japan's China aid policy has remained consistent since 1979, although the partner of Japan's engagement policy has shifted from an economically weak China which was *de facto* a strategic ally during the 1980s to a rapidly modernising China which has become a potential economic rival and recognised security threat from the mid-1990s onwards.

In seeking to identify the goals and interests associated with Japan's China ODA policy, this study also sought to identify the actors and institutions that actually formulate the policy. It was found that policy has been developed by a number of actors. Before the mid-1990s, bureaucrats of various central ministries and. in particular, those of the MOFA, dominated ODA policy-making within the Japanese government. From the mid-1990s, however, the process of making China ODA policy has been characterised by intense competition between officials of the MOFA and parliamentarians of the LDP. Since then, the balance of power in the formulation of official China ODA policy has largely shifted from MOFA bureaucrats to LDP parliamentarians, especially those who are members of the so-called *diplomatic tribe*. The enhanced foreign policy-making power of LDP politicians in turn significantly undermined the autonomy of MOFA officials in the formulation and implementation of China ODA policy.

The very necessity for Japan's China ODA policy-making to be flexible and expeditious in response to China's rapidly changing economic and social conditions further exposed the limitations of Japan's traditionally bureaucratic-centred ODA policy-making, encouraging a higher level of participation in policy-making by LDP parliamentarians, who can make decisions quickly and with more flexibility than MOFA bureaucrats. One clear manifestation of this change within the policy-making process can be seen in Japan's imposition of several aid sanctions on China from 1995 to 2000. Thus, the shift in the balance of ODA policy-making power opened the way for the Japanese government to use development aid not only as a financial incentive (carrot) to promote desirable developments in China that are perceived to be in Japan's national interests. but also as a strategic weapon (stick) to restrain China's militarisation and disruptive behaviour in the region.

The findings of my research have important implications for the literature of Japanese foreign policy in general, and of Japan's China policy in particular. In terms of foreign policy-making, this study bridges the gap between analytical approaches based on the rational actor model (the *mercantile realism* and the *proactive state* approaches described in Chapter 1) and the approach based on the government, or bureaucratic, politics model (the *institutional analysis* approach). On the one hand, we have seen that changes in Japan's perceived economic, political and strategic interests in relation to China have been the major factor responsible for changes in the policy goals of Japanese ODA provision to China. On the other hand, the book further argued that those changes in perceptions were primarily caused by, or at least facilitated by, the shift in the balance of foreign aid policy-making power from MOFA bureaucrats to LDP politicians since the mid-1990s. In this sense, the book emphasises that the actual implementation of Japan's ODA policy towards China is not determined by the Japanese government making rational decisions according to an overall plan, but rather to a critical degree by intense policy-making competition between MOFA bureaucrats and LDP politicians, who all engage in the policy-making process on the basis of their different perceptions of national, organisational and personal interests. The study further implies that the picture of Japanese foreign and foreign aid policy-making as bureaucrat-centred, which for some time has held sway, is no longer necessarily viable, in view of the functional changes in the LDP's and the MOFA's foreign aid policy-making roles and capabilities during the first half of the 1990s.

Has Japan's attempt to engage with China through ODA since 1979 been successful? The answer depends on the context within which the question is considered. It must be acknowledged that the provision of a massive amount of funds by Japan has facilitated the development of the Chinese economy and thus has also contributed to an improvement in the living conditions of many people in China. On the other hand, if the question is considered in the context of China's current domestic political conditions and its strategic behaviour, the answer is doubtless negative. In the long run, however, that, too, may change. Despite repeated political and other setbacks, China is becoming economically stable and socially complex, and it is moving, though very gradually, in a politically liberal and democratic direction. Only time will tell how the effects of Japan's provision of massive amount of development aid to China since 1979 should ultimately be judged.

Appendix 1

Yen loan projects in China, 1979–2000
(¥ million (US$ million))

No.	Project name	Amount
First yen loan package (1979–84)		
1	Shijiusuo Port Construction Project	42,945
2	Yanzhou–Shijiusuo Railway Construction Project	39,710
3	Beijing–Qinhuangdao Railway Construction Project	87,000
4	Hengyang–Guangzhou Railway Transportation Reinforcement Project	3,320
5	Qinhuangdao Port Expansion Project	27,785
6	Wuqiangxi Hydroelectric Power Project	140
7	Commodity Loans	130,000
	Total	330.900
		(3,244)
Second yen loan package (1985–89)		
8	Hengyang–Guangzhou Railway Transportation Reinforcement Project	70,294
9	Zhengzhou–Baoji Railway Electrification Project	69,191
10	Qinhuangdao Port China and D Berths Construction Project	22,000
11	Lianyungang Port Expansion Project	47,000
12	Qingdao Port Expansion Project	57,000
13	Tianjin, Shanghai and Guangzhou Telecommunication Expansion Project	35,000
14	Tianshenqqiao (Basuo) Hydroelectric Power Project	77,375
15	Wuqiangxi Hydroelectric Power Project	8,490
16	Datong–Qinhuangdao (East Section) Railway Construction Project	18,410
17	Guanyinge Multipurpose Dam Project	11,780
18	Beijing Subway Construction Project	4,000
19	State Economic Information System Project (Model Project)	3,770
20	Beijing Water Supply Project	15,480
21	Beijing Sewage Treatment Plant Construction Project	2,640
22	Urban Gas Project	14,990
23	Urban Water Supply Project	12,580
24	Export Industries Promotion Project	70,000
	Total	540.000
		(5,294)
Third yen loan package (1990–95)		
25	Wuqiangxi Hydroelectric Power Project	16,600
26	Guanyinge Multipurpose Dam Project	6,445
27	Three Cities Water Supply Project (Tianjin, Hefei, Anshan)	8,866

(Continued)

(Continued)

No.	Project name	Amount
28	Weihe Fertilizer Plant Construction Project	26,926
29	Inner Mongolia Chemical Fertilizer Plant Construction	21,412
30	Yunnan Fertilizer Plant Construction Project	14,068
31	Second Wuhan Yangtze River Bridge Construction Project	4,760
32	Huangshi Yangtze Bridge Construction Project	3,700
33	Shenzhen Dapeng Bay Yantian Port 1st Phase Project	14,681
34	Hainan Highway Development Project	12,955
35	Hainan Telecommunication Development Project	3,583
36	Nine Provinces and Cities Telecommunication Network Project	43,734
37	Air Navigation and Air Traffic Control Modernisation Project	21,003
38	Shenmu–Shuoxian Railway Construction Project	26,985
39	Qindao Highway Development Project	8,800
40	Qindao Telecommunication Development Project	4,034
41	Baoji–Zhongwei Railway Construction Project	29,800
42	Wuhan/Tianhe Aerodrome Construction Project	6,279
43	Hengshui–Shangqiu Railway Construction Project	23,603
44	Shisanling Pumped Storage Power Station Project	13,000
45	Tianshengqiao First Hydropower Project	40,600
46	Nanning–Kunming Railway Construction Project	57,696
47	Shijiu Port Second Phase Construction Project	6,089
48	Hefe–Tongling Highway and Bridge Construction Project	8,603
49	Second Wuhan Yangtze River Bridge Construction Project	4,764
50	Luzhai Fertilizer Plant Construction Project	4,764
51	Jiujiang Fertilizer Plant Construction Project	10,273
52	Beijing Subway Second Phase Construction Project	15,678
53	Tongyu River Irrigation Development Project	11,535
54	Urban Water Supply Project (Xiamen, Chongqing and Kunming)	10,403
55	Hainan Haikou Port Development Project	2,589
56	Hubei Ezhou Power Plant Project	31,892
57	Lianyungang Port Xugou Area First Phase Construction Project	5,900
58	Qinhuangdao Port E and F Berths Construction Project	6,459
59	Qiqihar Nenjing River Highway Bridge Construction Project	2,100
60	Beijing–Shenyang–Harbin Telecommunication System Project	7,200
61	Qinhuangdao Port 4th Stage Coal Terminal Construction Project	11,122
62	Wengfu Chemical Fertilizer Plant Construction Project	12,286
63	Fujian Province Zhang Quan Railway Construction Project	6,720
64	Qindao Development Water Supply and Sewage Project	2,513
65	Xi'an Water Supply Project	7,139
65	Beijing Capital Airport Terminal Area Expansion Project	21,541
66	Jiangxi Jiujiang Thermal Power Project	29,600
67	State Economic Information System Project	20,300
68	Sanhe Thermal Power Plant Project	24,600
69	Shanxi Heijin Thermal Power Project	24,600
70	Tianjin No. 3 Gasworks Project	5,722
71	Dalian Port Dayao Bay First Phase Construction Project	6,655
72	Shanghai Baoshan Port Infrastructure Improvement Project	13,506
73	Shanghai Baoshan Power Plant Infrastructure Improvement	17,493
74	Hainan Yangpu Development Project	4,300
75	Shuoxian–Hunghua Port Railway Construction Project	27,715
76	Xi'an–Ankang Railway Construction Project	19,789
	Total	809,973
		(7,941)

No.	Project name	Amount
Fourth yen loan package (1996–2000)		
77	Beijing Capital Airport Terminal Area Expansion Project	8,459
78	Shuoxian–Huanghua Railway Construction Project	44,286
79	Xi'an–Ankang Railway Construction Project	15,211
80	Guiyang–Loudi Railway Construction Project	29,960
81	Urumuqi International Airport Expansion Project	4,890
82	Lanzhou Zhongchuan Airport Expansion Project	6,338
83	Qingdao Port Second Phase Expansion Project	2,700
84	Guiyang–Xinzhai Highway Construction Project	14,968
85	Guangzhou–Kunming-Chengdu Optical Fibre Cable Construction	5,349
86	Lanzhou–Xining-Lhasa Optical Fibre Cable Construction	3,046
87	Interior Regions Telecommunications Network Expansion Project	15,003
88	Sanjiang Plain Agricultural Development Project	17,702
89	Sanjiang Plain Longtouqiao Reservoir Construction Project	3,000
90	Liaoning Baishi Reservoir Construction Project	8,000
91	Hohhot Water Supply Project	5,446
92	Beijing No. 9 Waterworks Expansion Project	14,680
93	Guiyang Water Supply Project	5,500
94	Zhanjiang Water Supply Project	5,519
95	Lanzhou Environmental Improvement Project	7,700
96	Shenyang Environmental Improvement Project	11,196
97	Hohhot and Baotou Atmospheric Pollution Improvement Project	15,629
98	Liuzhou Environmental Improvement Project	10,738
99	Shanghai Puding International Airport Construction Project	40,000
100	Huanghua Port Construction Project	15,400
101	Shaanxi Hancheng No. 2 Thermal Power Plant Construction Project	57,970
102	Shanxi Wangqu Thermal Power Plant Construction Project	57,082
103	Bensi Environmental Improvement Project	8,507
104	Huai River Henan Water Pollution Control Project	12,175
105	Xiang River Basin Hunan Environmental Improvement Project	11.853
106	Dalian Water Supply System Rehabilitation Project	5,500
107	Heilongjiang Songhua River Basin Environmental Improvement	10.541
108	Jilin Song Liao River Basin Environment Improvement Project	12.800
109	Shandong Yantai Water Supply and Water-Induced Disaster Management Project	6.008
110	Henan Panshitou Reservoir Construction Project	6,734
111	Wangque–Laiyang Transmission and Substation Project	17,629
112	Hunan Yuanshui River Basin Hydropower Development Project	17,664
113	Power Distribution System Rehabilitation Project	13,754
114	Hangzhou–Quzhou Expressway Construction Project	30,000
115	Wanxian–Liangping Highway Construction Project	20,000
116	Liangping–Changshou Highway Construction Project	24,000
117	Hainan East Expressway Expansion Project	5,274
118	Xinxiang–Zhengzhou Highway Construction Project	23,491
119	Guiyang Environment Model City Project	14,435
120	Dalian Environment Model City Project	8,517
121	Chongqing Environment Model City Project	7,701
122	Suzhou Water Environmental Improvement Project	6,261
123	Zhejiang Sewage Treatment Project	11,256
124	Guangxi Water Supply Project	3,641
125	Kunming Water Supply Project	20,903

(*Continued*)

(Continued)

No.	Project name	Amount
126	Chengdu Water Supply Project	7,293
127	Chongqing Water Supply Project	6,244
128	Jiangxi Water Supply Project	4,147
128	Hunan Urban Flood Control Project	24,000
129	Hubei Urban Flood Control Project	13,000
130	Jiangxi Urban Flood Control Project	11,000
131	Yellow River Delta Agricultural Development Project	8,904
132	Harbin Electric Network Construction Project	6,070
133	Tianjing Water Treatment Project	7,142
134	Dalian Water Supply and Wastewater Treatment Project	3,309
135	Changsha Water Supply Project	4,850
136	Yingkou Water Supply Project	2,504
137	Tangsha Water Supply Project	2,841
138	Shaanxi Loess Plateau Afforestation Project	4,200
139	Shanxi Loess Plateau Afforestation Project	4,200
140	Inner-Mongolia Loess Plateau Afforestation Project	3,600
141	Zipingpu Multi-Purpose Dam Construction Project	32,199
142	Gansu Water-Saving Irrigation Project	6,000
143	Xinjiang Water-Saving Irrigation Project	14,400
144	Chongqing Urban Railway Construction Project	27,108
145	Heilongqing Heihe-Bei'an Road Construction Project	12,608
146	Shangdong Tai'an Pumped Storage Power Station Project	18,000
147	Hubei Small-Scale Hydropower Project	9,152
148	Gansu Small-Scale Hydropower Project	6,543
149	Liaoning TV & Radio Infrastructure Improvement Project	3,210
150	Wuhan Urban Railway Construction Project	2,894
	Total	969,843
		(9,508)
Special yen loans (2000)		
151	Beijing Urban Railway Construction Project	14,111
152	Xi'an Xianyang International Airport Terminal Expansion Project	3,091
	Total	17,202
		(169)

Source: Adapted from Japan Bank for International Cooperation, *JBIC ODA Loans to the People's Republic of China*, Tokyo, 2001.

Appendix 2

Interviews conducted in Japan, 2000–01

The names of Japanese academics and Japanese journalists I interviewed are given in the conventional way with surname first followed by given name. The names of officials in central Japanese government ministries and agencies, Japanese politicians and a LDP official are not specified in this list due to considerations of confidentiality. Instead, they are identified by letters of the alphabet.

Academics and journalists

1   Inada Jūichi, a political economist at Senshū University and a senior research fellow at the Japan Institute of International Affairs, Tokyo (28 March 2001).
2   Kayahara Ikuo, a defence analyst specialising on the PRC, formerly in the Japanese Defence Agency and currently at Takushoku University, Tokyo (4 April 2001).
3   Kokubun Ryōsei, specialist on Chinese politics, professor and director of the Centre for Area Studies at Keiō University, Tokyo (15 March 2001).
4   Motoyoshi Tadahiko, a researcher on Japanese ODA policy at the National Diet Library, Tokyo (3 April 2001).
5   Nakagawa Junji, a specialist on Japanese foreign aid and international law at the University of Tokyo, Tokyo (22 March 2001).
6   Shimomura Yasutami, an economist at Hōsei University and former policy adviser to the Liberal Democratic Party, Tokyo (4 April 2001).
7   Soeya Yoshihide, a political scientist specialising in Sino-Japanese relations at Keiō University and former foreign policy adviser to the Liberal Democratic Party, Tokyo (28 March 2001).
8   Sugishita Tsuneo, former senior *Yomiuri shinbun* journalist and currently a scholar specialising in Japanese development aid at Ibaraki University, Mito (11 April 2001).
9   Watanabe Toshio, a prominent development economist and former ODA policy adviser to both the Ministry of Foreign Affairs and the Liberal Democratic Party, Tokyo (13 April 2001).
10 Yabuki Susumu, a China analyst at Yokohama City University and former policy adviser to the Ōhira Masayoshi government, Yokohama (23 March 2001).

Bureaucrats, politicians and party officials

11 A, a senior official of the Liberal Democratic Party, Tokyo (27 March 2001).

12 B, a senior official of the Japanese Ministry of Finance, Tokyo (13 April 2001).

13 C, an official of the Japanese Ministry of Foreign Affairs, Tokyo (26 March 2001), joint interview with D and E.

14 D, an official of the Japanese Ministry of Foreign Affairs, Tokyo (26 March 2001), joint interview with C and E.

15 E, an official of the Japanese Ministry of Foreign Affairs, Tokyo (26 March 2001), joint interview with C and D.

16 F, a senior official of the Japanese Ministry of Foreign Affairs, Tokyo (20 April 2000), first interview.

17 F, a senior official of the Japanese Ministry of Foreign Affairs, Tokyo (14 March 2001), second interview.

18 G, a Liberal Democratic Party parliamentarian, Tokyo (3 April 2001).

19 H, an official of the Japan International Cooperation Agency, Tokyo (28 March 2001).

20 I, a senior official of the Japan Bank for International Cooperation, Tokyo (4 April 2001).

Notes

1 Introduction

1 In this book, those aid figures which were given in Japanese yen in original sources are not converted into US dollars, due to large fluctuations in the exchange rates over the last two decades.

2 These are the latest figures available. See Ministry of Foreign Affairs, Japan, *Diplomatic Bluebook 2004*, Tokyo: Ministry of Foreign Affairs, 2004, p. 49; Gaimushō Chūgoku-ka, 'Saikin no Chūgoku jōsei to Nitchū kankei (Current Chinese Affairs and Japan–China Relations)', unpublished report, April 2000, p. 15; East Asia Analytical Unit, Department of Foreign Affairs and Trade, Australia, *Asia's Global Powers: China–Japan Relations in the 21st Century*, Canberra, 1996, p. 65.

3 I calculated these proportions by compiling statistics from Organisation for Economic Cooperation and Development (OECD), *Geographical Distribution of Financial Flows to Developing Countries* (various issues), Paris, 1981–2000. For more details of my statistical analysis of ODA flow to China between 1979 and 1998, see Chapter 5.

4 Grant Element (GE) is an index of financial terms of assistance. The grant element of a loan on a commercial basis (e.g. 10 per cent interest rate) is 0 per cent, and as the terms (interest rate, grace period, maturity) are more alleviated, the figure of the GE rises, reaching 100 per cent in the case of an outright grant. Rutherford M. Poats, *Twenty-five Years of Development Cooperation: A Review*, Paris: OECD, 1986, p. 17.

5 Development Assistance Committee, OECD, *Recommendation on Financial Terms and Conditions*, 1969, cited in David Arase, *Buying Power: The Political Economy of Japan's Foreign Aid*, London: Lynne Rienner Publishers, 1995, p. 9.

6 Hans Morgenthau, 'A Political Theory of Foreign Aid', *American Political Science Review*, vol. 56, no. 2, 1962, pp. 301–9.

7 Peter J. Schrader, Steven W. Hook and Bruce Taylor, 'Clarifying the Foreign Aid Puzzle: A Comparison of American, Japanese, French, and Swedish Aid Flows', *World Politics*, vol. 50, no. 2, January 1998, p. 319.

8 David Wright-Neville, *The Evolution of Japanese Foreign Aid 1955–1990*, Monograph No. 2, Melbourne: Monash Development Studies Centre, 1991, p. 37, drawing on Kweku Ampiah, 'A One Sided Partnership', *West Africa*, November 28–December 4, 1988, p. 2222; Nakane Chie, *Tekiō no jōken: Nihonteki renzoku no shikō (Conditions of Adaptation: Japanese Thought)*, Tokyo: Kōdansha, 1972, pp. 159–62.

9 Schrader, Hook and Taylor, 'Clarifying the Foreign Aid Puzzle', p. 301.

10 Duncan L. Clarke, 'US Security Assistance to Egypt and Israel: Politically Untouchable?', *Middle East Journal*, vol. 51, no. 2, Spring 1997, p. 201; Inada Jūichi, 'Nihon gaikō ni okeru enjo mondai no shosokumen (Several Aspects of Foreign Aid Issues in Japanese Diplomacy)', *Kokusai mondai*, no. 326, May 1987, p. 6.

11 Wendy Levy, 'Major Returns to Local Firms in Aid to China', *Insight: Australian Foreign Affairs and Trade Issues*, vol. 2, no. 11, July 1993, p. 13.

12 Yasuyuki Sawada and Hiroyuki Yamada, 'Japan's ODA and Poverty Reduction: A Cross-Donore Comparison and a Case Study of Malaysia', in Hirohisa Kohama (ed.) *External Factors for Asian Development*, Singapore: Institute of Southeast Asian Studies, 2003, pp. 47–69.

13 Schrader, Hook and Taylor, 'Clarifying the Foreign Aid Puzzle', p. 320. Some scholarly works that criticise Japan's ODA projects in a variety of recipient countries from a humanitarian perspective are: Murai Yoshinori, *Musekinin enjo taikoku Nihon* (Japan as an Irresponsible Foreign Aid Power), Tokyo: JICC shuppan-kyoku, 1989; 'Gaimushō no ODA rinen o tou? (Question the ODA Philosophy of the Ministry of Foreign Affairs?)' *Sekai*, no. 569, June 1992, pp. 315–24; also Sumi Kazuo, *ODA enjo no genjitsu* (Reality of ODA), Tokyo: Iwanami shinsho, 1989.

14 Arase. *Buying Power*, p. 14.

15 One scholarly work that does focus on Japan's ODA to China is Greg Story, 'Japan's Official Development Assistance to China: A Survey', Australia–Japan Research Centre: Australian National University, Pacific Economic Paper No. 150, 1987. However, as a relatively short working paper, it is restricted to a broad investigation of certain aspects of Japanese aid to China. Moreover, as it was published in 1987, it does not cover Japanese aid to China in the 1990s and the 2000s.

16 One such official report is: Kokusai kyōryoku ginkō, 'Chūgoku enshakkan no gaiyō (Summary of Japanese Yen Loans to China)', Tokyo, June 2001.

17 Interview with Kokubun Ryōsei, specialist on Chinese politics, professor and director of the Centre for Area Studies at Keiō University, Tokyo, 15 March 2001.

18 Allen S. Whiting, *China Eyes Japan*, Berkeley, CA: University of California Press, 1989, p. 123.

19 Interview with A, a senior official of the Liberal Democratic Party, Tokyo, 27 March 2001. This view is supported by Hashimoto Kōhei, 'Nihon no enjo seisaku kettei yōin (Determinants of Japan's Foreign Aid Policy)', in Hashimoto Kōhei (ed.) *Nihon no gaikō seisaku kettei yōin* (Domestic Determinants of Japanese Foreign Policy), Tokyo: PHP kenkyūjo, 1999, p. 350.

20 This view is expressed in the work of Whiting. For more detail, see *China Eyes Japan*, pp. 123, 213.

21 Robert M. Orr, Jr, *The Emergence of Japan's Foreign Aid Power*, New York: Columbia University Press, 1990, p. 73.

22 William J. Long, 'Nonproliferation as a Goal of Japanese Foreign Assistance Policy', *Asian Survey*, vol. 39, no. 2, 1999, pp. 328–47.

23 Gaimushō keizai kyōryoku kyoku (Economic Cooperation Bureau, Ministry of Foreign Affairs), *Wagakuni no seifu kaihatsu enjo* (Japan's ODA) *2000*, Tokyo, 2000, p. 155.

24 The three different types of ODA are discussed in detail in Chapter 5.

25 Zaidan hōjin kazankai (Kazankai Foundation) (ed.) *Chūgoku sōran 1998* (Biennial Comprehensive Analysis of China 1998), Tokyo: Zaidan hōjin kazankai, 1998, p. 385.

26 Ibid., pp. 11–12.

27 Gaimushō, '21seiki ni muketa tai-Chū keizai kyōryoku no arikata ni kansuru kondankai: Teigen (Policy Recommendation Report by the Committee on Japanese Economic Assistance to China for the 21st Century)', unpublished report, December 2000, p. 21.

28 Inada Jūichi, 'Tai-Chū ODA no keizaiteki shakaiteki hyōka ni tsuite (An Economic and Social Assessment of China ODA)', in Nihon kokusai mondai kenkyūjo (ed.) *Tai-Chū ODA no keizaiteki shakaiteki inpakuto ni tsuite no kisoteki chōsa* (Basic Research on the Economic and Social Impact of China ODA), unpublished report, Tokyo, 2000, p. 4.

29 The most prominent proponent of this view is Margee M. Ensign. See *Doing Good or Doing Well? Japan's Foreign Aid Program*, New York: Columbia University Press, 1992; also Neville, *The Evolution of Japanese Foreign Aid*.

30 Neville, *The Evolution of Japanese Foreign Aid*, p. 38.

31 When a recipient country is obliged to purchase goods and services associated with ODA projects from companies based in the donor country, it is called 'tied' ODA. If the ODA is free from any such condition, it is called 'untied' ODA. For more details, see Nishigaki Akira and Shimomura Yasutami, *The Economics of Development Assistance: Japan's ODA in a Symbiotic World*, Tokyo: LTCB International Library Foundation, 1999, pp. 98–9.

32 The 'neo-imperialism' argument articulated by Jon Halliday and Gavan McCormack is an extreme version of this view. Halliday and McCormack criticise Japanese reparations and aid provision to Southeast Asian countries in the 1950s and 1960s as an economic version of earlier Japanese imperialism. See *Japanese Imperialism Today: Co-Prosperity in Greater East Asia*, New York, London: Monthly Review Press, 1973, pp. 17–31.

33 William L. Brooks and Robert M. Orr, Jr, 'Japan's Foreign Economic Cooperation', *Asian Survey*, vol. 25, no. 3, March 1985, p. 339.

34 Kent E. Calder, 'Japanese Foreign Economic Policy Formation: Explaining the Reactive State', *World Politics*, vol. 40, no. 4, July 1988, pp. 517–41. For an archival document indicating the intention to forestall Communist revolution in Asia, see Gaimushō, 'Chūgoku mondai (China Issue)', Gaikō shiryō-kan (Diplomatic Record Office), Tokyo, Microfilm No: A'-0356, 1955.

35 Arase, *Buying Power*, p. 245.

36 Ibid., p. 4.

37 The most prominent proponent of this structural realism theory is Kenneth N. Waltz. See *Theory of International Politics*, Reading, MA: Addison-Wesley Pub. Co., 1979; 'Structural Realism after the Cold War', *International Security*, vol. 25, no. 1, Summer 2000, pp. 5–41.

38 Eric Heginbotham and Richard J. Samuels, 'Mercantile Realism and Japanese Foreign Policy', *International Security*, vol. 22, no. 4, Spring 1998, p. 172.

39 Ibid.

40 Ibid., p. 184.

41 Ibid., p. 172.

42 Ibid.

43 Ibid., p. 203.

44 Ibid., p. 194.

45 Paul M. Kennedy, *The Rise and Fall of the Great Powers*, New York: Random House, 1987, pp. 324, 332.

46 Heginbotham and Samuels, 'Mercantile Realism and Japanese Foreign Policy', p. 173.

47 Ibid., p. 202.

48 Henrik Schmiegelow and Michèle Schmiegelow, 'How Japan Affects the International System', *International Organisation*, vol. 44, no. 4, Autumn 1990, pp. 579–80.

49 For example, Calder, 'Japanese Foreign Economic Policy Formation'; Orr, *The Emergence of Japan's Foreign Aid Power*, pp. 103–36; Michael Blacker, 'Evaluating Japan's Diplomatic Performance', in Gerald L. Curtis (ed.) *Japan's Foreign Policy after the Cold War: Coping with Change*, 1993, pp. 1–42; also see Glenn D. Hook, Julie Gilson, Christopher W. Hughes and Hugo Dobson, *Japan's International Relations: Politics, Economics and Security*, London and New York: Routledge, 2001, pp. 69–71.

50 Calder, 'Japanese Foreign Economic Policy Formation', pp. 518, 519, 523.

51 Orr, *The Emergence of Japan's Foreign Aid Power*, p. 107.

52 Paul A. Summerville, 'The Politics of Self-Restraint: The Japanese State, and the Voluntary Export Restraint of Japanese Passenger Car Exports to the United States in 1981', unpublished PhD thesis, University of Tokyo, 1988, cited in Orr, *The Emergence of Japan's Foreign Aid Power*, p. 108.

53 Akitoshi Miyashita, '*Gaiatsu* and Japan's Foreign Aid: Rethinking the Reactive-Proactive Debate', *International Studies Quarterly*, vol. 43, no. 4, 1999, p. 695. Emphasis in original.

54 Yanai Shinichi, 'Chūgoku to no keizai kyōryoku ni tsuite (Japanese Economic Cooperation with China)', record of public lecture given by the then Director of the Economic Cooperation Bureau of the Ministry of Foreign Affairs, *Tōa*, no. 159, September 1980, pp. 79–81. West European countries also expressed a similar concern at that time. See *Asahi shinbun*, 7 December 1979.

55 Gaimushō keizai kyōryoku kyoku, *Wagakuni no seifu kaihatsu enjo 1999* (Japan's ODA 1999), Tokyo, 1999, p. 118. For a detailed treatment of this sanction, see Chapter 6.

56 Saori N. Katada, 'Why Did Japan Suspend Foreign Aid to China? Japan's Foreign Aid Decision-making and Source of Aid Sanction', *Social Science Japan Journal*, vol. 4, no. 1, 2001, p. 56.

57 Interview with F, a senior official of the Japanese Ministry of Foreign Affairs, Tokyo, 20 April 2000.

58 Dennis T. Yasutomo, *The Manner of Giving: Strategic Aid and Japanese Foreign Policy*, Lexington, MA and Toronto: Lexington Books, 1986, p. 9.

59 Dennis T. Yasutomo, *The New Multilateralism in Japan's Foreign Policy*, New York: St Martin's Press, 1995, pp. 36–48.

60 Akiko Fukushima, *Japanese Foreign Policy: the Emerging Logic of Multilateralism*, New York: Macmillan Press, 1999, pp. 108–11.

61 Ōhira sōri no seisaku kenkyū kai, Sōgō anzen hoshō kenkyū gurūpu, *Sōgō anzen hoshō kenkyū gurūpu hōkokusho* (Report of the Study Group on Comprehensive Security), Tokyo: Naikaku kanbō, July 1980, cited in Arase, *Buying Power*, p. 227.

62 Gaimushō keizai kyōryoku kyoku, *Keizai kyōryoku no rinen: Seifu kaihatsu enjo wa naze okonau no ka* (The Concept of Economic Cooperation: Why Implement Official Development Assistance?), Tokyo, 1981, p. 75. For more detailed discussion of the linkage between ODA and Japan's comprehensive security, see J.W.M. Chapman, R. Drifte and I.T.M. Gow, *Japan's Quest for Comprehensive Security: Defence–Diplomacy–Dependence*, New York: St Martin's Press, 1982, p. 95; also Akiko Fukushima, 'Official Development Assistance (ODA) as a Japanese Foreign Policy Tool', in Inoguchi Takashi and Purnendra Jain (eds) *Japanese Foreign Policy Today*, New York: Palgrave, 2000, p. 162.

63 Graham T. Allison, *Essence of Decision: Explaining the Cuban Missile Crisis*. Boston, MA: Little, Brown Company, 1971, pp. 10–36, 145–7; Graham T. Allison and Morton H. Halperin, 'Bureaucratic Politics: A Paradigm and Some Policy Implications', *World Politics*, vol. 24, Spring 1972, pp. 40–79.

64 Alan Rix, *Japan's Economic Aid: Policymaking and Politics*, London: Croom Helm, 1980; Orr, *The Emergence of Japan's Foreign Aid Power*.

65 Rix, *Japan's Economic Aid*, pp. 12, 118–19, 267.

66 Orr, *The Emergence of Japan's Foreign Aid Power*, p. 3.

67 The term 'four-ministry system (*yon shōchō taisei*)' was first used by Higashi Sadao. See *Seifu kaihatsu enjo* (Official Development Assistance), Tokyo: Keiō shobō shuppan, 1986.

68 Orr, *The Emergence of Japan's Foreign Aid Power*, pp. 1–18, 137–46.

69 Arase, *Buying Power*, p. 256.

70 Ibid., p. 2.

71 Ibid., p. 256. See also p. 233.

72 Ibid., p. 7.

73 Max Millikan and W.W. Rostow, 'A Proposal: Key to an Effective Foreign Policy', in US Senate, Special Committee to Study the Foreign Aid Program, *Compilation of Studies and Surveys*, Washington, DC: GPO, 1957, cited in Arase, *Buying Power*, p. 11.

74 Arase, *Buying Power*, p. 7.

75 See Reinhard Drifte, 'Japanese–Chinese Security Relations: The Japanese Way of Engagement', *Social Science Japan*, no. 21, September 2001, p. 26.

76 Ibid., p. 30. For details of the debate on engagement and containment of China, see Robert S. Ross, 'Beijing as a Conservative Power', *Foreign Affairs*, vol. 76, no. 2, March–April 1997, pp. 33–44; David Shambaugh, 'Containment or Engagement of China? Calculating Beijing's Response', *International Security*, vol. 21, no. 2, Fall 1996, pp. 180–209.

77 Sandra Wilson, *The Manchurian Crisis and Japanese Society, 1931–33*, London and New York: Routledge, 2002, p. 61.

78 Japanese official diplomatic documents are usually closed to the public until at least thirty years after the documents were initially issued. This is the reason that the archival documents used in this book were produced before the end of the 1960s.

79 Interview with Inada Jūichi, a political economist specialising on Japanese ODA policy at Senshū University and also a senior research fellow at the Japan Institute of International Affairs, Tokyo, 28 March 2001.

80 Marijke Breuning, 'Words and Deeds: Foreign Assistance Rhetoric and Policy Behaviour in the Netherlands, Belgium, and the United Kingdom', *International Studies Quarterly*, vol. 39, no. 2, June 1995, pp. 235–54.

81 For example, in 2001, the ODA budget ¥729 billion accounted for about 70 per cent of the total annual budget of the Ministry of Foreign Affairs. See *Asahi shinbun*, 29 August 2001.

2 Japan's pursuit of economic and political engagement with China, 1945–78

1 Paul J. Bailey, *Postwar Japan, 1945 to the Present*, Oxford: Blackwell Publishers, 1996, pp. 29–39, 41–52, 154–8; W.G. Beasley, *The Rise of Modern Japan*, London: Weidenfeld and Nicolson, Third Edition, 2000, pp. 213–26.

2 Michael Schaller, *The American Occupation of Japan: The Origins of the Cold War in Asia*, New York, Oxford: Oxford University Press, 1985, pp. 122–40.

3 See Gaimushō (Ministry of Foreign Affairs, Japan), 'Statement by General Frank R. McCoy, United States Representative on the Far Eastern Commission, Concerning Japanese Reparations and Level of Industry', Gaikō shiryō-kan (Diplomatic Record Office), Microfilm No: B'-0003 (12 May 1949).

4 Watanabe Akio, *Sengo Nihon no taigai seisaku: Kokusai kankei no henyō to Nihon no yakuwari* (Foreign Policy of Postwar Japan: Changes in International Relations and the Role of Japan), Tokyo: Yūhikaku-sensho, 1985, p. 24.

5 Gaimushō, 'Ashida shokan (The Ashida Memorandum)', handed from Japanese Foreign Minister Ashida Hitoshi to SCAP, Gaikō shiryō-kan, Microfilm No: B'0008 (13 September 1947); J.A.A. Stockwin, *The Japanese Socialist Party and Neutralism: A Study of a Political Party and Its Foreign Policy*, London, New York: Melbourne University Press, 1968, pp. 2–12.

6 Kazan-kai, 'Beikoku no Ajia senryaku to Nitchū jōyaku (US Asia Policy and the Japan-China Treaty)', *Tōa*, no. 137, November 1978, p. 43.

7 Hosoya Chihiro, 'Nichi-Bei-Chū sankyoku kankei no rekishi-teki kōzō (History of Japan–US–China Triangular Relations)', *Kokusai mondai*, no. 254, 1981, p. 3; see also Walter LaFeber, *The Clash: US–Japanese Relations throughout History*, New York, London: W.W. Norton & Company, 1997, p. 231.

8 Gaimushō, 'Chūkyō shōnin ni kansuru Hatoyama sōri genmei hōdō ni kansuru ken (Matters Concerning Prime Minister Hatoyama's Statement about Japan's Recognition of Communist China)', Gaikō shiryō-kan, Microfilm No: A'-0356 (21 February 1955).

9 Townsend Hoopes, *The Devil and John Foster Dulles*, London: Andre Deutsch, 1974, p. 107.

10 Hosoya, 'Nichi-Bei-Chū sankyoku kankei', p. 3; Schaller, *The American Occupation of Japan*, pp. 164–5, 189–90.

11 George P. Jan, 'Japan's Trade with Communist China', *Asian Survey*, vol. 9, no. 12, December 1969, pp. 902–3.

12 Ibid., p. 903.

13 Hosoya, 'Nichi-Bei-Chū sankyoku kankei', p. 6.

14 Jan, 'Japan's Trade with Communist China', p. 903.

15 Ibid.

16 Tanaka Akihiko, *Nitchū kankei 1945–1990 (Japan–China Relations 1945–1990)*, Tokyo: Tōkyō daigaku shuppan-kai, 1991, p. 45.

17 Gaimushō, 'Tōmen no tai-Chūkyō seisaku: niji-an (Immediate Policy towards Communist China: Second Draft)', Gaikō shiryō-kan, Microfilm No: A'-0356 (12 September 1955).

18 Ibid.

19 Jan, 'Japan's Trade with Communist China', p. 904.

20 Ibid.

21 Gaimushō, 'Tōmen no tai-Chūkyō seisaku: niji-an'.

22 Watanabe, *Sengo Nihon no taigai seisaku*, pp. 26–8.

23 Ibid., p. 47.

24 Gaimushō, 'Tōmen no tai-Chūkyō seisaku: niji-an'.

25 John Dower, *Empire and Aftermath: Yoshida Shigeru and the Japanese Experience, 1878–1954*, Cambridge, MA: Harvard University Press, 1988, pp. 485–8.

26 Quoted in Wolf Mendl, *Japan's Asia Policy: Regional Security and Global Interests*, London and New York: Routledge, 1995, p. 79.

27 Chen Zhaobin, 'Sengo Nihon no Chūgoku seisaku no genkei: 1950 nendai ni okeru "futatsu no Chūgoku" to "seikei-bunri"(The Origins of Japan's Postwar China Policy: the "Two China Policy" and the "Separation of Politics and Economy" during the 1950s)', *Shisō*, no. 887 May 1998, p. 28.

28 Dower, *Empire and Aftermath*, pp. 403–4; Okada Akira, 'Wagakuni no Chūgoku gaikō uramenshi (A Secret History of Japan's China Diplomacy)', *Tōa*, no. 368, February 1988, p. 88.

29 Tanaka, *Nitchū kankei*, pp. 35–8.

30 From Sebald to Secretary, No. 1167, Nov. 30, 1951, Box 3004, US National Archives, Washington, DC, cited in Chen, 'Sengo Nihon no Chūgoku seisaku', p. 30.

31 George P. Jan, 'The Japanese People and Japanese Policy toward Communist China', *Western Political Quarterly*, vol. 22, no. 3, September 1969, p. 607.

32 Gaimushō, 'Chūgoku mondai ni taisuru Yoshida sōri yori Daresu komon ate shokan (Memorandum from Prime Minister Yoshida to Dulles Regarding the China Issue)', Gaikō shiryō-kan, Microfilm No: A'-0009, handed from Iguchi, Vice-Minister of the Japanese Foreign Ministry, to Sebald, the US Ambassador to Japan (on 22 December 1951).

33 The Memorandum and the draft of the Memorandum (which has the same text but no date, address or signature) can be examined in the Gaikō shiryō-kan (Diplomatic Record Office) in Tokyo. See 'Chūgoku mondai ni taisuru Yoshida sōri yori Daresu komon ate shokan', pp. 70–2. For the Draft of the Memorandum see pp. 64–8 of the same document.

34 For more details, see Hoopes, *The Devil and John Foster Dulles*, p. 112; Okada, 'Wagakuni no Chūgoku gaikō uramenshi', p. 88; and Tanaka, *Nitchū kankei*, pp. 35–8.

35 Gaimushō, 'Chūgoku mondai'.

36 Gaimushō, 'Chūgoku mondai ni taisuru Yoshida sōri yori Daresu komon ate shokan'.

37 Tanaka, *Nitchū kankei*, pp. 46–7.

38 Hatano Sumio, 'Nitchū keizai kankei no tenkai (The Development of Japan–China Economic Relations)', in Masuda Hiroshi and Hatano Sumio (eds) *Ajia no naka no*

Nihon to Chūgoku: yūkō to masatsu no gendaishi (Japan and China in Asia: Recent History of Friendship and Confrontation), Tokyo: Yamakawa Shuppan-sha, 1995, pp. 249–50.

39 LaFeber, *The Clash*, p. 100.

40 Hatano, 'Nitchū keizai kankei no tenkai', p. 250.

41 Okada Akira, *Mizudori gaikō hiwa* (Secret Stories of the Waterfowl Diplomacy), Tokyo: Chūō kōronsha, 1983, p. 63.

42 Gaimushō, 'Nihon Chūkyō kankei zakken: Shōwa 35–40 nen (Documents Concerning Japan–Communist China Relations: 1960–65)', Gaikō shiryō-kan, Microfilm No: A'-0356 (undated).

43 Gaimushō, 'Chūgoku mondai kentō kai (Review Committee on the China Issue)', Gaikō shiryō-kan, Microfilm No: A'-0356 (31 August 1956).

44 For details of Kishi's bureaucratic and political career, see Kishi Nobusuke, Yatsugi Kazuo and Itō Takashi, *Kishi Nobusuke no kaisō* (The Memoirs of Kishi Nobusuke), Tokyo: Bungei shunjū, 1981.

45 Maurice Meisner, 'MAO Zedong', in Joel Krieger (ed.) *The Oxford Companion to Politics of the World*, New York, Oxford: Oxford University Press, 1993, p. 563.

46 Funabashi Yōichi, *Naibu: aru Chūgoku hōkoku* (*Inside: A China Report*), Tokyo: Asahi shinbun-sha, 1983, p. 33.

47 Hatano, 'Nitchū keizai kankei no tenkai', p. 250.

48 Chen, 'Sengo Nihon no Chūgoku seisaku', pp. 39–40.

49 George R. Packard III, *Protest in Tokyo: The Security Treaty Crisis of 1960*, Princeton, NJ: Princeton University Press, 1966, pp. 153–81.

50 Okada, *Mizudori gaikō hiwa*, p. 68.

51 Gaimushō, 'Tai Chūkyō shochi yōkō (Outline of Japan's Communist China Policy)', Gaikō shiryō-kan, Microfilm No: A'-0356 (10 October 1958).

52 Soeya Yoshihide, *Nihon gaikō to Chūgoku, 1945–1972* (Japanese Diplomacy and China, 1945–1972), Tokyo: Keiō daigaku shuppan-kai, 1995, p. 87.

53 Ibid.

54 Sadako Ogata, 'The Business Community and Japanese Foreign Policy: Normalisation of Relations with the People's Republic of China', in Robert A. Scalapino (ed.) *The Foreign Policy of Modern Japan*, Berkeley, CA: University of California Press, 1977, p. 180.

55 Ibid.

56 For more details about the informal channel between the CCP and the JCP in the 1960s, see Kōan chōsa-chō (Public Security Investigation Agency), *Nihon no naka no Chūkyo* (*Communist China in Japan*), 1967, p. 18, cited in Chae-Jin Lee, *Japan Faces China: Political and Economic Relations in the Postwar Era*, Baltimore, MD: The Johns Hopkins University Press, 1976, p. 233; *Asahi shinbun*, 14 June 1998; and Peter Berton, 'The Japanese Communist Party and Its Transformations', Working Paper No. 67, Japan Policy Research Institute, California, May 2000.

57 Gaimushō, 'Tōmen no tai-Chūkyō seisaku: niji-an'.

58 For more details of the political impact of the Sino-Soviet Alliance on Japan, see C.W. Braddick, *Japan and the Sino-Soviet Alliance 1950–1964: in the Shadow of the Monolith*, Houndmills, Basingstoke, Hampsher: Palgrave/Macmillan, 2004.

59 Gaimushō, 'Chū-So dōmei jōyaku no kaisetsu (Interpretations of the Sino-Soviet Treaty of Friendship and Alliance)', Gaikō shiryō-kan, Microfilm No: B'-0008 (14 February 1950).

60 Gaimushō, 'Chūkyō no genjō to sono taigai seisaku (The Current Situation in Communist China and Its Foreign Policy)', Gaikō shiryō-kan, Microfilm No: A'-0356 (26 May 1959).

61 Gaimushō, 'Wagakuni no tai-Chūgoku seisaku: chōki kihon seisaku (Japan's China Policy: Basic Long-Term Policy)', Gaikō shiryō-kan, Microfilm No: A'-0356 (14 July 1959).

62 Ogata, 'The Business Community and Japanese Foreign Policy', p. 181.
63 Ishii Akira, 'Chū-So kankei no 40-nen: byōdō na nikoku kankei o motomete (40 Years of Sino-Soviet Relations: In Search of an Equal Relationship)', *Kokusai mondai*, no. 354, September 1989, p. 12, 15.
64 Ibid., pp. 8–9.
65 Gaimushō, 'Chūkyō no genjō to sono taigai seisaku'.
66 Gaimushō, 'Tai Chūkyō shochi yōkō'.
67 Ogata, 'The Business Community and Japanese Foreign Policy', p. 181.
68 See Packard, *Protest in Tokyo*, pp. 300–2.
69 Tagawa Seiichi, *Nitchū kōshō hiroku: Tagawa nikki 14-nen no shōgen* (Secret Record of Japan–China Negotiations: 14 Years of Testimonies from the Tagawa Diary), Tokyo: Mainichi shinbun-sha, 1973, pp. 32–51.
70 Yoshihide Soeya, *Japan's Economic Diplomacy With China, 1945–1978*, Oxford: Clarendon Press, 1998, p. 62.
71 For more details about his role in re-establishing Sino-Japanese trade, see Tagawa Seiichi, *Matsumura Kenzō to Chūgoku* (Matsumura Kenzō and China), Tokyo: Yomiuri shinbun-sha, 1972.
72 Tanaka, *Nitchū kankei*, p. 55.
73 Soeya, *Japan's Economic Diplomacy*, pp. 79–105.
74 Tagawa, *Nitchū kōshō hiroku*, p. 33; Soeya, *Japan's Economic Diplomacy*, pp. 79–105.
75 Soeya, *Japan's Economic Diplomacy*, p. 46.
76 Michael Schaller, 'Altered States: The United States and Japan During the 1960s', in Diane B. Kunz (ed.) *The Diplomacy of the Cultural Decade: American Foreign Relations during the 1960s*, New York, 1994, cited in LaFeber, *The Clash*, p. 339.
77 Braddick, *Japan and the Sino-Soviet Alliance*, pp. 105–41.
78 Jan, 'Japan's Trade with Communist China', pp. 913, 918.
79 Soeya, *Japan's Economic Diplomacy*, pp. 62–3.
80 Tanaka, *Nitchū kankei*, p. 56.
81 Ibid., pp. 57–8.
82 William A. Joseph, 'Cultural Revolution', in Joel Krieger, William A. Joseph and James A. Paul (eds) *The Oxford Companion to Politics of the World*, New York and London: Oxford University Press, 1993, pp. 211–12.
83 *People's Daily*, 4 June 1967, cited in Tanaka, *Nitchū kankei*, p. 60.
84 Soeya, *Nihon gaikō to Chūgoku*, pp. 116–20.
85 Tagawa, *Nitchū kōshō hiroku*, p. 71.
86 For details of actual MT Trade negotiations held during this period, see Tagawa, *Nitchū kōshō hiroku*, pp. 144–60.
87 *Japan Times*, 29 August 1967; 'Konransuru Nitchū bōeki shōsha no uchimaku (An Inside Story of Japan–China Trade Firms in Disarray)', *Tōkyō keizai*, no. 3366, 1967, p. 55, cited in Soeya, *Japan's Economic Diplomacy*, p. 77.
88 Jan, 'Japan's Trade with Communist China', p. 918.
89 See, for example, Gaimushō, 'Tōmen no tai-Chūkyō seisaku: niji-an'.
90 Ibid.
91 Asahi shinbun-sha, *Shiryō: Nihon to Chūgoku '45–'71* (Documents: Japan and China '45–'71), Tokyo, 1972, p. 44.
92 Ibid., pp. 67–8.
93 Richard Nixon, *The Memoirs of Richard Nixon*, South Melbourne: Macmillan Company of Australia, 1978, p. 554.
94 Soeya Yoshihide, '1970-nendai no Bei-Chū kankei to Nihon gaikō (US–China Relations and Japanese Diplomacy in the 1970s)', in Nihon seiji gakkai (ed.), *Kiki no Nihon gaikō 70-nendai (Japanese Foreign Policy during the Crisis of the 1970s)*, Tokyo: Iwanami shoten, 1997, pp. 4–5.
95 See Nixon, *The Memoirs of Richard Nixon*, p. 555; Henry Kissinger, *White House Years*, London: Weidenfeld and Nicolson and Michael Joseph, 1979, p. 762.

96 Satō Eisaku. *Satō Eisaku nikki: dai yon-kan* (The Diary of Satō Eisaku: Volume Four), Tokyo: Asahi shinbun-sha, 1997. pp. 376–7.

97 Kissinger, *White House Years*, p. 772.

98 Okada, *Mizudori gaikō hiwa*, pp. 145–50; also Satō Eisaku, *Satō Eisaku nikki: dai go-kan* (The Diary of Satō Eisaku: Volume Five), Tokyo: Asahi shinbun-sha, 1997, pp. 42, 206.

99 Tanaka, *Nitchū kankei 1945–1990*, p. 73.

100 While he was in the prime minister's office, Satō frequently dispatched this person secretly to China to contact senior PRC leaders. See, for example, Satō, *Satō Eisaku nikki: dai yon-kan*, pp. 413, 419, 426, 455, 464, 474; also Satō, *Satō Eisaku nikki: dai go-kan*, pp. 27, 41, 78, 107, 112, 176, 273, 299, 337, 403, 435, 455, 461.

101 Kōji Nakamura, 'Twice a Loser', *Far Eastern Economic Review*, no. 47, 20 November 1971, p. 1, cited in Gene T. Hsiao, 'The Sino-Japanese Rapprochement: A Relationship of Ambivalence', *China Quarterly*, no. 57, January/March 1974, p. 107.

102 Okada, *Mizudori gaikō hiwa*, p. 164.

103 For details of the Foreign Ministry's assessment of the issue of China's UN membership, see Kissinger, *White House Years*, p. 772.

104 Nixon, *The Memoirs of Richard Nixon*, p. 555.

105 Soeya, *Nihon gaikō to Chūgoku*, p. 17.

106 Tanaka, *Nitchū kankei*, p. 72.

107 Sadako Ogata, *Normalisation with China: A Comparative Study of the US and Japanese Process*, Berkeley, CA: Institute of East Asian Studies, University of California, 1988, p. 37.

108 For more details of this election, see Haruhiro Fukui, 'Tanaka Goes to Peking: A Case Study in Foreign Policymaking', in T.J. Pempel (ed.) *Policymaking in Contemporary Japan*, Ithaca, NY and London: Cornell University Press, 1977, p. 72.

109 For further details of Chinese leaders' perspective on post-Satō Japanese politics, see Tagawa, *Nitchū kōshō hiroku*, pp. 310–30.

110 Ogata Sadako, 'Tai-Chū kokkō seijōka no Nichi-Bei hikaku (Normalisation with China: A Comparative Study of the US and Japanese Process)', *Kokusai mondai*, May 1981, no. 256, p. 68.

111 Tagawa, *Nitchū kōshō hiroku*, p. 343.

112 Betshi Yukio, 'Nitchū kokkō seijōka no seiji katei (The Political Process of Japan–China Diplomatic Normalisation)', *Kokusai seiji*, August 1980, p. 4.

113 Tagawa, *Nitchū kōshō hiroku*, p. 338.

114 Ibid., pp. 337, 343.

115 Besthi, 'Nitchū kokkō seijōka', p. 7.

116 Nixon, *The Memoirs of Richard Nixon*, p. 567; Kissinger, *White House Years*, p. 1089.

117 On the roles played by opposition party leaders, the business community, the bureaucracy, and public opinion in the process of normalisation, see Fukui, 'Tanaka Goes to Peking', pp. 72–98.

118 Yung H. Park, 'The "Anti-Hegemony" Controversy in Sino-Japanese Relations', *Pacific Affairs*, vol. 49, no. 3, Fall 1976, p. 486.

119 Soeya, *Japan's Economic Diplomacy with China*, p. 143.

120 John King Fairbank, *China: A New History*, Cambridge, MA and London: The Belknap Press of Harvard University Press, Third Printing, 1994, pp. 383–405. For the recollections of a Japanese engineer stationed in Wuhan city during the period of ascendancy of the Gang of Four, see Asakawa Hideji, 'Tai-Chū tekkō gijutsu kyōryoku ni tsuite (Regarding Japan's Steel Plant Technology Assistance to China)', *Tōa*, no. 175, January 1982, p. 69.

121 Chae-Jin Lee, 'The Making of the Sino-Japanese Peace and Friendship Treaty', *Pacific Affairs*, vol. 52, no. 3, Fall 1979, p. 422.

122 Park, 'The "Anti-hegemony" Controversy', p. 486.

123 Ibid., pp. 483–8.

124 For more details, see Li Kwok-sing, *A Glossary of Political Terms of the People's Republic of China*, Hong Kong: Chinese University Press, 1995, pp. 423–42; Fairbank, *China: A New History*, pp. 406–17.
125 Susumu Yabuki, *China's New Political Economy: The Giant Awakes*, Boulder, CO, San Francisco and Oxford: Westview Press, 1995, p. 167.
126 Okabe Tatsumi, 'Tenanmon jiken to kongo no Chūgoku (The Tiananmen Square Incident and China Hereafter)', *Kokusai mondai*, no. 358, January 1990, p. 14.
127 Yoichi Yokoi, 'Plant and Technology Contracts and the Changing Pattern of Economic Interdependence Between China and Japan', in Christopher Howe (ed.) *China and Japan: History, Trends, and Prospects*, Oxford: Clarendon Press, 1996, p. 136; see also Tanaka, *Nitchū kankei*, p. 108.
128 Kokubun Ryōsei, 'Chūgoku no taigai keizai seisaku kettei no seiji kōzō: puranto keiyaku chūdan kettei no baai (The Political Structure of Chinese Foreign Economic Policy-making: Decision-making for Plant Contract Cancellation)', in Okabe Tatsumi (ed.) *Chūgoku gaikō seisaku kettei no kōzō* (The Structure of Chinese Diplomatic Policymaking), Tokyo: Nihon kokusai mondai kenkyū-jo, 1983, p. 174.
129 Ibid.

3 Policy objectives and underlying interests since 1979

1 Interview with Inada Jūichi, a political economist at Senshū University and a senior research fellow at the Japan Institute of International Affairs, Tokyo, 28 March 2001. See also Allen S. Whiting, *China Eyes Japan*, Berkeley, CA: University of California Press, 1989, pp. 123, 213.
2 Interview with I, a senior official of the Japan Bank for International Cooperation, Tokyo, 4 April 2001; Hidenori Ijiri, 'Sino-Japanese Controversy since the 1972 Diplomatic Normalisation', in Christopher Howe (ed.) *China and Japan: History, Trends, and Prospects*, Oxford: Clarendon Press, 1996, pp. 73–4; Zaidan hōjin kazankai (Kazankai Foundation) (ed.) *Chūgoku sōran 1998* (Biennial Comprehensive Analysis at China 1998), Tokyo: Zaidan hōjin kazankai, 1998, p. 136.
3 Interview with I; also interview with C, D and E, three officials of the Japanese Ministry of Foreign Affairs, Tokyo, 26 March 2001.
4 Hashimoto Kōhei, 'Nihon no enjo seisaku kettei yōin (Determinants of Japan's Foreign Aid Policy)', in Hashimoto Kōhei (ed.) *Nihon no gaikō seisaku kettei yōin* (Domestic Determinants of Japanese Foreign Policy), Tokyo: PHP kenkyūjo, 1999, p. 350.
5 Interview with A, a senior official of the Liberal Democratic Party, Tokyo, 27 March 2001.
6 Asakawa Hideji, 'Tai-Chū tekkō gijutsu kyōryoku ni tsuite (Regarding Japan's Steel Plant Technology Assistance to China)', *Tōa*, no. 175, January 1982, p. 71.
7 Kokubun Ryōsei, 'Chūgoku no taigai keizai seisaku kettei no seiji kōzō: puranto keiyaku chūdan kettei no baai (The Political Structure of Chinese Foreign Economic Policy-Making: Decision-making for Plant Contract Cancellation)', in Okabe Tatsumi (ed.) *Chūgoku gaikō seisaku kettei no kōzō* (The Structure of Chinese Diplomatic Policymaking), Tokyo: Nihon kokusai mondai kenkyū-jo, 1983, p. 180.
8 Whiting, *China Eyes Japan*, p. 96.
9 Kojima Sueo, 'Shin-dankai ni haitta Nitchū keizai kankei (A New Stage of Japan–China Economic Relations)', *Tōa*, no. 197, November 1983, p. 29.
10 Kokubun, 'Chūgoku no taigai keizai seisaku kettei', p. 160.
11 Ibid., pp. 169–70.
12 Ibid., p. 173.
13 Ibid., p. 175.
14 Zaidan hōjin kazankai (ed.) *Chūgoku sōran 1998*, p. 385.
15 Economic Cooperation Bureau, Ministry of Foreign Affairs, *Japan's ODA Annual Report 1993*, Tokyo, 1994, p. 42.

16 Interview with F, a senior official of the Japanese Ministry of Foreign Affairs, 20 April 2000 (first interview).

17 Interview with Inada; interview with Soeya Yoshihide, a political scientist specialising in Sino-Japanese relations at Keiō University and former foreign policy adviser to the Liberal Democratic Party, Tokyo, 28 March 2001; also see Kazan-kai, 'Nitchū keizai kyōryoku no shin-dankai: Chūgoku no gendaika to enshakkan o megutte (The New Phase of Japan–China Economic Cooperation: Regarding Chinese Modernisation and the Yen Loans)', *Tōa*, no. 152, February 1980, pp. 37, 38, 39.

18 Interview with Inada.

19 Interview with Kayahara Ikuo, a defence analyst specialising on the PRC, formerly in the Japanese Defence Agency and currently at Takushoku University, Tokyo, 4 April 2001; also see Robert M. Orr, Jr, *The Emergence of Japan's Foreign Aid Power*, New York: Columbia University Press, 1990, p. 73.

20 Interview with Yabuki Susumu, a China analyst at Yokohama City University, Yokohama, 23 March 2001.

21 Interview with Kayahara; also see Kayahara Ikuo, 'Anzen hoshō kara mita Nitchū kankei (Security Perspective on Japan–China Relations)', *Chūgoku 21*, vol. 10, January 2001, p. 79; *Japan Times*, 11 September 1978.

22 For example. see William T. Tow, 'Sino-Japanese Security Cooperation: Evolution and Prospects', *Pacific Affairs*, vol. 56, no. 1, Spring 1983, pp. 60–1.

23 Interview with Inada; interview with Soeya; also interview with F, 14 March 2001 (second interview).

24 Herbert Yee and Ian Storey, 'Introduction', in Herbert Yee and Ian Storey (eds) *The China Threat: Perceptions, Myths and Reality*, London and New York: RoutledgeCurzon, 2002, p. 5.

25 Interview with F, 20 April 2000 (first interview).

26 Katō Hiroyuki, 'Chūchōki hatten senryaku no sakutei o megutte: "Chūgoku kyōiron" no keizaitei sokumen (Regarding the Formulation of Medium to Long-Term Development Strategy: The Economic Perspective of the "China Threat Thesis")', in Amako Satoshi (ed.) *Chūgoku wa kyōi ka?* (Is China a Threat?), Tokyo: Keisō shobō, 1997, p. 24.

27 Ibid.; also interview with Yabuki.

28 Interview with F, 14 March 2001 (second interview).

29 Zaidan hōjin kazankai (Kazankai Foundation) (ed.) *Chūgoku sōran 1978* (Biennial Comprehensive Analysis of China 1978), Tokyo: Zaidan hōjin kazankai, 1978, p. 140.

30 Interview with F, Tokyo, 14 March 2001 (second interview).

31 There are a number of outstanding law suits by Chinese war victims demanding that the Japanese government pay war compensation. For details of some of these law suits, see *Asahi shinbun*, 29 April 2002; *Yomiuri shinbun*, 27 August 2002.

32 Hasegawa Keitarō and Watanabe Toshio, *Yōsō no chōtaikoku Chūgoku* (Myth of Superpower China), Tokyo: Tokuma shoten, 1995, pp. 174–5.

33 For details of this view, see Amako Satoshi, 'Seiji taisei no kōzō teki henyō (Structural Change in the Chinese Political System)', in Mōri Kazuko (ed.) *Gendai Chūgoku no kōzō hendō* (Structural Change in Contemporary China), Tokyo: Tōkyō daigaku shuppan-kai, 2000, pp. 15–55. This view is also shared by some American foreign policy specialists on China: see *Ryūkyū shinpō*, 24 May 2002.

34 Interview with F, 14 March 2001 (second interview).

35 Tony Saich, 'Tiananmen Square' in Joel Krieger, William A. Joseph and James A. Paul (eds) *The Oxford Companion to Politics of the World*, New York and Oxford: Oxford University Press, 1993, pp. 910–11.

36 K.V. Kesavan, 'Japan and the Tiananmen Square Incident: Aspects of the Bilateral Relationship', *Asian Survey*, vol. 30, no. 7, July 1990, p. 671.

37 Tanaka Akihiko, *Nitchū kankei 1945–1990* (Japan–China Relations 1945–1990), Tokyo: Tōkyō daigaku shuppan-kai, 1991, p. 173.

38 Kesavan, 'Japan and the Tiananmen Square Incident', p. 672.

39 Quoted in Tanaka, *Nitchū kankei*, p. 176.

40 Tanaka Akihiko, 'Tenanmon jiken igo no Chūgoku o meguru kokusai kankyō (The International Environment Surrounding China after the Tiananmen Square Incident)', *Kokusai mondai*, no. 358, January 1990, p. 42.

41 Kesavan, 'Japan and the Tiananmen Square Incident', p. 673.

42 Tanaka, 'Tenanmon jiken igo no Chūgoku', p. 37.

43 Seungwon Suh, 'Tenanmon jiken ni okeru Nihon no tai-Chūgoku enshakkan seisaku, 1989–90 (Japan's Yen Loan Policy to China during the Tiananmen Square Incident, 1989–90)', *Hōgaku seijigaku ronkyū*, no. 29, Summer 1996, p. 264.

44 Tanaka, *Nitchū kankei*, p. 172.

45 Tanaka, 'Tenanmon jiken igo no Chūgoku', p. 42.

46 Tanaka, *Nitchū kankei*, p. 179.

47 Suh, 'Tenanmon jiken ni okeru', p. 274.

48 Okabe Tatsumi, 'Tenanmon jiken to kongo no Chūgoku (The Tiananmen Square Incident and China Hereafter)', *Kokusai mondai*, no. 358, January 1990, p. 16.

49 Kojima Tomoyuki, 'Koritsu kaihi wa Chūgoku no konran kenen de (Avoidance of Isolation by China's Own Effort)', *Tōa*, no. 277, July 1990, p. 50.

50 Kesavan, 'Japan and the Tiananmen Square Incident', p. 681.

51 See, for example, Peter J. Schrader, Steven W. Hook and Bruce Taylor, 'Clarifying the Foreign Aid Puzzle: A Comparison of American, Japanese, French, and Swedish Aid Flows', *World Politics*, vol. 50, no. 2, January 1998, pp. 311–14; also Margee M. Ensign, *Doing Good or Doing Well? Japan's Foreign Aid Program*, New York: Columbia University Press, 1992.

52 Yanai Shinichi, 'Chūgoku to no keizai kyōryoku ni tsuite (Japanese Economic Cooperation with China)', record of lecture given by the then Director of Gaimushō keizai kyōryoku kyoku (Economic Cooperation Bureau of the Foreign Ministry), *Tōa*, no. 159, September 1980, pp. 79–81.

53 Regarding the MOFA's official response to the commercial instrument argument, see Economic Cooperation Bureau, Ministry of Foreign Affairs, *Japan's ODA 1990*, Tokyo, 1991, pp. 19–20.

54 Saburō Ōkita, 'Japan, China and the United States: Economic Relations and Prospects', *Foreign Affairs*, vol. 57, no. 5, Summer 1979, p. 1100.

55 *Asahi shinbun*, 1 December 1979. For more details of the infrastructure developed by Japanese ODA, see Chapter 5.

56 *Asahi shinbun*, 4 December 1979.

57 Edward J. Lincoln, 'Japan's Rapidly Emerging Strategy Toward Asia', Technical Paper No. 58, Research Programme on Globalisation and Regionalisation, OECD, April 1992, pp. 9, 27–8.

58 Nihon bōeki shinkō kyōkai (JETRO), *Chūgoku deita fairu 1999/2000* (China Data File 1999/2000), Tokyo, 2000, p. 160.

59 Tanaka, *Nitchū kankei*, pp. 134–5.

60 Ibid., pp. 135–7, 170–1.

61 Gaimushō keizai kyōryoku kyoku (Economic Cooperation Bureau, Ministry of Foreign Affairs), *Wagakuni no seifu kaihatsu enjo 1994 (Japan's ODA 1994)*, Tokyo, 1994, pp. 97–8.

62 Shimomura Yasutami, Nakagawa Junji and Saitō Jun, *ODA taikō no seiji keizai gaku* (Political Economy of the ODA Charter), Tokyo: Yūhikaku, 1999, pp. 114–16.

63 See Takashi Inoguchi, *Japan's International Relations*, Boulder, CO: Westview Press, 1991, p. 150.

64 Gaimushō Chūgoku-ka (China Division, Ministry of Foreign Affairs), 'Saikin no Chūgoku jōsei to Nitchū kankei (Current Chinese Affairs and Japan–China Relations)', unpublished report, April 2000, pp. 6–10.

65 See Thomas J. Christensen, 'China, the US–Japan Alliance, and the Security Dilemma in East Asia', *International Security*, vol. 23, no. 4, Spring 1999, pp. 52–5.

66 For example, Nakajima Mineo, 'Chūgoku wa kyōi ka? (Is China a Threat to Japan?)', *Bōeigaku kenkyū*, no. 17, March 1997, p. 8; Katō Hiroyuki, 'Chū-chōki hatten

senryaku no sakutei o megutte (The Formation of Medium to Long-Term Development Strategy)', in Amako Satoshi (ed.) *Chūgoku wa kyōi ka?* (Is China a Threat to Japan?), Tokyo: Keisō shobō, 1997, p. 24; also Kojima Tomoyuki, 'Zaisei kiki no naka no kokubōhi zōdai (The Increase in Chinese Defence Expenditure in the Budget Crisis)', *Tōa*, no. 287, May 1991, p. 67.

67 Yee and Storey, 'Introduction', p. 2.

68 Takagi Seiichirō, 'Chūgoku no "keizai taikoku ka" to taigai kankei (China as an "Emerging Economic Power" and its Foreign Relations)', *Kokusai mondai*, no. 406, January 1994, p. 60.

69 For detailed analysis of PRC's military development and military policies over the last several decades, see Hiramatsu Shigeo, *Chūgoku no gunji ryoku* (China's Military Capability), Tokyo: Bunshun shinsho, 1999.

70 See *Asahi shinbun*, 7 March 2002; also *Yomiuri shinbun*, 7 March 2002.

71 See, for example, National Institute for Defence Studies, Japan, *East Asian Strategic Review 1998–1999*, Tokyo, 1999, pp. 139–42; Abe Junichi, 'Kaiyō o mezasu Chūgoku no gunji senryaku (China's Military Strategy Aiming at the Ocean)', *Kokusai mondai*, no. 430, January 1996, pp. 65–8; Kojima Tomoyuki, 'Chūgoku no seiji to gaikō wa fukuzatsu sakusō (Complicated Chinese Politics and Diplomacy)', *Tōa*, no. 344, February 1996, p. 60; also Kayahara Ikuo, 'Kenkoku 50 shūnen kinen gyōji kara mita Chūgoku seikyoku to kokubō kindaika (China's Political Affairs and Military Modernisation Observed from the 50th Anniversary Event of the National Founding)', *Bōei shisetsu to gijutsu*, vol. 10, no. 1, January 2000, pp. 52–64.

72 Komori Yoshihisa, 'Machigai darake no Chūgoku enjo (Japan's Mistaken China Aid)', *Chūō kōron*, March 2002, pp. 94–109; Hiramatsu Shigeo, 'Chūgokugun o tsuyokusuru ODA (The ODA which Makes the Chinese Military Stronger)', *Seiron*, November 2000, pp. 152–60.

73 Interview with F, 20 April 2000 (first interview); Yutaka Kawashima, *Japanese Foreign Policy at The Crossraods: Challenges and Options for the Twenty-First Century*, Washington, DC: Brookings Institution Press, 2003, pp. 95–110.

74 Economic Cooperation Bureau, Ministry of Foreign Affairs, *Japan's Official Development Assistance Annual Report 1998*, Tokyo, 1999, p. 151.

75 Shimomura, Nakagawa and Saitō, *ODA taikō no seiji keizai gaku*, pp. 83–4.

76 Ministry of Foreign Affairs, *Japan's ODA 1995*, Online. Available http://www. mofa.go.jp/policy/oda/summary/1995/2approaches.html (accessed 17 May 2001)

77 David Arase, 'A Militarised Japan?', *Journal of Strategic Studies*, vol. 18, no. 3, September 1995, p. 87.

78 Tejima Ryūichi, *1991-nen Nihon no haiboku* (Japan's Defeat in 1991), Tokyo: Shinchō-sha, 1993, p. 250.

79 J.A.A. Stockwin, *Governing Japan: Divided Politics in a Major Economy*, Oxford: Blackwell, Third Edition, 1999, p. 75; Kojima, 'Zaisei kiki no naka no kokubōhi zōdai', p. 67.

80 Shimomura, Nakagawa and Saitō, *ODA taikō no seiji keizai gaku*, pp. 81–2; Nakai Yoshifumi, '90 nendai Nitchū kankei no tenbō (Prospects for Japan–China Relations in the 1990s)', *Gaikō jihō*, no. 1339, June 1997, p. 47.

81 Shimomura, Nakagawa and Saitō, *ODA taikō no seiji keizai gaku*, p. 70.

82 Murai Yoshinori, *Musekinin enjo taikoku Nihon* (Japan as an Irresponsible Foreign Aid Power), Tokyo: JICC shuppan-kyoku, 1989, p. 83.

83 Shimomura, Nakagawa and Saitō, *ODA taikō no seiji keizai gaku*, p. 70.

84 See the result of a questionnaire to 122 Japanese foreign policy scholars in Nihon kokusai mondai kenkyūjo, '1990-nendai no kokusai kankei to Nihon (International Relations and Japan in the 1990s)', *Kokusai mondai*, no. 361, April 1990, pp. 44–76.

85 Shimomura, Nakagawa and Saitō, *ODA taikō no seiji keizai gaku*, p. 82.

86 Kimata Yōichirō, 'Seiji-teki kondishonariti toshite no Nihon no ODA yon-shishin (Japan's ODA Four Principles as Political Conditionality)', unpublished Masters Thesis, Yokohama kokuritsu daigaku, 1997, p. 45.

87 Shimomura, Nakagawa and Saitō, *ODA taikō no seiji keizai gaku*, pp. 83–7.
88 Ibid., p. 82.
89 The MOFA proclaimed that one of the main purposes in introducing the Charter was 'to garner Japanese people's understanding and support for the official development assistance.' Economic Cooperation Bureau, Ministry of Foreign Affairs, *Japan's Official Development Assistance 1993*, Tokyo, 1994, p. 33.
90 Shimomura, Nakagawa and Saitō, *ODA taikō no seiji keizai gaku*, pp. 84, 87.
91 *Chūgoku sōran 1998* (Biennial Comprehensive Analysis of China 1998), Tokyo: Zaidan hōjin kazankai, 1998, pp. 369–70.
92 Ibid., p. 355.
93 William H. Overholt, 'China's Economic Squeeze', *Orbis*, vol. 44, no. 1, Winter 2000, pp.13–34; Okada Tomihiro, '2010-nen no Chūgoku keizai zō (The Chinese Economy in 2010)', *Tōa*, no. 322, April 1994, pp. 21–36; Amako Satoshi, 'Chūgoku, Tenanmon jiken to sōgō kokuryoku (China, the Tiananmen Square Incident and Comprehensive National Power)', *Sekai*, no. 687, April 2001, p. 147; Inoguchi Takashi, 'Kaibutsu Chūgoku ni dō tsukiau noka? (How to Deal with a Monster China?)', *This is Yomiuri*, vol. 7, no. 6, September 1996, pp. 34–45; Lester Brown, *Who Will Feed China? Wake-up Call for a Small Planet*, New York: Norton, 1995; Paul Krugman, 'The Myth of Asia's Miracle', *Foreign Affairs*, vol. 73, no. 6, November/December 1994, pp. 62–78.
94 Kokusai kyōryoku jigyōdan (Japan International Cooperation Agency), *Dainiji Chūgoku kunibetsu enjo kenkyū kai hōkoku-sho* (Second Report by the China Aid Research Group), Tokyo, February 1999, pp. 15–25.
95 Ibid., p. 19.
96 Inada, 'Tai-Chū ODA no keizaiteki shakaiteki hyōka ni tsuite', pp. 3–4.
97 Nihon kokusai mondai kenkyūjo (ed.) *Tai-Chū ODA no keizaiteki shakaiteki inpakuto ni tsuite no kisoteki chōsa* (Basic Research on the Economic and Social Impact of China ODA), unpublished report, Tokyo, 2000, p. 2.
98 *Asahi shinbun*, 29 August 2001.
99 Saori N. Katada, 'New Courses in Japan's Foreign Aid Policy: More Humanitarian and More Nationalistic', in Saori N. Katada, Hanns W. Maull and Takashi Inoguchi (eds) *Global Governance: Germany and Japan in the International System*, Aldershot and Burlington: Ashgate, 2004, pp. 180, 191–4.
100 Saori N. Katada, 'Why Did Japan Suspend Foreign Aid to China? Japan's Foreign Aid Decision-making and Source of Aid Sanction', *Social Science Japan Journal*, vol. 4. no. 1, 2001, p. 53.
101 See *Yomiuri shinbun*, 20 December 2001.
102 Interview with Soeya.
103 For the argument that Japanese ODA has contributed to China's military modernisation, see Hiramatsu Shigeo, 'Tai-Chū ODA "gun-min ryōyō" no jittai (The "Military–Civilian Dual Use" of Japanese ODA by China)', *Tōa*, no. 400, October 2000, pp. 6–21.
104 International Monetary Fund, *Direction of Trade Statistics*, Washington, DC: IMF, 2003, pp. 158. 924.
105 *Yomiuri shinbun*, 28 August 2000.
106 Interview with Kokubun.
107 Economic Cooperation Bureau, Japanese Ministry of Foreign Affairs, *Japan's Official Development Assistance Annual Report 1999*, Tokyo, 2000, p. 163.

4 Aid policy-making: institutions, processes and power relations

1 Yasuo Takao, *National Integration and Local Power in Japan*, Aldershot, Brookfield, WI, Singapore and Sydney: Ashgate, 1999, p. 3.
2 Part of the argument in this chapter appears as Tsukasa Takamine, 'Domestic Determinants of Japan's China Aid Policy: The Changing Balance of Foreign Policymaking Power', *Japanese Studies*, vol. 22, no. 2, September 2002, pp. 191–206.

3 S. Hayden Lesbirel, *NIMBY Politics in Japan: Energy Siting and the Management of Environmental Conflict*, Ithaca, NY, London: Cornell University Press, 1998, pp. 9. 151–2.

4 Alan Rix, *Japan's Economic Aid: Policymaking and Politics*, London: Croom Helm, 1980; Robert M. Orr, Jr, *The Emergence of Japan's Foreign Aid Power*. New York: Columbia University Press, 1990.

5 For more details about *bureaucrat-centred Japanese policy-making*, see Fujiwara Hirotatsu, *Kanryō no kōzō* (The Structure of the Bureaucracy), Tokyo: Kōdansha gendai shinsho, *1974;* Tsuji Kiyoaki, *Shinban: Nihon kanryōsei no kenkyū* (An Analysis of the Japanese Bureaucratic System), Tokyo: Tōkyō daigaku shuppan-kai, 1969; and T.J. Pempel, 'The Bureaucratisation of Policymaking in Postwar Japan', *American Journal of Political Science*, vol. 18, November 1974, pp. 647–64.

6 At the time of writing this book, Japanese Prime Minister Koizumi Junichirō had announced his plan to establish a new prime minister's advisory committee on foreign affairs consisting of Japanese foreign policy specialists and academics. This indicates his willingness to enhance the foreign policy-making capability of the Prime Minister's Office, suggesting also that the current capability of the Office is considered to be weak. *Yomiuri shinbun*, 31 August 2001; also *Asahi shinbun*, 29 August 2001.

7 Interview with Motoyoshi Tadahiko, a researcher on Japanese foreign aid policy at the National Diet Library, Tokyo, 3 April 2001.

8 Interview with A, a senior official of the Liberal Democratic Party, Tokyo, 27 March 2001.

9 Masashi Nishihara, *The Japanese and Sukarno's Indonesia: Tokyo–Jakarta Relations, 1951–1966*, Honolulu, HI: University of Hawaii Press, 1976.

10 Interview with B, a senior official of the Japanese Ministry of Finance, Tokyo. 13 April 2001; also see Takenaka Heizō and Okamoto Yukio, 'Nihon no gaikō to seisaku kettei no arikata (Diplomacy and Policymaking in Japan)', *Keizai seminā*, no. 496, May 1996, pp. 28–36.

11 For contemporary Japanese pork-barrel politics, see Aurelia George Mulgan, *Japan's Failed Revolution: Koizumi and the Politics of Economic Reform*, Australia: Asia Pacific Press, 2002, pp. 69–98.

12 For more detail about the Japanese electoral system see J.A.A. Stockwin, *Governing Japan: Divided Politics in a Major Economy*, Oxford: Blackwell Publishers, Third Edition, 1999, pp. 113–31.

13 T.J. Pempel, 'Regime Shift: Japanese Politics in a Changing World Economy', *Journal of Japanese Studies*, vol. 23, no. 2, 1997, p. 399.

14 Raymond Christensen, 'The New Japanese Election System', *Pacific Affairs*, vol. 69, no. 1, 1996, p. 62.

15 Takao, *National Integration and Local Power in Japan*, p. 26.

16 Interview with A.

17 Stockwin, *Governing Japan*, p. 97.

18 See Haruhiro Fukui, 'Studies in Policymaking: A Review of the Literature', in T.J. Pempel (ed.) *Policymaking in Contemporary Japan*, Ithaca, NY and London: Cornell University Press, 1977, pp. 22–59.

19 According to one senior LDP official, senior MOFA bureaucrats also managed to silence officials of the LDP Policy Research Council who were opposing bureaucratic decisions by using their connections with factional bosses. Interview with A.

20 Takenaka and Okamoto, 'Nihon no gaikō', p. 30.

21 Satō Seizaburō and Matsuzaki Tetsuhisa, *Jimintō seiken* (Liberal Democratic Party Governments), Tokyo: Chūō kōronsha, 1986, pp. 83, 94. Satō and Matsuzaki point out that the degree of the LDP's policymaking dependence on central ministries was much higher than that of the government party of then West Germany.

22 Takenaka and Okamoto, 'Nihon no gaikō', p. 36. In 1997 the ministry had 5,094 staff (1,985 in Japan and 3,109 overseas). See MOFA, *Gaikō seisho 1998* (Diplomatic Bluebook 1998), Tokyo: Gaimushō, 1998, p. 148.

23 Kusano Atsushi, 'Yugin kikin tōgō to ODA (Merger between the Japan Export and Import Bank and the Overseas Economic Cooperation Fund, and ODA)', *Shōkun*, vol. 28, no. 5, p. 172.

24 Interview with B, a senior official in the Japanese Ministry of Finance, Tokyo, 13 April 2001.

25 Orr, *The Emergence of Japan's Foreign Aid Power*, p. 20.

26 Interview with B.

27 Interview with C, D and E, three officials of the Japanese Ministry of Foreign Affairs, Tokyo, 26 March 2001.

28 Interview with F, a senior official of the Japanese Ministry of Foreign Affairs, Tokyo, 20 April 2000 (first interview).

29 Interviews with Sugishita Tsuneo, former *Yomiuri shinbun* journalist and currently academic at Ibaraki University, Mito, 11 April 2001; interview with Soeya Yoshihide, a political scientist specialising in Sino-Japanese relations at Keiō University and former foreign policy adviser to the Liberal Democratic Party, Tokyo (28 March 2001); interview with Watanabe Toshio, a prominent Japanese development economist, Tokyo, 13 April 2001. Also, see Michael J. Green, *Japan's Reluctant Realism: Foreign Policy Challenge in an Era of Uncertain Power*, New York: Palgrave, 2001, p. 85–6.

30 Interview with Sugishita. Sugishita had reported ODA-related issues for many years before recently becoming a university academic, and he also gave testimony regarding Japanese ODA policy at a national Diet session in 1998. For details, see Sangiin kokusai mondai ni kansuru chōsa-kai (Research Committee on Foreign Affairs, Upper House), 'Sangiin taigai keizai kyōryoku ni kansuru shō iinkai kaigiroku (Record of the Upper House Sub-Committee on Foreign Economic Cooperation)', Tokyo, 27 February 1988.

31 Sakurai Yoshiko, 'Gaimushō Chaina sukūru (The China School of the Ministry of Foreign Affairs)', *Bungei shūnjū*, vol. 80, no. 8, September 2002, p. 135.

32 Haruhiro Fukui, *Party in Power: The Japanese Liberal–Democrats and Policy-making*, Los Angeles, CA: University of California Press, 1970, pp. 165–7.

33 Stockwin, *Governing Japan*, 1999, p. 96.

34 Interview with A.

35 Interview with A; also see Watanabe Akio, 'Gaikō seisaku no yukue to Gaimushō (The outlook for Foreign Policy and the Ministry of Foreign Affairs)', *Hōgaku seminā*, vol. 23, September 1983, pp. 43–4; Hatayama Noboru and Takenaka Heizō, 'Seisaku kettei ni okeru kanryō no yakuwari (Roles of Bureaucrats in Policy-making)', *Keizai seminā*, vol. 483, April 1995, p. 29.

36 The system elects 300 out of a total of 500 House of Representative seats by single-member, first-past-the post election, and the other 200 seats from 11 regional constituencies by proportional representation. Stockwin, *Governing Japan*, p. 83.

37 Christensen, 'The New Japanese Election System', pp. 62–4.

38 Interview with G, a Liberal Democratic Party parliamentarian, Tokyo, 3 April 2001.

39 Nakajima Kuniko, 'Nihon no gaikō seisaku kettei katei ni okeru Jiyūminshutō seimu chōsakai no yakuwari (The Role of the LDP Policy Research Council within the Process of Japanese Foreign Policy-making)', in Hashimoto Kōhei (ed.) *Nihon no gaikō seisaku kettei yōin* (Domestic Determinants of Japanese Foreign Policy), Tokyo: PHP kenkyūjo, 1999, p. 75.

40 Interview with Watanabe.

41 Interview with Sugishita.

42 Sōrifu (Prime Minister's Office), Japan, *Gaikō ni kansuru yoron chōsa* (Opinion Polls on Japanese Diplomacy), Tokyo: Sōrifu, 1998, pp. 48–51. The specific question, asked in the polls was: 'do you think that current Sino-Japanese relations are in good shape?'.

43 Ibid.

44 See Jimintō (LDP), 'Chūgoku ni taisuru keizai enjo oyobi kyōryoku no sōkatsu to shishin (Review and Guidelines of Japanese Economic Aid and Assistance to China)', unpublished policy recommendation report, December 2000, p. 3; Gaimushō (MOFA), '21seiki ni muketa taichū keizai kyōryoku no arikata ni kansuru kondankai: Teigen (Policy Recommendation Report by the Committee on Japanese Economic Assistance to China for the 21st Century)', unpublished report, December 2000, p. 4.

45 See, for example, National Bureau of Statistics of China, *China Statistical Yearbook 2001*, Beijing: China Statistic Press, 2001, pp. 250–2; Gaimushō, 'Saikin no Chūgoku jōsei to Nitchū kankei, (Currect Chinese Affairs and Japan–China Relations) unpublished report, April 2000, p. 8; also National Bureau of Statistics of China, *China Statistical Yearbook 2003*, Beijing: China Statistic Press, 2003, p. 284.

46 See Gaimushō, 'Saikin no Chūgoku keizai jōsei to Nitchū kankei', (Current Chinese Affairs and Japan–China Relations) unpublished report, November 1999, pp. 10–11; also *Asahi shinbun*, 13 October 2000.

47 *Yomiuri shinbun*, 8 December 2000; also LDP, 'Chūgoku ni taisuru keizai enjo', pp. 2–3.

48 The term Gross National Income (GNI) refers to GDP plus net receipts of primary income (compensation of employees and property income) from abroad. World Bank, *2004 World Bank Atlas*, Washington, DC, 2004, p. 58.

49 World Bank, *2004 World Bank Development Indicators*, Washington, DC, 2004, pp. 14–15; Gaimushō, '21seiki ni muketa taichū keizai kyōryoku', pp. 1–6; Jimintō, 'Chūgoku ni taisuru keizai enjo', p. 2.

50 Jimintō, 'Chūgoku ni taisuru keizai enjo', p. 3; Kojima Tomoyuki, 'Chūgoku o "sekinin aru taikoku" ni surutameni (In Order to Make China a 'Responsible Power')', *Gaikō fōramu*, no. 151, February 2001, p. 39. For details of Chinese foreign aid activities between 1979 and 1983, see Sakurai Toshihiro, 'Chūgoku no taigai enjo (China's Foreign Aid)', *Kikinchōsa kihō*, no. 49, June 1985, pp. 176–83.

51 Interview with Watanabe.

52 Interview with A.

53 Interview with G.

54 Interview with A.

55 His skill in coordinating political and bureaucratic interests is well described in: Nakajima, 'Nihon no gaikō seisaku kettei katei', pp. 92–3.

56 Interview with Inada Jūichi, a political economist at Senshū University and a senior research fellow at the Japan Institute of International Affairs, Tokyo (28 March 2001).

57 Interview with F, 14 March 2001 (second interview). For Takemi's perception of Sino-Japanese relations, see Takemi Keizō, 'Kokunai seji no dainamizumu to Nichi-Bei-Chū kankei (Dynamism of International Politics and Japan–US–China Relations)', unpublished report, 1999.

58 See, for example, Inoguchi Takashi and Iwai Tomoaki, *Zoku giin no kenkyū: Jimintō o gyūjiru shuyaku tachi* (Research on Zoku Parliamentarians: The Tribe which Dominates Liberal Democratic Party Governments), Tokyo: Nihon keizai shinbun-sha, 1987.

59 Ibid., p. 134.

60 Unlike ordinary yen loans, which are basically untied, special yen loans are tied to the interests of Japanese private companies. (Interview with B.)

61 Interview with A.

62 Michael J. Green, *Japan's Reluctant Realism: Foreign Policy Challenge in an Era of Uncertain Power*, New York: Palgrave, 2001, p. 82–4; Takemi Keizō, 'Nitchū nitai kankei ni okeru shinchū shintai ha no shūen (The End of Political Divisions between the Pro-China and Pro-Taiwan Group in Japanese Relations with China and Taiwan)', *Mondai to kenkyū*, vol. 26, no. 8, 1998, pp. 60–71.

63 Takemi, 'Nitchū nitai kankei', pp. 60–71.

64 Interview with A.
65 Interview with G. Notably, Nonaka Hiromu and Hayashi Yoshirō already retired from their positions as member of the Diet by the beginning of 2000s.
66 Takemi, 'Nitchū nitai kankei', pp. 61–5.
67 Michael J. Green and Benjamin L. Self, 'Japan's Changing China Policy: From Commercial Liberalism to Reluctant Realism', *Survival*, vol. 38, no. 2, Summer 1996, p. 45.
68 Masujima Toshiyuki, 'Gyōsei kaikaku o meguru sho-kōsatsu: Hashimoto gyōkaku o chūshin to shite (An Assessment of Administrative Reforms: With Particular Focus on the Hashimoto Reform)', *NIRA seisaku kenkyū*, vol. 11, no. 6, 1998, p. 28.
69 Shimomura Yasutami, Nakagawa Junji and Saitō Jun, *ODA taikō no seiji keizai gaku* (Political Economy of the Japanese ODA Charter), Tokyo: Yūhikaku, 1999, p. 85.
70 The business leaders who led the First, Second and Third Administrative Reform Councils were Dokō Toshio, Ōtsuki Bunpei, and Suzuki Eiji, respectively.
71 Interview with C, D and E; For a scholarly analysis about the three-ministerial ODA policy-making system, see Keiko Hirata, 'New Challenges to Japan's Aid: An Analysis of Aid Policy-making', *Pacific Affairs*, vol. 71, no. 3, pp. 311–34.
72 Masujima, 'Gyōsei kaikaku o meguru', pp. 28–9.
73 Interview with G.
74 Interview with C, D and E. In the interview, these three informants indirectly mentioned how MOFA bureaucrats are now struggling to control other related foreign policies without being influenced by LDP parliamentarians, particularly those who are members of the Division of Foreign Affairs within the LDP Policy Research Council.
75 Interview with Watanabe.
76 Interview with Watanabe; interview with Sugishita.
77 Interview with C, D and E.
78 Interview with H, an official of the Japan International Cooperation Agency, Tokyo, 28 March 2001.
79 Interview with G.
80 Interview with A.
81 Interview with A.
82 *Asahi shinbun*, 23 April 2001; *Yomiuri shinbun*, 23 April 2001. The Japanese government again granted a tourist visa for Lee Denghui in December 2004 despite China's opposition. See *The Japan Times*, 4 January 2005.
83 Interview with Watanabe; interview with Soeya.
84 See Gaimushō, '21seiki ni muketa taichū keizai kyōryoku', pp. 1–13 and Jimintō, 'Chūgoku ni taisuru keizai enjo', pp. 1–7. These internal reports were provided to me by my interviewees.
85 The MOF controls this bank. Its name was changed to the Japan Bank for International Cooperation (JBIC) after its merger with the OECF in 1999.
86 Jimintō, 'Chūgoku ni taisuru keizai enjo', pp. 1–4.
87 Ibid.
88 Gaimushō, '21seiki ni muketa taichū keizai kyōryoku', pp. 16–17.
89 Jimintō, 'Chūgoku ni taisuru keizai enjo', p. 3 and Gaimushō, '21seiki ni muketa taichū keizai kyōryoku', p. 4.
90 Jimintō, 'Chūgoku ni taisuru keizai enjo', p. 3.
91 Gaimushō, '21seiki ni muketa taichū keizai kyōryoku', pp. 12, 25–6.
92 Ibid., p. 13.
93 Jimintō, 'Chūgoku ni taisuru keizai enjo', pp. 2–3.
94 Interview with Nakagawa Junji, an ODA specialist at the University of Tokyo, Tokyo, 22 March 2001; interview with Soeya.

5 Yen loans to China: development, globalisation and interdependence

1 Nakagawa Kikuo, 'Gaikoku shikin dōnyū taisei (China's System for Introducing Foreign Currency)', *Kikinchōsa kihō*, no. 49, June 1985, pp. 99–100.
2 The reason that Arab countries are separated out in Table 5.1 is because unlike the other countries listed, they are not members of the OECD.
3 Hirota Kōki, 'Chūgoku ni taisuru gaikoku enjo no dōkō (The Trend of Foreign Aid to China)', *Kikinchōsa kihō*, no. 49, June 1985, p. 188.
4 See Organisation for Economic Cooperation and Development (OECD), *Geographical Distribution of Financial Flows to Developing Countries, 1994–1998*, Paris, 2000.
5 Kokusai kyōryoku jigyōdan (Japan International Cooperation Agency), *Chūgoku kunibetsu enjo kenkyū-kai hōkoku-sho* (Report by the China Aid Research Group), Tokyo, December 1991, p. 17.
6 Gaimushō Chūgoku-ka (China Division, Ministry of Foreign Affairs), 'Saikin no Chūgoku jōsei to Nitchū kankei (Current Chinese Affairs and Japan–China Relations)', unpublished report, February 2001, p. 19.
7 Gaimushō keizai kyōryoku kyoku (Economic Cooperation Bureau, Ministry of Foreign Affairs), *Wagakuni no seifu kaihatsu enjo no jishi jōkyō 1998* (The Implementation of Japanese Official Development Assistance in 1998), Tokyo, 1999, p. 102.
8 Japan International Cooperation Agency, *Annual Report 2001*, Tokyo, 2002, p. 63.
9 Gang Zhang, 'Rail Aid to China', in Marie Söderberg (ed.) *The Business of Japanese Foreign Aid: Five Case Studies from Asia*, London and New York: Routledge, 1996, pp. 252, 270.
10 Economic Cooperation Bureau, Ministry of Foreign Affairs, *Japan's ODA Annual Report 1998*, Tokyo, April 1999, p. 4.
11 Gaimushō Chūgoku-ka, 'Saikin no Chūgoku jōsei', p. 19.
12 Kokusai kyōryoku jigyōdan, *Chūgoku kunibetsu enjo*, p. 12.
13 Hanns Günther Hilpert and Nakagane Katsuji, 'Economic Relations: What Can We Learn from Trade and FDI?', in Marie Söderberg (ed.) *Chinese–Japanese Relations in the Twenty-first Century: Complementarity and Conflict*, London and New York: European Institute of Japanese Studies, 2002, p. 131.
14 Matsuo Watanabe, 'Official Development Assistance as a catalyst for Foreign Direct Investment and Industrial Agglomeration', in Hirohisa Kohama (ed.) *External Factors for Asian Development*, Singapore: Institute of Southeast Asian Studies, 2003, pp. 136–68.
15 Hilpert and Nakagane, 'Economic Relations: What Can We Learn from Trade and FDI?', p. 143.
16 Katsuji Nakagane, 'Japanese Direct Investment in China: Its Effect on China's Economic Development', in Hanns Günther Hilpert and Rene Haak (eds) *Japan and China: Cooperation, Competition and Conflict*, New York: Palgrave, 2002, pp. 52–71.
17 Thomas Chan, Noel Tracy and Zhui Wenhui, *China's Export Miracle, Origins, Results and Prospects*, Houndsmill, Basingstoke: Macmillan, 1999, pp. 136–9.
18 Zai-Chūgoku Nihonkoku taishikan keizaibu (Economics Division, Japanese Embassy in China), 'Saikin no Chūgoku keizai jōsei to Nitchū keizai kankei (Current Chinese Economic Affairs and Japan–China Relations)', unpublished report, January 2001, p. 10.
19 For details about Sino-European trade and investment relations, see Roger Strange, Jim Slater and Limin Wang (eds) *Trade and Investment in China: The European Experience*, London and New York: Routledge 1998.
20 The figures for creating this graph were adapted from Hilpert and Nakagane, 'Economic Relations: What Can We Learn from Trade and FDI?', p. 135.
21 Hilpert and Nakagane note that before the mid-1980s, when the Chinese market was largely closed to the outside world, there were 'apparently special links between Japan

and China and the very little trade China had was extremely biased towards Japan'. When China opened up to the world, however, its trade became more diversified. 'Consequently the bias towards Japan came down.' Hilpert and Nakagane, 'Economic Relations', p. 137.

22 For more detailed analysis about the impact of FDI and trade on the Chinese economic development, see Xiaolan Fu, *Exports, Foreign Direct Investment and Economic Development in China*, New York: Palgrave Macmillan, 2004.

23 Shimomura Yasutami, 'Nitchū keizai kankei: kōteki shikin kyōryoku no yakuwari no tenbō (Japan–China Economic Relations: A Perspective of the Role of Japan's Official Financial Assistance)', paper presented at the Liberal Democratic Party Review Committee on Economic Assistance to China, Tokyo, November 2000, p. 1.

24 National Bureau of Statistics of China, *China Statistical Yearbook 2001*, Beijing: China Statistics Press, 2001, p. 410; *China Statistical Yearbook 2003*, Beijing: China Statistics Press, 2003, p. 460.

25 Mark Beeson and Leong Liew, 'Capitalism in East Asia: The Political Economy of Business Organisation in Japan, Korea and China', in Mark Beeson (ed.) *Reconfiguring East Asia: Regional Institutions and Organisations After the Crisis*, London and New York: RoutledgeCurzon, 2002, p. 155. Emphasis in original.

26 Marie Söderberg, 'Shipping Aid to China', in Marie Söderberg (ed.) *The Business of Japanese Foreign Aid: Five Case Studies from Asia*, London and New York: Routledge, 1996, p. 213; also see Hilpert and Nakagane, 'Economic Relations', p. 130.

27 Japan Bank for International Cooperation, *Annual Report 2000*, Tokyo, 2001, pp. 10–11.

28 For further details of the procedures, see Marie Söderberg, 'Shipping Aid to China', pp. 216–21; also Zhang, 'Rail Aid to China', pp. 248–52.

29 The Policy Division (*seisaku-ka*) and the Development Finance Division (*kaihatsu kinyū-ka*) of the Finance Ministry check debt problems, and then, the Ministry's Budget Division (*sukei kyoku*) adds budget considerations to the list of proposed yen loan projects in China.

30 Interview with B, a senior official of the Japanese Ministry of Finance, Tokyo, 13 April 2001.

31 Zhang, 'Rail Aid to China', p. 268.

32 Gaimushō (Japanese Ministry of Foreign Affairs), '21seiki ni muketa taichū keizai kyōryoku no arikata ni kansuru kondankai: Teigen (Policy Recommendation Report by the MOFA Committee on Japanese Economic Assistance to China for the 21st Century)', unpublished report, December 2000, p. 25. For more details of the total project contracts of yen loans to China in 1999, including Japanese contracts, see Kokusai kyōryoku ginkō (Japan Bank for International Cooperation), 'Kokusai kyōryoku ginkō ga kanri o okonatteiru keiyaku: Heisei 11-nendo ban (Contracts Managed by the Japan Bank for International Cooperation: 1999)', unpublished report, Tokyo, 1999.

33 Yabuki Susumu, 'Chūgoku keizai no kokusaika (Internationalisation of the Chinese Economy)', *Gakushikai kaihō*, no. 830, January 2001, pp. 127–8.

34 Interview with A, a senior official of the Liberal Democratic Party, Tokyo, 27 March 2001.

35 Yanai Shinichi, 'Chūgoku to no keizai kyōryoku ni tsuite (Japanese Economic Cooperation with China)', record of public lecture given by the then Director of the Economic Cooperation Bureau of the Foreign Ministry, *Tōa*, no. 159, September 1980, p. 73.

36 Economic Cooperation Bureau, Ministry of Foreign Affairs, *Japan's Official Development Assistance Annual Report 1998*, Tokyo, 1999, p. 4.

37 Interview with G, a Liberal Democratic Party parliamentarian, Tokyo, 3 April 2001.

38 Interview with B. For details of the special yen loan projects in China ¥17.2 billion, which were actually implemented in 2000, see Japan Bank for International

Cooperation, *JBIC ODA Loans to the People's Republic of China*, Tokyo, 2001, p. 19.

39 Kusano Atsushi, 'Yugin kikin tōgō to ODA (Merger between the Japan Export and Import Bank and the Overseas Economic Cooperation Fund, and ODA)', *Shokun.* vol. 28, no. 5, May 1996, p. 178.

40 Gaimushō, '21seiki ni muketa taichū keizai kyōryoku', see footnote 32, 2000, p. 21.

41 *Yomiuri shinbun*, 3 August 1991.

42 Komori Yoshihisa, 'Machigai darake no Chūgoku enjo (Japan's Mistaken China Aid)'. *Chūō kōron*, March 2002, p. 101.

43 Jiyūminshutō (Liberal Democratic Party), 'Chūgoku ni taisuru keizai enjo oyobi kyōryoku no sōkatsu to shishin (Review and Guidelines of Japanese Economic Aid and Assistance to China)', unpublished policy recommendation report, December 2000, p. 1; see also the Export and Import Bank of Japan, *JEXIM 1999*, annual report, Tokyo, 2000, p. 57.

44 Kokusai kyōryoku ginkō (Japan Bank for International Cooperation), 'Kokusai kyōryoku ginkō no yakuwari to kinō (Role and Function of the Japan Bank for International Cooperation)', Tokyo: JBIC, November 2000, pp. 11–12.

45 Japan Bank for International Cooperation, *ODA Loan Report 2000*, Tokyo, 2001, p. 12.

46 I count social services projects and irrigation and flood control projects as environment-related projects because for these projects, the JBIC applied the special interest rate for environment projects, which is lower than that for other projects.

47 Japan Bank for International Cooperation, *ODA Loan Report 2001*, Tokyo, 2002, pp. 73–4. The details of city projects given below are drawn from this source.

48 Japan Bank for International Cooperation, *JBIC ODA Loans*, pp. 45–6.

49 Ibid., pp. 41–2.

50 Japan Bank for International Cooperation, *ODA Loan Report 2000*, p. 12.

6 Aid as a strategic tool: three cases of economic sanctions

1 National Bureau of Statistics of China, *China Statistical Yearbook 2001*, Beijing: China Statistics Press, 2001, pp. 250–2; *China Statistical Yearbook 2003* Beijing: China Statistics Press, 2003, p. 284; Gaimushō Chūgoku-ka (China Division, Ministry of Foreign Affairs), 'Saikin no Chūgoku jōsei to Nitchū kankei (Current Chinese Affairs and Japan–China Relations)', unpublished report, Tokyo, April 2000, p. 8; *Asahi shinbun*, 7 March 2002.

2 International Institute for Strategic Studies, *The Military Balance 2003–2004*, London: IISS, 2004, p. 222.

3 National Institute for Defence Studies, *East Asian Strategic Review 1998–1999*, Tokyo: National Institute for Defence Studies, 1999, pp. 139–41.

4 National Institute for Defence Studies, *East Asian Strategic Review 2004*, Tokyo: National Institute for Defence Studies, 2004, pp. 109–13.

5 Yamada Tatsuo, Amako Satoshi and Tanaka Akihiko, 'Henyōsuru Chūgoku to iu shisutemu: Nihon wa tsuyoki Chūgoku to ikani renkei subekika? (Changing China as a System: How Should Japan Engage with a Strong China?)', *Sekai*, March 1996, pp. 32–3.

6 Okabe Tatsumi, 'Kokusai seijigaku to Chūgoku gaikō (International Politics and Chinese Diplomacy)', in Nihon kokusai seiji gakkai (ed.) *Gurōbarizumu, rijonar-izumu, nashonarizumu* (Globalism, Regionalism and Nationalism), Tokyo: Nihon kokusai seiji gakkai, 1997, pp. 42–56.

7 *Yomiuri shinbun*, 19 July 2004.

8 Ebata Kensuke, 'Chūgoku no gunjiryoku to higashi Ajia no gunbi kindaika (Chinese Military Capability and the Military Modernisation of East Asia)', *Tōa*, no. 337, July 1995, pp. 13–16.

9 Kayahara Ikuo, 'Ajia chiiki no enerugii jukyū to Chūgoku no sekiyū mondai (The Demand and Supply of Energy in the Asia Region and China's Oil Problem)', *Bōei shisetsu to gijutsu*, vol. 11, no. 1, January 2001, pp. 54, 64.

10 Interview with F, a senior official of the Japanese Ministry of Foreign Affairs, Tokyo, 20 March 2000 (first interview).

11 Interview with Kayahara Ikuo, a Japanese defence analyst specialising on the PRC, formerly in the Japanese Defence Agency and currently at Takushoku University, Tokyo, 4 April 2001; interview with Yabuki Susumu, a China analyst at Yokohama City University, Yokohama, 23 March 2001; also see Handa Shigeru, 'Chūgoku Kitachōsen wa semete kuru no desuka? (Will China and North Korea attack Japan?)', *Sekai*, no. 701, May 2002, pp. 110–13.

12 See Mōri Kazuko, 'Futeikei no Ajia: Chūgoku wa kyōika? (Shapeless Asia: Is China a Threat?), *Sekai*, no. 620, March 1996, pp. 41–8; Amako Satoshi (ed.), *Chūgoku wa kyōi ka?* (Is China a Threat?)', Tokyo: Keisō shobō, 1997; Miyazaki Isamu, 'Watashitachi wa Chūgoku o tadashiku toraeteiruka? (Are We Looking at China Correctly?)', *Sekai*, no. 685, March 2001, pp. 81–7. For a similar view presented by a UK scholar, see Gerald Segal, 'Does China Matter?', *Foreign Affairs*, vol. 78, no. 5, September/October 1999, pp. 24–36.

13 Herbert Yee and Ian Storey, 'Introduction', in Herbert Yee and Ian Storey (eds) *The China Threat: Perceptions, Myths and Reality*, London and New York: RoutledgeCurzon, 2002, pp. 9–10; also see Wenran Jiang, 'The Japanese Assessment of the "China Threat" ', in the same volume, p. 158.

14 Interview with F, 20 March 2000 (first interview).

15 For more details of this opinion survey, see *Yomiuri shinbun*, 11 September 2002.

16 I created this illustration based on Japanese policy-makers' and academics' perceptions of China as presented in Amako Satoshi, 'Introduction', in Amako Satoshi (ed.) *Chūgoku wa kyōi ka?*, pp. 3–22.

17 For a detailed review of the literature on this point, see Richard Weitz, 'Meeting the China Challenge: Some Insights from Scenario-Based Planning', *The Journal of Strategic Studies*, vol. 24, no. 3, September 2001, pp. 19–48.

18 Shimomura Yasutami, Nakagawa Junji and Saitō Jun, *ODA taikō no seiji keizai gaku* (Political Economy of the ODA Charter), Tokyo: Yūhikaku, 1999, pp. 110–12.

19 The structure of this table was adapted from Junji Nakagawa, 'Legal Problems of Japanese ODA Guidelines', *Japanese Annual of International Law*, no. 36, 1994, pp. 76–99.

20 Gaimushō keizai kyōryoku kyoku (Economic Cooperation Bureau, Ministry of Foreign Affairs), *Wagakuni no seifu kaihatsu enjo 1994* (Japan's ODA 1994), Tokyo, 1994, pp. 98–9.

21 See Economic Cooperation Bureau, Ministry of Foreign Affairs, *Japan's ODA Annual Report 1998*, Tokyo. Online. Available http://www.mofa.go.jp/policy/oda/summary/1998 (accessed 30 August 2001).

22 Kimata Yōichirō, 'Seiji-teki kondishonariti to shite no Nihon no ODA yon shishin (Japan's Four ODA Principles as Political Conditionality)', unpublished Masters Thesis, Yokohama: Yokohama kokuritsu daigaku, 1997, p. 75.

23 Gaimushō keizai kyōryoku kyoku, *Wagakuni no seifu kaihatsu enjo 1994*, p. 99.

24 China consistently conducted one or two nuclear tests a year until it joined the Comprehensive Test Ban Treaty in 1996. Bōeichō (Japanese Defence Agency), *Nihon no bōei 2000* (Defence of Japan 2000), Tokyo, 2001, p. 53.

25 Economic Cooperation Bureau, Ministry of Foreign Affairs, *Japan's ODA 1996*, Tokyo. Online. Available http://www.mofa.go.jp/policy/oda/summary/ 1996/c_8.html (accessed 26 July 2001).

26 *Yomiuri shinbun*, 19 May 1995.

27 William J. Long, 'Nonproliferation as a Goal of Japanese Foreign Assistance Policy', *Asian Survey*, vol. 39, no. 2, 1999, p. 336.

28 *Yomiuri shinbun*, 19 May 1995.
29 Ibid.
30 Kimata, 'Seiji-teki kondishonariti to shite', pp. 75–6.
31 The reason given by the MOFA for exclusion of humanitarian aid from the sanction is: 'Suspension of aid to a developing country under the Four Principles is not necessarily intended to bring economic and social hardships to the poor people of the developing country. Therefore, when its aid has to be suspended, Japan excludes emergency and humanitarian aid that benefits the people of the country at large.' Economic Cooperation Bureau, Ministry of Foreign Affairs, *Japan's ODA 1995*, Tokyo. Online. Available http://www.mofa.go.jp/policy/oda/summary/1995/index.html (accessed 8 September 2001).
32 Gaimushō keizai kyōryoku kyoku (Economic Cooperation Bureau, Ministry of Foreign Affairs), *Wagakuni no seifu kaihatsu enjo 1999* (Japan's ODA 1999), Tokyo, 1999, p. 118.
33 Economic Cooperation Bureau, Ministry of Foreign Affairs, *Japan's ODA 1996*, Tokyo. Online. Available http://www.mofa.go.jp/policy/oda/summary/ 1996/c_8.html (accessed 17 September 2001).
34 Long, 'Nonproliferation as a Goal', p. 336.
35 *Yomiuri shinbun*, 27 August 1995.
36 *Yomiuri shinbun*, 30 August 1995; *Yomiuri shinbun*, 27 August 1995.
37 *Yomiuri shinbun*, 27 August 1995.
38 Kimata, 'Seiji-teki kondishonariti to shite', pp. 76–81.
39 Ibid., p. 79.
40 Although, as Long points out, the US and Belgium also temporarily suspended 'export credits' to China, such credits are not counted as foreign aid (ODA) but as other official flow (OOF). Long, 'Non-proliferation as a Goal', p. 335.
41 *Yomiuri shinbun*, 30 August 1995.
42 Saori N. Katada, 'Why Did Japan Suspend Foreign Aid to China? Japan's Foreign Aid Decision-making and Source of Aid Sanction', *Social Science Japan Journal*, vol. 4, no. 1, 2001, p. 47.
43 Kimata, 'Seiji-teki kondishonariti to shite', p. 79.
44 Shimomura, Nakagawa and Saitō, *ODA taikō no seiji keizai gaku*, p. 134.
45 Gaimushō, *Wagakuni no seifu kaihatsu enjo 1999*, p. 118.
46 Zaidan hōjin kazankai (Kazankai Foundation) (ed.) *Chūgoku sōran 1998* (Biennial Comprehensive Analysis of China 1998), Tokyo: Zaidan hōjin kazankai, 1998, p. 142.
47 Long, 'Nonproliferation as a Goal', p. 335.
48 Katada, 'Why Did Japan Suspend Foreign Aid?', pp. 46–7.
49 *Mainichi shinbun*, 11 June 1996.
50 China tried to justify these tests by emphasising that their purpose was solely for defence. Zaidan hōjin kazankai (ed.) *Chūgoku sōran 1998*, p. 141.
51 Kimata, 'Seiji-teki kondishonariti to shite', p. 83.
52 *Yomiuri shinbun*, 9 March 1996.
53 Zaidan hōjin kazankai (ed.) *Chūgoku sōran 1998*, p. 139.
54 *Yomiuri shinbun*, 9 March 1996.
55 Zaidan hōjin kazankai (ed.) *Chūgoku sōran 1998*, pp. 139–40
56 Reinhard Drifte, *Japan's Security Relations with China since 1989: From Balancing to Bandwagoning?*, London and New York: RouledgeCurzon, 2003, p. 65.
57 *Nikkei Weekly*, 18 March 1996.
58 Zaidan hōjin kazankai (ed.) *Chūgoku sōran 1998*, p. 140.
59 *Yomiuri shinbun*, 9 March 1996.
60 Zaidan hōjin kazankai (ed.) *Chūgoku sōran 1998*, pp. 140–2.
61 *Yomiuri shinbun*, 5 December 1996.
62 Zaidan hōjin kazankai (ed.) *Chūgoku sōran 1998*, p. 140.

190   *Notes*

63 Ibid.
64 Drifte, *Japan's Security Relations with China*, pp. 64–70.
65 Kimata, 'Seiji-teki kondishonariti to shite', pp. 80–1; Katada, 'Why Did Japan Suspend Foreign Aid?', p. 47.
66 Zaidan hōjin kazankai (ed.) *Chūgoku sōran 1998*, pp. 140, 142.
67 Interview with F, Tokyo, 14 March 2001 (second interview).
68 *Yomiuri shinbun*, 22 March 2002.
69 Tanaka Akihiko, *The New Middle Ages: The World System in the 21st Century*, Tokyo: The International House of Japan, 2002, pp. 185–6.
70 For more details of the MOFA's Taiwan policy in the 1950s, see Gaimushō (Ministry of Foreign Affairs, Japan), 'Chūgoku mondai (China Issue)', Gaikō shiryō-kan (Diplomatic Record Office), Microfilm No: A'-0356 (undated, but the context indicates that it was issued in 1955); also see Gaimushō, 'Wagakuni no tai-Chūgoku seisaku: chōki kihon seisaku (Japan's China Policy: Basic Long-Term Policy)', Gaikō shiryō-kan, Microfilm No: A'-0356 (14 July 1959).
71 *Asahi shinbun*, 27 March 1996.
72 See Kent E. Calder, 'The New Face of Northeast Asia', *Foreign Affairs*, vol. 80, no. 1, January–February 2001, pp. 108–9.
73 Michael J. Green, *Japan's Reluctant Realism: Foreign Policy Challenge in an Era of Uncertain Power*, New York: Palgrave, 2001, p. 84; Chien-peng Chung, *Domestic Politics, International Bargaining and China's Territorial Disputes*, London and New York: RoutledgeCurzon, 2004, pp. 26–60.
74 *Yomiuri shinbun*, 27 February 1992.
75 *Asahi shinbun*, 18 March 1992.
76 Michael J. Green and Benjamin L. Self, 'Japan's Changing China Policy: From Commercial Liberalism to Reluctant Realism', *Survival*, vol. 38, no. 2, Summer 1996, p. 37; also *Japan's Reluctant Realism*, p. 84–5.
77 Unryu Suganuma, *Sovereign Rights and Territorial Space in Sino-Japanese Relations: Irredentism and the Diaoyu/Senkaku Islands*, Honolulu, HI: University of Hawaii Press, 2000, pp. 34–5: *Yomiuri shinbun*, 4 January 2005.
78 Hiramatsu Shigeo, 'Kakudai suru Chūgoku no Higashi-Shinakai shinshutsu: shinshoku sareru wagakuni no keizai suiiki (Expanding Chinese Activities in the East China Sea: The Eroded Japanese Exclusive Economic Zone)', *Tōa*, no. 382, April 1999, pp. 6–23.
79 *Yomiuri shinbun*, 28 August 2000.
80 For example, see Bōeichō, *Nihon no bōei 2000*, pp. 54–6.
81 *Yomiuri shinbun*, 29 August 2000.
82 *Yomiuri shinbun*, 25 May 2000.
83 Bōeichō, *Nihon no bōei 2000*, pp. 55–6.
84 *Yomiuri shinbun*, 28 August 2000.
85 For details of these projects, see Japan Bank for International Cooperation, *JBIC ODA Loans to the People's Republic of China*, Tokyo, June 2001, pp. 30, 34.
86 Interview with A, a senior official of the Liberal Democratic Party, Tokyo, 27 March 2001.
87 *Yomiuri shinbun*, 28 August 2000.
88 *Asahi shinbun*, 31 August 2000.
89 *Sankei shinbun*, 30 August 2000.
90 *Asahi shinbun*, 30 August 2000.
91 *Asahi shinbun*, 31 August 2000.
92 *Yomiuri shinbun*, 28 August 2000.
93 *Sankei shinbun*, 7 June 2001; *Yomiuri shinbun*, 22 July 2004; and also *Asahi shinbun*, 11 June 2004.
94 Zaidan hōjin kazankai (ed.) *Chūgoku sōran 1998*, p. 142.

95 Mōri Kazuko, 'Sekai shisutemu no naka no Chūgoku (China in the World System)', *Kokusai mondai*, no. 418, January 1995, pp. 2–16.
96 Gaimushō keizai kyōryoku kyoku (Economic Cooperation Bureau, Ministry of Foreign Affairs), *Wagakuni no seifu kaihatsu enjo 1989* (Japan's ODA 1989), Tokyo, 1989, pp. 82–3.
97 Economic Cooperation Bureau, Ministry of Foreign Affairs, *Japan's ODA Annual Report 1998*, Tokyo. Online. Available http://www.mofa.go.jp/policy/oda/summary/ 1998 (accessed 15 October 2002).
98 Shimomura, Nakagawa and Saitō, *ODA taikō no seiji keizai gaku*, pp. 119–24.
99 Kimata, 'Seiji-teki kondishonariti to shite', p. 77.

7 The effects of Japan's aid policy to China and implications for bilateral relations

1 Inada Jūichi, 'Tai-Chū ODA no keizaiteki shakaiteki hyōka ni tsuite (An Economic and Social Assessment of China ODA)', in Nihon kokusai mondai kenkyūjo (ed.) *Tai-Chū ODA no keizai sakai inpakuto ni tsuiteno kisoteki chōsa* (Basic Research on the Economic and Social Impact of China ODA), unpublished report, Tokyo, 2000, p. 7.
2 Interview with F, a senior official of the Japanese Ministry of Foreign Affairs, Tokyo, 20 April 2000 (first interview).
3 Interview with C, D and E, three officials of the Ministry of Foreign Affairs, Tokyo, 26 March 2001.
4 Interview with Kokubun Ryōsei, professor and director of the Centre for Area Studies at Keiō University, Tokyo, 15 March 2001; also interview with Sugishita Tsuneo, former *Yomiuri shinbun* journalist specialising on Japanese ODA and currently an academic at Ibaraki University, Mito, 11 April 2001.
5 Interview with Inada Jūichi, a Japanese scholar at Senshū University and a senior research fellow at the Japan Institute of International Affairs, Tokyo, 28 March 2001.
6 For details, see World Bank, *2004 World Bank Development Indicators*, Washington, DC, 2004, pp. 238–41.
7 Ōkita Saburō, 'Japan, China and the United States: Economic Relations and Prospects', *Foreign Affairs*, Summer 1979, p. 1104.
8 Interview with Soeya Yoshihide, a political scientist specialising on Sino-Japanese relations at Keiō University, Tokyo, 2 April 2001.
9 Kobayashi Morinao, 'Nitchū keizai kyōryoku no genjō to hōto (Current Condition and Future Direction of Japanese Economic Assistance to China)', *Tōa*, no. 403, January 2001, p. 13.
10 Interview with Watanabe Toshio, a prominent development economist, Tokyo, 13 April 2001; interview with B, a senior official of the Ministry of Finance, Tokyo, 13 April 2001.
11 Interview with F, 20 April 2000 (first interview).
12 Interview with C, D and E.
13 Interview with Nakagawa Junji, an ODA specialist at the University of Tokyo, Tokyo, 22 March 2001.
14 See *Yomiuri shinbun*, 12 April 2002.
15 Ministry of Foreign Affairs, Japan, *Diplomatic Bluebook 2004*, Tokyo: Ministry of Foreign Affairs, 2004, pp. 46–7.
16 Interview with Yabuki Susumu, a specialist on Chinese political economy at Yokohama City University, Yokohama, 23 March 2001.
17 Interview with Soeya.
18 Interview with Kokubun.
19 Interview with Watanabe.

20 Interview with C, D and E.
21 Kokusai kyōryoku jigyōdan, *Chūgoku kunibetsu enjo kenkyū-kai hōkoku-sho* (Report from the China ODA Research Committee), Tokyo, 1991, pp. 86–91.
22 For example, see Gaimushō Chūgoku-ka, 'Saikin no Chūgoku jōsei to Nitchū kankei (Current Chinese Affairs and Japan–China Relations)', unpublished report, April 2000, p. 6.
23 Interview with I, a senior official of the Japan Bank for International Cooperation, Tokyo, 4 April 2001.
24 Allen S. Whiting, 'China's Use of Force, 1950–96, and Taiwan', *International Security*, vol. 26, no. 2, Fall 2001, p. 131.
25 Interview with Kokubun.
26 Views of Chinese sociologists are summarised in Hishida Masaharu, 'Kokka to shakai no kōsei (The Symbiosis Between State and Society)', in Mōri Kazuko (ed.) *Gendai Chūgoku no kōzō hendō* (Structural Change in Contemporary China), Tokyo: Tōkyō daigaku shuppan-kai, 2000, p. 60.
27 George Gilboy and Eric Heginbotham, 'China's Coming Transformation', *Foreign Affairs*, July/August 2001, pp. 29–30.
28 Interview with Inada; interview with Soeya.
29 Gilboy and Heginbotham, 'China's Coming Transformation', p. 30; see also Richard Robison and David S.G. Goodman (eds) *The New Rich in Asia: Mobile Phones, McDonalds and Middle Class Revolution*, London and New York: Routledge, 1996.
30 Interview with Inada.
31 Amako Satoshi, 'Nitchū kankei nijūisseiki e no teigen (A Recommendation for Japan–China Relations in the Twenty-first Century)', *Chūgoku 21*, vol. 10, January 2001, p. 58; also see Kamimura Kōji, 'Chūgoku hōdō (China Report)', *Sekai*, no. 685, March 2001, p. 116; also interview with F, 20 April 2000 (first interview).
32 For example, see 'Intellectuals in China Under Fire, Again: Free Expression Worries the Authorities', *The Economist*, vol. 373, no. 8405, December 2004, pp. 26–7.
33 Interview with Soeya.
34 According to Kokubun Ryōsei, the Chinese Communist Party's fear of Falun Gong is linked with the problems of unemployment in China-that is, jobless people join Falun Gong because there is no institutional framework through which the public can express its fear and anger. (Interview with Kokubun)
35 Interview with F, 20 April 2000 (first interview).
36 Interview with C, D and E.
37 Interview with Watanabe; also interview with Sugishita.
38 Interview with F, 20 April 2000 (first interview).
39 Interview with Watanabe.
40 For examples, see Yasunobu Satō, 'New Directions in Japanese Foreign Policy: Promoting Human Rights and Democracy in Asia – ODA Perspective', in Edward Friedman (ed.) *The Politics of Democratisation*, Boulder, CO, San Francisco, CA, Oxford: Westview Press, 1994, pp. 103–21; Kusano Atsushi, 'Kaihatsu enjo wa seijiteki minshuka o sokushin suru (Development Assistance will Promote Political Democratisation)', *Ekonomisuto*, vol. 70, no. 25, June 1992, pp. 34–7.
41 Interview with Inada; interview with Soeya; interview with Sugishita.
42 Interview with F, 14 March 2001 (second interview).
43 Interview with Yabuki.
44 Jagdish Bhagwati, 'Democracy and Development', *Journal of Democracy*, vol. 3, no. 3, July 1992, p. 40.
45 Francis Fukuyama, 'Capitalism and Democracy: The Missing Link', *Journal of Democracy*, vol. 3, no. 3, July 1992, p. 108.
46 Ibid.

47 Nakagane Katsuji, 'Chūgoku keizai: mittsu no tenkan ten (The Chinese Economy: Three Transformations)', in Mōri Kazuko (ed.) *Gendai Chūgoku no kōzō hendō* (Structural Change in Contemporary China), Tokyo: Tōkyō daigaku shuppan-kai, 2000, p. 120.

48 Fukuyama, 'Capitalism and Democracy', p. 108.

49 Bhagwati, 'Democracy and Development', p. 40.

50 Fukuyama, 'Capitalism and Democracy', p. 108.

51 Nakagane Katsuji, 'Chūgoku keizai', p. 120.

52 Fukuyama, 'Capitalism and Democracy', p. 108.

53 Minxin Pei, 'Social Takeover in China and the USSR', *Journal of Democracy*, vol. 3, no. 1, January 1992, p. 116.

54 Seymore M. Lipset, 'Some Social Requisites of Democracy: Economic Development and Political Legitimacy', *American Political Science Review*, vol. 53, no. 1, March 1959, pp. 69–105; for more in depth discussions about Lipset's propositions, see Ole Elgström and Goran Hyden (eds) *Development and Democracy: What Have We Learned About and How?*, London and New York: Routledge, 2002.

55 National Institute for Defence Studies, *East Asian Strategic Review 1998–1999*, Tokyo: National Institute for Defence Studies, 1999, p. 90.

56 Hishida, 'Kokka to shakai no kōsei', pp. 76–8.

57 Nakagane, 'Chūgoku keizai', pp. 120–1.

58 Interview with Soeya; interview with Watanabe.

59 Interview with Inada Jūichi.

60 Interview with Soeya; interview with F, 14 March 2001 (second interview).

61 Interview with F, 14 March 2001 (second interview).

62 For details of this view refer to Amako Satoshi, 'Seiji taisei no kōzō teki henyō (Structural Change in the Chinese Political System)', in Mōri Kazuko (ed.) *Gendai Chūgoku no kōzō hendō* (Structural Change in Contemporary China), Tokyo: Tōkyō daigaku shuppan-kai, 2000, pp. 15–55; this view is also shared by some American foreign policy specialists on China: see *Ryūkyū shinpō*, 24 May 2002.

63 For detailed discussion about China's new anti-Japanese nationalism, see Peter Hays Gries, *China's New Nationalism: Pride, Politics, and Diplomacy*, Berkeley, CA, Los Angeles, CA and London: University of California Press, 2004, pp. 69–98.

64 Nakajima Mineo, 'Chūgoku wa kyōi ka? (Is China a Threat to Japan?)', *Bōeigaku kenkyū*, no. 17, March 1997, p. 8.

65 Interview with F, 20 April 2000 (first interview).

66 Michael J. Green, *Japan's Reluctant Realism: Foreign Policy Challenge in an Era of Uncertain Power*, New York: Palgrave, 2001, p. 86.

67 *Asahi shinbun*, 18 August 2004; *Yomiuri shinbun*, 29 July 2004.

68 Interview with F (first interview).

69 Interview with Kokubun.

70 David Shambaugh, 'Facing Reality in China Policy', *Foreign Affairs*, January–February 2001, vol. 80, no. 1, p. 54; Minxin Pei, 'Social Takeover in China and the USSR', p. 116.

71 Interview with Watanabe.

72 Interview with Watanabe.

73 Interview with Soeya; interview with Watanabe.

74 Interview with Yabuki.

75 Tang Liang, 'Chūgoku nōson ni okeru senkyo kaikaku to seiji hendō (Chinese Village Elections and Political Change in Rural Areas)', *Ajia keizai*, vol. 42, no. 2, pp. 2–22.

76 Interview with F, 20 April 2000 (first interview).

77 Interview with Inada.

78 Gilboy and Heginbotham, 'China's Coming Transformation', p. 32.

79 Takemi Keizō, 'Nitchū nitai kankei ni okeru shinchū shintai ha no shūen (The End of Political Divisions between the Pro-China and Pro-Taiwan Groups in Japanese Relations with China and Taiwan)', *Mondai to kenkyū*, vol. 26, no. 8, 1998, pp. 65–7.

80 Sangiin gaimu iinkai (Foreign Affairs Committee, Upper House of the Diet), 'Chūgoku Taiwan jōsei ni kansuru ketsugi (The Resolution Concerning China–Taiwan Affairs)', Tokyo (6 May 1996).
81 Interview with Soeya.
82 Economic Cooperation Bureau, Japanese Ministry of Foreign Affairs, *Japan's Official Development Assistance Annual Report 1999*, Tokyo, 2000, p. 179.
83 Interview with H, an official of the Japan International Cooperation Agency, Tokyo, 28 March 2001. For more detail on the concept of *mentsu*, see Sonoda Shigeto, *Chūgoku jin no shinri to kōdō* (Psychology and Behaviour of Chinese People), Tokyo: NHK bukkusu, 2001.
84 Interview with Soeya.
85 Interview with Watanabe; interview with Soeya; also interview with Sugishita.
86 Wenran Jiang, 'The Japanese Assessment of the 'China Threat', in Herbert Yee and Ian Storey (eds) *The China Threat: Perceptions, Myths and Reality*, London and New York: RoutledgeCurzon, 2002, pp. 160–1.
87 Michael J. Green and Benjamin L. Self, 'Japan's Changing China Policy: From Commercial Liberalism to Reluctant Realism', *Survival*, vol. 38, no. 2, Summer 1996, p. 43; Morimoto Satoshi, 'TMD no seijigaku: Nichibei bōei kyōryoku gaidorain to Ajia-Taiheiyō no anzen hoshō (Politics of TMD: The Japan–US Defence Cooperation Guideline and Asia-Pacific Security)', *Tōa*, no. 385, July 1999, pp. 14–20.
88 *Yomiuri shinbun*, 20 February 2001.
89 *Yomiuri shinbun*, 25 May 2001.
90 *The Japan Times*, 29 March 2003; *Yomiuri shinbun*, 11 September 2002.
91 *Asahi shinbun*, 25 November 2004; *Yomiuri shinbun*, 29 July 2004.
92 Interview with Kokubun. Yabuki also expressed a similar view in my interview with him.
93 Interview with F, 20 April 2000 (first interview).
94 Interview with C, D and E; also interview with H.
95 For examples, see Gaimushō keizai kyōryoku kyoku, *Wagakuni no seifu kaihatsu enjo 2000* (Japan's ODA 2000), Tokyo, 2000, p. 349; Kokusai kyōryoku jigyōdan, *Dainiji Chūgoku kunibetsu kenkyū-kai hōkokusho* (Second Report by China Aid Research Group), Tokyo, 1999, pp. 27–9.
96 *Yomiuri shinbun*, 20 December 2001.
97 For more details of this opinion poll, see *Yomiuri shinbun*, 11 September 2002.
98 Interview with F, 14 March 2001 (second interview); interview with Kokubun.
99 Interview with F, 20 April 2000 (first interview); interview with Sugishita; interview with Soeya.
100 Walter Hatch and Kozo Yamamura, *Asia in Japan's Embrace: Building a Regional Production Alliance*, Cambridge: Cambridge University Press, 1996, p. 11.
101 Ibid.
102 Interview with C, D and E.
103 Interview with Soeya.
104 Interview with F, 20 March 2000 (first interview).
105 Amako Satoshi, 'Nitchū kankei nijūisseiki e no teigen', p. 54; also Sugishita interview.
106 *Asahi shinbun*, 21 July 2002.
107 Interview with Watanabe; interview with Soeya.
108 Interview with Watanabe.
109 Christopher Howe, 'The Changing Asian Environment of China's Economic Development: The Perspective from Japan, with Particular Reference to Foreign Direct Investment and Industrial Restructuring', in Robert Ash (ed.) *China's Integration in Asia: Economic Security and Strategic Issues*, Richmond, VA and Surrey: Curzon Press, 2002, pp. 3–38.
110 Interview with Soeya; also interview with Watanabe.

111 Interview with F, 20 April 2000 (first interview).
112 Interview with Watanabe.
113 Interview with Soeya.
114 Nakagawa Kikuo, 'Gaikoku shikin dōnyū taisei (China's System for Introducing Foreign Currency)', *Kikinchōsa kihō*, no. 49, June 1985, p. 109.
115 Kokusai kyōryoku jigyōdan, *Chūgoku kunibetsu enjo*, p. 254.
116 Interview with B; interview with Kokubun.
117 Interview with F, 20 April 2000 (first interview); interview with Yabuki.
118 Interview with B.
119 Interview with Inada; interview with Watanabe.
120 Inada, 'Tai-Chū ODA no keizaiteki shakaiteki hyōka ni tsuite', p. 9.
121 *Sankei shinbun*, 15 December 2004.
122 Watanabe Toshio and Tanaka Akihiko, 'Toketeyuku Chūgoku (Melting China)', *Voice*, October 1999, pp. 78–9.
123 *Asahi shinbun*, 6 March 2002.
124 This study is cited in Ishihara Kyōichi, 'Chūgoku ni okeru "seidoka sareta shijō keizai" no kōchiku no kanōsei (The Possibility of Creating an "Institutionalised Market Economy" in China)', *Kokusai mondai*, no. 492, March 2001, p. 14; also see Katō Hiroyuki, 'Kōzō tenkanki o mukaeta Chūgoku keizai (Chinese Economy Facing Structural Change)', *Kokusai mondai*, no. 478, January 2000, p. 45.
125 William H. Overholt, 'China's Economic Squeeze', *Orbis*, vol. 44, no. 1, Winter 2000, p. 25.
126 *Yomiuri shinbun*, 21 October 2004; 10 December 2004.
127 See *Yomiuri shinbun*, 21 March 2002; *Ryūkyū shinpō*, 3 March 2002.
128 For more details about this problem see Watanabe Toshio, 'Kokuyū kigyō kaikaku ga shippai ni owareba Chūgoku keizai wa kiki ni ochiiru (If the Reform of State-Owned Enterprises Fails, the Chinese Economy Will Face a Crisis)', *Nihon no ronten*, Bungei shunjūsha, 1999, pp. 144–7; Gilboy and Heginbotham, 'China's Coming Transformation', p. 32.
129 See World Bank, *2004 World Bank Atlas*, Washington, DC, 2004, pp. 54–8.
130 See Figure 6 in Sōrifu (Prime Minister's Office), *Gaikō ni kansuru yoron chōsa (Opinion Polls on Japanese Diplomacy)*, Tokyo. Online. Available http://www8.cao.go.jp/survey/h16/h16-gaikou/index.html (accessed on 31 January 2005).
131 *The Japan Times*, 30 November 2004; *Asahi shinbun*, 23 December 2004.
132 *Yomiuri shinbun*, 6 December 2004.
133 *Asahi shinbun*, 23 December 2004.

Bibliography

Archival sources

Gaimushō (Ministry of Foreign Affairs, Japan), 'Ashida shokan (The Ashida Memorandum)', handed from Japanese Foreign Minister Ashida Hitoshi to US General Icklberger, Gaikō shiryō-kan (Diplomatic Record Office), Microfilm No: B'0008 (13 September 1947).

——, 'Statement by General Frank R. McCoy, United States Representative on the Far Eastern Commission, Concerning Japanese Reparations and Level of Industry', Gaikō shiryō-kan (Diplomatic Record Office), Microfilm No: B'-0003 (12 May 1949).

——, 'Chū-So dōmei jōyaku no kaisetsu (Interpretations of the Sino–Soviet Treaty of Friendship and Alliance)', Gaikō shiryō-kan (Diplomatic Record Office), Microfilm No: B'-0008 (14 February 1950).

——, 'Chūgoku mondai ni taisuru Yoshida sōri yori Daresu komon ate shokan (from Prime Minister Yoshida to Dulles Regarding the China Issue)', handed from Iguchi, Vice-Minister of the Japanese Foreign Ministry, to Sebald, the US Ambassador to Japan, Gaikō shiryō-kan (Diplomatic Record Office), Microfilm No: A'-0009 (22 December 1951).

——, 'Chūgoku mondai ni taisuru Yoshida sōri shokan ni taisuru kakkoku no hannō (Foreign Responses to Prime Minister Yoshida's Memorandum Regarding the China Issue)', Gaikō shiryō-kan (Diplomatic Record Office), Microfilm No: A'-0009 (20 January 1952).

——, 'Chūgoku mondai (China Issue)', Gaikō shiryō-kan (Diplomatic Record Office), Tokyo, Microfilm No: A'-0356 (1955).

——, 'Chūkyō shōnin ni kansuru Hatoyama sōri genmei hōdō ni kansuru ken (Matters Concerning Prime Minister Hatoyama's Statement about Japan's Recognition of Communist China)', Gaikō shiryō-kan (Diplomatic Record Office), Microfilm No: A'-0356 (21 February 1955).

——, 'Tōmen no tai-Chūkyō seisaku: niji-an (Immediate Policy towards Communist China: Second Draft)', Gaikō shiryō-kan (Diplomatic Record Office), Microfilm No: A'-0356 (12 September 1955).

——, 'Chūgoku mondai (China Issue)', Gaikō shiryō-kan (Diplomatic Record Office), Microfilm No: A'-0356 (1955).

——, 'Chūgoku mondai kentō kai (Review Committee on the China Issue)', Gaikō shiryō-kan (Diplomatic Record Office), Microfilm No: A'-0356 (31 August 1956).

——, 'Tai Chūkyō shochi yōkō (Outline of Japan's Communist China Policy)', Gaikō shiryō-kan (Diplomatic Record Office), Microfilm No: A'-0356 (10 October 1958).

Gaimushō, 'Wagakuni no tai-Chūgoku seisaku: chōki kihon seisaku (Japan's China Policy: Basic Long-Term Policy)', Gaikō shiryō-kan (Diplomatic Record Office), Microfilm No: A'-0356 (14 July 1959).

——, 'Chūkyō no genjō to sono taigai seisaku (The Current Situation in Communist China and its Foreign Policy)', Gaikō shiryō-kan (Diplomatic Record Office), Microfilm No: A'-0356 (26 May 1959).

——, 'Beikoku no Chūgoku seisaku (US China Policy)', Gaikō shiryō-kan (Diplomatic Record Office), Microfilm No: A'-0356 (28 January 1961).

——, 'Nihon no torubeki kihonteki tachiba (Japan's Basic Stance)', Gaikō shiryō-kan (Diplomatic Record Office), Microfilm No: A'-0356 (30 January 1961).

——, 'Nihon Chūkyō kankei zakken: Shōwa 35-40 nen (Documents concerning Japan–Communist China Relations: 1960–1965)', Gaikō shiryō-kan (Diplomatic Record Office), Microfilm No: A'-0356 (undated).

Official publications

Bōeichō (Japanese Defence Agency), *Nihon no bōei 2000* (Defence of Japan 2000), Tokyo, 2000.

Development Assistance Committee, OECD, *Recommendation on Financial Terms and Conditions*, Paris, 1969.

East Asia Analytical Unit, Department of Foreign Affairs and Trade, Australia, *Asia's Global Powers: China–Japan Relations in the 21st Century*, Canberra, 1996.

Economic Cooperation Bureau, Ministry of Foreign Affairs, *Japan's Official Development Assistance 1990*, Tokyo, 1991

——, *Japan's Official Development Assistance Annual Report 1993*, Tokyo, 1994.

——, *Japan's Official Development Assistance Annual Report 1995*, Tokyo, 1996.

——, *Japan's Official Development Assistance Annual Report 1998*, Tokyo, 1999.

——, *Japan's Official Development Assistance Annual Report 1999*, Tokyo, 2000.

——, *Japan's Official Development Assistance: White Paper 2001*, Tokyo, 2002.

——, *Japan's Official Development Assistance: White Paper 2001*, Tokyo, 2002.

——, *Japan's Official Development Assistance: White Paper 2001*, Tokyo, 2002.

——, *Japan's Official Development Assistance: White Paper 2002*, Tokyo, 2003.

Export and Import Bank of Japan, *JEXIM 1999*, annual report, Tokyo, 2000.

Gaimushō, *Gaikō Seisho 1998* (Diplomatic Bluebook 1998), Tokyo: Gaimushō, 1998.

Gaimushō keizai kyōryoku kyoku (Economic Cooperation Bureau, Ministry of Foreign Affairs), *Keizai kyōryoku no rinen: Seifu kaihatsu enjo wa naze okonau no ka* (The Concept of Economic Cooperation: Why Implement Official Development Assistance?), Tokyo, 1981.

——, *Wagakuni no seifu kaihatsu enjo 1984* (Japan's ODA 1984), Tokyo, 1984.

——, *Wagakuni no seifu kaihatsu enjo 1989* (Japan's ODA 1989), Tokyo, 1989.

——, *Wagakuni no seifu kaihatsu enjo 1994* (Japan's ODA 1994), Tokyo, 1994.

——, *Wagakuni no seifu kaihatsu enjo 1999* (Japan's ODA 1999), Tokyo, 1999.

——, *Wagakuni no seifu kaihatsu enjo no jishi jōkyō 1998* (The Implementation of Japanese Official Development Assistance in 1998), Tokyo, 1999.

——, *Wagakuni no seifu kaihatsu enjo 2000* (Japan's ODA 2000), Tokyo, 2000.

International Monetary Fund, *Direction of Trade Statistics*, Washington, DC, 1981–2001, 2003.

——, *International Financial Statistics*, Washington, DC, 2001.

Japan Bank for International Cooperation, *Annual Report 2000*, Tokyo, 2001.
——. *JBIC ODA Loans to the People's Republic of China*, Tokyo, 2001.
——, *ODA Loan Report 2000*, Tokyo, 2001.
Japan International Cooperation Agency, *Annual Report 2001*, Tokyo, 2002.
Kōan chōsa-chō (Public Security Investigation Agency), *Nihon no naka no Chūkyo* (Communist China in Japan), Tokyo, 1967.
Kokusai kyōryoku ginkō (Japan Bank for International Cooperation), *Kokusai kyōryoku ginkō no yakuwari to kinō* (Role and Function of the Japan Bank for International Cooperation), Tokyo, November 2000, pp. 1–28.
——, Chūgoku enshakkan no gaiyō (Summary of Japanese Yen Loans to China), Tokyo, June 2001.
Kokusai kyōryoku jigyōdan (Japan International Cooperation Agency), *Chūgoku kunibetsu enjo kenkyū-kai hōkoku-sho* (Report by the China Aid Research Group), Tokyo, 1991.
——, *Dainiji Chūgoku kunibetsu kenkyū-kai hōkoku-sho* (Second Report by China Aid Research Group), Tokyo, 1999.
Liberal Democratic Party, 'Foreign Policy: Japan's Strategy Towards the Asia-Pacific Region', Tokyo: LDP, 1997.
Ministry of Foreign Affairs, Japan, *Diplomatic Bluebook 2003*, Tokyo: Ministry of Foreign Affairs, 2003.
——, Japan, *Diplomatic Bluebook 2004*, Tokyo: Ministry of Foreign Affairs, 2004.
National Bureau of Statistics of China, *China Statistical Yearbook 1999*, Beijing: China Statistics Press, 1999.
——, *China Statistical Yearbook 2001*, Beijing: China Statistics Press. 2001.
——, *China Statistical Yearbook 2003*, Beijing: China Statistics Press, 2003.
National Institute for Defence Studies. *East Asian Strategic Review 1998–1999*, Tokyo: National Institute for Defence Studies. 1999.
——, *East Asian Strategic Review 2004*, Tokyo: National Institute for Defence Studies. 2004.
Nihon bōeki shinkō kyōkai (JETRO), *Chūgoku deita fairu 1999/2000* (China Data File 1999/2000), Tokyo, 2000.
Ōhira sōri no seisaku kenkyū kai, Sōgō anzen hoshō kenkyū gurūpu, *Sōgō anzen hoshō kenkyū gurūpu hōkokusho* (Report of the Study Group on Comprehensive Security), Tokyo: Naikaku kanbō, July 1980.
Organization for Economic Cooperation and Development (OECD), *Geographical Distribution of Financial Flows to Developing Countries, 1977/1980*, Paris, 1981.
——, *Geographical Distribution of Financial Flows to Developing Countries, 1982/1985*, Paris, 1985.
——, *Geographical Distribution of Financial Flows to Developing Countries, 1984/1987*, Paris, 1989.
——, *Geographical Distribution of Financial Flows to Developing Countries, 1986/1989*, Paris, 1991.
——, *Geographical Distribution of Financial Flows to Developing Countries, 1987/1990*, Paris, 1992.
——, *Geographical Distribution of Financial Flows to Aid Recipients, 1990–1994*, Paris, 1996.
——, *Geographical Distribution of Financial Flows to Aid Recipients, 1994–1998*, Paris, 2000.
Sōrifu (Prime Minister's Office), Japan, *Gaikō ni kansuru yoron chōsa* (Opinion Polls on Japanese Diplomacy), Tokyo: Sōrifu, 1998.
Sōrifu, *Gaikō ni kansuru yoron chōsa* (Opinion Polls on Japanese Diplomacy), Tokyo: Sōrifu, 1999.

——, *Gaikō ni kansuru yoron chōsa* (Opinion Polls on Japanese Diplomacy), Tokyo: Sōrifu, 2004.

World Bank, *1999 World Bank Atlas*, Washington, DC, 1999.

——, *2004 World Bank Atlas*, Washington, DC, 2004.

——, *2004 World Bank Development Indicators*, Washington, DC, 2004.

Zaimushō (Japanese Ministry of Finance), *Kanzei nenpō Heisei 12-nen ban* (Customs Annual Report 2000), Tokyo, 2000.

Newspapers

Asahi shinbun, 1979–2004.
Japan Times, 1978–2005.
Mainichi shinbun, 1996.
Nikkei Weekly, 1996.
Ryūkyū shinpō, 2002.
Sankei shinbun, 2000–2004.
Yomiuri shinbun, 1979–2005.

Unpublished theses and reports

Gaimushō (Japanese Ministry of Foreign Affairs), '21seiki ni muketa tai-Chū keizai kyōryoku no arikata ni kansuru kondankai: Teigen (Policy Recommendation Report by the MOFA Committee on Japanese Economic Assistance to China for the 21st Century)', unpublished report, December 2000, pp. 1–30.

Gaimushō Chūgoku-ka (China Division, Ministry of Foreign Affairs), 'Saikin no Chūgoku jōsei to Nitchū kankei (Current Chinese Affairs and Japan–China Relations)', unpublished report, April 2000, pp. 1–20.

——, 'Saikin no Chūgoku jōsei to Nitchū kankei (Current Chinese Affairs and Japan–China Relations)', unpublished report, February 2001, pp. 1–24.

Gaimushō keizai kyōryoku kyoku (Economic Cooperation Bureau, Ministry of Foreign Affairs), 'Taichū keizai kyōryoku (Japan's Economic Cooperation with China)', unpublished report, 2000, pp. 1–3.

Inada Jūichi, 'Tai-Chū ODA no keizaiteki shakaiteki hyōka ni tsuite (An Economic and Social Assessment of China ODA)', in Nihon kokusai mondai kenkyūjo (ed.), *Tai-Chū ODA no keizai sakai inpakuto ni tsuiteno kisoteki chōsa* (Basic Research on the Economic and Social Impact of China ODA), unpublished report, Tokyo, 2000, pp. 1–10.

Jimintō (Liberal Democratic Party), 'Chūgoku ni taisuru keizai enjo oyobi kyōryoku no sōkatsu to shishin (Review and Guidelines of Japanese Economic Aid and Assistance to China)', unpublished policy recommendation report, December 2000, pp. 1–7.

Kimata Yōichirō, 'Seiji-teki kondishonariti toshite no Nihon no ODA yon-shishin (Japan's Four ODA Principles as Political Conditionality)', unpublished Master's Thesis, Yokohama: Yokohama kokuritsu daigaku, 1997.

Keidanren (Federation of Economic Organizations), '21-seiki no Nitchū kankei o kangaeru (Assessing Sino–Japanese Relations in the 21st Century)', unpublished report, Tokyo, February 2001, pp. 1–15.

Kokusai kyōryoku ginkō (Japan Bank for International Cooperation), 'Kokusai kyōryoku ginkō ga kanri o okonatteiru keiyaku: Heisei 11-nendo ban (Contracts Managed by the Japan Bank for International Cooperation: 1999)', unpublished report, Tokyo, 1999.

Nihon kokusai mondai kenkyūjo (ed.) *Tai-Chū ODA no keizaiteki sakaiteki inpakuto ni tsuite no kisoteki chōsa* (Basic Research on the Economic and Social Impact of China ODA), unpublished report, Tokyo, 2000.

Sangiin gaimu iinkai (Foreign Affairs Committee, Upper House of the Diet),'Chūgoku Taiwan jōsei ni kansuru ketsugi (The Resolution Concerning China–Taiwan Affairs)', Tokyo, 6 May 1996.

Sangiin kokusai mondai ni kansuru chōsa-kai (Research Committee on Foreign Affairs, Upper House), 'Sangiin taigai keizai kyōryoku ni kansuru shō iinkai kaigiroku (Record of the Upper House Sub-Committee on Foreign Economic Cooperation)', Tokyo, 27 February 1988.

Shimomura Yasutami, 'Nitchū keizai kankei: kōteki shikin kyōryoku no yakuwari no tenbō (Japan–China Economic Relations: A Perspective on the Role of Japan's Official Financial Assistance)', paper presented at the Liberal Democratic Party Review Committee on Economic Assistance to China, Tokyo, November 2000, pp. 1–5.

Summerville, Paul A., 'The Politics of Self-Restraint: The Japanese State, and the Voluntary Export Restraint of Japanese Passenger Car Exports to the United States in 1981', unpublished PhD thesis, University of Tokyo, 1998.

Takemi Keizō, 'Kokunai seji no dainamizumu to Nichi-Bei-Chū kankei (Dynamism of International Politics and Japan–US–China Relations)', unpublished report, 1999.

Zai-Chūgoku Nihonkoku taishikan keizaibu (Economics Division, Japanese Embassy in China), 'Saikin no Chūgoku keizai jōsei to Nitchū keizai kankei (Current Chinese Economic Affairs and Japan–China Economic Relations)', unpublished report, November 1999, pp. 1–15.

——, 'Saikin no Chūgoku keizai jōsei to Nitchū keizai kankei (Current Chinese Economic Affairs and Japan–China Economic Relations)', unpublished report, January 2001. pp. 1–20.

Books and articles

Abe Junichi, 'Kaiyō o mezasu Chūgoku no gunji senryaku (China's Military Strategy Aiming at the Ocean)', *Kokusai mondai*, no. 430, January 1996, pp. 58–73.

Allison, Graham T., *Essence of Decision: Explaining the Cuban Missile Crisis*, Boston, MA: Little, Brown Company, 1971.

Allison, Graham T. and Morton H. Halperin, 'Bureaucratic Politics: A Paradigm and Some Policy Implications', *World Politics*, vol. 24, Spring 1972, pp. 40–79.

Amako Satoshi (ed.) *Chūgoku wa kyōi ka?* (Is China a Threat?), Tokyo: Keisō shobō, 1997.

——, 'Introduction', in Amako Satoshi (ed.) *Chūgoku wa kyōi ka?* (Is China a threat?), Tokyo: Keisōshobō, 1997, pp. 3–22.

——, 'Seiji taisei no kōzō teki henyō (Structural Change in the Chinese Political System)', in Mōri Kazuko (ed.) *Gendai Chūgoku no kōzō hendō* (Structural Change in Contemporary China), Tokyo: Tōkyō daigaku shuppan-kai, 2000, pp. 15–55.

——, 'Nitchū kankei nijūisseiki e no teigen (A Recommendation for Japan–China Relations in the Twenty-first Century)', *Chūgoku 21*, vol. 10, January 2001, pp. 43–60.

——, 'Chūgoku, Tenanmon jiken to sōgō kokuryoku (China, the Tiananmen Square Incident and Comprehensive National Power)', *Sekai*, no. 687, April 2001, pp. 146–51.

Ampiah, Kweku, 'A One Sided Partnership', *West Africa*, November 28–December 4, 1988, pp. 2221–38.

Arase, David, *Buying Power: The Political Economy of Japan's Foreign Aid*, London: Lynne Rienner Publishers, 1995.

——, 'A Militarised Japan?', *Journal of Strategic Studies*, vol. 18, no. 3, September 1995, pp. 84–103.

Asahi shinbunsha, *Shiryō: Nihon to Chūgoku '45–'71* (Documents: Japan and China '45–'71), Tokyo, 1972.

Asakawa Hideji, 'Tai-Chū tekkō gijutsu kyōryoku ni tsuite (Regarding Japan's Steel Plant Technology Assistance to China)', *Tōa*, no. 175, January 1982, pp. 64–81.

Ash, Robert (eds) *China's Integration in Asia: Economic Security and Strategic Issues*, Richmond, VA and Surrey: Curzon Press, 2002.

Bailey, Paul J., *Postwar Japan: 1945 to the Present*, Oxford: Blackwell Publishers, 1996.

Beasley, W.G., *The Rise of Modern Japan*, London: Weidenfeld and Nicolson, Third Edition, 2000.

Beer, Lawrence W., 'Some Dimensions of Japan's Present and Potential Relations with Communist China', *Asian Survey*, vol. 9, no. 3, March 1969, pp. 163–77.

Beeson, Mark (ed.) *Reconfiguring East Asia: Regional Institutions and Organisations After the Crisis*, London and New York: RoutledgeCurzon, 2002.

Beeson, Mark and Leong Liew, 'Capitalism in East Asia: the Political Economy of Business Organisation in Japan, Korea and China', in Beeson, Mark (ed.) *Reconfiguring East Asia: Regional Institutions and Organisations After the Crisis*, London and New York: RoutledgeCurzon, 2002, pp. 139–58.

Berton, Peter, 'The Japanese Communist Party and Its Transformations', Working Paper No. 67, Japan Policy Research Institute, Cardiff, CA, May 2000.

Betshi Yukio, 'Nitchū kokkō seijōka no seiji katei (The Political Process of Japan–China Diplomatic Normalisation)', *Kokusai seiji*, August 1980, pp. 1–18.

Bhagwati, Jagdish, 'Democracy and Development', *Journal of Democracy*, vol. 3, no. 3, July 1992, pp. 37–44.

Blacker, Michael, 'Evaluating Japan's Diplomatic Performance', in Gerald L. Curtis (ed.) *Japan's Foreign Policy after the Cold War: Coping with Change*, Armonk, NY: M.E. Sharpe, 1993, pp. 1–42.

Braddick, C.W., *Japan and the Sino–Soviet Alliance 1950–1964: in the Shadow of the Monolith*, Houndmills, Basingstoke, Hampsher: Palgrave/Macmillan, 2004.

Breuning, Marijke, 'Words and Deeds: Foreign Assistance Rhetoric and Policy Behaviour in the Netherlands, Belgium, and the United Kingdom', *International Studies Quarterly*, vol. 39, no. 2, June 1995, pp. 235–54.

Brooks, William L. and Robert M. Orr Jr, 'Japan's Foreign Economic Cooperation', *Asian Survey*, vol. 25, no. 3, March 1985, pp. 322–40.

Brown, Lester R., *Who Will Feed China? Wake-up Call for a Small Planet*, New York: W.W. Norton, 1995.

Calder, Kent E., 'Japanese Foreign Economic Policy Formation: Explaining the Reactive State', *World Politics*, vol. 40, no. 4, July 1988, pp. 517–41.

——, 'The New Face of Northeast Asia', *Foreign Affairs*, vol. 80, no. 1, January–February 2001, pp. 106–22.

Chan, Thomas, Noel Tracy and Zhui Wenhui, *China's Export Miracle, Origins, Results and Prospects*, Houndsmill, Basingstoke: Macmillan, 1999.

Chapman, J.W.M., R. Drifte and I.T.M. Gow, *Japan's Quest for Comprehensive Security: Defence–Diplomacy–Dependence*, New York: St Martin's Press, 1982.

Chen Zhaobin, 'Sengo Nihon no Chūgoku seisaku no genkei: 1950 nendai ni okeru "futatsu no Chūgoku" to "seikei-bunri" (The Origins of Japan's Postwar China Policy: the "Two China Policy" and the "Separation of Politics and Economy" during the 1950s)', *Shisō*, no. 887, May 1998, pp. 27–44.

Christensen, Raymond, 'The New Japanese Election System', *Pacific Affairs*, vol. 69, no. 1, 1996, pp. 49–70.

Christensen, Thomas J., 'China, the US–Japan Alliance, and the Security Dilemma in East Asia', *International Security*, vol. 23, no. 4, Spring 1999, pp. 49–80.

Chung, Chien-peng, *Domestic Politics, International Bargaining and China's Territorial Disputes*, London and New York: RoutledgeCurzon, 2004.

Clarke, Duncan L., 'US Security Assistance to Egypt and Israel: Politically Untouchable?', *Middle East Journal*, vol. 51, no. 2, Spring 1997, pp. 200–14.

Dower, John, *Empire and Aftermath: Yoshida Shigeru and the Japanese Experience, 1878–1954*, Cambridge, MA: Harvard University Press, 1988.

Drifte, Reinhard, 'Japanese–Chinese Security Relations: The Japanese Way of Engagement', *Social Science Japan*, no. 21, September 2001, pp. 26–31.

——, *Japan's Security Relations with China since 1989: From balancing to bandwagoning?*, London and New York: RouledgeCurzon, 2003.

Ebata Kensuke, 'Chūgoku no gunjiryoku to higashi Ajia no gunbi kindaika (Chinese Military Capability and the Military Modernisation of East Asia)', *Tōa*, no. 337, July 1995, pp. 6–25.

Elgström, Ole and Goran Hyden (eds) *Development and Democracy: What Have We Learned About and How?*, London and New York: Routledge, 2002.

Ensign, Margee M., *Doing Good or Doing Well? Japan's Foreign Aid Program*, New York: Columbia University Press, 1992.

Fairbank, John King, *China: A New History*, Cambridge, MA and London: The Belknap Press of Harvard University Press, Third Printing, 1994.

Fu, Xiaolan, *Exports, Foreign Direct Investment and Economic Development in China*, New York: Palgrave Macmillan, 2004.

Fujiwara Hirotatsu, *Kanryō no kōzō* (The Structure of the Bureaucracy), Tokyo: Kōdan-sha gendai shinsho, 1974.

Fukui, Haruhiro, *Party in Power: The Japanese Liberal–Democrats and Policy-making*. Los Angeles, CA: University of California Press, 1970.

——, 'Studies in Policymaking: A Review of the Literature', in T.J. Pempel (ed.) *Policymaking in Contemporary Japan*, Ithaca, NY and London: Cornell University Press, 1977, pp. 22–59.

——, 'Tanaka Goes to Peking: A Case Study in Foreign Policymaking', in T.J. Pempel (ed.) *Policymaking in Contemporary Japan*, Ithaca, NY and London: Cornell University Press, 1977, pp. 61–102.

Fukushima, Akiko, *Japanese Foreign Policy: the Emerging Logic of Multilateralism*, New York: Macmillan Press, 1999.

——, 'Official Development Assistance (ODA) as a Japanese Foreign Policy Tool', in Inoguchi Takashi and Purnendra Jain (eds) *Japanese Foreign Policy Today*, New York: Palgrave, 2000, pp. 152–74.

Fukuyama, Francis, 'Capitalism and Democracy: The Missing Link', *Journal of Democracy*, vol. 3, no. 3, July 1992, pp. 100–10.

Funabashi Yōichi, *Naibu: aru Chūgoku hōkoku* (Inside: A China Report), Tokyo: Asahi shinbun-sha, 1983.

Gilboy, George and Eric Heginbotham, 'China's Coming Transformation', *Foreign Affairs*, July/August 2001, pp. 26–39.

Green, Michael J., *Japan's Reluctant Realism: Foreign Policy Challenge in an Era of Uncertain Power*, New York: Palgrave, 2001.

Green, Michael J. and Benjamin L. Self, 'Japan's Changing China Policy: From Commercial Liberalism to Reluctant Realism', *Survival*, vol. 38, no. 2, Summer 1996, pp. 35–58.

Gries, Peter Hays, *China's New Nationalism: Pride, Politics, and Diplomacy*, Berkeley, CA, Los Angeles, CA and London: University of California Press, 2004.

Halliday, Jon and Gavan McCormack, *Japanese Imperialism Today: Co-Prosperity in Greater East Asia*, New York, London: Monthly Review Press, 1973.

Handa Shigeru, 'Chūgoku Kitachōsen wa semete kuru no desuka? (Will China and North Korea attack Japan?)', *Sekai*, no. 701, May 2002, pp. 110–13.

Hasegawa Keitarō and Watanabe Toshio, *Yōsō no chōtaikoku Chūgoku* (Myth of Superpower China), Tokyo: Tokuma shoten, 1995.

Hashimoto Kōhei, 'Nihon no enjo seisaku kettei yōin (Determinants of Japan's Foreign Aid Policy', in Hashimoto Kōhei (ed.) *Nihon no gaikō seisaku kettei yōin* (Domestic Determinants of Japanese Foreign Policy), Tokyo: PHP kenkyūjo, 1999, pp. 337–83.

—— (ed.) *Nihon no gaikō seisaku kettei yōin* (Domestic Determinants of Japanese Foreign Policy), Tokyo: PHP kenkyūjo, 1999.

Hatano Sumio, 'Nitchū keizai kankei no tenkai (The Development of Japan–China Economic Relations)', in Masuda Hiroshi and Hatano Sumio (eds) *Ajia no naka no Nihon to Chūgoku: yūkō to masatsu no gendaishi* (Japan and China in Asia: Recent History of Friendship and Confrontation), Tokyo: Yamakawa Shuppan-sha, 1995, pp. 247–67.

Hatayama Noboru and Takenaka Heizō, 'Seisaku kettei ni okeru kanryō no yakuwari (Roles of Bureaucrats in Policy-making)', *Keizai seminā*, vol. 483, April 1995, pp. 26–35.

Hatch, Walter and Kozo Yamamura, *Asia in Japan's Embrace: Building a Regional Production Alliance*, Cambridge: Cambridge University Press, 1996.

Heginbotham, Eric and Richard J. Samuels, 'Mercantile Realism and Japanese Foreign Policy', *International Security*, vol. 22, no. 4, Spring 1998, pp. 171–203.

Higashi Sadao, *Seifu kaihatsu enjo* (Official Development Assistance), Tokyo: Keiō shobō shuppan, 1986.

Hilpert, Hanns Günther and Nakagane Katsuji, 'Economic Relations: What Can We Learn from Trade and FDI?', in Marie Söderberg (ed.) *Chinese–Japanese Relations in the Twenty-first Century: Complementarity and Conflict*, London and New York: European Institute of Japanese Studies, 2002, pp. 130–53.

Hiramatsu Shigeo, *Chūgoku no gunji ryoku* (China's Military Capability), Tokyo: Bunshun shinsho, 1999.

——, 'Kakudai suru Chūgoku no Higashi-Shinakai shinshutsu: shinshoku sareru wagakuni no keizai suiiki (Expanding Chinese Activities in the East China Sea: The Eroded Japanese Exclusive Economic Zone)', *Tōa*, no. 382, April 1999, pp. 6–23.

——, 'Tai-Chū ODA "gun-min ryōyō" no jittai (The "Military–Civilian Dual Use" of Japanese ODA by China)', *Tōa*, no. 400, October 2000, pp. 6–21.

——, 'Chūgokugun o tsuyokusuru ODA (The ODA which Makes the Chinese Military Stronger)', *Seiron*, November 2000, pp. 152–60.

Hirata, Keiko, 'New Challenges to Japan's Aid: An Analysis of Aid Policy-making', *Pacific Affairs*, vol. 71, no. 3, pp. 311–34.

Hirota Kōki, 'Chūgoku ni taisuru gaikoku enjo no dōkō (The Trend of Foreign Aid to China)', *Kikinchōsa kihō*, no. 49, June 1985, pp. 184–8.

Hishida Masaharu, 'Kokka to shakai no kōsei (The Symbiosis Between State and Society)', in Mōri Kazuko (ed.) *Gendai Chūgoku no kōzō hendō* (Structural Change in Contemporary China), Tokyo: Tōkō daigaku shuppan-kai, 2000, pp. 57–90.

Hook, Glenn D, Julie Gilson, Christopher W. Hughes and Hugo Dobson, *Japan's International Relations: Politics, Economics and Security*, London and New York: Routledge, 2001.

Hoopes, Townsend, *The Devil and John Foster Dulles*, London: Andre Deutsch, 1973.

Hosoya Chihiro, 'Nichi-Bei-Chū sankyoku kankei no rekishi-teki kōzō (History of Japan–US–China Triangular Relations)', *Kokusai mondai*, no. 254, 1981, pp. 2–13.

Howe, Christopher (ed.) *China and Japan: History, Trends, and Prospects*, Oxford: Clarendon Press, 1996.

——, 'The Changing Asian Environment of China's Economic Development: The Perspective from Japan, with Particular Reference to Foreign Direct Investment and Industrial Restructuring', in Robert Ash (ed.) *China's Integration in Asia: Economic Security and Strategic Issues*, Richmond, VA and Surrey: Curzon Press, 2002, pp. 3–38.

Hsiao, Gene T., 'The Sino-Japanese Rapprochement: A Relationship of Ambivalence', *China Quarterly*, no. 57, January/March 1974, pp. 101–23.

Igarashi Hitoshi, 'Gendai Nihon no seisaku kettei katei to Jimintō (Policy-making in Contemporary Japan and the Liberal Democratic Party)', *Kenkyū shiryō geppō*, vol. 319, June 1985, pp. 1–17.

Ijiri, Hidenori, 'Sino–Japanese Controversy since the 1972 Diplomatic Normalisation', in Christopher Howe (ed.) *China and Japan: History, Trends, and Prospects*, Oxford: Clarendon Press, 1996, pp. 60–82.

Inada, Jūichi., 'Nihon gaikō ni okeru enjo mondai no shosokumen (Several Aspects of Foreign Aid Issues in Japanese Diplomacy)', *Kokusai mondai*, no. 326, May 1987, pp. 2–20.

Inoguchi Takashi, *Gendai Nihon seiji-keizai no kōzō* (The Structure of the Contemporary Japanese Political Economy), Tokyo: Tōyō keizai shinpō-sha, 1983.

——, *Japan's International Relations*, Boulder, CO: Westview Press, 1991.

——, 'Kaibutsu Chūgoku ni dō tsukiau noka? (How to Deal with a Monster China?)', *This is Yomiuri*, vol. 7, no. 6, September 1996, pp. 34–45.

Inoguchi Takashi and Iwai Tomoaki, *Zoku giin no kenkyū: Jimintō o gyūjiru shuyaku tachi* (Research on Zoku Parliamentarians: The Tribe which Dominates Liberal Democratic Party Governments), Tokyo: Nihon keizai shinbun-sha, 1987.

Inoguchi Takashi and Purnendra Jain (eds.) *Japanese Foreign Policy Today*, New York: Palgrave, 2000.

'Intellectuals in China Under Fire, Again: Free Expression Worries the Authorities', *The Economist*, vol. 373, no. 8405, December 2004, pp. 26–7.

International Institute for Strategic Studies, *The Military Balance 2003–2004*, London: IISS, 2004.

Ishihara Kyōichi, 'Chūgoku ni okeru "seidoka sareta shijō keizai" no kōchiku no kanōsei (The Possibility of Creating an "Institutionalised Market Economy" in China)', *Kokusai mondai*, no. 492, March 2001, pp. 2–16.

Ishii Akira, 'Chū-So kankei no 40-nen: byōdō na nikoku kankei o motomete (The 40 Years of Sino–Soviet Relations: In Search of an Equal Relationship)', *Kokusai mondai*, no. 354, September 1989, pp. 2–16.

Jan, George P., 'The Japanese People and Japanese Policy toward Communist China', *Western Political Quarterly*, vol. 22, no. 3, September 1969, pp. 605–21.

Jan, George P., 'Japan's Trade with Communist China', *Asian Survey*, vol. 9, no. 12, December 1969, pp. 900–18.

Jiang, Wenran, 'The Japanese Assessment of the "China Threat"' in Herbert Yee and Ian Storey (eds) *The China Threat: Perceptions, Myths and Reality*, London and New York: RoutledgeCurzon, 2002, pp. 150–65.

Joel Krieger, William A. Joseph and James A. Paul (eds), *The Oxford Companion to Politics of the World*, New York and London: Oxford University Press, 1993.

Joseph, William A., 'Cultural Revolution', in Joel Krieger William A. Joseph and James A. Paul (eds) *The Oxford Companion to Politics of the World*, New York and London: Oxford University Press, 1993, pp. 211–2.

Kamimura Kōji, 'Chūgoku hōdō (China Report)', *Sekai*, no. 685, March 2001, pp. 112–16.

Katada, Saori N., 'Why Did Japan Suspend Foreign Aid to China? Japan's Foreign Aid Decision-making and Source of Aid Sanction', *Social Science Japan Journal*, vol. 4, no. 1, April 2001, pp. 39–58.

——, 'New Cources in Japan's Foreign Aid Policy: More Humanitarian and More Nationalistic', in Saori N. Katada, Hanns W. Maull and Takashi Inoguchi (eds) *Global Governance: Germany and Japan in the International System*, Aldershot and Burlington: Ashgate, 2004, pp. 179–98.

Katō Hiroyuki, 'Chū-chōki hatten senryaku no sakutei o megutte: "Chūgoku Kyōiron" no keizaitei sokumen (Regarding the Formulation of Medium to Long-Term Development Strategy: The Economic Perspective on the "China Threat Thesis")', in Amako Satoshi (ed.) *Chūgoku wa kyōi ka?* (Is China a Threat?), Tokyo: Keisō shobō, 1997, pp. 23–45.

——, 'Kōzō tenkanki o mukaeta Chūgoku keizai (Chinese Economy Facing Structural Change)', *Kokusai mondai*, no. 478, January 2000, pp. 38–52.

Kawashima, Yutaka, *Japanese Foreign Policy at The Crossraods: Challenges and options for the Twenty-First Century*, Washington, DC: Brookings Institution Press, 2003.

Kayahara Ikuo, 'Kenkoku 50 shūnen kinen gyōji kara mita Chūgoku seikyoku to kokubō kindaika (China's Political Affairs and Military Modernisation Observed from the 50th Anniversary Event of the National Founding)', *Bōeishisetsu to gijutsu*, vol. 10, no. 1, January 2000, pp. 52–64.

——, 'Anzen hoshō kara mita Nitchū kankei (Security Perspective on Japan–China Relations)', *Chūgoku 21*, vol. 10, January 2001, pp. 75–96.

——, 'Ajia chiiki no enerugii jukyū to Chūgoku no sekiyū mondai (The Demand and Supply of Energy in the Asia Region and China's Oil Problem)', *Bōei shisetsu to gijutsu*, vol. 11, no. 1, January 2001, pp. 54–70.

Kennedy, Paul M., *The Rise and Fall of the Great Powers*, New York: Random House, 1987.

Kesavan, K.V., 'Japan and the Tiananmen Square Incident: Aspects of the Bilateral Relationship', *Asian Survey*, vol. 30, no. 7, July 1990, pp. 669–81.

Kishi Nobusuke, Yatsugi Kazuo and Itō Takashi, *Kishi Nobusuke no kaisō* (The Memoirs of Kishi Nobusuke), Tokyo: Bungei shunjū, 1981.

Kissinger, Henry, *White House Years*, London: Weidenfeld and Nicolson and Michael Joseph, 1979.

Kobayashi Mamoru, 'Henyō suru Chūgoku no yukue (Future Outlook of Changing China)', *Gaikō fōramu*, no. 151, February 2001, pp. 58–69.

Kobayashi Morinao, 'Nitchū keizai kyōryoku no genjō to hōto (Current Condition and Future Direction of Japanese Economic Assistance to China)', *Tōa*, no. 403, January 2001, pp. 7–18.

Kojima Sueo, 'Shin-dankai ni haitta Nitchū keizai kankei (A New Stage of Japan–China Economic Relations)', *Tōa*, no. 197, November 1983, pp. 23–39.

Kojima Tomoyuki, 'Mata kurikaesareru kyōkasho mondai (A Report of the Textbook Issue)', *Tōa*, no. 230, August 1986, pp. 40–51.

——, 'Koritsu kaihi wa Chūgoku no konran kenen de (Avoidance of Isolation by China's Own Effort)', *Tōa*, no. 277, July 1990, pp. 39–52.

——, 'Zaisei kiki no naka no kokubōhi zōdai (The Increase in Chinese Defence Expenditure in the Budget Crisis)', *Tōa*, no. 287, May 1991, pp. 54–75.

——, 'Chūgoku no seiji to gaikō wa fukuzatsu sakusō (Complicated Chinese Politics and Diplomacy)', *Tōa*, no. 344, February 1996, pp. 46–62.

——, 'Chūgoku o "sekinin aru taikoku" ni surutamени (In Order to Make China a "Responsible Power")', *Gaikō Fōramu*, no. 151, February 2001, pp. 38–45.

Kokubun Ryōsei, 'Chūgoku no taigai keizai seisaku kettei no seiji kōzō: puranto keiyaku chūdan kettei no baai (The Political Structure of Chinese Foreign Economic Policy-Making: Decision-making for Plant Contract Cancellation)', in Okabe Tatsumi (ed.) *Chūgoku gaikō seisaku kettei no kōzō* (The Structure of Chinese Diplomatic Policymaking), Tokyo: Nihon kokusai mondai kenkyū-jo, 1983, pp. 153–84.

Komori Yoshihisa, 'Machigai darake no Chūgoku enjo (Japan's Mistaken China Aid)', *Chūō kōron*, March 2002, pp. 94–109.

'Konransuru Nitchū bōeki shōsha no uchimaku (An Inside Story of Japan–China Trade Firms in Disarray)', *Tokyo keizai*, no. 3366, 1967.

Krugman, Paul, 'The Myth of Asia's Miracle', *Foreign Affairs*, vol. 73, no. 6, November/December 1994, pp. 62–78.

Kunz, Diane B. (ed.) *The Diplomacy of the Cultural Decades: American Foreign Relations during the 1960s*, New York, 1994.

Kusano Atsushi, 'Kaihatsu enjo wa seijiteki minshuka o sokushin suru (Development Assistance will Promote Political Democratisation)', *Ekonomisuto*, vol. 70, no. 25, June 1992, pp. 34–7.

——, 'Yugin kikin tōgō to ODA (Merger between the Japan Export and Import Bank and the Overseas Economic Cooperation Fund, and ODA)', *Shokun*, vol. 28, no. 5, May 1996, pp. 170–80.

LaFeber, Walter, *The Clash: US–Japanese Relations throughout History*, New York, and London: W.W. Norton & Company, 1997.

Lee, Chae-Jin, *Japan Faces China: Political and Economic Relations in the Postwar Era*, Baltimore, MD: The Johns Hopkins University Press, 1976.

——, 'The Making of the Sino-Japanese Peace and Friendship Treaty', *Pacific Affairs*, vol. 52, no. 3, Fall 1979, pp. 420–46.

Lesbirel, S. Hayden, *NIMBY Politics in Japan: Energy Siting and the Management of Environmental Conflict*, Ithaca, NY, London: Cornell University Press, 1998.

Levy, Wendy, 'Major Returns to Local Firms in Aid to China', *Insight: Australian Foreign Affairs and Trade Issues*, vol. 2, no. 11, July 1993, pp. 13–14.

Li, Kwok-sing, *A Glossary of Political Terms of the People's Republic of China*, Hong Kong: Chinese University Press, 1995.

Liang, Tang, 'Chūgoku nōson ni okeru senkyo kaikaku to seiji hendō (Chinese Village Elections and Political Change in Rural Areas)', *Ajia keizai*, vol. 42, no. 2, pp. 2–22.

Lincoln, Edward J., 'Japan's Rapidly Emerging Strategy Toward Asia', Technical Paper no. 58, Research Programme on Globalisation and Regionalisation, OECD, April 1992, pp. 9–28.

Lipset, Seymore, 'Some Social Requisites of Democracy: Economic Development and Political Legitimacy', *American Political Science Review*, vol. 53, no. 1, March 1959, pp. 69–105.

Long, William J., 'Nonproliferation as a Goal of Japanese Foreign Assistance Policy', *Asian Survey*, vol. 39, no. 2, March–April 1999, pp. 328–47.

Masuda Hiroshi and Hatano Sumio (eds) *Ajia no naka no Nihon to Chūgoku: yūkō to masatsu no gendaishi (Japan and China in Asia: Recent History of Friendship and Confrontation)*, Tokyo: Yamakawa shuppan-sha,1995.

Masujima Toshiyuki, 'Gyōsei kaikaku o meguru sho-kōsatsu: Hashimoto gyōkaku o chūshin to shite (An Assessment of Administrative Reforms: With Particular Focus on the Hashimoto Reform)', *NIRA seisaku kenkyū*, vol. 11, no. 6, 1998, pp. 28–37.

Meisner, Maurice, 'MAO Zedong', in Joel Krieger (ed.) *The Oxford Companion to Politics of the World*, New York and Oxford: Oxford University Press, 1993, p. 563.

Mendl, Wolf, *Issues in Japan's China Policy*, London: Royal Institute of International Affairs, 1978.

——, *Japan's Asia Policy: Regional Security and Global Interests*, London and New York: Routledge, 1995.

Meyer, Armin H., *Assignment Tokyo*, Indianapolis: Bobbs-Merrill, 1974.

Millikan, Max and W.W. Rostow, 'A Proposal: Key to an Effective Foreign Policy', US Senate, Special Committee to Study the Foreign Aid Program, Compilation of Studies and Surveys, Washington, DC: GPO, 1957.

Miyake Takao, 'Nitchū bōeki no genjō to shōrai (Current Condition and the Future of Japan–China Trade)', *Chūō kōron*, vol. 76, no. 9, September 1961, pp. 154–60.

Miyashita, Akitoshi, 'Gaiatsu and Japan's Foreign Aid: Rethinking the Reactive–Proactive Debate', *International Studies Quarterly*, vol. 43, no. 4, 1999, pp. 695–732.

Miyazaki Isamu, 'Watashitachi wa Chūgoku o tadashiku toraeteiruka? (Are We Look at China Correctly?)', *Sekai*, no. 685, March 2001, pp. 81–7.

Morgenthau, Hans, 'A Political Theory of Foreign Aid', *American Political Science Review*, vol. 56, no. 2, 1962, pp. 301–9.

Mōri Kazuko, 'Sekai shisutemu no naka no Chūgoku (China in the World System)', *Kokusai mondai*, no. 418, January 1995, pp. 2–16.

——, 'Futeikei no Ajia: Chūgoku wa kyōika? (Shapeless Asia: Is China a Threat?)', *Sekai*, no. 620, March 1996, pp. 41–8.

—— (ed.), *Gendai Chūgoku no kōzō hendō* (Structural Change in Contemporary China), Tokyo: Tōkyō daigaku shuppan-kai, 2000.

Morimoto Satoshi, 'TMD no seijigaku: Nichibei bōei kyōryoku gaidorain to Ajia-Taiheiyō no anzen hoshō (Politics of TMD: the Japan–US Defence Cooperation Guideline and Asia-Pacific Security)', *Tōa*, no. 385, July 1999, pp. 6–20.

Mulgan, Aurelia George, *Japan's Failed Revolution: Koizumi and the Politics of Economic Reform*, Australia: Asia Pacific Press, 2002.

Murai Yoshinori, *Musekinin enjo taikoku Nihon* (Japan as an Irresponsible Foreign Aid Power), Tokyo: JICC shuppan-kyoku, 1989.

——, 'Gaimushō no ODA rinen o tou? (Question the ODA Philosophy of the Ministry of Foreign Affairs?)' *Sekai*, no. 569, June 1992, pp. 315–24.

Nakagane Katsuji, 'Chūgoku keizai: mittsu no tenkan ten (The Chinese Economy: Three Transformations)', in Mōri Kazuko (ed.) *Gendai Chūgoku no kōzō hendō* (Structural Change in Contemporary China), Tokyo: Tōkyō daigaku shuppan-kai, 2000, pp. 91–126.

——, 'Japanese Direct Investment in China: Its Effect on China's Economic Development', in Hanns Günther Hilpert and Rene Haak (eds) *Japan and China: Cooperation, Competition and Conflict*, New York: Palgrave, 2002, pp. 52–71.

Nakagawa, Junji, 'Legal Problems of Japanese ODA Guidelines', *Japanese Journal of International Law*, no. 36, 1994, pp. 76–99.

Nakagawa Kikuo, 'Gaikoku shikin dōnyū taisei (China's System for Introducing Foreign Currency)', *Kikinchōsa kihō*, no. 49, June 1985, pp. 99–109.

Nakai Yoshifumi, '90 nendai Nitchū kankei no tenbō (Prospect of Japan–China Relations in the 1990s)', *Gaikō jihō*, no. 1339, June 1997, pp. 31–48.

Nakajima Kuniko, 'Nihon no gaikō seisaku kettei katei ni okeru Jiyūminshutō seimu chōsakai no yakuwari (The Role of the LDP Policy Research Council within the Process of Japanese Foreign Policy-making)', in Hashimoto Kōhei (ed.) *Nihon no gaikō seisaku kettei yōin* (Domestic Determinants of Japanese Foreign Policy), Tokyo: PHP kenkyūjo, 1999, pp. 70–108.

Nakajima Mineo, 'Chūgoku wa kyōi ka? (Is China a Threat to Japan?)', *Bōeigaku kenkyū*. no. 17, March 1997, pp. 1–18.

Nakamaru Itaru, 'Jyūnan de kidōsei ni tonda ODA kaikaku (ODA Reform that has Flexibility and Mobility)', *Gekkan jiyūminshu*, no. 547, October 1998, pp. 88–103.

Nakamura, Kōji, 'Twice a Loser', *Far Eastern Economic Review*, no. 47, 20 November 1971, p. 1.

Nakane Chie, *Tekiō no jōken: Nihonteki renzoku no shikō* (Conditions of Adaptation: Japanese Thought), Tokyo: Kōdansha, 1972.

Nihon kokusai mondai kenkyūjo, '1990-nendai no kokusai kankei to Nihon (International Relations and Japan in the 1990s)', *Kokusai mondai*, no. 361, April 1990, pp. 44–76.

Nishigaki, Akira and Shimomura Yasutami, *The Economics of Development Assistance: Japan's ODA in a Symbiotic World*, Tokyo: LTCB International Library Foundation, 1999.

Nishihara, Masashi, *The Japanese and Sukarno's Indonesia: Tokyo–Jakarta Relations, 1951–1966*, Honolulu, HI: University Press of Hawaii, 1976.

Nixon, Richard, *The Memoirs of Richard Nixon*, South Melbourne: Macmillan Company of Australia. 1978.

Ogata, Sadako, 'The Business Community and Japanese Foreign Policy: Normalisation of Relations with the People's Republic of China', in Robert A. Scalapino, (ed.) *The Foreign Policy of Modern Japan*, Berkeley, CA: University of California Press, 1977, pp. 175–203.

——, 'Tai-Chū kokkō seijōka no Nichi-Bei hikaku (Normalisation with China: A Comparative Study of the US and Japanese Process)', *Kokusai mondai*, May 1981. no. 256, pp. 62–77.

——, *Normalisation with China: A Comparative Study of the US and Japanese Process*, Berkeley, CA: Institute of East Asian Studies, University of California, 1988.

Okabe Tatsumi (ed.) *Chūgoku gaikō seisaku kettei no kōzō* (The Structure of Chinese Diplomatic Policymaking), Tokyo: Nihon kokusai mondai kenkyū-jo, 1983.

——, 'Tenanmon jiken to kongo no Chūgoku (The Tiananmen Square Incident and China Hereafter)', *Kokusai mondai*, no. 358, January 1990, pp. 2–16.

——, 'Kokusai seijigaku to Chūgoku gaikō (International Politics and Chinese Diplomacy)', in Nihon kokusai seiji gakkai (ed.) *Gurōbarizumu, rijonarizumu, nashonarizumu (Globalism, Regionalism and Nationalism)*, Tokyo: Nihon kokusai seiji gakkai, 1997, pp. 42–56.

Okada Akira, *Mizudori gaikō hiwa* (Secret Stories of the Waterfowl Diplomacy), Tokyo: Chūōkōron-sha, 1983.

——, 'Mizudori gaikō hiwa no zahyō kara kokusai jōsei o tenbou suru (Viewing International Affairs from the Perspective of the Waterfowl Diplomacy)', *Tōa*, no. 200, February 1984, pp. 69–83.

Okada Akira, 'Wagakuni no Chūgoku gaikō uramenshi (A Secret History of Japan's China Diplomacy)', *Tōa*, no. 368, February 1988, pp. 79–97.

Okada Tomihiro, '2010-nen no Chūgoku keizai zō (The Chinese Economy in 2010)', *Tōa*, no. 322, April 1994, pp. 21–36.

Ōkita, Saburō, 'Japan, China and the United States: Economic Relations and Prospects', *Foreign Affairs*, Summer 1979, pp. 1090–110.

Orr, Robert M., Jr, *The Emergence of Japan's Foreign Aid Power*, New York: Columbia University Press. 1990.

Overholt, William H., 'China's Economic Squeeze', *Orbis*, vol. 44, no. 1, Winter 2000, pp. 13–33.

Packard, George R., *Protest in Tokyo: The Security Treaty Crisis of 1960*, Princeton, NJ: Princeton University Press, 1966.

Park, Yung H., 'The "Anti-Hegemony" Controversy in Sino-Japanese Relations', *Pacific Affairs*, vol. 49, no. 3, Fall 1976, pp. 476–91.

Pei, Minxin, 'Social Takeover in China and the USSR', *Journal of Democracy*, vol. 3, no. 1, January 1992, pp. 109–18.

Pempel, T.J., 'The Bureaucratisation of Policymaking in Postwar Japan', *American Journal of Political Science*, vol.18, November 1974, pp. 647–64.

—— (ed.), *Policymaking in Contemporary Japan*, Ithaca, NY and London: Cornell University Press, 1977.

——, 'Regime Shift: Japanese Politics in a Changing World Economy', *Journal of Japanese Studies*, vol. 23, no. 2, 1997, pp. 333–62.

Poats, Rutherford M., *Twenty-five Years of Development Cooperation: A Review*, Paris: OECD, 1986.

Rix, Alan, *Japan's Economic Aid: Policymaking and Politics*, London: Croom Helm, 1980.

Robison, Richard and David S.G. Goodman (eds) *The New Rich in Asia: Mobile Phones, McDonalds and Middle Class Revolution*, London and New York: Routledge, 1996.

Rose, Caroline, *Interpreting History in Sino-Japanese Relations: A Case Study in Political Decision Making*, London: Routledge, 1998.

Ross, Robert S., 'Beijing as a Conservative Power', *Foreign Affairs*, vol. 76, no. 2. March–April 1997, pp. 33–44.

Saich, Tony, 'Tiananmen Square' in Joel Krieger, William A. Joseph and James A. Paul (eds) *The Oxford Companion to Politics of the World*, New York and Oxford: Oxford University Press, 1993, pp. 910–11.

Sakurai Toshihiro, 'Chūgoku no taigai enjo (China's Foreign Aid)'. *Kikinchōsa kihō*. no. 49, June 1985, pp. 176–83.

Sakurai Yoshiko, 'Gaimushō Chaina sukūru (The China School of the Ministry of Foreign Affairs)', *Bungei shūnjū*, vol. 80, no. 8, September 2002, pp. 130–3.

Satō Eisaku, *Satō Eisaku nikki: dai go-kan* (The Diary of Satō Eisaku: Volume Five). Tokyo: Asahi shinbun-sha, 1997.

——, *Satō Eisaku nikki: dai yon-kan* (The Diary of Satō Eisaku: Volume Four). Tokyo: Asahi shinbun-sha, 1997.

Satō Seizaburō and Matsuzaki Tetsuhisa, *Jimintō seiken* (Liberal Democratic Party Governments), Tokyo: Chūōkōronsha, 1986.

Satō, Yasunobu, 'New Directions in Japanese Foreign Policy: Promoting Human Rights and Democracy in Asia – ODA Perspective', in Edward Friedman (ed.) *The Politics of Democratisation*, Boulder, CO, San Francisco, CA, Oxford: Westview Press, 1994, pp. 103–21.

Sawada, Yasuyuki and Hiroyuki Yamada, 'Japan's ODA and Poverty Reduction: A Cross-Donore Comparison and a Case Study of Malaysia', in Hirohisa Kohama (ed.) *External Factors for Asian Development*, Singapore: Institute of Southeast Asian Studies, 2003, pp. 47–69.

Scalapino, Robert A. (ed.) *The Foreign Policy of Modern Japan*, Berkeley, CA: University of California Press, 1977.

Schaller, Michael, *The American Occupation of Japan: The Origins of the Cold War in Asia*, New York, Oxford: Oxford University Press, 1985.

——, 'Altered States: The United States and Japan During the 1960s', in Diane B. Kunz (ed.) *The Diplomacy of the Cultural Decade: American Foreign Relations During the 1960s*, New York, 1994.

Schmiegelow, Henrik and Michèle Schmiegelow, 'How Japan Affects the International System', *International Organization*, vol. 44, no. 4, Autumn 1990, pp. 553–88.

Schrader, Peter J., Steven W. Hook and Bruce Taylor, 'Clarifying the Foreign Aid Puzzle: A Comparison of American, Japanese, French, and Swedish Aid Flows', *World Politics*, vol. 50, no. 2, January 1998, pp. 294–323.

Segal, Gerald, 'Does China Matter?', *Foreign Affairs*, vol. 78, no. 5, September/October 1999, pp. 24–36.

Shambaugh, David, 'Containment or Engagement of China? Calculating Beijing's Response', *International Security*, vol. 21, no. 2, Fall 1996, pp. 180–209.

——, 'Facing Reality in China Policy', *Foreign Affairs*, vol. 80, no. 1, January–February 2001, pp. 50–64.

Shimomura Yasutami, Nakagawa Junji and Saitō Jun, *ODA taikō no seiji keizai gaku* (*Political Economy of the ODA Charter*), Tokyo: Yūhikaku, 1999.

Söderberg, Marie (ed.) *The Business of Japanese Foreign Aid: Five Case Studies from Asia*, London and New York: Routledge, 1996.

——, 'Shipping Aid to China', in Marie Söderberg (ed.) *The Business of Japanese Foreign Aid: Five Case Studies from Asia*, London and New York, Routledge, 1996, pp. 211–44.

—— (ed.) *Chinese–Japanese Relations in the Twenty-first Century: Complementarity and Conflict*, London and New York: European Institute of Japanese Studies, 2002.

Soeya Yoshihide, *Nihon gaikō to Chūgoku, 1945–1972* (Japanese Diplomacy and China, 1945–1972), Tokyo: Keiō daigaku shuppan-kai, 1995.

——, '1970-nendai no Bei-Chū kankei to Nihon gaikō (US–China Relations and Japanese Diplomacy in the 1970s)', in Nihon seiji gakkai (ed.) *Kiki no Nihon gaikō 70-nendai* (*Japanese Foreign Policy during the Crisis of the 1970s*), Tokyo: Iwanami shoten, 1997, pp. 3–20.

——, *Japan's Economic Diplomacy With China, 1945–1978*, Oxford: Clarendon Press, 1998.

Sonoda Shigeto, *Chūgoku jin no shinri to kōdō* (Psychology and Behaviour of Chinese People), Tokyo: NHK bukkusu, 2001.

Stockwin, J.A.A., *The Japanese Socialist Party and Neutralism: A Study of a Political Party and Its Foreign Policy*, London, New York: Melbourne University Press, 1968.

——, *Governing Japan: Divided Politics in a Major Economy*, Oxford: Blackwell Publishers, Third Edition, 1999.

Story, Greg, 'Japan's Official Development Assistance to China: A Survey', Australia–Japan Research Centre: Australian National University, Pacific Economic Paper, no. 150, 1987.

Strange, Roger, Jim Slater and Limin Wang (eds) *Trade and Investment in China: The European Experience*, London and New York: Routledge, 1998.

Suganuma, Unryu, *Sovereign Rights and Territorial Space in Sino-Japanese Relations: Irredentism and the Diaoyu/Senkaku Islands*, Honolulu, HI: University of Hawaii Press, 2000.

Suh Seungwon, 'Tenanmon jiken ni okeru Nihon no tai-Chūgoku enshakkan seisaku, 1989–90 (Japan's Yen Loan Policy to China during the Tiananmen Square Incident, 1989–90)', *Hōgaku seijigaku ronkyū*, no. 29, Summer 1996, pp. 249–87.

Sumi Kazuo, *ODA enjo no genjitsu* (Reality of ODA), Tokyo: Iwanami shinsho, 1989.

Szonyi, Michael, 'China: The Years Ahead', *International Journal*, vol. 55, no. 3, Summer 2000, pp. 475–84.

Tagawa Seiichi, *Matsumura Kenzō to Chūgoku* (Matsumura Kenzō and China), Tokyo: Yomiuri shinbunsha, 1972.

——, *Nitchū kōshō hiroku: Tagawa nikki 14-nen no shōgen* (Secret Record of Japan–China Negotiations: 14 Years of Testimonies from the Tagawa Diary), Tokyo: Mainichi shinbun-sha, 1973.

Takagi Seiichirō, 'Chūgoku no "keizai taikoku ka" to taigai kankei (China as an "Emerging an Economic Power" and its Foreign Relations)', *Kokusai mondai*, no. 406, January 1994, pp. 60–76.

Takamine, Tsukasa, 'Domestic Determinants of Japan's China Aid Policy: The Changing Balance of Foreign Policymaking Power', *Japanese Studies*, vol. 22, no. 2, September 2002, pp. 191–206.

Takao, Yasuo, *National Integration and Local Power in Japan*, Aldershot, Brookfield USA, Singapore and Sydney: Ashgate, 1999.

Takemi Keizō, 'Nitchū nitai kankei ni okeru shinchū shintai ha no shūen (The End of Political Divisions between the Pro-China and Pro-Taiwan Groups in Japanese Relations with China and Taiwan)', *Mondai to kenkyū*, vol. 26, no. 8, 1998, pp. 60–71.

Takenaka Heizō and Okamoto Yukio, 'Nihon no gaikō to seisaku kettei no arikata (Diplomacy and Policymaking in Japan)', *Keizai seminā*, no. 496, May 1996, pp. 28–36.

Tanaka Akihiko, 'Tenanmon jiken igo no Chūgoku o meguru kokusai kankyō (The International Environment Surrounding China after the Tiananmen Square Incident)', *Kokusai mondai*, no. 358, January 1990, pp. 30–45.

——, *Nitchū kankei 1945–1990* (Japan–China Relations 1945–1990), Tokyo: Tōkyō daigaku shuppan-kai, 1991.

——, *The New Middle Ages: The World System in the 21st Century*, Tokyo: The International House of Japan, 2002.

Tejima Ryūichi, *1991-nen Nihon no haiboku* (Japan's Defeat in 1991), Tokyo: Shinchō-sha, 1993.

Tow, William T., 'Sino-Japanese Security Cooperation: Evolution and Prospects', *Pacific Affairs*, vol. 56, no. 1, Spring 1983, pp. 51–83.

Tsuji Kiyoaki, *Shinban: Nihon kanryōsei no kenkyū* (An Analysis of the Japanese Bureaucratic System), Tokyo: Tōdai shuppan-kai, 1969.

Uchida Kenzō, 'Kanryō shudō kara Jimintō seichō shudōno jidaie (From the Era of Ministry Officials to the Era of the LDP Policy Research Council)', *Nihon keizai kenkyū sentā kaihō*, no. 458, 1984.

Wall, David, *The Charity of Nations: The Political Economy of Foreign Aid*, London: Macmillan, 1973.

Waltz, Kenneth N., *Theory of International Politics*, Reading, MA: Addison-Wesley Pub. Co., 1979.

——, 'Structural Realism after the Cold War', *International Security*, vol. 25, no. 1, Summer 2000, pp. 5–41.

Watanabe Akio, 'Gaikō seisaku no yukue to Gaimushō (The Outlook for Foreign Policy and the Ministry of Foreign Affairs)', *Hōgaku semina*, vol. 23, September 1983, pp. 38–45.

——, *Sengo Nihon no taigai seisaku: Kokusai kankei no henyō to Nihon no yakuwari* (*Foreign Policy of Postwar Japan: Changes in International Relations and the Role of Japan*), Tokyo: Yūhikaku-sensho, 1985.

Watanabe, Matsuo, 'Official Development Assistance as a catalyst for Foreign Direct Investment and Industrial Agglomeration', in Hirohisa Kohama (ed.) *External Factors for Asian Development*, Singapore: Institute of Southeast Asian Studies, 2003, pp. 136–68.

Watanabe Toshio, 'Kokuyū kigyō kaikaku ga shippai ni owareba Chūgoku keizai wa kiki ni ochiiru (If the Reform of State-Owned Enterprises Fails, the Chinese Economy Will Face a Crisis)', *Nihon no ronten*, Bungei shunjūsha, 1999, pp. 144–7.

Watanabe Toshio and Tanaka Akihiko, 'Toketeyuku Chūgoku (Melting China)', *Voice*, October 1999, pp. 72–82.

Weitz, Richard, 'Meeting the China Challenge: Some Insights from Scenario-Based Planning', *The Journal of Strategic Studies*, vol. 24, no. 3, September 2001, pp. 19–48.

Whiting, Allen S., *China Eyes Japan*, Berkeley, CA: University of California Press, 1989.

——, 'China's Use of Force, 1950–96, and Taiwan', *International Security*, vol. 26, no. 2. Fall 2001, pp. 103–31.

Wilson, Sandra, *The Manchurian Crisis and Japanese Society, 1931–33*, London and New York: Routledge, 2002.

Wright-Neville, David, *The Evolution of Japanese Foreign Aid 1955–1990*, Monograph No. 2, Melbourne: Monash Development Studies Centre, 1991.

Yabuki, Susumu, *China's New Political Economy: The Giant Awakes*, Boulder, CO, Oxford and San Francisco, CA: Westview Press, 1995.

——, 'Chūgoku keizai no kokusaika (Internationalisation of the Chinese Economy)', *Gakushikai kaihō*, no. 830, January 2001, pp. 110–28.

Yajima Tsuguo, 'Waga kuni no tai-Chūgoku keizai-gijutsu kyōryoku no rekishi to tenbō (The History and Future of Japan's Techno-economic Cooperation with China)'. *Chūgoku to higashi Ajia*, no. 43, March 1999, pp. 6–37.

Yamada Tatsuo, Amako Satoshi and Tanaka Akihiko, 'Henyōsuru Chūgoku to iu shisutemu: Nihon wa tsuyoki Chūgoku to ikani renkei subekika? (Changing China as a System: How Should Japan Engage with a Strong China?)', *Sekai*, March 1996, pp. 23–40.

Yanai Shinichi, 'Chūgoku to no keizai kyōryoku ni tsuite (Japanese Economic Cooperation with China)', record of lecture given by the then Director of Gaimushō keizai kyōryoku kyoku (Economic Cooperation Bureau of the Foreign Ministry), *Tōa*, no. 159, September 1980, pp. 79–81.

Yasutomo, Dennis T., *The Manner of Giving: Strategic Aid and Japanese Foreign Policy*, Lexington, MA and Toronto: Lexington Books, 1986.

——, *The New Multilateralism in Japan's Foreign Policy*, New York: St Martin's Press, 1995.

Yee, Herbert and Ian Storey 'Introduction', in Herbert Yee and Ian Storey (eds) *The China Threat: Perceptions, Myths and Reality*, London and New York: RoutledgeCurzon. 2002, pp. 1–19.

Yokoi, Yoichi, 'Plant and Technology Contracts and the Changing Pattern of Economic Interdependence Between China and Japan', in Christopher Howe (ed.) *China and Japan: History, Trends, and Prospects*, Oxford: Clarendon Press, 1996, pp. 127–46.

Yokoyama Hiroaki, 'Chūgoku e no "oime" to Nakasone gaikō (The Feeling of Guilt towards China and Nakasone Diplomacy)', *Tōa*, no. 304, October 1992, pp. 9–28.

Zaidan hōjin kazankai (Kazankai Foundation) 'Beikoku no Ajia senryaku to Nitchū jōyaku (The US Asia Policy and the Japan–China Treaty)', *Tōa*, no. 137, November 1978, pp. 41–53.

—— (ed.) *Chūgoku sōran 1978* (Biennial Comprehensive Analysis of China 1978), Tokyo: Zaidan hōjin kazankai, 1978.

—— (ed.) *Chūgoku sōran 1998* (Biennial Comprehensive Analysis of China 1998), Tokyo: Zaidan hōjin kazankai, 1998.

Zhang, Gang, 'Rail Aid to China', in Marie Söderberg (ed.) *The Business of Japanese Foreign Aid: Five Case Studies from Asia*, London and New York: Routledge, 1996, pp. 245–76.

Index

226   *Index*

For Product Safety Concerns and Information please contact our EU
representative GPSR@taylorandfrancis.com
Taylor & Francis Verlag GmbH, Kaufingerstraße 24, 80331 München, Germany

* 9 7 8 0 4 1 5 5 1 1 4 6 9 *